'Masculinity' first year ...

p5 — New paradigm of masculini[ty],
informed by older paradigms.

to Roytovste: "an ascent from some primordial collective
psychological soup to a sharply defined
+ p7.
individual identity." → we must get
away from this sort of history.

n 7. Halpern: "the multiplicity of possible historical connections
between sex + identity".

[Ch. 2] — On proliferation of penis discourse
1650 - 1750: -

p15. End of 1600s, ← knight is the result of
subj. of penis enters   this.
public debate p38 knight brings
                  he penis into
And/Mod. grand narrative discussion for Does the penis
                  first time represent maleness,
         → (How) knight questions   masculinity?
         (un)levering of the
         penis. — p34 → p20. For
                → False   Stephanson 1650-1750
                 enforced   period is a period
                 polarity.   when the erect member
* length's Progress   did = the man — literal
                         + symbolic close together!
* Text as / posthetic/debatable Knight + Freud question that
 make author ... — p16.   p33 Precursors to knight
      → form his book as   on Phallus.
       his body !!
"is represented.

p + p 48.

p42 : C18 medical science narrows down what

(*) maleness is - to reproductive organs : biological
view of masculinity: overmedicalization of
masculinity. Maleness accounted for by
condition of male genitalia.

p44. Stephanson's argument is that the penis/phallus
weren't always split: cf. 1650-1750.
My argument is to show that Knight + Freud
respond to those 1650-1750 discussions, and
question the links between male brain and
male physical body / penis.

p 45 - Ancient-Modern Grand Narrative

p 47 : Boords: academic discourses finds it
difficult to keep the male body in view -
ends up abstracting it, towards the phallus.
—> Stephanson weaves the history of
biological essentialism, —> but at the
same time, the links between male mind +
penis is undermined, complicated -
cf. arbor vitae + porn discourses show the
penis as phallus - "fractured" masculinity

and p65 — p 158 (167-8)
— wrong
and RPK —> phallus
(*)(*) P68-9.
p72-3.

The Yard of Wit

p 237, n. 63: On absence of consideration of penis in academic discourse

p 83 ff. IMPOTENCE TRIALS — erection wrong
↑ sign of virility ⊛
— 86-87

④ De Graaf's (17 ff.) inflating of cadaverous phallus → living phallus on a dead man —
Graaf's "museum" — p 80
→ Phallus + the Museum —
RPK ⊛

The Yard of Wit

Male Creativity and Sexuality, 1650–1750

RAYMOND STEPHANSON

PENN

University of Pennsylvania Press

Philadelphia

10   9   8   7   6   5   4   3   2   1

Published by
University of Pennsylvania Press
Philadelphia, Pennsylvania 19104-4011

Library of Congress Cataloging-in-Publication Data
Stephanson, Raymond.
  The yard of wit : male creativity and sexuality, 1650–1750 / Raymond Stephanson.
    p.   cm.
  ISBN 0-8122-3758-7 (cloth : alk. paper)
  Includes bibliographical references (p.) and index.
  1. Pope, Alexander, 1688–1744—Authorship. 2. English literature—18th century—History
and criticism. 3. Masculinity in literature. 4. English literature—Male authors—History and
criticism. 5. English literature—Early modern, 1500–1700—History and criticism. 6. Authors,
English—Early modern, 1500–1700—Psychology. 7. Authors, English—18th century—Psychology.
8. Male authors, English—Sexual behavior. 9. Male authors, English—Psychology. 10. Creation
(Literary, artistic, etc.). 11. Body, Human, in literature. 12. Generative organs, Male. 13. Men
in literature. 14. Sex in literature. 15. Creative ability. I. Title.
PR448.M37 S74   2004
820.9'353—dc22   2003055566

For Lesley, Stella, and Eric

Contents

Illustrations

Preface

Pope's penis: to suggest that the yard of Alexander the Little reveals something important about the culture of eighteenth-century male creativity will doubtless strike some readers as a preposterous and needless prurience. Yet it is clear that the links between male writing and contexts of masculinity and the male body—particularly genitalia—played a significant role in the self-fashioning of several generations of male authors from ca. 1650–1750. This book is about the collective structures of male creativity for the period—particularly its somatic and sexual discourses—with Alexander Pope as primary example.

My project started out as a study of how Pope fashioned his own poetical sensibility *as a man*: Why were his comments about poetry and creativity so often associated with sexuality? What impact did his many friendships, especially with older men, have in shaping his sense of himself as a poet? Why did his self-conscious dramatizations of the poetic imagination gravitate toward the body (Belinda's and Eloisa's, for example, or his own twisted frame)? What methodology might explain his investment of eros in both his male friends and his poems? What was one to make of the fact that his enemies so often attacked his writing and personality through ritualistic castration gestures or scathing belittlement of his genitals, and why did modern scholarship largely ignore this side of the Pope quarry? What was one to make of his handling of sexualized female Muses which he often projected onto himself or male friends, and why did he use tropes of the creative brain as womb? What did it mean for this diminutive man to say that "he pleas'd by manly ways," and what sort of phallic strut might inform his public self-portraiture? What were the cultural subtexts of Colley Cibber's embarrassing anecdote in 1742 about Pope's supposed visit to a whorehouse as a young man? I wanted a clearer sense of the connections between Pope's creativity and his masculinity.

Before long it was clear that such questions were related to the larger literary culture of other writers, that how Pope fantasized the symbolic landscape of male writing in his most self-conscious moments—both the interior site of creativity as well as his public status within the literary marketplace—was inescapably embedded within the collective norms and attitudes of male literary culture understood in its broadest sense. The scope of my book changed accordingly, and I sought answers to a question deceptively simple and yet richly entangled within deeper paradigms: how did male writers of the period, not just Pope, imagine the origins, nature, and structures of their own creativity, or what William Collins referred to as the "poetical character" (the phrase comes from his pindaric "Ode on the Poetical Character," that beautiful mid-century lyric about the origins and mythopoeic properties of the creative imagination)?

One answer is that male literary culture of the period depended on a shared symbolic and metaphorical system to fashion a myth about its own creativity, often linking itself to the material realms of Enlightenment sexuality. There were other kinds of figurative linkage, of course—to politics, wealth, land, law, the nervous system—but male authors also typically constructed notions of their own poetic imagination, the origins of their creativity, and their life-long writerly output as masculine sexual dramas. Encoded at a casual but nonetheless deep level of cultural utterance in the later seventeenth and eighteenth centuries is a collective imaginative approach by male writers to questions about their craft, their intimate spaces of inspiration, and their sometimes unstable position within the larger group of other men. These gestures inhabited a metaphorized vocabulary of male sexuality and masculinity which—I shall be arguing—were in significant ways the foundations upon which the symbolic codes of male creativity and male literary communities were built.

Another answer is that the discourses linking creativity and sexuality functioned within the hierarchical dynamics and power structures of male literary communities—that is, within the homosocial domains of male friendship, or in its shadow form, male competition. This is not to forget or dismiss the increasing role played by a female readership at this time, or to underestimate the impact of the new wave of female authors. But for male writers roughly contemporary with the life of Pope, one's authority within literary and critical circles was often specifically linked to being a man whose "manly" qualities—whether literal or figurative—were valued by other men who themselves occupied positions of influence by virtue of their own homosocial connections. Notions of literary authority, in other words, were frequently grounded on a dynamic of homocentric inclusion (or exclusion) whose subtext was an acceptable masculinity—visceral, social, or literary (ideally, all three)—and whose praxis was often linked to the bonds of friendship with other men. Within these homosocial contexts and hierarchies questions of male creativity were given definition, value, and status.

A third answer is that collective notions of the poetical character depended on how male writers metaphorized their literary "labor," both as an internalized imaginative act and as an object of readerly attention. A significant aspect of the history of authorial self-representation is that men were concerned about how their creativity was perceived, and writers of all stripes—famous ones like Pope, up-and-comers like Mark Akenside, hacks such as Ned Ward—tried to shape and control the figurative definitions that would be associated with their creative efforts.

This study, then, is essentially an inventory of how the male literary culture ca. 1650–1750 deployed self-conscious and well-recognized sets of metaphors and allegories to talk of male creativity, both its internal character and its status in public. A rhetorical stock-taking, if you will, this book concentrates on how and why male writers linked their authorial work to male and female groins, genitalia, reproductive and erotic acts, and how these figurative gestures played a role within homosocial hierarchies in the larger literary community. As an investigation of cultural discourses of and about male creativity, my chapters try to identify the shared vocabulary of metaphorical codes among male writers of very different sorts, as well as to speculate on how changing cultural perceptions of the status of the "literary"— both professional and economic—account for variations in how these collective tropes were used. The result, I hope, will be a better understanding of how Enlightenment notions of male creativity were constructed and how they changed, although I will refer to examples and writers before and after the period 1650–1750 to suggest the continuity of many of these verbal codes.

There is another more personal side to the genesis of this book, one that illuminates the fascinating, and uneasy, professional politics of my subject matter. In the mid-1990s when I was asked at eighteenth-century studies conferences about the work I was doing, my "Pope and sex" rejoinder was often politely treated as an unnecessary and surprising prurience or simply as a non-starter, since, as we were all supposed to know, Pope did not have one—a real sex life, that is. Case closed. The conversation topic shifted, usually to Pope's representations of female sexuality. I then took to explaining that I wanted to describe how male bodies, friendship, and genitalia were linked to notions of male creativity, and that Pope was of enormous importance in such a study, especially treatments of his penis. I quickly discovered that many people were embarrassed by my subject, and instead of engaging with it they sometimes simplistically interpreted my interest as a sign of my sexual orientation or, alternatively, as an unwelcome entry onto turf then owned by feminists and gay historians. It struck me that part of what was going on here was symptomatic of a general academic reluctance to study male genitals or to keep the historical subject of the sexualized male body in focus without digressing from it.

Other experiences seemed, amusingly, to confirm this reluctance: my male friends at the University of Saskatchewan joked for years that I was "working on Pope's penis" (on informal days, "Pope's dick"), and counted on me to supply the occasional racy photocopied engraving of something salacious from the period, but they seemed uncomfortable whenever I talked seriously about my subject, preferring humor and the light porn images from the past. My feminist friends were convinced I was working on eighteenth-century masculinity, trying to make a difference, and when one missed a paper I gave to our Department of Women's and Gender Studies on "Men & 'Yard'-Work in the 17th-18th Centuries," a polite, handwritten message regretted that she had missed my talk on men's domestic labor. Those who had attended seemed politely mystified by my interest in impotence trials, looking for ways to transpose my materials onto the female body.

Other anecdotes tell different, but related, stories. The three times I gave conference papers on aspects of the pregnant male brain-womb, I seemed to be in my audience's good books. The three times I spoke on aspects related to the Enlightenment penis and reproductive system, I was given the impression by several established male academics that I had come close to doing something personally obscene in public. More recently it was intimated by a sophisticated conference-goer that both sex *and* the body were now old fashioned topics, that those in the know had moved on to fresher and more sumptuous academic game, and that female bodies were, anyhow, much more interesting than male. I began to wonder why there was so persistent a dodging of an obvious subject through substitution, humor, denial, or deferral. Why, I asked myself, was it so difficult to have scholarly discussion about the cultural history of men's crotches?

These anecdotes—which I offer in good humor—contain interesting signs, it seems to me, of a nervous academic reluctance about the sexualized male body and its cultural symbolisms in history. The reasons for such uneasiness are complex, of course, but they are also part of our historical inheritance from the eighteenth century's troubled musings about the sexualized connection of male body and mind. That male academics in particular are so reluctant to examine the history of the discursive site where the symbolic phallus tends to be preferred over their penises is perhaps not so surprising. But these hesitations are the result of historical legacies, and if there is a secondary purpose to this book it is to throw open the larger question of how the Enlightenment dislocation of the biological yard from the cultural phallus-as-commodity haunts individual male experience even today, although it would take another book to explore this historical continuity.

Things have changed a great deal since these personal experiences in the mid and later 1990s, as the many notes to this book will suggest. The resistance evident in the anecdotes above has given way to more candid inquiry, especially with the advent of Enlightenment "male studies" which has corrected and replaced many anachronisms and misreadings of the eighteenth-century male. In this new climate, my argument that the period witnessed the advent of a new Priapus of the literary marketplace may raise fewer eyebrows, and my claim that there is a new commercial traffic in creativity-genitalia imagery—or what my book calls "the yard of wit"—may seem less perverse than it did five or ten years ago.

We are the inheritors of these historical developments, but it seems to me that we are still in the early stages of recovering the variety of sexualized tropes, rhetorical gestures, and cultural narratives which informed part of a collective literary self-fashioning and an emergent literary consumerism, not to mention a revised symbolism of the male body. This book documents an important part of this history.

Chapter 1

Introduction: Male Creativity and Its Changing Contexts

Discourses about male creativity were fundamentally influenced by three historical transformations: (1) a revised cultural understanding of masculinity as an interiorized sexual identity; (2) a new kind of interest in the male body as the site where masculinity would be registered, with particular emphasis on the connections between the organs of generation and the mind; and (3) the commodification of the literary in an emergent capitalist print culture. The most significant result for ideas of male creativity and the poetical character was that male genitalia were increasingly seen as the symbolic commodities of both masculinity and male literary labor. More specifically, traditional creativity/procreativity tropes were affected by these transformations, and cultural understanding of the literal and figurative connections between creative male mind and reproductive systems—both male and female—were rewritten in ways that reflected newer physiological theories as well as the new economic value of literary production. The same is true for non-procreative, eroticized tropes for creativity—sexy female Muses, erections—which became rhetorical markers for the inner site of one's inspiration as well as the public status of one's writing in the literary marketplace. These collective metaphorical equations played a significant role in establishing widespread associations of the male mind as sexualized body, which in turn became rhetorical commodities very likely to yield a profit for authors and booksellers. Pope became the first public emblem of these developments, symbolizing the new commercial traffic in the yard of wit.

New Commodities: Masculinity, Male Bodies, Literary Labor

How we understand the links between creativity and manliness has everything to do with basic assumptions about the defining features of masculinity for this period, which were far from stable. As scholars know, histories of Enlightenment men and maleness are about masculinities rather than a single universal type; about fluid and often permeable gender boundaries; about social, economic, and political forces as well as sexual behavior; about transitions and consolidations of the categories of maleness rather than transhistorical modes; and about the relationship between public representations and actual behavior. Historians seem agreed that eighteenth-century maleness was subject to a variety of new configurations and developments. Perhaps the most difficult question of all has been the debate about when and how there might have been a shift from "masculinity" understood and experienced as social reputation to "masculinity" as an interiorized sense of personal identity defined increasingly by sexuality. John Tosh has framed the historical question and its interpretive difficulty concisely:

All that can be said with confidence is that a fundamental shift occurred between the seventeenth and twentieth centuries. In the sixteenth and seventeenth centuries masculinity was regarded as a matter of reputation; it had first to be earned from one's peers and then guarded jealously against defamation. . . . In the twentieth century, by contrast, masculinity has come to be experienced as an aspect of subjectivity, sensitive to social codes no doubt, but rooted in the individual's interiority; an "insecure" masculinity is one which is assailed by inner doubt (particularly about sexuality) rather than by threats and aspersions from other men. . . . Was the period 1750–1850, so crucial for the development of class identities, also critical in the gradual transition from masculinity as reputation to masculinity as interiority?[1]

At first glance, one might be tempted to say "yes," and then look for specific discursive evidence and individual case studies which would substantiate the general claim that the eighteenth century witnesses the emergence of a new configuration for masculine identity in which selfhood becomes an internalized sexual identity variously construed across a range of acceptable and transgressive modes. Anthony Fletcher has made such arguments easier by pointing out "that the word masculinity, meaning 'the quality or condition of being masculine,' had its first recorded usage in England in 1748." His acknowledgment that "New words enter the language as people feel the insufficiency of current speech to express something they want to encapsulate" might suggest that the word enters common usage precisely in order to name this new sense of interiority. But Fletcher also cautions us about the difficulties of proof: "How far among men living in the Victorian period, let alone during the seventeenth or eighteenth centuries, it [masculinity] involved an internalised identity—an interiority of the mind and emotions—as opposed to a sense of role-playing—is very hard for the historian to judge."[2] Tosh goes so far as to suggest that, even by the nineteenth century, "It is hard to see compelling evidence for a new sense of interiority."[3]

A different reservation has been issued by Tim Hitchcock and Michèle Cohen in the introductory essay to their important collection of studies of Enlightenment maleness. The historical development of masculinity in this period, they say, is as complex, contradictory, and variable as that of femininity, and therefore is not well-accounted for by simplistic models of historical change:

The model of a straightforward transition from a single early modern masculinity based on social reputation to a modern version in which men defined themselves through sexual behaviour (both heterosexual and homosexual) and through their control of women (newly confined to the domestic sphere) can now be seen to be inadequate. Such a model assumes that the main problems masculinity engages with are sexual and patriarchal in nature and that there exists a single unified masculinity available for historical analysis.[4]

The question then: is there sufficient evidence to mark the eighteenth century as the period when masculinity moves from social to internal positioning, and how might this be reflected in self-conscious literary commentary? The cautions and reservations of these prominent social historians are especially important challenges because the work of the majority of scholars in the field has assumed there is considerable evidence for such claims.

Indeed, a good deal of scholarship in the last decade has tried to recover and describe the subjectivities or internalized identity-markers of various kinds of men and masculinities. Although there are now too many good publications to provide an assessment of each, the following brief selection will give some sense of how vigorously scholars have proceeded under the assumption that a newer sense of an internalized sexual identity explains much about the history of Enlightenment masculinities. First, there are those historians after Foucault whose work has helped to frame fundamental questions about categories, cultural paradigms, and historical contexts, and without which much subsequent scholarship might have been inconceivable. The work of Randolph Trumbach, for instance, has been important for providing a significant array of empirical, archival data about the new-style sodomite-molly which has made possible more nuanced readings of the subjective space of individual self-identification.[5] G. S. Rousseau, likewise, has opened up significant conceptual questions about gender identification and sexual identities in the past, offering a powerful counter-balance to heterosexist assumptions about history, biography, and sexual stereotypes.[6] One of the foundational claims of Thomas Laqueur's *Making Sex: Body and Gender from the Greeks to Freud*[7]—that the idea of "sexuality" as a fundamental constituent of identity does not become a particularly meaningful concept until the eighteenth century—has convinced many that the late seventeenth and eighteenth centuries are the birthplace of an interiorized, sexualized sense of a

masculine self. Also important is Michael McKeon's "Historicizing Patriarchy: The Emergence of Gender Difference in England, 1660–1760,"[8]
whose astute theoretical observations on the historical overlap and differences of male sexual identity and class identity have prevented an
over-simplified isolation of sex and gender matters from other material contexts within which identity-questions are inevitably embedded.

   These influential conceptual assessments of the historical terrain are
widely referred to and have, in different ways, encouraged more specific reconstructions of internalized male identities, either of individual men or of homosocial sub-sets. Kristina Straub's important
study, *Sexual Suspects: Eighteenth-Century Players and Sexual Ideology*,[9] is
in part an examination of the problematic ways in which discourses
about the sexuality of male actors was a site of cultural struggle over
how normative and transgressive male sexual identities would come to
be defined. Jill Campbell has written persuasively about gender and
identity in Fielding's writing, arguing that his contemporaries were
"engaged in a process of reformulating the import of gendered identity in the course of the eighteenth century," and that Fielding himself
harbored a suspicion "that the apparently most personal and essential
aspects of identity may be revealed as artificial and contingent constructs."[10] Straub's and Campbell's studies are useful reminders of the
complex and self-conscious responses by individual male authors and
actors whose lives appear to have been suspended between old and
new paradigms for acceptable masculine self-identification. In an earlier essay of my own, I tried to account for the ways in which the apparently sexualized rhetoric between predominantly heterosexual
male friends might have been part of how an internalized masculine
identity was experienced—a male subjectivity, in other words, whose
nuances were recognizable in the eighteenth century and before but
which are now lost to us.[11] More recently, Shawn Lisa Maurer has
done much to explain how the domestication of masculinity in the
new social periodical helped to provide the contexts which would lead
to the internalization of "the bourgeois family man . . . as the proto-
type of desirable masculinity."[12] In his impressive reading of male-
male relationships and identities in eighteenth-century homoerotic
culture, George Haggerty has made a convincing case for "how sexuality became a feature of Enlightenment subjectivity and why gender codification became the central marker for difference, the central
dichotomonic legacy of early modern culture." In a subtle discussion
of Beckford, Haggerty argues "that we can discover in this case—in
Beckford's writing, in the press, and in the popular response to his
situation—the beginnings of a particular kind of male homosexual
sensibility."[13] Philip Carter's recent essay on Boswell examines "the

various styles of manliness that Boswell was keen to develop, and some of the personality types that he was eager to impersonate," such as "sense, self-control, moderation, independence, refinement and sentiment." Carter suggests that while "Boswell considered sex an important part of his adult identity and his understanding of manliness, both as a universal and personal category. . . . he did not do so to the exclusion of other manifestations of manly behaviour." Carter concludes that "the value of the case study is not just in setting out what ideals were to be emulated, but also how effectively these were either put into practice or complicated by other forms of social identification."[14]

Whatever masculinity-as-identity might have been as it left social markers to become an interiorized mentality, studies such as these—written mainly by literary critics—claim that the period roughly 1650–1800 was developing a new idiom, new discourses, new stereotypes and prejudices about how maleness and masculinity were to be defined, understood, represented, or how they might have been experienced and internalized as identity. This is not to say that such studies ignore the social and reputational dimensions of what "masculinity" might have meant, but rather they emphasize that being "manly" and exhibiting a masculine character were increasingly derived from a sexualized inner self. Still, the cautions of social historians are salutary, I think, because they warn us of the dangers of oversimplification and the subtle anachronisms that can be brought about by an over-magnification of a single facet such as sexual identity. Such cautions also remind us that what we actually mean by "masculinity" itself as a changing historical thing still needs further elaboration.

My own position is that an interiorized sense of maleness-as-sexualized-identity *is* emerging at this time, although still informed variously by older paradigms based on social hierarchy and reputation. I agree with David M. Halperin's point that the large-scale cultural transformations and reorganizations which accompanied the shift to industrialization and the emergence of a capitalist economy also had significant impact on "the various relations among sexual roles, sexual object-choices, sexual categories, sexual behaviors, and sexual identities in bourgeois Europe between the end of the seventeenth century and the beginning of the twentieth. Sex takes on new social and individual functions, and it assumes a new importance in defining and normalizing the modern self."[15] However, because the period is clearly one of changing sex and gender attitudes, one must approach questions of identity with an awareness that such a concept is likely in transition as well, and our readings of the evidence must therefore allow for the play of older modes and stereotypes as they are modified, blended with the new, or finally eliminated. On shifting

ground of this sort, the subject "masculinity" becomes particularly difficult to come at or catch, and certainly easy to oversimplify. The main challenge right now, as it seems to me, is to incorporate the best macro- and micro-studies of this complex history—both the social, hierarchical, reputational structures and the interiorized sexual, psychological self-identificatory evidence—in order to chart a history which can simultaneously reveal older and newer modes, eclectic blends and mixes, the variable relationship of sexual acts and sexual identities, and the uneven shifts and accommodations which can make it difficult to differentiate between older and newer discourses.

In his study of masculinity in the sixteenth and early seventeenth centuries, Mark Breitenberg has spoken of the difficulty which faces the social or literary historian in sketching what he calls a "nascent interiority." While his remarks are about the need to historicize or translate psychoanalytical approaches—which see identity as mental or psychic conditions—into Renaissance social phenomena, his distinction is helpful to the point I want to make about the period which concerns this book:

> While psychoanalysis locates subjectivity in the individual's psychic struggle, the early modern period discovers identity in the more public context we associate with shame cultures, where such factors as property, reputation and status are pre-eminent. Indeed, quite possibly psychoanalysis articulates what was only beginning to emerge, or perhaps, submerge, in the early modern period. Hamlet is a useful figure for this nascent interiority: his dilemma is surely the result of social factors (loss of place, public title), but his response appears to us as familiar for its interior manifestations.[16]

Breitenberg's "nascent interiority" is a useful heuristic device for imagining a flexible model of historical transition which embraces both macro- and micro-approaches to Enlightenment masculinities, as well as acknowledging the nearly always psychologized and sexualized conceptualization of such matters as the historically-inherited norm of the late twentieth and twenty-first centuries. In other words, for studies of Enlightenment masculinities to progress we need to balance the modern psychological privileging of subjective individualism in the history of selfhood—an assumption Roy Porter has described as the "question-begging and self-serving leftover of Victorian fanfares of progress" which discovers "an ascent from some primordial collective psychological soup to a sharply defined individual identity"[17]—with the ways in which masculinity, to quote sociologist R. W. Connell, is always "deeply enmeshed in the history of institutions and of economic structures. Masculinity is not just an idea in the head, or a personal identity. It is also extended in the world, merged in organized social relations.

To understand masculinity historically we must study changes in those social relations."[18] The history of masculine identity, then, must be wary of some exclusive interpretive attachment either to external pressures of rank, reputation, and shame, or to newly fashioned internal self-identifications based on sexual character. The historical record points to a far more complex reality.

David Halperin has framed the interpretive difficulty and challenge in a slightly different manner, but one which similarly recognizes the anachronistic and transhistorical tendencies of much recent work. Our modern model of identity—tied, he says, to a notion of a psychologized sexual subjectivity—is one which "knits up desire, its objects, sexual behavior, gender identity, reproductive function, mental health, erotic sensibility, personal style, and degrees of normality or deviance into an individuating, normativizing feature of the personality called 'sexuality' or 'sexual orientation.' " Such a model, he writes, "is inconceivable" before the nineteenth century, but he hastens to add that this does not mean that it was impossible "for sexual acts to be linked in various ways with a sexual disposition or sexual subjectivity well before the nineteenth century." What we must bring to our studies of these pre-1800 historical matters, he suggests, is a far more nuanced sense of the wide array of possible relationships between sexuality and notions of identity:

What my argument does do, I hope, is to encourage us to inquire into the construction of sexual identities before the emergence of sexual orientations, and to do this *without* recurring to modern notions of sexuality or sexual orientation and thereby contributing to a kind of antihistoricist backlash. Perhaps we need to supplement our notion of sexual identity with a more refined concept of, say, partial identity, emergent identity, transient identity, semi-identity, incomplete identity, proto-identity, or sub-identity. In any case, my intent is not to reinstall a notion of sexual identity as a historical category so much as to indicate *the multiplicity of possible historical connections between sex and identity*, a multiplicity whose existence has been obscured by the necessary but narrowly focused, totalizing critique of sexual identity as a unitary concept.[19]

The value of Halperin's "partial identity" and Breitenberg's "nascent interiority" is that they foreground the problems of historical variability, fluidity, and unevenness in the very categories we attempt to grasp. As current scholarship tries to trace the various ways an interiorized sexuality-as-self emerged, we must be wary of simplistic before-and-after concepts: i.e., before 1800 sexual acts did not necessarily reflect a sexual identity or orientation, and after 1800 they did; or, before 1700 or 1750 or 1800 male identity was social and reputational, and after one of these dates it was interiorized. Even the common-sense position that male identity always has and continues to reveal a dynamic rather than stable exchange between external and internal identificatory structures is also prey to sophisticated anachronism which assumes there is a core identity inside. Such assumptions must also be tested against the fact that eighteenth-century notions of selfhood and identity, as E. J. Hundert has argued, also included analogies of the self as actor, masquerading theatrically in a newly commercialized world which offered a variety of moral and psychological roles to be enacted: "Eighteenth-century thinkers were thus faced with the argument that character itself was in essence a social artifact, a construct existing in an intersubjective space of the demands of others, and within which a person's identity was of necessity devised."[20]

I set forth these complex historical issues at some length because a study of male discourses about the poetical character can contribute to our understanding of developments and changes in Enlightenment masculinity. A working assumption of this book is that the "literary" does not merely issue from or come after "history," the text-world of the creative imagination serving as convenient mirror or second-order reflector of a historical real-world. And male literary communities—whether high or low, Scriblerian or Grubstreet, Whig or Tory—are no more separable or sealed off from the making of cultural history than scientific, political, religious, or military communities. Both the poetical character and the male writerly cadres with which I am concerned were in some important ways constitutive of cultural reality and its most typical habits of perception, and we do well not to underestimate the anthropological evidence which resides in the literary record. What remains still largely unexplored territory are the ways in which male literary communities reveal (perhaps more clearly than other homosocial groupings) the dynamic interplay of socially- and internally-located concepts of masculinity and manliness. Because male creativity itself was already conceptualized as having the double aspects of interior mental activity and public status, the links between notions of creativity and masculinity were situated at the nexus of social and psychologized constructions. That is, the poetical character was collectively understood as both an internal site of creativity within the male writer's mind, as well as a commodity within the competitive marketplace of letters which situated and ranked authors publicly in hierarchies of worth or monetary value. In turn, this double sense—of internal and reputational status—was accompanied by a parallel formation in which the interior place of male creativity was imaged primarily as a sexual site, and one's relative position in the public hierarchy of male authors was importantly connected to one's perceived manliness as a writer within a network of homosocial connections. For historians of the Enlightenment, these collective representations of the poetical character *as an aspect* of masculinity offer a rich archive about how male identity, sexuality, homosocial relations, and creativity intermingled in the cultural imaginary both as social and interiorized realities.

One of the most far-reaching implications of the gradual shifting from masculinity as reputation to masculinity as sexualized interiority is the new importance of the male body. There is perhaps nothing surprising in this: as notions of masculine identity were increasingly derived from constructions of a sexualized inner self, the male body and its sexuality became more than ever the sites where masculinity would be registered. And yet there is an astonishing lack of work on these issues, which seems clearly related to the general academic reluctance to make the history of the male body a legitimate scholarly subject. Taken for granted in ways the female body never is, and too often dismissed or reduced to simplistic notions of embodiment-as-patriarchy, the male body would appear not to have had a history at all until very recently; or so the academic record would imply. An emerging scholarship has already begun to fill in some of the blanks,[21] although very little work has been done on the reconfigured links and widespread associations between genital physiology and male mind—newer associations that Chapter 2 will explore. The ways in which young men learned to acquire a masculine identity involved many contexts of experience, behavior, and appropriate social interaction; maleness depended on one's birth, economic station, and on one's work status or professional pursuit. Increasingly, however, a newly-sexualized brain or male character would supply an important marker of masculinity as well, but one understood as an interiorized identity dependent on a specifically male physiology which originated in a revised set of cultural symbols for the male organs of generation, sexual and erotic inclination, and reproductive potency. The shift in the ways male genitalia were understood helps to explain why a sexual sensibility came to be seen as a dominant category of mind or a masculine identity. In short, the constitution and condition of the male body itself came to be increasingly essential categories in how maleness and masculinity were defined, and have much to tell us about the historical transition from primarily social and reputational contexts to internal identifications of the uniquely sexualized male self.

The new physiology, as Laqueur and others have shown, intensified the connections between masculinity and male sexual function. At the heart of this historical reconstruction is the claim that it is not until the late seventeenth and eighteenth centuries that a biological notion of male sexuality was widely imagined as constitutive of masculine psychological reality. Reproductive biology, in other words, appeared more than ever one of the primary sites of an essentialized maleness whose consciousness and experiential history might be understood as linked

to the condition and activities of the sexual parts. This gradual recon-
ceptualization of masculinity in relation to the male body is evident
not only in the histories of medicine ca. 1650–1750—both scientific
and popular manifestations—and in pornography,[22] but also in self-
conscious commentary about male creativity. Detailed analysis of these
somatic and sexual discourses will be offered in Chapter 2, where a
handful of important historical questions will be answered: How were
male organs of generation understood in medical traditions and in the
non-scientific population at large? Were the cultural associations and
symbols for this period different from earlier cultural systems? In
what specific ways were male genitalia linked to the brain and ideas of
masculinity? Why is there such a remarkable increase in public references to male genitalia in this period, especially to the penis? Is there
an underlying logic or single structure to this period's literal and symbolic use of male genitalia?

That the very seat of male thought or identity could be shaped by a
man's physical condition or sexual organs is arguably one of the most
significant results of late seventeenth- and eighteenth-century medical
and non-medical developments, not least because it helps to explain
the early formation of the concept of an essentialized male consciousness as sexually defined—the model inherited by modern western culture. The refashioned links between male brain/mind and body were
part of the newer symbolic terrain within which one might have internalized one's sense of identity as a man or imagined such an interior
identity in other men, and these Enlightenment equations reflect a variety of reorganizations of the concept of masculinity as a biological and
social entity. However, male mind/male genitalia associations were no
simple matter. Newer notions of masculinity-as-sexualized-embodiment
were characterized by ambiguity and differential symbolizing, especially when it came to the penis, or, what the period also called the
yard, the privy member, tarse, pintle, or pego. Medical, pornographic,
legal, and other non-literary discourses tell a similar story, that there
was a perceived instability of male subjectivity as it might be grounded
by reference to "the yard." The penis-mind connection was especially
vexed, being understood as either a direct or an inverse relationship,
with mental capacity either the result of genital capacity *or* of genital
deficiency. Even physiological accounts of the causes of erections made
connections of a sexualized male body and masculine identity a trouble-
some issue, with tumescence often the result of imaginative caprice or
mechanical/biological triggers rather than the will. The most striking development was that the yard was often viewed as a separate symbolic
commodity even while attached to real men. The historical record suggests that the Enlightenment yard was often a problematic emblem of
male identity because its function could be related either to a collective

uneasiness about mind-body relationships or to the psychological com-plexities of individual male will and the instability of the conditions of desiring.

If newer notions of masculine identity and sexualized male bodies were important in the cultural landscape affecting literary discourses, there was another historical development whose impact was monu-mental, forever altering the very idea of the "literary." I mean the commodification of literature which characterizes the history of print culture for this period—that well-known gradual shifting from older forms of male patronage to a literary marketplace in which writers and their books were being newly defined as consumer products with a potential economic value. In this newer capitalist milieu the dignity of male authorship and the enigmatic nature of the imaginative act would be sorely tested and modified, subject increasingly to a com-mercialized evaluation which affected the ways in which the poetical character was understood and represented. The fascinating history of the relationship between notions of the author as materially transcen-dent creator-genius and author as cultural commodity whose imagi-nation was for sale has received a variety of excellent analyses.[23] The explanations are now familiar ones: with the professionalization of imaginative writing from the late seventeenth century, the image of the independent author-gentleman was now also reducible to crass commercial object. The poetical character was for sale, too, victim of a meteoric literary capitalism whose effects are still evident in notions of aesthetic value today. Different explanations have been offered for how various kinds of writers responded to the commodification of their own works and status as authors, but a common thread of argu-ment is that male writers combatted their entry into the marketplace of letters by differentiating their own creative genius from the hirelings, hacks, and literary prostitutes who depended on a paying public. How-ever, little work has been done on the connections of literary commod-ification and masculinity or male bodies. While important studies have been published on the interrelationship of female authorship, female bodies, female sexuality and literary commodification, there exists no comparable body of scholarship for the men who were affected by the new economy of letters.

The important exception is Linda Zionkowski's *Men's Work: Gender, Class, and the Professionalization of Poetry, 1660–1784*,[24] an enormously helpful account of the shift from late seventeenth-century notions of the male poet as the materially aloof or self-indulgent aristocrat to mid- and later eighteenth-century models of the poet as the professionally-engaged author in the marketplace. What particularly distinguishes her book are carefully reasoned accounts of how changing concepts of the poet were also linked to maleness and rank:

the period saw the emergence of a new "stereotype of manliness" that took as its reference point the market rather than the court, the bourgeois or economic man rather than the gentleman or aristocrat. . . . whether these poets viewed themselves as professionals engaged in commercial literary culture or vehemently rejected that identification, their verse constituted an important arena for conflicting definitions of masculinity—definitions that, in turn, legitimized particular forms of literary production and certain configurations of literary careers. (5)

In eloquent chapters about Rochester, Oldham, Dryden, Pope, Gray, and Johnson, Zionkowski convincingly shows "the extent to which a change in idealizations of manhood accompanied the shift toward the market in literature" (98), so that by mid-century writers had begun "to associate masculinity and cultural power with commercial success, while characterizing poets' detachment from the market [her prime example is Gray] as an infantile, or effeminate, dependence upon others" (132). By the time we get to Samuel Johnson, she argues, "the gentleman writing from idleness and leisure inhabits a category separate from and inferior to that of the professional man of letters, who lives upon his talents" (182). Her book also examines some aspects of how these important transitions were accompanied by sexual and eroticized tropes about the male poet's relationship to his readers or an emergent capitalist marketplace of letters.

My interests are similar to Zionkowski's, but our emphasis and angle of perspective are very different. I am much more interested in how the sexualized male body and issues of masculinity-as-embodiment are related to redefined notions of the literary and of male creativity. Indeed, I want to suggest that there is an important historical convergence, a double commodification of literature *and* of masculinity as the sexualized male body. My book will argue that the perceived conjunction of the "literary" and the "manly" was being refashioned at a time when masculinity and literary labor were both becoming commodities—as ideas, discourses, processes. As male minds, brains, characters—literary or otherwise—came to be associated more intensely with the male reproductive system, men found themselves the object of a synecdochic gesture in which they were reduced to and commodified as their genitalia, most often "the yard." At the same time, idealized notions of male authors and their books were being reduced and commodified as economic items in a literary marketplace where male creativity in turn could also be represented as genitalia in a kind of cultural shorthand. Both the "literary" and the "manly" circulated in a newer economy where they were being given a revised cultural capital as things. The two kinds of commodification are clearly homologous and related in the sense that male genitalia became the essentialized commodity—literal and symbolic—of both masculinity and male creativity.

phallus = material man
phallus = textual man.

Heads and Groins

These changing cultural equations had important implications for discourses of male wit and literary production, especially for the traditional creativity/procreativity tropes which so dominate the history of metaphors for mental invention. The parts and organs of the human body have always been objects of metaphorization, reflecting not only specific historical conceptualizations of the physiological interrelatedness of body systems, but also culturally specific ideas about religious, social, political, or gender hierarchies.[25] But it was the figurative conjunction of heads and groins which were most congenial to ideas of literary activity. Head-groin associations had been around since classical times, but unlike other tropes for creativity, the connections of these two highly symbolic body parts called attention to the ways in which creative energies might be embodied or contain a sexual element. Such was the case with the head and brain of Enlightenment male writers, whose creativity—both as an internal mental event, and as a textual product increasingly located in a public print culture—was often imagined and written about as though it were akin to a sexual or reproductive act, something that might be explained with reference to genitalia or one of several theories of generation. Heads and groins, that is, became a heavily freighted cultural imagery for notions about male creativity and sexuality, and Chapter 3 examines their rhetorical traffic.

A pre-Enlightenment history of procreative motifs associated with mental labor and creative invention is easy enough to find, well known to scholars, and I need not itemize its most famous examples here. As is well known, from classical times the male's fertile intellect or imagination had been likened to the fecund female, whose pregnant womb became a metaphor for male creativity. But while the conjunction of the sexually-procreative and mentally-creative is hardly new, there is in the Enlightenment a unique reconfiguration of these traditional discourses which depended on newer embryological debates (especially ovist versus animalculist preformationism, and preformationism versus epigeneticism) and on the newer conceptual associations of male brain and sexualized male body. That is, the metaphors of embodiment used to characterize creative acts no longer relied so exclusively on hackneyed classical myth or quaint poeticisms but now grounded themselves in revised physiological assumptions which were quickly entering the wider domain of public thought and stereotypes. The best known of these analogies—the idea of pregnant male poets and their brain-wombs (with the book or work of art as child)—is prominent in self-conscious literary commentaries written by men during the late seventeenth and eighteenth centuries, but has received only limited attention despite the rich anthropological evidence it includes.[26] Classical creativity/procreativity tropes had encouraged the connection of male brains and female groins, thereby sexualizing the male creative principle as both a heterosexual idea and a transvestite embodiment. The transgendered dramatization of male wit as pregnant woman or eroticized female Muse included a misogynistic gesture, certainly, in which female as fleshy materiality, passive reproductive vessel, or prostitute could reflect the new literary commercialism. But these transvestite renderings enabled other discourses about the traffic in male creativity, especially in erotically-charged, epicoene exchanges between men when they discussed the nature or status of literary endeavors.[27] Part of an older rhetoric of male friendship, the presentation of self as a sexy or fecund female was a convenient vehicle for reflecting one's homosocial status among friends or male competitors where one's value as a writer could be voiced as a type of female objectification or passive sexuality; in this sense, male author as reproductive female Muse served as a marker of one's masculinity. The heterosexual aspect of the trope—male poet's erotic relationship with his female Muse—also called attention to the conjunction of the male body and creativity by making a successful imaginative outcome dependent on male sexual ability. These head-groin associations would be much affected by the historical transformations I sketched above, particularly when it came to representations of the economic value of literary "labor."

More specifically, the first two sections of Chapter 3 examine the cultural underpinnings which might explain why the inner site of male creativity was so frequently imagined as a uterus, and why the male author's entrance into, and public status within, the republic of letters was so often metaphorized as a young lady's precarious position in a male sexual economy. Indeed, reproductive tropes—whether of pregnant male brains, the birth of the child-book, the begetting and birthing of the male writer himself—are so common that their presence has been largely taken for granted. Similarly, male self-projection as female—whether as woman about to give birth, eroticized Muse, chaste or prostituted young country lass—is so frequent and casual a rhetorical gesture in the period as to seem trite and without significance, except perhaps as evidence of a thoughtless male appropriation of matters female, or worse, of a systemic misogyny. I will be arguing instead that the implications of these well-known tropes and analogies have much to tell us about the deep-level constructions of male creativity as cultural subject within a newly-commodified world of letters, as well as about the competitive structure of male literary communities. These two sections will offer a variety of answers to a difficult question: why is the female Other in her reproductive and erotic capacities so often the metaphorical terrain onto which an entire male literary culture would map a symbolic understanding of itself? As we will see, these related metaphors allowed male writers to articulate a positive identity about themselves, their art, and their relationship to literary traditions and readers. But in a rapidly expanding print culture in which devaluation of various kinds was frequently decried, these metapoetic narratives were also used to sustain and dramatize a hierarchy among male writers, providing familiar allegorizations and rhetorical codes by which a logic of inclusion and exclusion would prevail. I will argue that tropes of male brain-wombs and female Muses allowed several generations of writers to respond to changed perceptions of the value and status of their literary labor.

The companion trope—the male mind as somehow about male reproductive parts—is so much a part of our own gender slang and stereotypes about men today ("dickhead," "he's got balls," to take two examples) that one might assume the Enlightenment conjunction has been well studied. And yet, curiously, it has so far not engaged serious or sustained scholarly attention despite the fact that cultural connections of male imagination, wit, fancy, the poetical character and the genitals—especially the penis—constituted one of the most important revised and expanded discourses on male creativity as it was conceptualized in the period. Classical images associating mental creation with male genitalia are outnumbered by brain-womb/Muses before the seventeenth century, but the newer physiological models explaining male mind/body interrelationships would dramatically open up the ways the poetical character would be seen as an aspect of male embodiment. The last three sections of Chapter 3 are about the literal and figurative uses of male genitalia to characterize something about the male imagination, a male writer's public status, or his response to his own commodification in a newer, capitalist print-culture. Self-conscious narratives about the poetical character were frequently invested with yard-wit equations or with reference to the stones or seed and, not surprisingly, these links were part of the larger set of cultural formations and reflective of its ambiguities. The creative imagination as yard could take several forms: wit could be metaphorized variously as getting it up, as coitus, masturbation, ejaculation; the male poet's head might be imaged as a displaced privy member; the written work could be figured as male genitalia, something subject to expurgation which in turn was figured as a castration; pens and quills could be hard or soft yards spilling ink, semen, or urine; occasionally, the underlying subject of male writing itself was represented as a non-procreative phallus. Complex exchange principles sometimes prevailed in which yards had to be traded, lost, or denied for male wit to appear at all. Male writing might be linked to a heterosexual copulatory power or an apparently homoerotic exchange. In some instances, poet-yard equations provided an idealized mythos of an independent creative power under the sign *not* of Apollo and the Muses but of Priapus or some heightened epicoene begetting. In others, poet-yard tropes might circulate within the larger literary community as a kind of rhetorical prop or identifying shorthand which could be purloined maliciously or used combatively to enter the lists in which hierarchy, reputations, and collective standards among male writers might be fashioned and fought over. Tropes of poet-as-pintle or wit-as-yard were also used to figure an autonomous, self-generating male creativity which sometimes replaced heterosexual myths of the creative act with an exclusive homosocial drama which included ideas of autogenesis, autoeroticism, or male-male begetting. And of course male genitalia were used literally or figuratively in disputes between literary antagonists in the public realm, providing an accessible vehicle for sometimes preposterous comedy or vicious humiliation, as for instance in Colley Cibber's whorehouse anecdote which so deeply embarrassed Pope in the early 1740s. Predictably, the record of literary usage is varied and often contradictory, reflecting the differential equations and oppositions of non-literary discourses.

Heads and groins: associations of the two constitute an important rhetorical record of the collective response by authors to the history of their own commodification. What is striking about an inventory of creativity-sexuality conjunctions for male writing is the breadth and variety of vehicles drawn from contexts of masculinity and the male body. Genitalia, reproductive function (or dysfunction), transvestite gestures, birthing tropes, sexual engagements with Muses, erotic inclination, urinary flow, emasculation, libidinal deviance, and so forth—all these embodiments played a role in an authorial self-fashioning that informed the response of several generations of male writers who defended the idea of authorial independence and dignity while at the same time serving a newer capitalist mode which committed them to debased notions of literary value. Taken together, however, these collective narratives reflected a variety of ambiguities, not only about the cultural position of literature, authors, and literary tradition in the new marketplace, but also about the semiotic landscape which defined and, in a sense, normalized the perceived connection between male body and mind.

The two metaphorical economies organized around female wombs/Muses and male genitalia had complex and differential functions. The most obvious was in gender matters, where the heterosexual model apparently resident in tropes of creative male brain as female groin was really about homosocial realities for male writers, with femaleness only temporarily appropriated. That is, the female principle—whether literal or figurative, whether female Muse, pregnant womb, male poet as young virgin, male friend as epicoene lover—was simultaneously deployed, appropriated, and disposed of by male writers whose eye was on the peer group of other men. The two economies were different schema for arriving at the same result: a collective mythologizing of the poetical character which served as the underlying appeal to the community of other male writers for inclusion, approval, and authentication. But other functions reveal collective anxieties, especially when it came to ideas of the transfer of creativity from the interior mental place to its plight in the public domain—a source of considerable ambiguity when it came to sexual metaphors. With the inner site of creative energy characterized as somehow equivalent to genitalia, the public circulation of oneself as male poet was also represented as a symbolic circulation and potential loss of one's sexuality. Just as the male poet's entry into the literary community could be likened to the plight of the young virgin who entered an adult world where sexual compromise and violation were likely, so too with the wit-yard tropes, where such entry was metaphorized as equivalent to putting one's privy member in public circulation where it could be bought and sold, laughed at or admired, figuratively castrated, and owned by others.

One result was that head-groin associations changed over time. For example, the shift from ideas of autonomous gentleman author to professional writer in the marketplace was accompanied by a changing figurative embodiment: that is, the new traffic in male creativity was less frequently imaged as an immaculate patriarchal birthing or phallic self-sufficiency, and more often reflected by an imagery of precarious and painstaking reproductive "labor" or of potentially defective male genitalia. Chapter 3 will also investigate how tropes linking brains and genitalia sometimes reflected desires for a transcendent autonomy or independence from the emerging economic realities of the literary marketplace; at other times they offered metaphorical props perfectly suited to the new exchange principles. These two metaphorical systems thus served a double function, both as markers of a newer literary commercialism as well as an idealized resistance to the capitalist milieu where the status of literary labor was in transition. Often these competing functions clashed within the same work, signs of a larger ambiguity about the changing socio-economic position of authors and their writing.

Another result was that male writers such as Pope sometimes represented the poetical character as simultaneously about male sexual power and loss, as both an eroticized prowess and a sexual vulnerability. Head-groin metaphors contained contradictory possibilities about sexualized wit, presenting its origins as an erotic energy but often portraying its manifestation as an erotic depletion. The links between a writer's brain and his genitalia were sometimes characterized as forms of exchange, displacement, or compensation, which in turn might dramatize his imagination as an instance of stifled or rejected sexuality, or of missing yards. With male genitalia as the essentialized commodity of both masculinity and male creativity, the shifts from conception to execution, from private site to public expression, or from inner creative autonomy to marketplace dependency could be represented as a sexual depletion and loss, despite collective myths and meta-narratives to the contrary.

There was another sense in which connections of creative male mind and organs of generation harbored a significant ambiguity, and that was in the relative sway which either the symbolic head or groin might have over the other. In a culture for which mind and personality were seen to reside in the brain, the inclusion of another body part as symbolic site of male essence—whether yard, stones, or seed— always entailed a potential instability or splitting of selfhood because the part in question might be either synonymous with soul/mind/will or somehow at odds. The possibility of such alienation or disjunction played a role in how masculinity-as-sexualized-interiority was understood, and the underlying genital source of male identity was sometimes represented as a threat to traditional mind-body hierarchies, and in the literary realm as an anxiety that the groin's influence on the creative mind might issue in an unthinkable transgression.

Associations of the male writer's skull with male and female groins became a convenient token for his status in the literary world, a symbolic commodity in an increasingly commercialized publishing realm where literature and authors alike were being bought and sold. The author's head was subjected to a cultural metaphorization which articulated not one but a variety of collective formations ranging from the internal site of mental creativity to the sometimes fractious position of the writer in the public domain of literary hierarchies and marketplaces where the figure of the professional writer was emerging. Clustering around references to the male writer's head and brain was a collective sexualized vocabulary signaling a variety of important differences—of talent, homosocial rank, and relative position and value as a commodity. In the new marketplace of literary labor, poets' heads and groins were becoming things of commercial traffic.

The Exemplary Pope

Alexander Pope is my touchstone for these historical developments, and his example will haunt the conceptual parameters of this book just as his life, reputation, and writing forever changed and defined the eighteenth-century literary realm. Pope's impact was enormous, influencing the scene of professional writing during his lifetime and well into the nineteenth century. He was in many ways symbolic of the poetical character itself, a public icon exemplifying male genius, literary fame and wealth, and the cultural status of the new professional author. No wonder eighteenth-century readers and writers referred to him more often than any other of their contemporaries. True, he cannot be perfectly typical of the several generations of male writers that this book is about, writers whose status, interests, peer group, subject-matter, nationality, profession, education, and age are in many instances quite different. Still, Alexander the Little, in some ways so very different—an unmarried, four-foot six-inch hunchback, denied so many official possibilities because of his Catholicism, and yet the most famous eighteenth-century poet—is in other ways exemplary of the new convergence of masculinity, sexuality, and male creativity.

What makes Pope so important to a study such as this is that, perhaps more than for other writers of the period, his creativity was experienced by him and perceived by others as a palpable aspect of his masculinity—physical, social, sexual. And because his life and career straddled the historical transition from older to newer notions of masculinity, his correspondence, poetry, and comments by contemporaries allow us to see how the maleness-creativity conjunction was defined both by one's rank and homosocial connections—that is, manliness as public, reputational—as well as by an interiorized masculinity-as-sexual-embodiment. Pope's body is also immensely important because his anatomical predicament called special attention to the reconfigured connections between male mind and body, which in turn were often projected onto his creativity as sexual or genital conditions. Indeed, Pope himself eroticized the poetical character almost obsessively, using the head-groin metaphors I have sketched above as well as other sexual gestures. Most important, his historical role in the gradual commercializing of the literary domain had a double aspect: not only was he one of the first professional writers to benefit hugely from the new marketplace of letters he so often derided, but he became an object of commodification himself, not only as target of a Pope-bashing industry which made money for others, but also as a cultural emblem of the male author whose creativity and masculinity both were defined against his sexualized body. This book will use a wide variety of men to make my case about the history of male creativity for this period—from friends of Pope such as Wycherley and Cromwell to enemies like Curll, Cibber, or Ned Ward; from important figures on either side of Pope such as Oldham and Dryden or Wilkes and Sterne—but I use Pope's example as primary evidence, especially in Chapter 4, because he is so often paradigmatic of the complex intersection of male bodies, sexuality, and the poetical character.

Saving specific analysis of Pope and his contemporaries for the last chapter, I extend these preliminary observations about where his cultural exemplarity as sexualized male author can be discovered: (1) in his use of the two metaphorical economies; (2) in eroticized discussions of poetry in his correspondence with older male friends; and (3) in the literal and figurative function of Pope's head and groin when they were publicly associated with his writing.

Sexual matters were often located by Pope at the site of creativity and in commentary about the poetical character, where ideas of the eroticized male body and genital urges were significant adjuncts of how he imagined the nature of his own poetic inspiration and output. Two brief examples will illustrate. First, in his earliest letter to the aging William Wycherley, the sixteen-year-old Pope applied a traditional reproductive trope to the poetical character, using the well-worn association of mental creativity with birthing: "True Wit," he writes, "may be defin'd a Justness of Thought, and a Facility of Expression; or (in the Midwives phrase) a perfect Conception, with an easy Delivery."[28] Second, in the summer of 1707, when he was nineteen, Pope addressed and mailed a verse epistle to his friend Henry Cromwell (London dandy and rake, cousin of Oliver, and nearly thirty years older than the young poet). The poem was published piratically by Edmund Curll in his *Miscellanea* (postdated 1727, but published in 1726) and then again in 1735 in his unauthorized *Mr. Pope's Literary Correspondence*, although Pope never acknowledged it as his own. Humorously distinguishing himself from the poetasters whose rhymes would offend the hard-of-hearing Cromwell, the teenaged Alexander makes his mock-humble case, comparing himself to one Pentlow, who was, according to Curll's 1735 note, "A Gamester remarkable for his *Virile* Parts, which he us'd to be fond of Shewing":

> I hope, you think me none of those
> Who shew their Parts as *Pentlow* does,
> I but lug out to one or two
> Such Friends, if such there are, as you. (*Corr.* 1: 26, 12 or 13 July 1707)

In this cheeky analogy, questions of manliness, friendship, and poetry are tumbled into an outrageous scenario of Pope's well-hung wit which is lugged out only for close male friends who can appreciate the difference between small and large Wits, between "remarkable . . . *Virile* Parts" promiscuously displayed to all or privately unbuttoned for friends only. The lines contain a bawdy and impolite mélange of penises, wit, male friends, genital exhibitionism, and an implied hierarchy within male literary communities. Together, both examples reflect in their different ways a convergence of masculinity, homosocial relations, sexuality, and cultural constructions of male creativity. One can approach these metaphors as instances of Pope's personal difference, marshaling biographical facts which link the sexual content of the tropes to his impoverished sex life, unfortunate physical limitations, unmarried status, or other aspects of his apparent marginalization; and of course about the uniqueness of Pope in many of these respects there can be little doubt.[29] But I want to suggest that what we often view as most unique about Pope can also be understood as intensified or exaggerated symptoms of underlying cultural structures. The two deployments above are of course intimately tied to Pope's idiosyncratic interest in matters sexual—both his lifelong penchant for erotic subject matter as well as his heterosexual disappointments as he aged—but they are not wholly exclusive to Pope, being also representative of similar rhetorical equations used by his contemporaries.

This fortuitous convergence of the biographically unique but culturally exemplary Pope is most helpfully present in the ways he located his eroticized creativity in the homosocial context of male friends, especially in his teens and early twenties. As is now generally accepted, the story about Pope and poetry and sex goes far beyond his experience of heterosexual fantasies and disappointments, and must include discussion of relationships with the men he loved—usually older men (Caryll senior, Garth, Wycherley, Walsh, Trumbull, Cromwell) who offered the young poet another context through which the male creativity-sexuality conjunction would be voiced. In these relationships we can see an older model of masculinity dependent on rank and reputation, one in which young Alexander's entries into manhood and the public realm of male authorship were interconnected. The patronizing and protective milieu of older male friends provided the young poet a means of approaching a world of manly competence at a time when his adolescent sex-drive was beginning to be linked closely to his budding literary ambitions. Aspects of male friendship, that is, compensated the absence of wife or lover, but they also affected the ways Pope understood his creativity as a sexualized energy. And in the male culture of the late seventeenth and early eighteenth centuries—when Pope grew up and entered the republic of letters—the power relations and social hierarchy which were so important to collective notions of both manliness and male authorial stature were often characterized by eroticized metaphors and narratives, part of an older cultural model of male friendship which encouraged sexualized locutions and gestures of narrative transvestism between men. Writers of Pope's day incorporated certain of these epicoene and homosocial elements in their self-conscious remarks about male creativity and in allegories about the poetical character. One result can be seen in sometimes elaborate figurative gesturing and eroticized rhetorical flourishes, as in the following letter to Pope (in his early twenties) from the older Cromwell, who explains that Wycherley feels particular affection for Pope—whom he has not seen for some time—and is keen to receive his young friend:

Mr. *Wycherley* has, I believe, sent you two or three letters of invitation; but you, like the Fair, will be long sollicited before you yield, to make the favour the more acceptable to the Lover. He is much yours by his talk; for that un-bounded Genius which has rang'd at large like a libertine, now seems confin'd to you: and I shou'd take him for your Mistress too by your simile of the Sun and Earth [i.e., in an earlier letter, Pope said that he was to Wycherley as the earth to the sun: "the Earth . . . is clearer, or gloomier, just as the Sun is brighter, or more overcast"]: 'Tis very fine, but inverted by the application; for the gaiety of your fancy, and the drooping of his by the withdrawing of your lustre, perswades me it wou'd be juster by the reverse. Oh happy Favourite of the Muses! how *per-noctare*, all night long with them? but alas! you do but toy, but skirmish with them, and decline a close Engagement. (*Corr.* 1: 136, 7 December 1711)

Cromwell's epistolary wit may be exaggerated, combining an older rhetorical posturing with the locker-room strut of the libertine, but the passage contains a typical intersection of discursive elements which shaped collective constructions of male creativity. First, the beloved male friend as mistress or female lover, here twice used—initially, Wycherley the lusty libertine returning to his lover, the feminized Pope; then Wycherley-as-Mistress to the masculinized but stand-offish Pope. Second, the male writer as phallus-poet, as sexual favorite of the female Muses—here, the endless staying power of poet-Pope is flatteringly presented as a copulatory tease. Third, a clear articulation of masculine hierarchy, with Wycherley (in his early seventies) given preeminence as older male to feminized mistress-Pope, but the younger poet's brilliant wit still acknowledged.

What we are seeing here are revealing aspects of the male literary community into which Pope sought entry, and of the ways he experienced the reception of his poetic creativity as an eroticized feature of masculinity and its hierarchies. For Wycherley and his contemporaries, poetic energies and ambitions were effortlessly coupled with a variety of libidinal analogies and sexual tropes, thus encouraging an epicoene banter between males when they talked about their authorship or writing. For young Pope, these discursive repertories must have provided some compensation for his increasingly doubtful heterosexual accomplishments, but they also reinforced the connection of his poetry to his masculinity, sexual competence, and relative position in a male hierarchy. Homosociality, sex, and the poetical character converged again and again in Pope's early exchanges about his own poetic practice, as they do in this example, providing us an important glimpse into the historical conjunction of male creativity and masculinity. But while the status of young Alexander's auspicious wit was subject to the power dynamics of rank and homosocial connections, his stature as a male would also be heightened by an impressive literary debut whose genius was metaphorized as a type of manliness or a potent form of sexual energy. My point about this kind of evidence is that Pope's early career especially reflects an older model of masculinity as reputation and rank, and that his exchanges with other men underscore the importance of homosocial contexts within which a sexualized male creativity was fashioned and articulated.

Finally, as exemplary of sexualized male creativity, Pope's body was turned into a commodity, an item for sale and also a symbolic imaging of his creativity. Although we are more accustomed, perhaps, to thinking of this gifted hunchback as sadly unique or unfortunately deformed, in fact Pope's dwarfed body and literary fame became emblems of the new marketplace of letters. Helen Deutsch has shrewdly described the complex interface of Pope's body and his authorial power, and of the textual struggle to control representations of the relationship of his deformity and poetry. Describing Pope's references to his own deformed body as a kind of pre-emptive strike against a public pruriently keen about the connections between physical deformity and human character, Deutsch reminds us that "the market for Pope's poetry was inseparable from a thriving market for images of the poet. Portraying Pope was something of a national pastime." In a capitalist market where physical images of Pope's head and ideas of his body were of interest to consumers, the poet waged "war with a contemporary reading (and lampooning) public . . . for the power of self-representation," and he did so not by trying "to write himself out of his body, rather he silences his audience by making his body visible."[30] G. S. Rousseau has more recently argued how Pope must have painfully felt the parallels of his own deficient body to the castrato of Italian opera—symbol of both feminized sexual deficiency and of a commercial star-culture in the burgeoning world of consumerist leisure: "opera's sexual symbols and . . . its sexual politics . . . particularly spoke to the dwarfish Pope of impaired genitals who saw, or was forced to see, himself reflected in its eunuchs and castrati."[31] Deutsch and Rousseau both recognize the powerful connections among Pope's body, creativity and market forces, reading his literal and symbolic deformity in poems and letters as acts of controlled self-exposure, over-compensation, internalized self-hatred, or masculine self-possession. But to these eloquent readings of Pope's body and culture I want to add that associations of his physical condition and creativity, especially later in his life, were used publicly by others to gain profit or fame in ways that suggest the newer model of masculinity as sexualized interiority. The head and groin of Alexander the Little, that is, served as an exemplary association of the male mind as sexualized body; and in turn, the public conjunction of his poetry and penis also represented the commercialization of the association itself, the commodification of the discourse equating male sexuality and creativity.

And indeed Pope's head and groin were used variously by others for profit. In the summer of 1735 when Edmund Curll moved his printing shop to Rose Street in Covent Garden, his new shop sign was "Pope's Head," a sarcastic business gesture signaling the wily Curll's commercial investment in his enemy, whose head represented a significant source of Curll's profit. But the most famous example came in 1742, when Cibber's published account of a sordid whorehouse visit was followed quickly by several engravings and other pamphlet satires. Cibber's comic tribunal brought Pope's penis into the public glare—as did rumors of his urinary stricture—throwing into relief the cultural linkage of male genitalia and male creativity as interrelated print-culture commodities. I can think of no author before Pope whose poetic stature, reputation, and accomplishment were publicly imaged as questions about his privy members, with public speculation about the actual condition of his yard. Having tried all his life, not always successfully, to control images of his physicality, the ailing Pope was now faced with the prospect that his public image as poet, as a man, would be contaminated and rent by a crude equation with his pego. In a literary-historical moment of unusual spectacularization, the literal and figurative cultural connections of male genitalia and male creativity were made clear, and publicly situated on the body of England's best-known poet. More dramatically than other writers in the period 1650–1750, Pope is exemplary of the double commodification of the "manly" and the "literary" as yard.

Chapter 2
Masculinity as Male Genitalia

[handwritten annotation: 1650–1750 → a proliferation of discourse on the penis/phallus]

The underlying premises of this chapter can be summarized as fol-lows: (1) there is an unprecedented proliferation of male genitalia as subject matter ca. 1650–1750; (2) discourses of the penis/phallus which emerged in this period reflect uncertainty about the relationship of soft penis and phallus as that connection represented a range of possi-bilities for defining maleness or some facet of masculine identity; and (3) the newer equations—many of which we have unknowingly inher-ited—linking the male brain and mind to the condition of male privy members often viewed the yard as the physiological or psychological essence of maleness even while they symbolically separated the yard from the bodies of real men. One of the larger goals of this chapter, then, is to historicize the cultural function of male genitalia in the En-lightenment, and to examine literary and non-literary usage which might reveal discursive paradigms and their uneven and sometimes contradictory deployment in representative texts and contexts. I will suggest that these developments reflect the early modern origins of our now habitual separation of literal and symbolic genitalia, of the mundane penis—hardly ever a focus outside urology or Viagra ads—from the obsessively metaphorized and over-determined Phallus.

A simple historical question: why is it that from roughly the second half of the seventeenth century the penis, whether limp or erect (less often the testicles and semen), emerges as a common trope and fre-quent subject in public discussion, despite the fact that such reference was considered impolite? There are, of course, countless references to male genitalia in the written and representational records of earlier periods in Western culture, but not since classical times had men's sexual parts been so often the focus of public discourse.[1] A cursory inventory of examples will provide initial substance for this claim. Consider, for instance, the gossip and the many poems on affairs of state which talk of Charles II's wandering pintle; the libertine yard of Restoration stage rakes (e.g., from the opening scene of Wycherley's *The Country Wife* the audience's attention is captured by competing stories about Horner's penis); the scores of imperfect enjoyment and premature ejaculation poems; talking penis poems such as Pope's *Sober Advice from Horace*[2] in which the personified penis speaks to its owner; works such as *The Members to Their Soveraign* (1726, supposedly by Matthew Prior), the anonymous but possibly Rochesterian "One Writing Against His Prick" (late seventeenth century), and Sade's *Juli-ette* (1791), in which men talk to their personified yards; the many dildo stories, from Rochester's well-known "Signior Dildo" (1673), to Samuel Butler's lesser-known *Dildoides* (first published 1706), to the now almost forgotten *The Cabinet of Love* (1721) and *Monsieur Thing's Origin: Or, Seignior D---o's Adventures in Britain* (1722); the sublime phal-lus and the limp penises of pornography as they are offered up in Cleland's *Memoirs of a Woman of Pleasure* (1748–49); the many bawdy poems like *The Natural History of the Arbor Vitae: Or, The Tree of Life* (1732), *Teague-Root Display'd* (1746), "The Geranium" (n.d., attributed to Richard Brinsley Sheridan), or James Perry's *Mimosa: Or, The Sen-sitive Plant* (1779) which rely on botanical metaphors of the penis/ phallus as plant or tree; the notorious impotence trials in France and England in which the condition of the husband's genitals was the primary focus of crowded courtroom debate and widely read trial reports; nuanced literary associations of the problematic penis and artistry as in Sterne's *Tristram Shandy* (1759–65); the sharp increase of medical literature about male reproductive organs and venereal dis-ease, with an attendant rise in the quantity of anatomical illustrations. Can one make up a comparable list for any period of English history before 1650 in which attention to male genitalia is so prominent? What does such a proliferation tell us about the cultural status of male genitalia?

My claim about a proliferation of the penis-as-public-subject in the late seventeenth and eighteenth centuries can be substantiated in other ways as well. Consider the curious allusion to Pope's penis and urinary tract which appeared in an eighty-four page pornographic narrative of 1741, comically entitled *A Voyage to Lethe; By Capt. Samuel Cock* . . . .[3] The anonymous Gulliverian voyage was one of a handful of extended geographical metaphors in the still emerging world of eighteenth cen-tury pornography which spoke of penises, vaginas, and copulation in a barely-disguised lingo of navigation and exploration.[4] When Cap-tain Cock and his crew reach their destination, a palace (the willingly penetrated vagina), female hostess Voluptuaria provides them a guided tour. Just before she euphemistically compares the lengths and abili-ties of the yards of well-known men in London (Captain Cock's being the most impressive), Voluptuaria admits to a desire for a visit from the famous poet, Alexander Pope: "I confess likewise I have been very ambitious of a Visit from the great Poet of *Twickenham*, but I must after all approve his Wisdom in despising my Palace, since it would be Madness in him to attempt a Voyage hither in the leaky Condition his Cockboat is in" (30).

This curious reference to Pope raises several questions: Why should the condition of Pope's urinary tract come up as a subject in pornography in 1741? Would a public reference such as this have been typical or even possible to find a hundred and fifty or two hundred years earlier? And what, finally, are the latent cultural attitudes implied in the juxtaposition of male poet and his ailing yard? One answer is that Pope's treatment at the hands of Dr. Cheselden in August 1740 for a strangury (a urethral stricture characterized by slow and painful emission of urine) had become public knowledge and was being comically exploited by an author who insinuated, in the interests of his phallic theme, that Pope's "leaky . . . Cockboat" was the result of an earlier sexual encounter leading to an unfortunate gonorrhea. A crude tabloid raciness, in other words, targeting famous people in the marketplace of gossip, might help sales. Another answer is suggested by my initial list of examples above: within an historical context in which public attention to the penis as a topic seems to become increasingly important, it is not so surprising to find a smutty short story conjuring up the great poet's leaky penis in a surrealistic landscape of willing cunt-palaces and the crude navigations of tumescent cock-boats. But perhaps most important, this pornographer's technique of making his male figures meaningful only as they have a phallic identity (whether potent or impotent, well-hung or short, poxed or sound) is linked historically to the examples above as a sign that male identity and masculinity itself were increasingly being defined by the male reproductive system (which in turn had been given its own complex set of narratives and codes). This is not to say that the period ca. 1650–1750 has no links with the past, or that it bears no similarity to twentieth- and twenty-first century symbolisms which connect male genitalia to male identity. Rather, I want to suggest that the subject "penis/phallus" (as well as stones and seed) functions variously in history, depending on the discursive formations generated by the changing ideological requirements of different cultures at different historical moments. I want to argue, as well, that the world roughly contemporaneous with the life of Pope was preoccupied by the problematic relationship of maleness and the yard in ways that do not characterize earlier periods.

I emphasize the historical specificity of these issues because the penis has been plagued by a twentieth- and twenty-first century ahistoricism. Dominated as we still are by Freudian, Lacanian, and feminist readings of "the Phallus," one can see the contemporary tendency to take the penis out of history altogether and metaphorize it in the name of some theoretical or political agenda. During the period we are concerned with here, literal and symbolic senses were not yet separated in the stark manner they have since come to be, and the erect phallus within metaphorical equations still had reference to the biological and temporal realms of real penises attached to men, and to a host of other historical conditions (political, social, professional, intellectual) which affected the make-up of what was then a newer cultural symbolism. Lacanian and feminist approaches to the penis—to indulge in some risky generalization—have been largely preoccupied with a disembodied, metaphorized "Phallus" which has little to do with the individual experience of having had a penis (whether flaccid or erect), and is very often uninformed by a notion of historical constructedness. This is not to dismiss the important contributions made by the larger theoretical orientation of psychoanalytical and feminist methodologies, both of which have done much in the last decades to open up important interpretive possibilities which can supplement historical analyses of sex and gender. One of the deep ironies, however, is that the poststructuralist Phallus—detached from men's bodies, pried away from history—has also done much to obscure the complex historical discourses associated with the male reproductive system in general, and the penis in particular. By theorizing "the Phallus" as transcendental signifier of an original (and now missing) desire, or, as the phallogocentric discourse of Patriarchy itself, these sophisticated academic constructs have worked against the possibility of tracing a history of symbolisms associated with the penis. As a metaphor for a linguistic concept, or as a synecdoche for the paternal metaphor, "the Phallus" has proven to be an illuminating new category; for a history of male bodies, on the other hand, it has been a stumbling block, lacking a properly historical and material account of how the physiological has been transformed variously, at different historical moments, into the symbolic.

Predictably, notions of male creativity were affected by the discursive variety and ambiguity which informed a newer symbolic language for the male organs of generation. Indeed, the "literary" was an important vehicle for the proliferation and development of these discourses in the public imaginary, making accessible through the pleasures of wit the various tropes and rhetorical gestures which marked these discourses. A publication such as *A Voyage to Lethe* will make little claim upon literary greatness, and yet it is one of many examples in which a cultural "logic" is at work even in so bawdy a gesture as the juxtaposition of poet Pope and his ailing yard. But in order to investigate the important implications for male creativity and the poetical character we need to map the conceptual shifts and discursive formations by which Pope's culture gave meaning to the male reproductive system.

The first section of this chapter will sketch the dominant cultural constructions which informed Enlightenment treatments of male organs of generation, first as they were inherited from classical medical traditions and modified to suit a newer medicalized sexuality, and then as they appeared in non-medical narratives as problematic cultural issues. I will be arguing that in these early modern formulations the most far-reaching implication would be the physiological links between the genitals and the brain—particularly the brain-testicles homology—and that newer models of brain-genitalia correspondences raised questions about how male consciousness might be informed by the organs of generation, which in turn intensified the perceived links between the reproductive system and an essentialized maleness.

The second section explores the "problematic penis," the site of competing cultural equations of male body and mind. The historical evidence suggests that there were a variety of discursive formations which commodified the male as his penis. However, despite the diversity of specific deployments, there appears to be a deep-level set of cultural equations characterized by three intersecting categories, which I investigate in sections three through five: the ways the relationship between soft penis and erection was conceptualized; the question of whether the head-genitals relationship was conceived as a directly or inversely proportional one; the implications of a notion of an enigmatic yard in which the relationship of penis and mind was severed, leaving two separate systems in which the yard was incommensurate or enigmatically at odds with male will or identity.

More specifically, cultural conceptualizations of the relationship between soft and turgid penis were not limited to a privileging of the symbolically detached phallus, but rather the potent erection as self-contained symbol was found along with a discourse about the temporal drama of the yard in the lives and on the bodies of individual men. That is, there was a recognition that the process of tumescence and detumescence has different figurative possibilities than does the phallus separated imaginatively from the penis, and the presence of both discursive modes is typical of the period, reflecting an uncertainty about how the relationship of soft and erect tarse might be representative of masculine identity or mind. As well, various mind-yard equations reflected competing definitional systems: in directly proportional formulations, the turgid member was seen as a synecdoche for the power of male will, virility, or social and political sway, and the castrated, impotent, or small-yarded male was representative of forms of failure or mental lack; in inverse modes, however, the large penis was the sign of a fool, and a genital deficiency (castration, impotence, small penis) was compensated by mental capacity. Finally, the yard was sometimes viewed as an irrational and ungovernable Other, at odds with male will, and commodified as a thing to be owned or exchanged by others without reference to the male self or character to which it was attached. In medical debates about what caused an erection, it was agreed that not the will but the subversive imagination was the source, thus associating turgid tarse and wit with irrational bodily forces threatening to overwhelm the typical hierarchy of mind over body. Moreover, new medical techniques for "blowing up" the cut-off penis of cadavers contributed to concepts of the autonomous phallus severed from the conscious mind. The erect privy member as symbolic commodity was evident not only in anatomical explorations, but also in the tumescence of hanged criminals and in the function and status of dildoes. Section six examines several outcomes of these ambiguous symbolic practices as they figured in the notorious impotence trials. In these highly public tribunals, the vexed cultural meanings of the penis were reflected in the startling proposition that the erected yard is *not* the conclusive sign of male virility, thus destabilizing a notion of masculine identity as it might be proven in relation to the phallus.

A fascinating cultural logic emerged from these competing discourses, one which we have inherited and now largely take for granted: masculinity and male identity were increasingly understood as being intimately defined by one's groin; this meant that male genitalia—the yard in particular—gained status as the new commodity representing maleness; but the yard-as-masculinity synecdoche included a tendency to separate men from the body part that had also become the key symbol of maleness itself; this commodification of the yard resulted in a new and fractured form of self-consciousness for individual men in which the experiencing self (particular man with penis) had to engage with the experience of self as commodity (yard = maleness). This fracture is symptomatic of later developments (such as Lacanian and feminist psychoanalysis) in which the symbolic freight of the phallus-as-commodity overwhelms the historical record of men and their bodies.

Male Brain-Male Genitalia Interrelationships: Stones and Seed

Prior to the seventeenth century, the yard, stones, and seed were an important adjunct of masculinity, but not necessarily the most important signs of maleness. Male organs of generation were simply one of a variety of social markers acting as a subset of male privilege as citizen, father, patriarchal agent, or legal entity—bodily signs, in other words, which, along with other attributes (lineage in particular), entitled the owner to a position somewhere on a gendered socio-political hierarchy but did not by themselves constitute some essentialized male identity anchored ontologically to biological sex. I need not rehearse the arguments provided by Sander L. Gilman and Thomas Laqueur which trace the cultural manifestations of male and female sexuality within a one-sex, one-flesh corporeal model before the eighteenth century.[5] Suffice it to say that before seventeenth-century physiology precipitated a paradigmatic shift from a hierarchical model of biological sex (in which female genitalia were an inverted, colder, less perfect version of male genitalia) to one based on essential biological difference (of sexual organs, nervous systems, skeletons), the privy parts of men served variously as symbolic tokens of a culturally construed masculinity and therefore of a superior position on the scale of being. But it would not be until the seventeenth and eighteenth centuries that a biological notion of male sexuality was widely imagined as constitutive of masculine psychological reality, and that the male reproductive system would become one of the primary sites of an essentialized maleness, with the yard as the key symbol of that essence.

This is not to suggest that classical medicine and early cultural constructions of the significance of male genitalia did not make important links to masculinity; the testes, yard, and seed were obviously tied to matters of gender before 1650, and invested with cultural symbolism which would be inherited by Pope's culture, although modified by a newer physiological symbolism which would replace the older equations. One way to assess the nature of this transmission is to ask what it was that mainstream Enlightenment commentaries found most distinctive about the representational qualities in classical medical theories and older social values. What, in other words, struck the moderns as typical in the older symbolism, and how did they both identify with and differentiate themselves from the figurations of bygone traditions?

Seventeenth and eighteenth-century "high" medical treatises and "low" popular sexologies are particularly revealing in this regard, nearly always glancing back at the ways an older symbolism converted biology into culture.[6] A typical example from the medical literature is Regnier De Graaf's *Tractatus De Virorum Organis Generationi Inservientibus* (1668), the longest medical treatise on male genitalia of the period, frequently cited by subsequent medical writers, and having the distinction of being perhaps the most significant compendium of received medical beliefs about the male organs of generation in the seventeenth and eighteenth centuries. In a more comprehensive manner than most, De Graaf's 160–page treatise included retrospective anthropological nods to older classical theories as well as careful references to all of the significant medical theorists of the sixteenth and seventeenth centuries.[7] Introducing the genital parts outside the cavity of

the abdomen, De Graaf begins with "the *testes*, i.e., 'witnesses,' either because they provide evidence of virility, in as much as from them we recognize a man capable of generating offspring, or because, among the Romans, no one was allowed to make a will unless he had witnesses and these were of the male sex."[8] De Graaf's contemporaries (and the eighteenth-century physiologists to follow) would repeat the testes-as-virility formula, of course, and a rhetoric of "witnessing" would be repeated with few variations by "high" and "low" treatises alike. But his etymological precision is also a means of differentiating the symbolic value which the possession of testicles had earlier signified from the modernness of his own analysis, which I shall consider more fully below. What Enlightenment writers most noticed about the early formulations of masculinity and testicles was the symbolic emphasis placed on them as signs of acceptable oath-taking, the right to bear witness, and reliable testimony. The "testes" are so called, Thomas Gibson wrote in *The Anatomy of Humane Bodies Epitomized* (1682), "either because they testifie one to be a man, or because amongst the Romans none was admitted to bear witness but he that had them."[9] The twentieth edition of Venette's *Conjugal Love or, The Pleasures of the Marriage Bed Considered* (1750) reflected that "it was not allowable formerly, in the courts of justice, at Rome, for any man to bear witness against another, except his testicles were entire."[10] And Voltaire would point to another ancient meaning, to be found in the Old Testament, of touching another man's testicles as a gesture of promise-making: "It was a mark of respect, a symbol of fidelity, as formerly our feudal lords put their hands between those [thighs] of their paramount lords."[11]

This thread of anthropological reportage characterizes Enlightenment understanding of earlier cultural constructions of the stones as biological signs of reproductive ability but also of a certain kind of homosocial privilege involving legal capacity or gestures of fidelity. The most colorful and perversely allegorized variation of these older conceptualizations comes in John Marten's *A Treatise of all the Degrees and Symptoms of the Venereal Disease* (6th ed., 1708), which tells of "one *Combalus*" who castrated himself:

because he perceiving himself to be affected by *Stratonice*, the Wife of the King of *Assyria*, who he was to attend upon in some Progress she made, after he had secretly Castrated himself, Sealed up his *Testicles* in a Box, and deliver'd it unto the King, to be kept as some Jewels of value enclos'd; and afterwards when he was suspected of Incontinency with the Queen, he was acquitted of the Accusation, by that pledge of Fidelity he left in the Custody of the King, when the Box came to be open'd.[12]

Swearing on the testicles as a gesture or "witness" of fidelity is here carried to a preposterous narrative pitch, but Marten's anecdotal sensationalism is nevertheless consistent with the examples above, and marks one of the typical narrative tactics by which Enlightenment writers would distinguish an older symbolism associated with male genitalia. When we examine the underlying codes of seventeenth and eighteenth-century commentary below, we will see that the testes no longer have a dominant sense of male legal status but rather are situated among a hierarchy of bodily organs whose closest relative is the brain. And the testicles-brain homology, as one might expect, represents a significant shift in symbolic emphasis, with important implications for how masculinity and male identity would be figured.

A similar retrospective is to be found in introductions to the yard, in which the moderns briefly recount the mythical, military, or racial symbolism most prominent in earlier constructions. Although the classical deity Priapus is not a significant presence in seventeenth and eighteenth-century uses of mythology, it is this older ithyphallic god of fertility which Enlightenment treatises associate with the emphasis of a classical symbolism.[13] Montaigne, one of Pope's favorite writers, reminded the reader in his essay "Upon Some Verses of Virgil" that the ancients commonly deified the erect penis:

> The Aegyptian dames in their Bacchanalian feasts wore a wooden one about their necks, exquisitely fashioned, as huge and heavy as every one could conveniently beare. . . . The greatest and wisest matrons of Rome were honoured for offring flowers and garlands to God Priapus. And when their Virgins were married, they (during the nuptials) were made to sit upon their privities.[14]

John Marten's *Gonosologium Novum* (1709) would similarly recall that "The Ancients ranked the *Yard* of Man among the number of their *Gods*,"[15] as would Voltaire: "The Egyptians were so far from attaching any depravity to what we dare neither uncover nor name that they carried in procession a large image, named *phallum*, of the virile member, to thank the gods for their goodness in making this member serve for the propagation of mankind."[16] De Graaf would isolate the same symbolism in his characterization of an earlier cultural construction of the penis, but with the addition of military and racial contexts:

> How much esteem and dignity the male member enjoyed among the Egyptians as well as among not a few other peoples can be seen in Riolan's *Anthropographia* (2.30). . . . [De Graaf quotes verses which refer to the public decoration by reputable women of a huge artificial phallus carried through the main square.] A story told by van Linschoten in his *Itinerario* is also worthy of note. The Kaffir peoples of Ethiopia, who dwell on the sea coast at the Cape of Good Hope, are constantly engaged in wars with one another. Victorious warriors cut off the penises of those they have slain or captured, dry them out and regularly offer them to their king in the presence of the other noblemen in this fashion: they each take a number of penises in their mouths and spit them out at the feet of the king, who gathers them together, picks them up

[handwritten: → Priority catg? between ancient (=modern ancients – 1600s w-ancient ancients?) and modernity:]

34 Chapter 2 *[handwritten: in former times, penis was a direct sign of status – whereas in modern times, things are more tricky]*

and restores them to the victorious warriors as royal gifts; the warriors string them together to form necklaces which they hang from the necks of their betrothed or their wives. (45)

The racialized image of penis-spitting African tribesmen is as startling, perhaps, as Marten's testicles-in-a-box anecdote, especially when contrasted to De Graaf's medicalized penis, but it also indicates the range of an older symbolism which associated male genitalia with contexts of military victory, war trophies, or aggressive penile display.[17] And the anthropological account also anticipates early modern racial stereotyping which would assign the threateningly over-sized or grotesquely infibulated penis to primitive non-white males. Certainly the phallus as scepter, weapon, or castrated trophy can be found in the seventeenth and eighteenth-century records, particularly around Charles II's notoriously phallic reign, and, forms of priapic worship are still evident in pornographic works such as John Oldham's *Sardanapalus* (late 1670s),[18] Alexis Piron's *Ode à Priape* (1710),[19] and John Wilkes's *Veni Creator; Or, The Maid's Prayer* (1750s)[20]; but Pope's culture had assigned to the penis/phallus a new role whose symbolism was about a potentially problematic masculine identity rather than externalized signs of mythical generation, military prowess, or the racially exotic and monstrous. For the ancients, both the yard and stones were relatively direct signs of status or legal character; for the moderns, signification could be a more difficult matter, especially when the relationship between groin and mental identity was viewed as an inverse or incommensurate one.

[handwritten marginalia: No. ancient vs modern]

I dwell on the historical and anthropological note-taking of these Enlightenment commentators to illustrate just how self-conscious they were about the older constructions of the meaningfulness of male genitalia. In the cases of the testicles and penis, earlier representations were either no longer a part of the insistent medicalization of physiological systems within the new health sciences, or their legal, social, and military metaphors had been absorbed but largely rewritten within a newer cultural mapping of the human body as machine.[21] Semen was another matter, however. Despite debates by classical medical theorists about the make-up of male seed, its genesis, and its function, older morphological models had nevertheless produced two generally agreed-upon concepts which were to be absorbed almost completely by the new physiology and its popular transmission, either literally or figuratively: semen was (along with animal spirits) one of the most spiritous and vital fluids, and therefore exceedingly important to the well-being of the male body; and the production of seed and its discharge were linked directly to the brain.[22] In both instances, the moderns would medicalize and concentrate these beliefs through a newer physiology which increasingly located an essentialized maleness exclusively within the microscopic workings of the tubes, glands, tissue, and fluids of the parts of generation. The new constructs of male reproductive biology would recall the older medical symbolism while ushering in very different cultural contexts and symbolic codes.

From the earliest narratives of its essence, sperm was seen as a vital pneuma associated with heat, fire, fertile foam, and an ineffable admixture of spirit and matter.[23] A liquid with a supreme generative power, seed had acquired the status of a life-force itself. The new physiology and the sexologies repeat this conceptual rhetoric with approval. On the refinement of semen in the epididymis, De Graaf writes that the watery parts of the seminal liquid "foam more as they pass through the tubules and bestow final perfection upon them, a process which we believe Hippocrates to have understood similarly to ourselves where he says that foam is of 'the essence of semen' " (32); he concludes that "the most noble" semen "is a hot and humid spiritous body produced in the testicles or a body full of spirit capable of generating a soul" (44). Paraphrasing Hippocrates, Samuel Tissot's *Onanism: or, A Treatise Upon the Disorders Produced by Masturbation* (4th ed., 1772) ranks "the seminal Liquor . . . [as] the most valuable" of bodily humors, and, with Galen's authority, calls it "the most subtle . . . vital spirit. . . . the Essential Oil of the animal liquors" (48–9, 52). Venette's encomium is also typical, claiming of "*Sperma*" that "The moisture from whence the seed is derived . . . is the most refined and noblest part of the human frame, containing, in itself, the whole nature and complexion of every part of the body; or in other words, being the very essence of man" (38–9). Other medical treatises offer up a similar rhetorical palette of heightened agency, privileged status, or sublime creativity: Joseph Cam's *A Practical Treatise: Or, Second Thoughts on the Consequences of the Venereal Disease* (3rd ed., 1729) registers a sense of awe that "such noble Virtues are hoarded up in that Matter elaborated by the Testicles" (2); Robert James's *A Medicinal Dictionary* (1745) calls semen "the Flower, and choicest Part of the Blood, and nervous Fluid";[24] and Pierre-Louis Moreau de Maupertuis's *The Earthly Venus* (1753) asks whether "the seminal spirits" are "not the fire sung by poets as having been stolen from the gods by Prometheus."[25] By far the most remarkable eighteenth-century appreciation of the power of the seminal liquor is to be found in James Graham's end-of-century *A New and Curious Treatise of the Nature and Effects of Simple Earth, Water and Air* (1793):

The seminal principle, or luminous, ever-active balsam of life, is the grand staff, strength, all-animating vital source or principle of the beauty, vigour and serenity, both of body and of mind. Without a full and genial tide of this rich, vivifying luminous principle, continually circulating in every part of the system, it is absolutely impossible that either man or woman can enjoy either health, strength, spirits or happiness. (27)[26]

The rhetorical dimension is an important aspect of how the moderns would keep alive older ideas of sperm as a male quintessence linked to a semi-divine realm of spiritual fluids. But the verbal vehicles of this conceptual tradition were carried over into the literary realm as well, where semen as a sublimely-charged synecdoche of male creativity reflected a larger tendency to equate maleness with genitalia. In one of the few successfully concluded imperfect enjoyment poems of the Restoration—an anonymous poem entitled "The Lost Opportunity Recovered," printed in *Wit and Drollery. Jovial Poems* (1682)— Lysander, the premature ejaculator, returns the morning after to his Cloris (a married woman) and, "With a proud Courage and with stiffness blest, / Foaming with Love he makes to Beauty's Lap" for a second encounter. Engaging more efficaciously this time, Lysander recovers his tumescence, ejaculates, and his paramour "wip'd away those drops of Liquid Fire."[27] Nearly a century later Claude Quillet's *The Joys of Hymen, Or, the Conjugal Directory: A Poem, in Three Books* (1768) prescribed nothing less than a personal technology for the most favorable production of sperm, as well as specific recommendations about the best time for intercourse. One must avoid the venereal act after the evening meal, "Fresh from the festal board," to allow proper time for the decoction of semen from the newly supplied blood:

> For sages say, the warm and active juice,
> Which purple wines and Ceres gifts produce;
> The kindly strength which feeds the genial flame
> Of love, or nourishes the vital frame:
> All these (a rude and undigested heap)
> Digestive pow'rs will ripen while you sleep;
> Strain through unnumber'd tubes the flowing tide,
> And blood from Chyle, and sperm from blood divide.[28]

According to this physiologically nuanced poet, morning is the ideal moment to discharge "love's warm balm." Leaving aside the timing of intercourse or the happy recoveries of premature ejaculators, however, one can easily discover a vocabulary of liquid fire, genial flame, foaming energy, or spiritous fluid permeating the seed-lingo in non-medical narratives throughout the period under discussion. Swift uses the spirit-semen equation satirically in *A Tale of a Tub and A Discourse Concerning the Mechanical Operation of the Spirit*,[29] as does Pope in an allegedly suppressed conclusion to "Epistle to Miss Blount, on her leaving the Town, after the Coronation."[30] John Cleland's Fanny Hill rapturously describes male ejaculate as "his soul distil'd," "the spermatic injection . . . spurting liquid fire," and, in the novel's last sexual act, the beloved Charles's orgasm is attended by "my dear love's liquid emanation of himself."[31]

This last passage from *Fanny Hill* clearly indicates the direction which Enlightenment writers would take in their refitted use of classical medical beliefs, and points to another set of beliefs about the value of semen and its effects, namely, the *aura seminalis* as productive of masculinity itself. In the overall economy of bodily fluids (blood, lymph, milk, menses, sweat, tears, urine, phlegm), seed had always been ranked highly, placed on a par with animal spirits. Part of the reason for this was that semen was viewed as an especially concentrated liquid whose powerful presence (or excessive loss) was not to be underestimated. Recounting earlier theories, De Graaf noted that "Some even think that a single drachm of semen is the equivalent of twenty of blood" (44). The sexologies made greater claims: "if we believe Avicenna," Venette would explain, one unit of seed is the equivalent of "forty times the quantity of blood" (172); predictably enough, Tissot's anti-masturbation tract would repeat the more exaggerated claim, reminding the reader "that physicians of all ages have been unanimously of opinion, that the loss of an ounce of this humour would weaken more than that of forty ounces of blood" (2). For the seventeenth and eighteenth century medical experts, however, male seed would hold precedence as a fluid also because it was a chemical agent of maleness itself. As "the heaviest humour in the human body," according to Albrecht von Haller's *First Lines of Physiology* (1747), seed's function went beyond creative discharge, being "absorbed again into the blood, where it produces wonderful changes."[32] It was the *aura seminalis*, after all, which explained the journey from boyhood to virile manhood, altering the voice and skin, producing body hair, giving rise to physical strength and courage. Described at times as almost a world-soul or fiery emanation of divine-like spirit, semen was also a concentrated, essentialized masculinity—each drop a distilled and heated liquid carrying within it the potential code, as it were, of a male identity.

Indeed, one of the striking features of Enlightenment medical narratives is that it is not the yard or testicles but the seed which evoked an overall heightening of rhetoric. An important cause of this medico-scientific wonder is surely the improvement of microscopes and the discovery of sperm in the 1670s by Ham and Leeuwenhoek, the latter an acquaintance of De Graaf (both lived in Delft).[33] As Marjorie Nicolson and John Harley Warner have demonstrated, the larger cultural effects

which microscopic visions had on the collective imagination ought not
to be underestimated,[34] and in the case of Leeuwenhoek's animalcules,
homunculi, or spermatic worms (see Figure 1)—"spermatozoa" would
not be used until the 1820s—the imaginative appeal is particularly
noteworthy given the fact that it was *not* the animalculist but the ovist
school of preformationist thought which dominated embryology from
the late seventeenth until well into the eighteenth century.[35] That is,
although the miniature human was thought by most to reside within
the egg, where its unfolding and growth would somehow be triggered
by male semen, and, although a majority of the medico-scientific community was skeptical of animalculist arguments, the idea of the sperm
as homunculus or preformed human-ness (particularly maleness)
nevertheless held a wide imaginative appeal throughout the same period, showing up not only in animated debates published in the *Philosophical Transactions*,[36] but also in accounts of intense personal curiosity
by non-scientists such as Charles II, who in the mid-1680s commanded Robert Hooke, Curator of the Royal Society, to demonstrate
these animalcula, or by the twenty-nine year-old Pope, who with his
mother visited one Mr. Hatton "who is . . . curious in microscopes and
showed my mother some of the *semen masculinum*, with animascula [sic]
in it" (*Corr.* 1: 465, Pope to Caryll, 18 February 1717/18). Popular versions of sperm-as-man showed up in print as well, most famously in
the first two chapters of *Tristram Shandy*, but also in novels such as *The
History of the Human Heart* (1749) or in "Sir" John Hill's spoof of
sperm-catching machines in *Lucine sine Concubitu* (1750). The reasons
for this appeal are not simply the new imaginative venue provided by
the microscope, however; the image of the teeming seminal fluid—
each drop containing the compacted human being, usually imagined
male—also maintained the larger ideological construct of a superior
male creativity not just at the macro levels of art, politics, and material
sway, but now also at the micro level of the nearly invisible processes of
life-giving itself. What microscopes brought to discourses about sperm
was visible proof of maleness in its smallest constituent form. These
conceptual images—sperm as male spirit, animalcule as tiny man—
gave dramatic substance to the idea that masculinity and male identity
itself were directly dependent on the man's genitals and, by extension,
that in the mysterious and spiritous inner workings of the organs of
generation could be found an essential truth about the male mind.

   But in seventeenth and eighteenth century medical models, no
theory about sperm was more important than the brain-testicles homology, which functioned *not* as a direct but an inverse relationship.
The origins of the homology can be explained partly as the legacy of
classical medical theorists, the majority of whom believed that semen

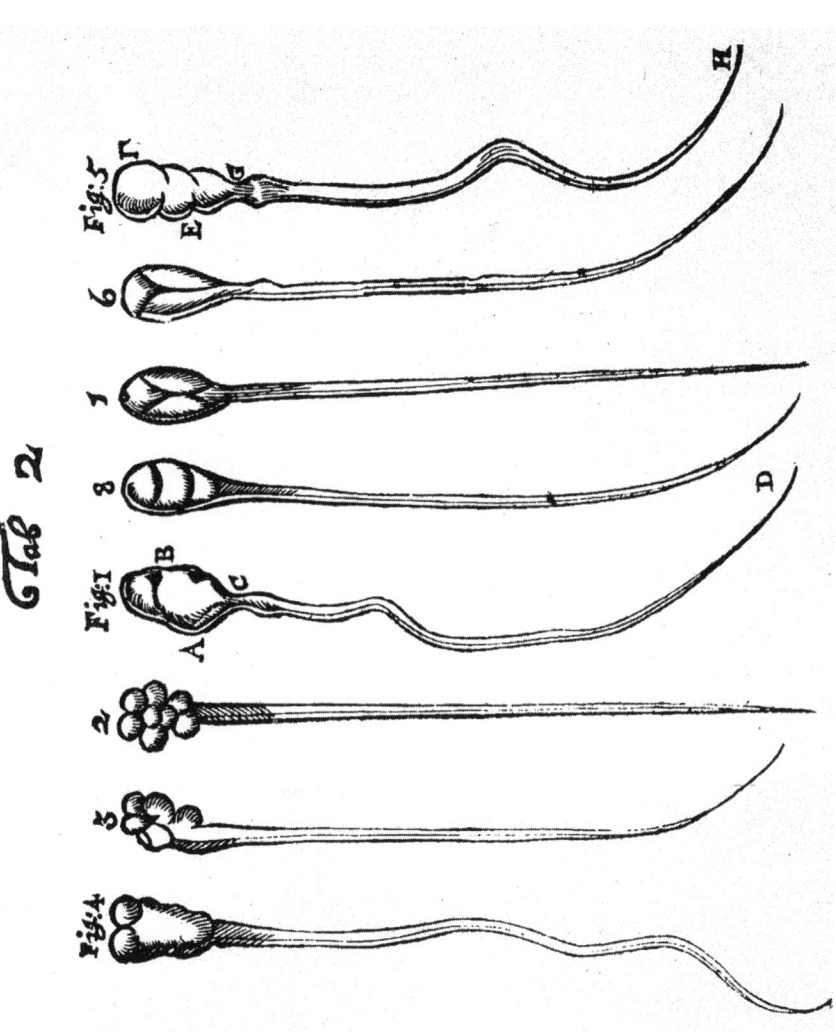

Figure 1. Leeuwenhoek's drawings of spermatozoa, "Observations Di. Anthonii Leewenhoeck, de prognatis è Semine genitali Animalculis," *Philosophical Transactions*, No. 142, 1678. Courtesy of The Wellcome Library, London.

originated in the brain,[37] and that excessive seminal loss would therefore debilitate the brain. Tissot's anti-masturbatory tract cites this model
of inverse relationship as a historic remnant of classical thought: "Hippocrates thought it was extracted from all the body, and particularly
the head. . . . Galen is of this opinion . . . [that] When a person loses
his seed . . . he loses at the same time the vital spirit: so that it is not astonishing that too frequent coition should enervate, as the body is
thereby deprived of the purest of its humours" (48–49). Venette, likewise, would acknowledge the literalism of the ancients' notion of a
balanced fluid economy, reporting that "The brain . . . has been diminished to that degree in some lascivious men, according to Galen,
that it has not been bigger than one's fist" (162–63). The force of the
older model is evident in other sexologies, as well, which sometimes
appear to accept the classical theory without modification, as does
Marten's *Gonosologium Novum* in accounting for one of the causes of
impotence:

So will a man's being wounded behind the Ears . . . whereby certain branches
of the Jugular Veins and Arteries that are there have been cut; so that after
those Vessels have been cicatriz'd, there follows an interception of the Seminal
Matter downwards, and also of the community, which ought of necessity to be
between the Brain and the *Testicles*; so that when the Conduits or Passages are
stopp'd, the Stones or *Testicles* cannot any more receive either Matter or lively
Spirits from the Brain in so great quantity, as it was wont. (41)

As these passages suggest, the older thesis survived in the sexologies, which offered readers a simplistic literal version of the brain-
sperm connection: interrupt the downward flow from brain to testicles
and sperm would be deficient; discharge too much sperm and suffer
a brain-drain (usually figured as lassitude, headache, blurred vision,
dizziness, stupidity; sometimes as madness or death, as in the anti-
masturbation diatribes). But the brain-testes homology was also intensified by newer studies in reproductive physiology such as De Graaf's
which, having explained the confection of semen as a refinement of
blood within the testes (see his *Tractatus* 29–32) rather than of nervous
fluid or blood within the brain, were now more keenly interested in
the physiological dynamics by which blood and animal spirits were
shared by brain and testicles. One result was that the literalism of the
classical linkage of brain and sperm was replaced by a homology in
which brain and testicles were seen to have a correspondence of structure and function—that is, the brain produced animal spirits from the
blood just as the testicles produced semen from the blood. As Jean
Baptiste Verduc put it in *A Treatise of the Parts of a Human Body* (1704),
"nothing can give us a clearer Idea of the vast Activity of the Seed,
than the Similitude, which is betwixt those Parts which prepare the

Seed, and the Brain. These two parts in short, have in a manner the same Structure; they both consist of several small Pipes which suck in the most spiritous parts from the Mass of the Blood; and so we may say that the Testicles are in a manner a second Brain, since they do filtrate as the Brain doth, a Liquor which is almost as penetrating, and as spiritous as the Animal Spirits."[38]

Of course, the shift from literal to homologous connection did not happen in a vacuum, and depended on parallel developments in neuroanatomy and new theories about cerebral and neurological function, particularly as they were set forth by Thomas Willis, arguably the most significant neurophysiologist of the early modern period.[39] In writing of the nerves which affected the testicles, and wanting to correct the erroneous belief that semen was derived from nervous fluid in the brain, Willis offered an account of the interrelationship of seed, blood, animal spirits, brain, and testes which provided the dominant conceptualization of such matters through much of the eighteenth century. Excessive discharge of semen, he reasoned, produces a general debility of brain and nerves because the replenishment of seed requires an immediate flow of blood and animal spirits to the genital area, thus temporarily robbing the brain of its own requirements.[40] But while Willis's and De Graaf's physiological models helped to banish older connections in favor of the more complex similitude later described by Verduc, what they retained from classical assumptions was the notion that brain and testicles were still linked by a complex fluid economy which functioned as an inverse hydraulic relationship. As major physiological entities in the hierarchy of bodily organs, the brain and testicles shared the same system of fluids, competing for animal spirits or vital matter in the blood; according to nearly every commentator in the seventeenth and eighteenth centuries, maximum health and stability were achieved for each organ and for the body as a whole when a happy physiological balance of fluid-making and fluid-use could be maintained. Within what has been called "the sublime order of the spermatic economy,"[41] this meant neither the excessive discharge nor prolonged retention of semen. Reflecting the state of knowledge at mid-century, Robert James's *A Medicinal Dictionary* (1745) would present the orthodox view that "Retention of the Semen induces a Torpor and languid State of the Body, and often lays a Foundation for terrible nervous Disorders. . . . Venery ought to be only moderately used, lest too great an Evacuation of the Semen should prove prejudicial to Health. . . . Nor should Persons indulge themselves in Venery after strong Application of Mind" (3: s.v. "VENUS"). A balanced fluid economy assured health, and this entailed occasional rather than frequent sexual intercourse; masturbatory emission was unnecessarily wasteful and potentially harmful. Excessive venery might not shrink one's brain to the size of a fist, as Galen had warned, but it would surely interfere with a man's ability to think.

But the inverse relationship of brain and testicles via sperm was not merely a mechanical matter. What was most significant about the updated use of classical literalism was the newer conceptualization of the relationship of male body and male mind encouraged by the homology itself. And in this regard, the impact of Willis's neurophysiological theories are particularly important. Because concepts of mind and soul were now commonly localized as brain and nervous system, the newer male brain-male genitalia correspondences—whether direct or inverse—were not simply issues of animal health, but also raised important questions about how masculine consciousness might be informed by the organs of generation. The seventeenth and eighteenth centuries had inherited from classical medical models an identification of maleness with the reproductive system, but the meaning of that system had changed as a result of improved physiological experimentation, the advent of the microscope in medicine, and new embryological and neurological speculation. The older symbolism, as we have seen, was about hierarchy and analogy in which seed, yard, and testes were one of many markers linking the man to issues of legitimacy or power within the frameworks of law, citizenship, paternity, or reproductive potency. The medicalized version of the moderns absorbed some of these older constructions, but now viewed genitalia as an important effect on the brain/mind; reproductive biology, in other words, was generating a model of an essentialized maleness whose consciousness and experiential history might be understood as linked to the condition and activities of the sexual parts.

But it is in the non-medical discourses that we find the larger cultural ramifications of how the genitals-mind correspondences were absorbed and then played out through a variety of verbal codes, many of which informed the self-mythologizing narratives of male literary communities. From the most simplistic mechanical versions of the equation to the sophisticated adaptations of Laurence Sterne, the historical record reflects an interest in this newly sexualized male brain whose sensibility and deepest thinking could be understood as inescapably linked to the privy parts. As we will see, the interrelated head and groin were often conceived in subtle symbolic terms, as in Diderot's epistolary observation that "Il y a un peu de testicule au fond de nos sentiments les plus sublimes et de notre tendresse la plus epurée" ["There is a bit of testicle at the bottom of our most sublime feelings and our purest tenderness"].[42] This is a complex notion, intimating a deep link between mental conception or sensibility and the generative production of spiritous seed in the testes. In this symbolic short-hand, creative acts are not about male brain-wombs but rather the microscopic making of the seminal liquor which expands and unfolds as a male principle of body and mind. Sterne offers up his own comic redaction of the brain-testes homology in Walter's meditations on the seat of the soul, one of whose possibilities is the "very thin, subtle and very fragrant juice which *Coglionissimo* [big balls] *Borri*, the great *Milaneze* physician, affirms, in a letter to *Bartholine*, to have discovered in the cellulae of the occipital parts of the cerebellum."[43] Hilariously blurring the distinction between semen and neurospinal fluid, Sterne implies that great thoughts about the brain—indeed, the soul itself—might come from the personified testicles of the good Italian doctor. Satirists such as Swift would also come to the mind-genitals equation with a sophisticated sense of their interaction, even though his put-down of the Fanatic would depend on the crudest reduction of intellect and spirit into lust and sperm:

the Seed or Principle, which has ever put Men upon *Visions* in Things *Invisible*, is of a Corporeal Nature: For the profounder *Chymists* inform us, that the Strongest *Spirits* may be extracted from *Human Flesh*. Besides, the Spinal Marrow, being nothing else but a Continuation of the Brain, must needs create a very free Communication between the Superior Faculties and those below: And thus the *Thorn in the Flesh* serves for a *Spur* to the *Spirit*. I think, it is agreed among Physicians, that nothing affects the Head so much, as a tentiginous Humor, repelled and elated to the upper Region, found by daily practice, to run frequently up into Madness. . . . I have been informed by certain Sanguine Brethren of the first Class, that in the Height and *Orgasmus* of their Spiritual exercise it has been frequent with them *****; immediately after which, they found the *Spirit* to relax and flag of a sudden with the Nerves, and they were forced to hasten to a Conclusion. (*A Discourse Concerning the Mechanical Operation of the Spirit*)[44]

In this comical parley of body and mind, Swift anatomizes religious hypocrisy by deploying iatromechanical concepts which transformed mind and body into simple machine laws. However, he also insinuates an inescapable presence of a genital sexuality as it will affect the farthest reaches of mind into philosophy, religion, and the visionary. While Swift might parody "mechanical operations" as a methodology for investigating the interface of body and mind, his own ironic play with "Spirit"—as ineffable mind/soul, animal spirits, or sperm—points to the complex linkage of consciousness, nervous system, and libido.

That the very seat of male thought or masculine identity could be influenced or even defined by a man's sexual organs is a significant historical formation, but in this early phase the newer symbolism which came into being was characterized by contradictoriness. As we have seen, the conceptualization of the traffic between brain and genitalia contained a fundamental tension: on the one hand, the relationship could be a directly proportional one in which the presence and activity of testicles, yard, and seed created and defined a physical and mental maleness itself (as with notions of *aura seminalis*); on the other, the mind-genitalia connection could be inversely proportional (as with the brain-testicles homology), which meant a potential antagonism between genital and mental performance. These contradictory views existed simultaneously in the medical and sexological treatises, and their alternative (and highly problematic) implications for notions of masculinity and male identity are never clearly resolved. The non-medical discourses are likewise uncertain about the significantly different ramifications of these two models, sometimes exemplifying both systems within a single text. Unlike high and low medical narratives, however, the other discourses provide a clearer picture of how these competing concepts might have informed cultural constructions at large, the first model of direct relationship allowing for equations of male mental capacity with lust, reproductive potency, phallic size, or excessive intercourse (think, for instance, of the libertine sexual energy of the witty Restoration stage-rake). The second model of inverse proportion offered either/or scenarios in which one could possess either heightened mental or genital ability but not both at the same time, allowing for complex exchanges in which large amounts of wit or intellect might compensate a missing phallicism and vice versa.

The medical commentaries intensified the link between the male reproductive system and an essentialized maleness, refining the conceptual bridging between genitalia and the male mind in particular. But they are also witness to the uneasy and uneven cultural terrain as a newer symbolism about the male organs of generation came into being. As we turn now to the moderns' approaches to the penis/phallus, we will see that the most problematic and contradictory features of the genitals-mind models were shifted onto the yard.

The Problematic Penis and Male Identity

As I have suggested, the penis is problematic in the twofold sense that Enlightenment usage was differential and ambiguous, and that the subject "the penis" has been plagued by a twentieth- and twenty-first century ahistoricism. The history of the penis, I am arguing, has not been well served by current theory. At the heart of my quarrel with psychoanalytical and feminist methodologies is their tendency to separate the penis and the phallus, forgetting that in so doing they are participating in a history of such splitting which privileges the metaphorized erection. An almost obsessive attention to the phallus as symbol has created the illusion that we are studying the cultural implications of male genitalia, when in fact we have focused on a single aspect—the erection as abstract idea—all but ignoring the relationship of hard and soft penis with its implications for studies of the male body. Lacan, as is well known, insists that the phallus is not a penis, but rather "the privileged signifier of that mark in which the role of the logos is joined with the advent of desire." Lacan's phallus is thus a linguistic concept, "a sign of the latency with which any signifiable is struck," and a symbolic attribute no more in the possession of men than of women, both of whom will experience not the transcendental expression of a unitary, integrated self—one version of "having" the Phallus—but rather a perpetual "play of displacement and condensation . . . [which] marks his [or her] relation as a subject to the signifier."[45] Occupying a symbolic role *qua* signifier at the level of desire in general, Lacan's phallus is thus to be carefully distinguished from the mundane penis, whose cultural and representational function is all but dismissed. Feminist critiques of the Lacanian phallus have exposed the rhetorical slight of hand which places Lacan himself at the center of definitional power whose patriarchal authority cannot be confronted.[46] But feminist psychoanalytical frameworks have tended to follow Lacan in their absorption with the metaphorical phallus, as well as in their reluctance to recognize the value, or indeed the necessity, of reconstructing a history of penis-phallus conceptualizations which would explain why we have arrived at our current mode of privileging an ahistorical, symbolic phallus over the material penis.

There are signs that this theoretical myopia is giving way to a historical curiosity. David M. Friedman's recent popularized approach in *A Mind of Its Own: A Cultural History of the Penis*[47] suggests a mainstream interest in such a history. But scholars have also begun to speculate about a history of penis-phallus relationships in western culture, wondering why and when the penis and phallus came to be separated symbolically, with the latter becoming an intellectual icon and the former a taboo or at best an impolite subject not quite fit for professional academic discussion. One version of this historicization is the difficult question of how to explain the historical distance and differences between the early phallus worshipers of classical periods and the all but invisible phallus of postmodern theory and psychoanalysis. Jean-Joseph Goux has considered the differences between the symbolic "phallophorism of antiquity" (i.e., rites of Osiris, figures of Hermes and Dionysius) and the "modern phallocentrism" of psychoanalysis and philosophy, suggesting that "The modern phallus is a deciphered phallus. . . . The phallus is rediscovered, but, being no longer religious, sacred, ritualized, figural, it is no longer the same. It is unconscious and structural. There is a major difference between a culture which reserves a mythico-ritual place for the phallic emblem, and one which has a need for the experience and theoretical reconstruction of psychoanalysis to uncover the role and function of the phallus."[48] Daniel Boyarin argues in a different vein that "The phallus became the phallus, i.e., became separated from the penis by being veiled in the Mysteries of late antiquity," and that "it is the ideological separation of phallus from penis, produced in history, but forgotten as history, that enables the phallus [in its Lacanian and feminist senses] to do its work, that founds the Dominant Fiction." For Boyarin, "Historicizing 'the phallus' thus becomes crucial to a political retrieval of the entire psychoanalytic project."[49] Paul Smith has likewise called for a renovation of the psychoanalytical by the historical: "the task of historicizing the preoedipal must take on the same importance as the task of historicizing the monolithic psychoanalytical metaphor of the phallus: the imaginary is only ever constructed through phenomenologically available matter which is variable across history, and the body itself is also variably constructed across history."[50] Given the sweeping nature of these remarks, how does one begin to imagine the Enlightenment in some grand narrative about the history of male genitalia? Late seventeenth- and eighteenth-century culture certainly had its own array of symbols for the erect penis, and compared to earlier cultural formulations around the penis-phallus relationship, Enlightenment discourses are increasingly the site of a symbolic maleness recognizably modern—one in which the flaccid privy member was separated and understood as symbolically different from the stiffened yard. But in contrast to today's current focus, the connections among symbolic, biological, and historical realms were then more palpable and not yet abstracted and rewritten within the disembodied and sometimes unreachable terrain of modern psychoanalysis or the reductionist caricatures of some feminisms.

But historicizing the symbolic phallus is only one important new line of inquiry. Another arises from the recognition that a history of penis-phallus relationships as they are variously conceptualized at different times is also an important aspect of the history of masculinity and the male body. Susan Bordo has recently warned of the consequences of using

the most abstract and attenuated forms of the phallus . . . such as the "phallogocentrism" that deconstructionists and feminists have claimed runs throughout Western philosophy, science, and religion. . . . I have avoided dealing with these kinds of arguments here (although I have made them myself in other contexts) precisely because they move discussion of the phallus so extremely far afield from the male body, and I fear they will pull me into an abstract realm where I would be vulnerable to the very disease that I would be diagnosing.[51]

While she does not pursue her study of male bodies outside the twentieth century, Bordo recognizes that "the symbol emerged historically . . .
out of forms of reverence that *did* have reference to biology," and that
the connection of the penises of real men to the symbolic cultural level
of ideas ought not to be underestimated if we want to understand the
history of male flesh as it might have been occupied and experienced
by men, or if we wish to understand the relationship of individual men
to the cultural metaphorization of the male body: "The phallus," she
writes, "haunts the penis. Paradoxically, at the same time the penis . . .
also haunts phallic authority, threatens its undoing."[52] As Bordo real-
izes, a good deal of academic discourse has demonstrated, somewhat
paradoxically, how difficult it has been to keep the male body in view
while studying the penis-phallus as subject.

This emergent intellectual and historical curiosity about male genitalia will perhaps reverse current academic trends, reminding us that
there is a history of the relationship between the soft and hard penis—
not only experiential but cultural—that the combined process of erigibility and detumescence has also been symbolized variously throughout
history (as have testicles and semen), and that such investigations will
have much to tell us about why male genitalia have come to play the
part they have in postmodern psychoanalytical and feminist theory.

What made the penis such a metaphorically preeminent and culturally problematized physical site? For one thing, the yard was the seat
of pleasure whose sensitivity made it the exterior part most experien-
tially representative of internal reproductive physiology. Visually the
penis was also a dramatic physical feature of the loins, capable of size-
change, urination, and ejaculation. It was popularly viewed as the most
active genital part and thus the vagaries of its condition and multiple
function made it a particularly convenient vehicle for a variety of symbolic registers, despite the elaboration of the role of testes, glands, fluid
systems, and micro-vessels provided by the physiologists. Moreover,
the glans was understood as having a high proportion of extremely sensitive nerves, and the heightened responsiveness to stimulation helped
to make the connection of the yard to the nervous system and brain a
relatively easy matter.[53] The ability of the limp penis to become erect
could easily be metaphorized, with successful or unsuccessful tumescence having obvious implications for the male's status within psycho-
sexual, social, political, or literary contexts, as well as for the plight of
male desire itself. Its diseases, too—chancres, lues, gleets, stranguries,
priapisms—were easily converted into social and moral tokens, evidence
of the failure of masculine will, of social or political immorality, or
even of a national decline.[54] Of the external organs of generation, the
yard appeared to have the most complex role—and thus the greatest

grand narrative

range for metaphorical use—and in non-medical discourses it was the penis which typically represented the reproductive system as a whole in the genitalia-mind correspondences.

To expand our answers to why the penis became so prominent a sign we must also investigate the influence of larger cultural contexts, ranging from the history of masculinity and the emergence of pornography, to legal proceedings and literary practices, and even to political and nationalistic currents. If one were to search for some master category which explained the reasons of such a convergence, one might point to the well-known historical shifting through the seventeenth century from notions of the individual as an integrated part of an organic cosmos governed by God's will to a self increasingly defined by inner physiological and external material conditions within a mechanized cosmos. In this context of paradigmatic change, one can view the proliferation of the yard-male identity equation as a specific version of the newly quantifiable self subject to forms of mechanical measurement.

And there were other macro contexts of historical change which contributed to this convergence. For instance, the male body was being culturally repositioned as a symbolic entity in response to large-scale social shifts, with the result that the reproductively potent penis became one symbol by which several value-systems would be defined. As Michael McKeon has argued, a significant feature of attacks on aristocratic ideology through the eighteenth century was the dismantling of the notion that birth determined worth, "that honor is biologically inherited." The dynamics of what McKeon calls "a dissection of the cadaver of male aristocracy" included three relocations relevant to my discussion: "honor" was increasingly lodged in the idea of the domestic female; the perceived sterility and effete corruption of the male aristocrat "was reembodied in the effeminate nonmale, the 'unreproductive' sodomite"; personal worth and internal value would now be found in the sentimental man of public virtue, "defined by his economic activity, his occupational status, and his heterosexuality."[55] To these careful assessments I would add that if an eighteenth-century norm of masculinity depended increasingly on differentiating the effete sterility of aristocrat or molly from the heterosexual male within the family unit, then one of the governing bodily signs of this new male was the reproductively potent penis which authenticated social and sexual norms at which the sodomitical aristocrat either failed or transgressed. A biological essentialism, in other words, which had once propped up an aristocratic hierarchy of worth and honor, was now rewritten as a gendered distinction among kinds of males, whose heterosexual phallicism was central to a definition of the "normal" self.[56]

The penis could define male identity in other ways, as well, with a non-reproductive sexual competence becoming a basic measure of a man's personality. Leo Braudy has approached late seventeenth-century premature ejaculation poems in this way, suggesting that the period's near obsession with the idea of impotence represents "one of the earliest modern examples of the ambiguous relation between the male sexual body and the male sense of personal identity that will become one of the main themes of writing in western literature." The specific significance of a poem such as Rochester's "The Imperfect Enjoyment," he writes, is that "the man has become the prick," and the larger historical import of Rochester's work as a whole is that it "helps mark a historical moment in which masculinity was becoming not the God-given portion of every male but an aspect of character primarily defined by sexual accomplishment and performance, constantly needing to be reattained."[57] While Braudy does not explore other discourses in which man-as-penis becomes a more common trope, he is right in marking this literary fashion as a historical example of new ways by which maleness would be essentialized. One might add that within the empirical culture of the new science, the medicalization of sexuality made such quantitative appreciations almost predictable. In the hands of De Graaf and other anatomists, the organs of generation and coition received the kind of empirical dissecting, inflating, mapping, and measuring never before so anatomically precise; it is therefore not surprising to discover that in a culture for which "sexuality" had been reified as a category, the quantitative and mechanical approaches of human biology would support a vocabulary of size, prowess, frequency, and potency.[58]

The proliferation of the penis as public subject appears in some unlikely places, as well, informing aspects of eighteenth-century English nationalism which (among other strategies) used the sexually potent *English* penis to valorize a national identity, morality, and even a made-in-Britain aesthetic sensibility. In writing of Fielding and popular Italian castrati such as Farinelli, Jill Campbell has examined the ways in which the castrato's testicular loss was viewed in general as a phallic deficiency, which in turn "provided an occasion to isolate, and to literalize, to make explicit, the cultural significances of the phallus itself: in considering the nature of the castrato's loss, the satirists at times assume the phallus to be the guarantor of everything from moral discourse to English currency to English-ness."[59] Moreover, theatrical instances of the erect, limp, or missing penis—as it is figured in Restoration stage-rakes and eunuchs—has also been explained as the metaphorical centering of political and gender anxieties following the Civil War, particularly as these upheavals might have produced a so-called "crisis" in masculinity.[60]

The symbolic function of the male organs of generation, and the yard in particular, can also be understood in relation to pornography and the libertine quality of Charles II's court. As a relatively new and subversive genre initially combining political and religious satire with the more intimate narrative potential of the novel, pornography increasingly turned away from its satirical ethos toward the narrower domain of private sexual titillation in which pornographers sought for ways to raise the yards of their male readers, thus linking the imaginative act more intimately with a phallic response. Samuel Pepys would privately masturbate during his reading of *L'Escole des Filles*, writing in code that the salacious descriptions "did hazer my prick para stand all the while, and una vez decharger."[61] Seed and testicles do not disappear in the sexual configurations of pornography, but it is the phallus—both as the sought-after object of many erotic episodes, as well as the masturbated penis of the reader—that is privileged. The early modern "invention of pornography," to use Lynn Hunt's phrase, can thus be viewed as a new literary or subliterary genre devoted almost exclusively to stimulating the nervous connections between men's brains and their pricks, although matters are somewhat more complicated than this, as we will see.

Older formulations of the penis as power, trophy, or political might can also be found in notorious anecdotes about the libertine aggression of rakes such as Rochester, or in the publicly discussed royal pintle of Charles II, whose monarchy was often figured as an endless swiving, as in Rochester's cheeky poem, "On King Charles": "His sceptre and his prick are of a length; / And she that plays with one may sway the other."[62] Remarkable imagery indeed, not only as a courtier's playful but potentially dangerous critique of Charles's privileging of penis over politics, but also as an instance of the extent to which this culture would personify a single part of the male body, transforming penises into a large variety of symbols for male spheres of action. The ups and downs of the yard, as well as its contact with the world of others through intercourse, made it a convenient vehicle for a wide range of usage in the affairs of men, from the in-close physiological workings of reproduction and sexual pleasure in medical books and sexologies; to the careers of kings, the hypocrisy of aristocrats and randy clergymen in gossip and pornography; to new gender roles for men; and to an increasingly democratized male body politic. To this list we will later add male literary communities, for whom the yard and its doings often symbolized something about the creative energy within the poet's brain.

So what was problematic or unstable about specific representations of the penis/phallus? In this gathering of new and refurbished symbols, what were the implications for concepts of maleness? As we turn now from brief sketches of the macro contexts of symbolic usage to closer scrutiny of representative textual evidence in the next three sections, we encounter a sprawling inventory ranging from literal to figurative, from biological marker to socio-sexual status, from youth to old age, from the privy member as "hard" sign of male will and power to the symbol of an irrational Other outside one's control. But despite the diversity of specific deployments, there appears to be a deep-level set of cultural equations whose intersecting and often oppositional structures relate to the conceptual linkage between male mind and yard.

The Erection and the Penis

It is important that we resist our postmodern tendency to consider only the already symbolic phallus and ignore the literal penis, a slippage or act of convenient blindness of which seventeenth and eighteenth-century writers cannot often be accused.[63] The historical record for this period suggests that there were two different ways of imagining the relationship of the soft yard to the erect pintle: either they were linked together as part of a single process of tumescence and detumescence, symbolizing a wide range of masculine experience from puberty to old age; or, the penis was separated or sharply differentiated from the phallus, with the former marginalized as a sign of male failure and the phallus left as a sign of male will and power. Indeed, one of the striking features of the record is the attention given to the first formulation. The period's symbolic equations, in other words, do not always begin and end with the already engorged yard, but frequently include the circumstances within which the penis stiffens or resumes its accustomed flaccidity. The Enlightenment penis, one might say, is significantly present in cultural representations of male genitalia, and not removed peremptorily from the site of symbolic formation—as in current academic approaches—to some invisible place detached from the phallus, or simplistically resituated in a visible but negative category of male failure such as impotence. Of course, hard and soft yards could signify opposite conditions about masculine capability, with hardened member a synecdoche for male power and limp pizzle the satirized plight of fumbler or premature ejaculator, but penis and phallus were not always separated in this fashion, and indeed often linked as a variable process representative of some aspect of male embodiment in time.

The combined process of tumescence and detumescence clearly has a different set of figurative possibilities than does the already erect, symbolically detached yard, which tends to represent a static condition of empowerment. The erigibility and softening of the yard, by

contrast, represent the variability of masculine experience as it is related to the material realms of sex, desire, age, health, social and economic station. The significance of this second representational scheme
is that the biological penis often foregrounds the unique subjectivity of
particular kinds of men, throwing into relief the uneven conjunction
of male sexuality and historical contingencies; the phallus-by-itself, on
the other hand, is often presented as symbolically distinct from the
male who owns it, even though it might represent masculine power.
These two modes are frequently juxtaposed in the discourses ca.
1650–1750, and their jostling suggests uncertainty about what kind of
symbolic equations ought to prevail: defining maleness against a relatively narrow phallic emblem? or broadening the typology so as to reflect a greater variety of maleness? The second option entails much
greater range, of course, but also a higher probability of problems or
failure. And yet the writers of this period frequently eschew an exclusive equation of the unitary Phallus-as-Man and write instead about
the rising-and-falling penises-of-men. From the urinary to the ejaculatory, from the limp to the poxed, from the hormonal vigor of youth to
aged impotence, from satyriasis to due benevolence, from cantharides
to flagellated readiness—the Enlightenment yard was often a problematic emblem of male identity because its function could be related
to the psychological and physical complexities of individual men.

A good place to begin is with the pornographic tradition, the genre
we most often associate with an uncomplicated phallicism. The period's most famous pornographic novel—John Cleland's *Memoirs of a
Woman of Pleasure* (1748–49)—illustrates that phallic modes were frequently attended by the variable and sometimes idiosyncratic realities
of penises. While the powerful erection is at the center of the three-
dozen scenes which make up his plot, Cleland is not unmindful of the
penis, and the novel offers a typology of yards suggesting a far greater
range of male subjectivity than the always-hard, symbolically-ready
erection represents. Moreover, as Peter Sabor has pointed out in the
introduction to his edition of the novel, "Cleland's world is assuredly
not the 'pornotopia' that Stephen Marcus defines [in which] 'All men
in it are always and infinitely potent' " (xxi–xxii). Fanny's epistolary
account presents a sequence of men who are largely defined by the
variable connection of their yards to their mental constitutions: the
impotent older male (15–16) and premature ejaculator (19); the "short-
liv'd erection" (139) of Norbert, the thirty year-old debauchee; the
punishingly-achieved erections and emissions of Barvile, the young
flagellant (143–52); the "sickly appetite" of "a grave, staid, solemn, el-
derly gentleman," whose fetishes include hair-combing and biting off
the finger-tips of Fanny's gloves (153); the "middle-siz'd . . . red-topt

ivory toy" (158) of the teenaged mollies.[64] That some of these examples turn the men into objects of satire or negative treatment at the same time as they exist for the purpose of prurient titillation, is clear enough. But one must also ponder the larger implications of these representations in which the process of tumescence and detumescence—whether frustrated or deviant—characterizes the identity of these men.[65] Why it is that the phallic imagery of Enlightenment pornography is so often bracketed by the unstable psychological and material conditions upon which male sexuality and erections depend?

It seems to me that the presence of these two modes of representation is typical of the period, and the sign of a larger cultural hesitation about how to give symbolic substance to the new equations of male minds and genitalia. Something similar can be found in the popular tradition of facetiae, bawdy songs, ribald jests, riddles, and extended metaphors which take the yard as subject. The "arbor vitae" treatises, for example—those not so subtle analogies of the penis as shrub, tree, or sensitive plant[66]—contain predictable gestures of phallic competence and over-sized glory set against sodomites, fumblers, or the poxed; but noteworthy is how frequently a "history" of the penis/phallus is made a part of these humorous treatments, making space for descriptions of the process of tumescence and detumescence as well as for often matter-of-fact references to aging, impotence, flagellation, aphrodisiacs. The culture of Pope's day seems interested simultaneously in glorifying the potent erection as a self-contained symbol and yet representing the yard as playing a sometimes problematic role in the history of individual men.

The presence of both modes can be found in other kinds of narratives and discourses as well, in which the relationship of the yard to blunt realities of money, beauty, or the unpredictable world of sexual desire is the subject. For example, in his satirical argument in favor of dildoes—objects which, from one vantage-point, are a mock-perfect instance of the symbolically-detached phallus—Samuel Butler's outrageous *Dildoides* (written in the 1670s; first published in 1706) makes the non-satirical point that "Woman must have both Youth and Beauty / E're the damn'd P—ck will do his duty, / And then Sometimes he scarce will stand too / Tho' you apply your Misses' hand to." Stirrings of the yard can be fussier and even more venal than this, however, "For wicked Pintles have no mind t'her / Who has no Mony, nor no Joynture." Notwithstanding the misogynistic measure of the sometimes fickle prick against artificial "Man in this Epitome,"[67] Butler's treatment is linked to many other portrayals of the penis as symbolic of the vagaries of male desire and circumstance, in which possibilities of tumescence intersect crudely with economic opportunism, hygiene, or a limited staying-power: "Dildo has nose, but cannot Smell, / No Stench can his great Courage quell: / At sight of Plaisters hee'l not fail, / Nor faintly ask what do you Ail?" "Which of us able to Prevent is / His Girle from Lying with his Prentice, / Unlesse we other means Provide / For Nature to be satisfy'd? / And what more Proper, than this Engine, / Which wou'd outdo 'em, shou'd three men Joyne" (1–2, 6). Butler's comical poem reaches a significant balancing of representational possibilities: although the second of the orators convinces the crowd of citizens to burn the dildoes lest "Idolatry . . . fill the Land, / And all True Pricks forget to Stand" (7), the first orator offers practical arguments in favor of dildoes, which are not bothered by health, smell, money, age, beauty, or desire in the ordinary ways that real yards are. Ultimately the poem chooses the real over the artificial phallus, but not before it has demonstrated the problematic relationship of soft and stiff yards.

Homosocial contexts, likewise, also hosted the juxtaposition of these two modes, as in a letter from the thirty-seven year-old Pope, who writes to thank Fortescue for "the fine Scollops" he has sent: "Those you favor me with are very safe arrived & have done me no little credit with the Dutchess of Hamilton. Alas! with any Female they will do me little credit, if I eat them myself: I have no way so good to please 'em, as by presenting 'em with any thing rather than with my self." In this example, the meaning and functioning of the yard are linked politely to psychosexual matters of acceptance, which here circulates maddeningly just out of Pope's reach; he is permitted to be the generous giver of the aphrodisiac scallops, but any presentation of his own stimulated yard will be ignored or shunned, the cursed result of his misshapen body. And yet in the very next paragraph Pope compensates for this rejection, juxtaposing a homosocial fantasy of his own phallic competence and sway: "Dr. Arbuthnot is highly mindful of you. He has (with my Consent) put a Joke upon Gay & me, out of pure disposition to give him joy & gladness. Gay is made to believe that I had a Clap, of which I fancy you'l hear his Sentiments in that ludicrous way, which God has given him to excell all others in" (*Corr.* 2: 290, 18 March 1724/5). As is often the case in examples from this period, the two modes of penis/phallus relationship accompany one another, offering very different and alternating possibilities of how a man might be defined or understood in relation to his yard.

John Armstrong's *The Oeconomy of Love* (1736) is a perfect example of a non-pornographic treatise in which "the tumid Wonder"[68] represents not a static emblem of symbolic power, but the variable phases of maleness from sexual maturation and the growth of pubic hair, to the teenager's first wet dreams and intercourse, to the dangers of masturbation, and finally to the sexual frustrations of old age, impotence, and the attempt by "Flagellation, and the rage of Blows, / To rouse the *Venus* loitering in his Veins!" (54, ll. 528–9)—or, in a last desperate attempt to stimulate an erection, the use of aphrodisiacs such as "*Orchis*," "*Satyrion*" (a member of the orchid family), "*Eryngo*" (candied sea holly), "*Cantharides*" (Spanish flies) (55, ll. 550–5). The figure of the aged male has received little study for this period, except for passing reference to satirical versions of the impotent or cuckolded fumbler. And yet the story is a more complex one, as Armstrong's treatment suggests, and the temporal realities of the yard included sometimes moving and nostalgic accounts of desires which have outlived the aging body's ability, as in Robert Herrick's "To His Mistresses":

> Old I am, and cannot do
> That I was accustomed to.
> Bring your magics, spells, and charms,
> To enflesh my thighs and arms;
> Is there no way to beget
> In my limbs their former heat?
> Aeson had, as poets feign,
> Baths that made him young again:
> Find that medicine, if you can,
> For your dry, decrepit man
> Who would fain his strength renew,
> Were it but to pleasure you.[69]

Or, the careful attentions of the young lady in Rochester's "A Song of a Young Lady. To her Ancient Lover":

> Thy nobler part, which but to name
> In our sex would be counted shame,
> By Age's frozen grasp possessed,
> From his ice shall be released,
> And, soothed by my reviving hand,
> In former warmth and vigour stand.[70]

These kinds of examples, both pornographic and non-pornographic, serve to remind us that penises were often represented as meaningful in relation to contexts of male life; that stiffened or slack yards often reflected the varieties of male experience in time rather than parts to be measured or indexed against an emblematized phallic standard which was totemically separate from the individual male body and will, but still applicable to one's stature or value within the cultural subset of maleness.[71] And it is worth noting that conditions in which there was difficulty achieving or maintaining an erection were not always or exclusively the object of satire or contempt. If one desired an erection, it was of course agreeable to be able to have one; if one could not, or if one depended on idiosyncratic erotic aids, this culture afforded not a single but a double symbolic register.

These two very different ways of imagining the relationship of the soft penis to the erection suggest a semiotic tug-of-war in which the yard could have meaning either as it was defined by the life-situation of the male, or as it defined maleness itself. Unlike the late twentieth- and twenty-first century, this earlier period had not yet narrowed its penis-symbolism exclusively to a disembodied Phallus; eighteenth-century pornography was not obsessed—as is the case with our current video porn—with the "money shot";[72] representations of the yard—however impolite as a topic of discussion—involved a variety of contexts whose symbolic possibilities were not uniformly the result of a phallus separated imaginatively from the penis.

Mind-Yard Connections: Direct and Inverse

Within such diversity, other kinds of oppositional structures are visible, particularly around the relationship of a man's head and his genitals. Stiff pricks, of course—the bigger the better—could function unambiguously as signs of masculine capability, with turgid member a synecdoche for the power of male will, a marker of masculine stature, a guarantor of virility or masculinity itself. Ideas of privileged political power lurk even in some of the slang terms, such as "privy member." This relatively uncomplicated equation can be described briefly.

The erection served variously as a directly proportional sign of the successful will and assertiveness of the male brain or of the masculine character. The mind's ability to raise the yard was a token of the man's knowledge of and power over a material world of others, as is reflected in the sexual connotations of the phrase "To Know." Johnson's dictionary-gloss is coy—"6. To converse with another sex"—but his biblical example—"And Adam *knew* Eve his wife"—makes plain the associations of mind, erection, knowledge, and copulatory power-over. As a mark of stature in the gender hierarchy, the metaphor was certainly used before 1650, as in Ben Jonson's *Every Man in His Humour* (1598) in which the jealous Kitely bemoans his lack of psychological strength as "want[ing] the mindes erection."[73] At mid-century Hobbes would describe the human "*Desire*, to know why, and how" or "CURIOSITY" as "a Lust of the mind, that by a perseverance of delight in the continuall and indefatigable generation of Knowledge, exceedeth the short vehemence of any carnall pleasure."[74] If Hobbes's conceit imagined the figuratively endless phallic pleasures of mental procreation, at century's end John Dennis would rely on the metaphorical structure for an exaggerated compliment to Dryden:

Since I came to this place I have taken up my Pen several times in order to write to you, but have constantly at the very Beginning found myself Damp'd and Disabled; upon which I have been apt to believe that extraordinary Esteem may sometimes make the Mind as Impotent as Violent Love does the Body. . . . I have heard of more than one lusty Gallant, who, tho he could at any time with Readiness and Vigour possess the Woman whom he lov'd but moderately, yet when he has been about to give his darling Mistriss, whom he has vehemently and long desir'd, the first last Proof of his Passion, has found on a sudden that his Body has Jaded and Grown resty under his Soul, and gone backward the faster, the more he has spurr'd it forward. Esteem has wrought a like effect upon my Mind.[75]

In this flourish, Dennis's pretense that his phallic mind has been overcome by his esteem is transparent flattery whose own wit serves as a sign of his potent yard-brain.

   Laurence Sterne would later offer his own idiosyncratic concoction for the connection of yard-brain to knowing and knowledge, reminding his reader that "it so happens and ever must, says *Prignitz*, that the excellency of the nose is in a direct arithmetical proportion to the excellency of the wearer's fancy" (3: 38, 173–74). In so equating the capacity of heated imagination and euphemistic nose, Tristram announces one of the primary structures of the novel in which the mental and creative abilities of the male characters—Walter, Toby, Tristram himself—are framed by the copulatory and reproductive strengths of the yard, which the mischievous Sterne invites the reader to imagine at every conceivable moment. Thus, two chapters later:

The gift of ratiocination and making syllogisms,—I mean in man,—for in superior classes of beings, such as angels and spirits,—'tis all done, may it please your worships, as they tell me, by INTUITION;—and beings inferior, as your worships all know,——syllogize by their noses. (3: 40, 177)

In this comic synthesis, the nose-penis *is* mental capacity (notwithstanding the phallic incompetence of the Shandy males), and Sterne is unable to resist tweaking the nose of the great Locke, whose chapter on reason (*Essay Concerning Human Understanding* Bk. 4, Ch. 17, Sect. 18) is ludicrously reduced to a measure by cocks:

The gift of doing it as it should be, amongst us,—or the great and principal act of ratiocination in man, as logicians tell us, is the finding out the agreement or disagreement of two ideas one with another, by the intervention of a third; (called the *medius terminus*) just as a man, as *Locke* well observes, by a yard, finds two men's nine-pin-alleys to be of the same length. (3: 40, 177)[76]

   If rampant yard could signify the power of male "knowing," it could also be figured as a sublime object of desire itself—the "pride of nature, and its richest master-piece," according to Cleland's Fanny Hill

(46)—which promised other forms of knowledge and pleasure to those who subjected themselves to its power. Thus, in a translation of Nicolas Chorier's pornographic *Satyra Sotadica* (1659 or 1660), the mother of the just-married and now-deflowered fifteen year-old Octavia solemnly lectures her daughter on the virtues brought by the enormous member of "thy dear *Philander*": "thou art now born to a new Life. . . . Thy Wit and Understanding will clear up with thy Enjoyments, for that very Engine that opens our Bodies, will do the same to our Minds."77 This promised "knowing," however, is about female acquiescence to a symbolic male authority which resides in the exaggerated phallus. The yard, as Fanny Hill recognizes, is not simply a "label of manhood" (165) but, in its hardened glory, can be "an object of terror and delight" (73), "the king member" (110), or the "scepter-member, which commands us all" (183). In this direct equation of erect penis and masculine character the stiffened tarse becomes on one occasion nothing less than a "plenipotentiary instrument" (113). The phallus has become the man, a genital envoy invested with the full power and authority of the male, with its/his ability to "know" women or to elicit a sublime curiosity in them signs of the man's will and power over bodies, language, and desire itself.

As Cleland's metaphors suggest, the brain-phallus equation was also used as a measure of political might, where "the king member" signaled the sway and dominion of the monarch. Charles II's private sexuality and public political role met often in such formulas—"His sceptre and his prick are of a length," to take Rochester's famous barb—where the king's pretensions to godhood or potential for tyranny and absolutism were figured by the powerful rule of the over-sized royal yard. Oldham's *Sardanapalus* (late 1670s) alludes to Charles's sceptre-phallus, linking political might to "thy Soveraign Pr-k's Prerogative":

> Methinks I see thee now in full Seraglio stand,
> With Love's great Scepter in thy hand,
> And over all its Spacious Realm thy Power extend:
> Ten Thousand Maids lye prostrate at thy Feet,
> Ready thy Pintle's high Commands to meet;
> . . . .
> Far as wide Nature spreads her Thighs,
> Thy Tarse's vast Dominion lyes:
> All Womankind acknowledge its great Sway,
> And all to its large Treasury their Tribute pay,
> Pay Custom of their unprohibited Commodities.78

However preposterous the image, royal command and dominion here reside in the tarse, which embodies the king's rule over Nature herself. More exaggerated yet are the opening lines of the obscene closet drama, the Rochesterian *Sodom* (1684), in which the hard penis of

King Bolloximian (read Charles II) literally replaces both crown and sceptre:

> Thus in the zenith of my lust I reign,
> I drink to swive, and swive to drink again.
> Let other monarchs who their sceptres bear,
> To keep their subjects less in love than fear,
> Be slaves to crowns—my nation shall be free.
> My pintle only shall my sceptre be.
> My laws shall act more pleasure than command,
> And with my prick I'll govern all the land.[79]

As Harold Weber has noted, the king "insists that political power can be understood and expressed only as a manifestation of his royal phallus, the male organ that generates and sustains the patriarchal structures of society."[80] But the figurative traffic between mind and yard is equally clear: because the erect pintle perfectly reflects the royal will and character, it is an even better symbol than the sceptre and crown it replaces, serving as instrument of the sovereign's power and as surrogate for the royal mind itself.

The non-royal yard must not be forgotten in this context. Although hardly the only marker in the hierarchy of masculinity, the privy member of the well-hung gentleman or genteel whoremaster could add to one's stature. Bolingbroke and Bathurst were both noted for their phallic exploits, causing friend Pope to commemorate the sexual appetites of both in his *Sober Advice from Horace*. But their notorious cocksmanship was also appreciated as an extra mark of their status among men. For someone like the passionate Alexander, whose erotic yearnings are so palpable in his poetry and letters, Bolingbroke represented a masculine model of the many things he admired or wanted for himself, including libidinal self-indulgence. As Brean Hammond has noted astutely, " 'all accomplish'd St. John' was everything that Pope aspired to be in his imagination," and if, "ludicrously, in spite of Pope's actual physical incapacities, the poet liked to imagine himself something of a rake," "in Bolingbroke he found the genuine article."[81] St. John's phallic prowess was an extra badge of virility and manliness, his ambitious yard conferring a distinction of desirable masculinity which would gather respect even from other men.

Something similar is evident in Pope's representations of Bathurst's copious swiving, which is presented humorously as being in competition with Pope's loving friendship:

There was a Man in the Land of Twitnam, called Pope. He was a Servant of the Lord Bathurst of those days, a Patriarch of great Eminence, for getting children, at home & abroad. But . . . his Love for strange women, caused the said Lord to forget all his Friends of the Male-Sex; insomuch that he knew not, nor once rememberd, there was such a man in the Land of Twitnam as aforesaid. It were to be wisht, he would come & see; or if nothing else will move him, there are certain Handmaids belonging to the said Pope which are comely in their goings, yea which go comelily. (*Corr.* 2: 292, 1725?)

In these epicoene romps, Pope's mock-jealous desire for Bathurst's love takes a backseat to the escapades of the Lord's yard, which has been diverted by countless mistresses. The poet slyly suggests that it is only through the Lord's aroused member that a person—whether mistress or male friend—can engage Bathurst's attention, and Pope comically offers up his Handmaids for the friend's phallic pleasures, if only to provide the occasion for a meeting of friends. However tongue-in-cheek these libertine insinuations, the flattery is real enough, depending on the equation of male authority or stature of character with potent yard. Adding to his other manly accomplishments, Lord Bathurst's ambitious phallicism distinguishes his desirability to women and other men alike; to defer to the noble yard is, by Pope's neat epicoene logic, to "converse with" Lord Bathurst himself.

Biographical and autobiographical domains yield other versions of the erection as measure of selfhood and worth, as in the case of Horace Walpole's jealous care of Lord Lincoln's reputedly gargantuan member, or in the obsessive self-regard of James Boswell. The homosexually-inclined Walpole was, according to a recent biographer, a "size queen"[82] obsessed with the beloved Lincoln's potency and genital dimensions. At a public masquerade night in February 1743, Horace explained to Mann,

I dressed myself in an Indian dress, and after he [Lincoln] was come thither . . . made him three low bows, and kneeling down, took a letter out of my bosom, wrapped in Persian silk, and laid it on my head. . . . They persuaded him to take it: it was a Persian letter from Kouli Kan. . . . here it is: "Highly favored *among women* . . . We have heard prodigious things of thee: they say, thy vigour is nine times beyond that of our prophet . . . Most potent Lord, we have sent thee as a mark of our grace fifty of the most beautiful maidens of Persia. . . . Adieu! happy young man! May thy days be as long as thy manhood, and may thy manhood continue more piercing than Zufager, that sword of Hali which had two points."[83]

Although there are some similarities here to Pope's epicoene play with friend Bathurst, Walpole's risqué public gesture is more psychologically complex, involving both the exhibitionist display of Walpole's wit, as well as an attempt to embarrass Lincoln, who "stared violently." But there is an underlying jealousy here as well, in which the clever Walpole indecorously calls attention to the penis of his well-hung friend in order to assert a humorous mastery over it by invoking it publicly at his own will. Having conjured up Lincoln's yard, so to

speak, for the amusement of the assembly, Walpole's seraglio impersonation archly insinuates some intimate knowledge, and therefore token ownership, of Lincoln's "vigour." And "to know" the phallus, by
this psychological circuitry, is to own the man, even though the letters
indicate that Lincoln was the dominant one in the relationship, and
the infatuated Horace a passive, emotionally needy lover sometimes
desperate for a reciprocated passion from the apparently bisexual
Lincoln. My larger point about these examples is that, however different the personal circumstances between Pope's epicoene friendships
and Walpole's sodomitical passion, their writing sometimes shared a
metaphorical economy in which the stiff prick could take on symbolic
properties which represented the power or desirability of the beloved
male, whose very being and stature were in turn equated with the
turgid yard.

To take one final example of direct mind-yard equations we can
look at autobiographical remarks by Boswell, whose compulsive phi-
landering is sometimes attended by a narcissistic phallicism in which
size and staying-power provide reassurances of his male worth. The
occasions are often crude and potentially dangerous: "I picked up a
girl in the Strand; went into a court with intention to enjoy her in ar-
mour. But she had none. I toyed with her. She wondered at my size,
and said if I ever took a girl's maidenhead, I would make her squeak.
I gave her a shilling." But at times his almost autoerotic textual reca-
pitulations are dramatically extended, as they are with "Louisa" (actually Anne Lewis), "a handsome actress of Covent Garden Theatre":

Proud of my godlike vigour, I soon resumed the noble game. I was in full glow
of health. Sobriety had preserved me from effeminacy and weakness, and my
bounding blood beat quick and high alarms. A more voluptuous night I never
enjoyed. Five times was I fairly lost in supreme rapture. Louisa was madly
fond of me; she declared I was a prodigy, and asked me if this was not extraordinary for human nature. I said twice as much might be, but this was not,
although in my own mind I was somewhat proud of my performance. She
said it was what there was no just reason to be proud of. But I told her I could
not help it. She said it was what we had in common with the beasts. I said no.
For we had it highly improved by the pleasures of sentiment. I asked her what
she thought enough. She gently chid me for asking such questions, but said
two times.[84]

What is interesting here is the curious logic of the Boswellian measure. For Louisa, five times "lost in supreme rapture" makes Boswell
a prodigy. For his own part (having wisely abstained from alcohol),
Boswell's "godlike vigour" makes him "somewhat proud of my performance." And yet, ludicrously, he will set the bench-mark for "extraordinary" phallic accomplishment at ten orgasms.[85] In this exaggerated
priapic grid, size and number define the man, whose redoubtable

tarse moves him upward on the scale of manliness from the beastly to the godlike with each additional encounter. Boswell's five times is not extraordinary in this hierarchy, he claims, even if it is for Louisa, whose measure of the prodigious is to be tupped more than twice. Boswell situates his own performance against the idealized, always-ready priapic engine whose ten-fold capacity is more about the totemic erection than it is about the real penis. But these exaggerations also allow Boswell to attach his own considerable sexual appetite to the symbolic phallus, sign of male will, mental and physical strength, or desirability of character. Boswell's godlike vigor would prove short-lived, however; days later came the "sorrow" of "Signor Gonorrhoea" (49, January 1763), and with it the entry of the other representational mode I described in the last section.

If the erection functioned variously as a directly proportional sign of the successful intentionality, knowledge, or assertiveness of the masculine character, then within this logic the castrated, impotent, or small-yarded man predictably embodied a semiotic stamp of male failure ranging from literary satires to the more complex imperfect enjoyment traditions to personal lampoons. These negative contexts are well known and need no further elaboration here.[86]

Far more complex is the inverse relationship of male mind and groin in which the prodigious yard is a mark of idiocy, deformity, or compensation for the male who is in some sense deficient. The medical and sexological traditions are one vehicle for this structure. For instance, Jane Sharp's *The Midwives Book* (1671): "Some men, but chiefly fools, have Yards so long that they are useless for generation" (22); Thomas Gibson's *The Anatomy of Humane Bodies Epitomized* (1697): "But it is generally observed to be larger in short Men, and such as are not much given to Venery; also in those that have high and long Noses, and that are stupid and half witted" (160); John Marten's *A Treatise of all the Degrees and Symptoms of the Venereal Disease* (1708): "And we observe here, that little Men, deform'd Men, and Block-heads, (those of little Wit) are better provided in those Parts, than large Men, and others" (367); commenting on Heliogabalus's preference for soldiers with large members, Venette remarks that "he did not suspect at the same time that these long-penised people were the most befuddled and stupid of men."[87] Although De Graaf had dismissed some of these equations as silly (including the midwife's knotting of the umbilical cord as a determinant of penis size [see 46]), the notion that fools were more likely to possess the over-sized privy member persisted as an alternate structure to the direct model. One of the most famous examples is Cleland's *"Good-natur'd Dick"* (160), simple-minded owner of the biggest erection in *Fanny Hill*. Louisa, Fanny's colleague, has "conceiv'd a strange longing to be satisfy'd, whether the general rule held good with regard to this changeling and how far nature had made him amends in her best bodily gifts, for her denial of the sublimer intellectual ones" (161). True to form, Nature has given the idiot a phallus "of so tremendous a size, that prepar'd as we were to see something extraordinary, it still, out of measure surpass'd our expectation, and astonish'd even me, who had not been us'd to trade in trifles." The "enormous" breadth and "prodigious" length "complet[ed] the proof of his being a natural . . . since it was full manifest that he inherited, and largely too, the prerogative of majesty, which distinguishes that otherwise most unfortunate condition, and gives rise to the vulgar saying, 'That a fool's bauble is a lady's play fellow' " (162). Linking the epic tool of simple Dick to a tumescent majesty void of thought, Cleland presents this yard as the mechanically aroused flesh of "the man machine" (163), the La Mettrian figure whose gargantuan yard functions not as sign of mental preeminence but as meaty object serving the erotic convenience of lusty Louisa.

Like Cleland's novel, the arbor vitae tradition includes both direct and inverse relationships, the latter associated in particular with the boorish and ill-educated Irishman, whose prominently large "tree of life" is compensatory for his other deficiencies, social and intellectual. Thus, according to *The Natural History of the Arbor Vitae* (1732), "The height here in *England* rarely passes nine [inches] . . . whereas in *Ireland* it comes to far greater dimensions, is so good, that many of the natives entirely subsist upon it, and when transplanted, have been sometimes known to raise good houses with single plants of this sort" (5).[88] Rochester's "Signior Dildo" includes the same principle—"Our dainty fine duchesses have got a trick / To dote on a fool for the sake of his prick" (ll. 37–8)—as does Defoe's Roxana: "for I had now five Children by him; the only Work (perhaps) that Fools are good for."[89]

But inverse relationships went beyond the association of well-hung but stupid, short, long-nosed, deformed, or Irish men. Importantly, the man who was impotent or small-yarded or castrated could also be linked to an aspect of mental ability or creativity which was sometimes viewed as natural compensation for a phallic deficiency. S. A. D. Tissot's *An Essay on Diseases Incidental to Literary and Sedentary Persons* (English trans. 1768) is one instance of the inverse mind-genitalia relationship in a literary context. Writing of the various deleterious effects brought on the body by excessive intellectual or creative application, Tissot observes that

The seminal fluid, which has been thought by some great men not to be very different from the nervous liquor, is likewise depriv'd of its force; and upon this principle, and from an accurate consideration of what each part in a father contributes to the formation of a son, it perhaps is not badly accounted for, why strong and illustrious sons are seldom the offspring of illustrious men: for the *punctum saliens* is contaminated at the first moment of life, whence it receives an injury which is not afterwards to be repair'd by any art; and whilst the mind of the father was entirely given up to meditation, and his corporeal functions totally neglected, the vivifying liquor was perhaps defrauded of that part of elaboration which it should have had from the brain, so as to give a proper tone to the brain of the embryo.[90]

Strikingly similar to the bungled begetting of Tristram by cerebral Walter Shandy, Tissot's illustrous man is capable of great thought at the expense of reproductive potency.

The castrato is another example—here, non-literary but brutally literal—of an inverse principle by which smaller or absent genitalia are offset by greater mental or creative power. Indeed, the castrato is not a product of Nature but a man-made artistic instrument of exquisite music proving one of her underlying truths about the relationship of phallus to mind: the enchanting, mellifluous voice of a Carlo Broschi (Farinelli), Nicolo Grimaldi (Nicolini), Giovanni Grossi (Siface), Francesco Bernardi (Senesino), or Giusto Ferdinando Tenducci was a direct result of testicular loss, infantile penis, and by extension an absent phallicism.[91] And the trade-off, according to Charles Ancillon's *Traité des Eunuques* (1707; translated in 1718 for Curll as *Eunuchism Display'd*), could be phenomenal, as in the case of Pauluccio's voice which "had all the warblings and Turns of a Nightingal, but with only this difference, that it was much finer, and did not a Man know the contrary, he would believe it impossible such Tone could proceed from the Throat of any Thing that was human" (31). An inspired and moving male art, in other words, could be engineered with one crushing action or stroke of a blade, sacrificing genitalia in the interests of a commercialized male creativity.

This is not to say that the cultural milieu of Pope's day preferred little pricks (as fourth-century Athenians did, according to Eva Keuls[92]) or that eighteenth-century men sought impotence and castration as assurance of their mental preeminence. The presence of these inverse models suggests rather that the value or stature of the male mind in relation to the yard did not conform to a single standard of definition; that the tarse sometimes functioned within complex exchange systems in which masculine ability and worth could be defined as the result of a diminished phallicism; that the large erection could be antithetical to a heightened operation of mind. Moreover, one must ponder the co-presence of direct and inverse models, often simultaneously at work in the same textual system (e.g., *Fanny Hill*, *Tristram Shandy*) or within the oeuvre of an author (e.g., Rochester, Pope). That castrati could be seen as both unmanly, effeminized eunuch-figures of immense creative talent *as well as* able copulatory agents who could provide pleasure without risk, says something about the cultural and discursive ambiguities I am trying to chart in this chapter, and is linked to the competing models simultaneously present in other places, such as in *Tristram Shandy* ("the excellency of the nose [penis] is in a direct arithmetical proportion to the excellency of the wearer's fancy" [3: 38, 173–74] versus Tristram's own aesthetic sensibility which is inversely related to his phallic incompetence) or in Wycherley's *The Country Wife* (the phallic wit of the horny Horner versus the facade of Horner the witty eunuch). This interplay of direct and inverse modes is related to the contrasting representational schemes outlined in the last section, in which the phallus-by-itself was frequently juxtaposed with the biological and temporal penis. In both instances we see competing systems which complicated the penis as a symbol of the man or of some condition of maleness. But underneath both was a collective uneasiness about the mind-body connection. Lurking continually in these oppositional structures was the potential for the yard to overwhelm the mind and, in turn, the man himself.

Enigmatic Yard Versus Mind

Some of the most revealing mind-yard formulations were vexed by paradox and ambiguity, for the penis also represented a problematic juncture of body and mind. The degree to which the yard was subordinate to a man's will was unpredictable, and the extent to which erections appeared to have a life of their own—autonomous and independent of their owners—or even to take over and control the male mind itself, posed complex implications. The enigmatic or unruly penis was nothing new. Montaigne had acknowledged the history of the phallus as powerful male symbol of generation, mythologized in the older figure of Priapus; but he also provided two other contexts of meaning for the yard which are pertinent: "The Gods (saith Plato) have furnished man with a disobedient, skittish, and tyrannical member; which like an untamed furious-beast, attempteth by the violence of his appetite to bring all things under his becke"; "love is nothing else but an insatiate thirst of enjoying a greedily desired subject. Nor Venus that good huswife, other then a tickling delight of emptying ones seminary vessels: as is the pleasure which nature giveth us to discharge other parts, which becommeth faulty by immoderation and defective by indiscretion."[93] The two senses here—lustful phallus as irrational physical drive prevailing over the man, as mere physiological function mechanically propelled—anticipate another discourse ca. 1650–1750 in which the meaning of the yard is that it escapes man's control altogether.

The simplest version of the enigmatic yard is that it somehow commandeers the male mind, thus making the man a mere subset of the penis. The threat of one's privy member becoming the master category which ruled body *and* mind represented a potentially chaotic state of affairs in which the most complex and creative modes of male sensibility, self-control, or power were mere trifles in comparison with the overwhelming demands of one's pintle. In a perverse metaphorical sense, the penis becomes larger than the man, the part over-taking the whole, leaving a comically diminished maleness which exists only to serve the now over-grown and imperious pego.[94]

The figure of the man led by his own domineering yard can be found in satire and in mechanical accounts of the male sex drive. Not surprisingly, Charles II's copious swiving was treated in this fashion, as in the anonymous "An Historical Poem" (1680)—"The poor Priapus King, led by the nose, / Looks as one set up for to scare the crows"—or in John Lacy's "Satire" (1677): "Was ever prince's soul so meanly poor, / To be enslav'd to ev'ry little whore? / The seaman's needle points always to the pole, / But thine still points to ev'ry craving hole."[95] As Rachel Weil has shrewdly noted about satirical treatments of Charles II's body, "the king's penis is sometimes equated with his sovereign power, and, at other times, his penis appears to represent his point of vulnerability and his *illusion* of power."[96] The political implication of the part ruling the whole was also extended to Pope's friend Bolingbroke, lampooned as a man whose influential position as Secretary of State under Queen Anne (from 1710) was certain to be compromised by the fact that he would be led by his prick:

At the latter End of Queen *Anne*'s Reign, a certain Viscount had the *Reputation* of *deflowering* far and near; the Elegance of whose Taste was esteem'd such, that it was rather a Recommendation, than an Impediment to the Woman's *Marriage*, or her future *keeping*, if she had but once pass'd the *Hand* and *Seal* of Mr. *Secret—ry*. A merry but true Story, is related on that Occasion, *viz.* a Courtezan being met in the *Mall* by a Gentleman, he ask'd *whether she had heard the News——pray what is it?——Why, your old Friend* H——ry St. J—hn, *is made S—c—y of St——e. What may that be worth*, says the Lady——*Perhaps about* 10000£. *a Year.——By G-d I'm glad to hear it with all my Soul, for the Wh—res will get every Penny of it.*[97]

Noteworthy is how quickly one context for the phallus—as marker of male power, mental capacity, or stature of character—could be transformed into its negative counterpart. To make things worse, this submission to the penis was compounded by a further loss of control in the penis submitting to women. Matters of government, kingship, official service on behalf of the state—these were precariously embodied in men who, like Charles or Bolingbroke, were ruled by their privy members. The immediate implications of political instability and unpredictable authority were obvious, but underneath was a deeper question: did a man's brain or will have control over the penis/phallus, or did the yard represent an enigmatic bodily force which chaotically threatened the traditional hierarchy of mind over body?

Mechanical and physiological accounts of the temporary demands of aroused penises recognized that lust was apt to outweigh will, that erections could in a sense empty and occupy the mind. In 1724, for example, Bernard Mandeville's *A Modest Defence of Publick Stews* painted a picture of the mind at the mercy of the groin: "for let a Man have ever so much Business, it can't stop the Circulation of his Blood, or prevent the Seminal Secretion: for Sleeping or Waking, the *Spermaticks* will do their Office." And for the "Man of Pleasure" whose mind succumbs too readily to every venereal twitch of the loins, eventually "their Lust lies chiefly in their Brain, kept alive by the Impression of former Ideas. . . . [I]n time," the witty Mandeville concludes, "it [lust] changes its Residence from the *Glans Penis* to the *Glandula Penealis*."[98] In this humorous word-play the brain becomes a surrogate site for the yard's activities, producing a dangerous mental obsession and a debilitated nervous constitution. A related question about the power of genitals over mind is offered in *An Essay Upon Improving and Adding, to the Strength of Great-Britain and Ireland, By Fornication* (1735), written by Daniel Maclauchlan: "How often do we find our Bodies impregnated with such great Quantities of Seed and animal Spirits, as seize our Hearts, and touch our Brains, to that Degree, we cannot help poring continually upon the fair Objects of our Desire."[99] There are literary versions of the yard-over-mind idea, of course, as in *Consummation: Or, the Rape of Adonis* (1741, published by Edmund Curll), in which an unwilling boy-Adonis is sexually assaulted by the older Venus, who manually stimulates his member and then initiates intercourse against his will:

> Her fair Right-hand, that trembled with Delight,
> Soft-touch'd the mystic Source of genial Might:
> The potent Touch awak'd the drousy Pow'r,
> As the warm Ray revives the drooping Flow'r:
> The wanton Fair, in various Nature wise,
> Perceiv'd the Subject of Enjoyments rise
> . . . .
> Thus as she press'd him close and closer still,
> Nature consents in spite of wayward Will.[100]

Interesting here is the idea that the penis erecting as phallus is Nature itself, a powerful physical force that can easily over-ride the male will, which within this logic becomes a superficial, disruptible thing at the mercy of the libido. John Cleland's *Memoirs of a Coxcomb* (1751) acknowledges the same subordination. About to fornicate with the older

and unattractive Lady Oldborough, the young Sir William Delamore
comments on his irrepressible phallic mode:

But as I was now in the pride of my spring, well-bottomed, and my blood fer-
mented so strongly in my veins as to threaten the bursting its turgid and distended channels, so that love was rather a natural want in me, than merely a
debauch of imagination, the sympathy of organs established between the two
sexes, sensibly exerted itself, and drove all delicacy or distinction of persons
out of my head.[101]

In these various formulations, the relationship between flesh and
mind is mechanically simple, the occasion in which the phallus domi-
nates, unceremoniously preempting the conscious will or reason.

A more problematic version of this insistent, unruly yard is that it
somehow has always already framed the context of male thought or
consciousness, thus replacing the brain's governorship with a phallic
mode whose enigmatic surges both overtake male will and mysteriously provide the basis of thought. Ideas become, in this sense, barely
disguised gestures of the powerful organ below, a case of the yard using the head as a mouthpiece. A light-hearted example is the anonymous "No true Love between Man and Woman" (1694), in which the
ultimate source of male sentiment and perhaps even the most serious
intellectual operations are attributed to the pintle:

> When a Man to a Woman comes creeping and cringing,
> And spends his high Raptures on her Nose and her Eyes;
> 'Tis *Priapus* inspires the Talkative Engine,
> And all for the sake of her lilly white Thighs.
> Your Vows and Protests, your Oaths all and some,
> Ask *Solon*, *Lycurgus*, both Learned and Smart;
> They'll tell you the place from whence they all come,
> Is half a Yard almost below the Heart.[102]

A more serious use of this concept informs the anthropological essentialism of Richard Payne Knight's *Discourse on the Worship of Priapus* . . .
(1786–87), which assumes that even the highest influences of culture
and education cannot finally suppress an underlying phallic character:

Men, considered collectively, are at all times the same animals, employing the
same organs, and endowed with the same faculties: their passions, prejudices,
and conceptions, will of course be formed upon the same internal principles,
although directed to various ends, and modified in various ways, by the variety of external circumstances operating upon them. Education and science
may correct, restrain, and extend; but neither can annihilate or create: they
may turn and embellish the currents; but can neither stop nor enlarge the
springs, which, continuing to flow with a perpetual and equal tide, return to
their ancient channels, when the causes that perverted them are withdrawn.[103]

But underneath these discursive strands and lurking images of seminal flow is a highly problematic set of implications: if the deepest origins of male mental conception or masculine sensibility are to be found in the penis and its adjunct parts; if it is indeed the case that " 'Tis *Priapus* inspires the Talkative Engine"; and if the penis/phallus is not subject to a man's conscious control but capable of subjecting the man himself, part ruling the whole—then the yard can also be figured as the irrational and ungovernable Other within the man, the bodily part which threatens to become autonomous, attached to but somehow independent of the man, prevailing over him and his mind in enigmatic fashion as though it were a separate entity.

The paradoxical condition of the yard as both subject to and yet not subject to the will, as both attached to the man as part of the whole and yet curiously disjunct from mind, is an important aspect of medical debates and explanations about what exactly caused an erection. As John Yolton and others have pointed out, concepts of action, the nature of muscular motion, the source of movement in the animal body, and involuntary as opposed to voluntary movement were the difficult questions in accounts of the connection between the mechanism of the body and conscious control. By willing my arm to move, how in fact does it do so? What causes muscular motion in parts of the body that appear to be insensible to mind or voluntary action?[104] Debates about the nature of animal motion were immensely important because they were so often about the place and function of mind or "soul" in the body. One version of the debate relevant to the erigibility of the yard was the general controversy over irritability and sensibility which, by the middle of the eighteenth century, was characterized most prominently by the opposition of Albrecht von Haller and Robert Whytt.[105] In his *A Dissertation on the Sensible and Irritable Parts of Animals* (1753; trans. 1755), Haller had made the following distinction: "I call that part of the human body irritable, which becomes shorter upon being touched. . . . I call that a sensible part of the human body, which upon being touched transmits the impression of it to the soul; and in brutes, in whom the existence of a soul is not so clear, I call those parts sensible, the Irritation of which occasions evident signs of pain and disquiet in the animal" (658–9). Performing nearly two hundred vivisections on animals, Haller concluded that muscle fibers were informed by an inherent irritability while nerve fibers were characterized by sensibility, and his *Dissertation* offered an inventory of bodily parts and organs whose reactive capacity placed them in one or the other category. Significantly, the parts most highly irritable were associated with the mechanical operations and unconscious movements of the animal machine (heart, diaphragm, intestines), actions over which the mind or soul had no direct control through the nervous system and its fibers. Many of the vital organs, he argued, had little or no sensibility, functioning independently of the will, mind, or soul; indeed, some parts were capable of continued contraction (however temporary) when they were removed from the body or their connection to the brain was severed. Whytt's *Essay on Vital and Other Involuntary Motions of Animals* (1751) represented a competing position in which irritability depended on sensibility: the bodily mechanism was ultimately informed by a soul which was in turn coextensive with the body and nervous system. Contraction could not result from a mere mechanical stimulus alone; it required the initiative of the soul, which was somehow distributed and could feel unconsciously throughout the body. At stake in these debates was nothing less than the role of soul or mind in physiology, with important theological issues which need not concern us here. More important for the subject of this chapter, the debate also held some interesting implications for the meaning of erections, the causes of which provided a neat focusing of the ambiguities of the mind-body relationship.

Was the stiffened yard a case of involuntary response or willed action? Was tumescence an instance of irritability or sensibility? The physiology of the erection was certainly well understood by the time De Graaf wrote his treatise on male genitalia, with the mechanical function of muscles, nerves, and constricted blood-flow carefully described. However, the more difficult question—what, then, caused the physiological process which hardened the penis?—offered no easy answers, leaving a muddle of explanations which simply reinforced the idea of the enigmatic yard. Some sense of the frustrated puzzlement which the action of tumescence elicited can be found in Haller's uncertain hovering over the issue:

> But, though you may conjecture the soul to be the cause of the nervous motion, you cannot do the same with regard to that arising from the vis insita [i.e., an inherent excitability independent of nervous system and mind]. The heart and intestines, also the organs of generation, are governed by a vis insita, and by stimuli. These powers do not arise from the will; nor are they lessened, or excited, or suppressed, or changed by the same. No custom nor art can make these organs subject to the will, which have their motions from a vis insita. . . . The cause [of erection] is love, the desire of pleasure, the friction of the glans, various irritations of the bladder, testicles, seminal vessels, urethra, from the urine, from abundance of good seed, from the venereal poison, from cantharides, whipping with rods, or convulsion of the nerves. (*First Lines of Physiology*, 1: 237–38; 2: 181)

Despite his materialist bent here, Haller elsewhere acknowledges that tumescence is more complex than an irritable response-mechanism independent of mind and will, or a simple case of nerves mechanically constricting the veins leading to penis. In *A Dissertation on the Sensible and Irritable Parts of Animals*, he writes that "The *penis*, which has likewise a great deal of skin, and receives a greater number of nerves than any other part of the body of an equal size, has also a proportionable degree of sensibility" (673), thus linking it to the voluntary category of muscular motion produced by brain, mind, or soul. For Haller, the erection seems a problematic instance of mixed categories, and in his final remarks about the privy member he returns to the irritability of the yard, suggesting that its complex status perhaps makes it a special case:

The Irritability of the genitals seems to be of a particular nature, in so far as voluptuous ideas are the most proper *stimulus* to put them in motion. However so far it resembles that of the other parts, as it is rendered active and produces an erection, if it is excited by a quantity of urine, or *semen*, the acrimony of cantharides, or the sharp discharge of a *gonnorrhoea*. But in whatever manner these irritations are produced, the effect of them is always to constrict the veins, and to retard the motion of the blood through them. (682–3)

Taken together, this collection of Hallerian analyses suggests an uncertainty in his thought: like other highly irritable organs and bodily parts, the yard is stimulated mechanically to erection without the conscious direction of the will (as in Venus's manual friction of Adonis's member); and yet the brain and mind are clearly involved in erection somehow, since "love," "desire of pleasure," and "voluptuous ideas" can trigger tumescence, and are signs of the yard's sensibility. Noteworthy in Haller's formulations is that the will has no direct access to or control over the erection, although he does not say what part of the mind does.

Whytt tackles the same problem in his *Essay on Vital and Other Involuntary Motions of Animals*, trying to explain how the process of tumescence is attributable to mind and yet simultaneously not subject to conscious control:

We cannot, by an effort of the will, either command or restrain the erection of the *penis*; and yet it is evidently owing to the mind; for sudden fear, or any thing which fixes our attention strongly and all at once, makes this member quickly subside, though it were ever so fully erected. The titillation, therefore, of the *vesiculae seminales* by the semen, lascivious thoughts, and other causes, only produce the erection of the *penis*, as they necessarily excite the mind to determine the blood in greater quantity into the cells. . . . As the erection of the *penis* often proceeds from lascivious thoughts, it must be ascribed, in these cases at least, to the mind, notwithstanding our being equally unconscious of her influence exerted here, as in producing the contraction of the heart. (314, 301; quoted in Rodgers, 127–28)

Positioned enigmatically at the juncture of body and mind, the raised
yard could be achieved through the mind's "lascivious thoughts" but
not through the will; and, to make matters more vexing still, this operation of mind was "unconscious." As James Rodgers and Sander
Gilman have noted, Whytt's explanation (and the Haller-Whytt debate in general) located the erection on ambiguous ground between
involuntary response and willed action, with the accompanying assumption "that there is a place within the mind of which the conscious
mind is not sensible" (Gilman, 196). In Whytt's argument, Rodgers
explains, "The mind . . . is necessary to control erection, yet the mind
itself is in this case beyond conscious control. There is no question of a
mindless, mechanical irritability at work, and yet Whytt insists that the
mind is insensible of its own working" (128).

So where do Whytt's "lascivious thoughts" or Haller's "voluptuous
ideas" originate? Clearly it was the imagination, as Hermann Boerhaave argued: "The Muscles concerned in this Action, are not to be
reckoned among the Class of vital or spontaneous Muscles, since of
themselves they do not act in the most healthy Man; but they are
rather in a Class *sui generis*, being under the influence of the Imagination. The Will has no influence either to suppress, excite, or diminish
their Action."[106] By associating the enigmatic erection with the imagination, the physiological discourses provided another version of the
idea that the yard mysteriously informs the mind and rules over the
man. The imagination was, after all, a mental capacity still linked by
many to a potentially dangerous lack of control in which the higher-
order functions of reason and will were usurped by an idiosyncratic
imaging faculty associated with appetites, passions, and the body. Seen
negatively in this way, the imagination was thus at the mercy of lower
forces which, in the case of the imperious yard, welled-up mysteriously into the mind, powerfully over-taking the will. Erections might
require an energy of mind, but they also signaled an unstable re-
arrangement of mental categories in which the man gave himself over
to the mind's dark underbelly: an imagination subject to unconscious
physical impetus and characterized by a lawless coupling of ideas.
There was another side of the erection-imagination nexus, however,
as we will see in the next chapter, for these physiological discourses lo-
cating the cause of erection in the imagination were a short step away
from constructions of male creativity and the imagination as inherently sexual sites.

Physiological theories about the causes of erection are related to the
non-medical examples of the enigmatic yard in the sense that they
view the penis as being in opposition to and incommensurate with
male will. The yard is acknowledged as a defining part of masculinity
and male identity, certainly, but in these configurations it is also an un-

ruly and problematic member, threateningly Other in its capacity to stand outside the will. Although a deep-seated connection of mind and penis through the imagination is acknowledged, this mysterious linkage also suggested an internal divisiveness or potential fragmentariness within, as though the phallus contained or represented a principle of alterity, a separate self with a mind and will of its own. The concept of the autonomous yard severed from the conscious mind had literal and figurative manifestations, from the cut-off penises in medical explorations, to the erections of hanged men, to dildoes.

Anatomical illustrations of the dissected yard present a curious case. As Sander Gilman has pointed out, one of the striking features of this visual discourse is that the "penis is represented within the eighteenth-century anatomical and medical treatises as erect."[107] There are two reasons for this, one of them a sign of a shift in the division of knowledge, and the other a mechanical offshoot of a new technology for studying the genitalia. Barbara Stafford has persuasively linked the graphic amputation and pictorial relief of particular organs, physiological systems, and bodily zones to a wide-spread abstraction of knowledge informing the burgeoning encyclopedist and mathematical obsession for standardized images and the reduction of complex realities to an inventory of definitional abstracts and numbered codes. "This textbook method of diagrammatic characterization," she observes, "led to the dismantling of the body into detachable heads, feet, arms, and legs collected from different sources, pieced together, and reduced into a composite figure."[108] Although she has little to say about male genitalia, the isolated penis of the anatomical illustrations is part of this new culture which increasingly disseminated knowledge and information through abstract diagram and the abbreviated lexical entry. As a subset of such division, the erect yard in medical pictures testifies to the entry of "sexuality" as a scientific subject in its own right, with distended, dissected rod-in-relief an emblem of the procreative mystery in men (for women it was the womb) which the life-sciences sought to isolate and explain.

For the point at hand, however, the technological innovations in anatomical studies of genitalia are more important than this well-known aspect of the history of knowledge, and we return to that central figure, Regnier De Graaf. His *De Usu Siphonis in Anatomia* (1668, published with *Tractatus de Virorum Organis Generationi Inservientibus*) was the first significant description of the use of the injection method in anatomy before Thomas Pole's general treatise in English on the subject in 1790. Although he did not invent the syringe, De Graaf's practical improvements of them led to instruments which were still being used almost without modification in the mid-nineteenth century.[109] De Graaf was one of the first to use injections to explore the complex

connections among the vas deferens, seminal vesicles, and the urethra. By forcing liquid (usually water or mercury) through these tubes
as well as through the spermatic artery, lymphatic vessels, and the
ducts of the prostate, he improved upon existing explanations of male
reproductive parts. Moreover, by injecting the vessels with wax or inflating them with air (see Figure 2; F represents "the seminal vesicles
distended with air"), specific features could be isolated and physiological theories proved. More dramatically, De Graaf perfected a method
of "blowing up" the penis with air or liquid (often by injecting the internal iliac artery) and then tying it off and letting it dry, thus allowing
examination of the yard in its erect state. Illustrations of this technique are found in many treatises, as in James Drake's *Anthropologia
Nova; Or, A New System of Anatomy* (1707). Figure 3 shows "The Fore-
part of the Human *Penis* prepared with *Mercury*" (273), with letter F
indicating "A Blow-Pipe in the *Urethra*" (273). The lesser representation, "Fig. II," shows "The two *Corpora Cavernosa Penis*, and that of the
Urethra, after a Transverse Section, when Inflated and dry'd" (274).
Perhaps the most comprehensive illustration of the De Graafian technique is William Cowper's "An Account of two Glands and their Excretory Ducts lately discover'd in Human Bodies" (see Figure 4). Published
in *Philosophical Transactions*, November 1699, No. 258, the figure clari-
fies the technical procedure for blowing-up the penis: letter I shows
"The Bulb of the Cavernous Body of the *Urethra* partly distended with
Wind" (368); P marks "The Ligature made to prevent the Wind from
passing out of the Cavernous Body of the *Urethra* and its Bulb," and Q
shows "The Aperture by which the Inflation was made" (369). After
De Graaf's innovations it was possible to create erections in cadavers
and in penises cut off from corpses. This ingenious technology is relevant to the cultural context of the enigmatic yard. If experiments with
the irritability of fibers and organs had demonstrated temporary motion or contraction of physical parts severed from the nervous system
and brain, thereby throwing into relief the troubling possibility of
some life-principle severed from mind and soul, then here was a striking literal version of the phallus as autonomous Other, completely detached from the male will and dramatically severed from the rest of
the male body. In short, a clinical method had been invented by which
the privy member could be raised even after death.

De Graaf's detailed instructions on how to prepare the cut-off yard
for medical observation may well be the first written account of its
kind, and it is repeated verbatim by a variety of eighteenth-century
medical treatises.[110] No one has discussed this important segment of
the *Tractatus*, which in fact sets forth a technology of erection which
does not require the man at all—not brain, body, will, or identity:

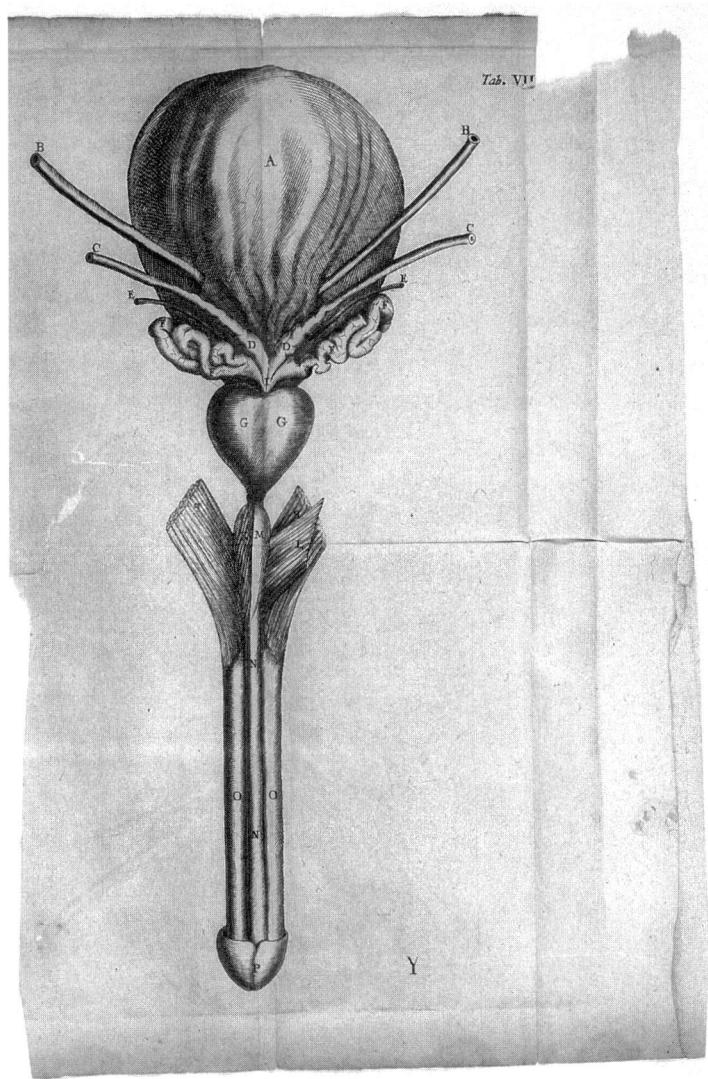

Figure 2. Human penis, urinary bladder, vasa deferentia, seminal vesicles, and prostate gland as they look from behind. Regnier De Graaf, plate VII, *Tractatus De Virorum Organis Generationi Inservientibus* (1668). Courtesy of The Wellcome Library, London.

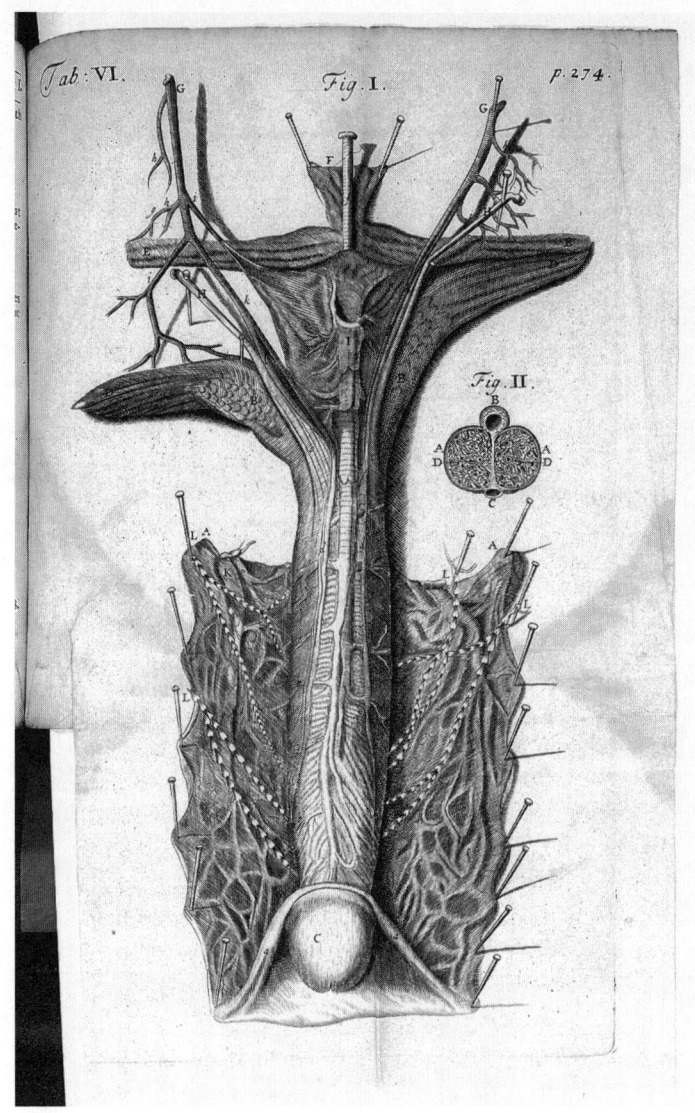

Figure 3. "The Fore-part of the Human *Penis* prepared with *Mercury*." James Drake, plate VI, *Anthropologia Nova, Or, A New System of Anatomy* (1707). Courtesy of The Wellcome Library, London.

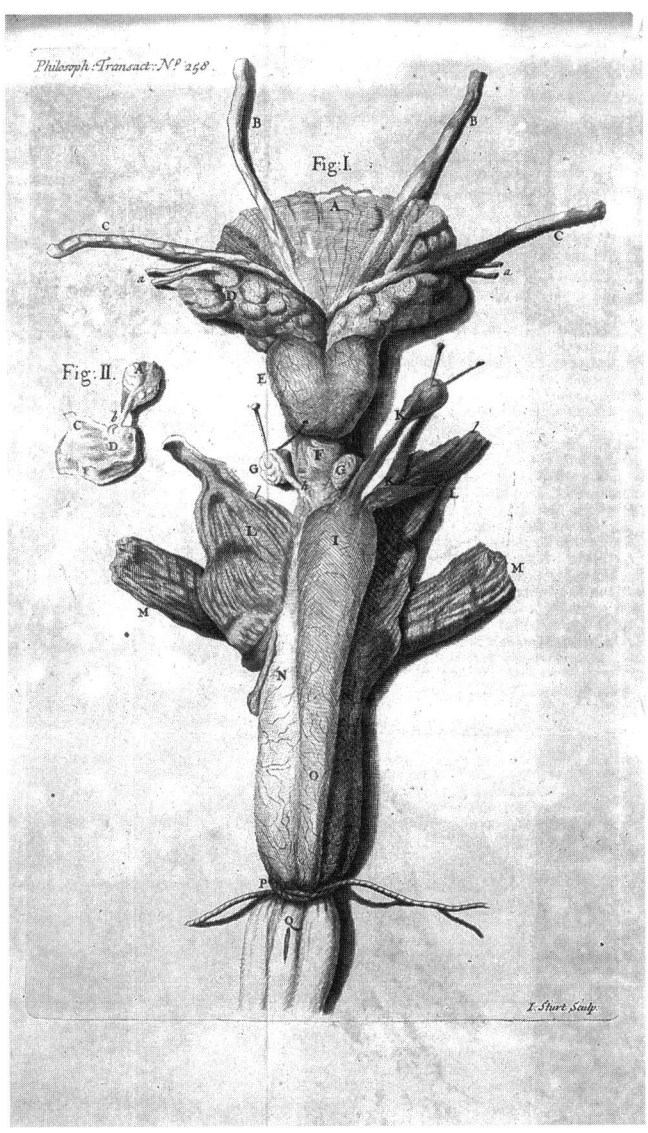

Figure 4. Glands and excretory ducts of the human penis. William Cowper, "An Account of two Glands and their Excretory Ducts lately discover'd in Human Bodies," *Philosophical Transactions*, No. 258, 1699. Courtesy of The Wellcome Library, London.

you should prepare a penis in the following way. First, gently express the blood which is always inside in more or less copious quantities and then insert a tube into the spongy substance, where it approaches most closely the bones of the pubis. Half fill the cavity of the penis with water with the aid of a syringe and shake gently. When the water has run out stained with blood, fill again with fresh water and repeat the operation three or four times until the water is no longer stained with blood when it comes out. As soon as you see this, gently express between two pieces of lint the quantity of water contained in the corpora nervosa [i.e., corpora cavernosa]. Finally, distend the penis, by inflating it, until it reaches its natural size. To be preserved at this size it should be tied up. A penis blown up in this way or dried out, you can examine at will; everything is clearly and distinctly visible in its natural position, i.e., in the sort of position it has during the sexual act. . . . it matters little whether the flaccid penis is large or small, since its size depends merely on the greater or smaller amount of blood in the corpora nervosa. We assert this the more freely because we have sometimes dissected cadavers in which the penis appeared at first glance to be quite small but when inflated on the sly extended like a "fearful, ugly, monstrous giant bereft of sight," to use Ausonius' joke. (*Cent. Nupt.* v. 1270), 47–48)

In this remarkable passage several things are detectable, not only medical mechanics but also a set of underlying cultural assumptions about the yard which link De Graaf and his medical milieu to popular discourses. Noteworthy is the twice-used "natural" in the first paragraph, an interesting slippage in the scientific mode letting in some of the cultural shadings and discursive modulations we have already seen. While De Graaf is suggesting that a proper study can only be conducted on the erect member, the passage also insinuates that the blown-up yard represents a norm, that the phallus and not the penis constitutes the "natural size" and "natural position." Of course, nothing could be more unnatural than the cut-off, lifeless, mechanically erected yard of anatomical investigation, and yet the Dutch doctor's textual practices are similar to those discourses which privilege hard phallus over mundane penis, separating the autonomous yard—now conveniently and permanently erect for study—from the man who owned it. De Graaf's "natural position," as we will see in a moment, is curiously similar to discourses about dildoes in which the detached, stiffened prick is commodified as an item for use and transaction, with actual man, male mind, or masculine sensibility nowhere to be found.

    De Graaf's sense of humor in the second paragraph represents a different and more complex slippage. In *Cento Nuptialis* the witty Ausonius had used the idea of the one-eyed Cyclops blinded by Odysseus to refer to the bridegroom's penis at the moment of penetration, but De Graaf's application is heavily freighted, projecting enigmatic life onto the now potent, cyclopean phallus whose monstrous presence transcends even the lifeless corpse. In this tangled allusive moment, the language of De Graaf's mechanical explanation is overtaken by another kind of discourse which converts the medicalized penis of anatomical scrutiny into a personified entity invested with its own autonomous status. The mechanically-induced erection of the cadaver—it is hard to know what to make of "inflated on the sly"—turns into a fearful, brute power ominously resident and alive in the distended yard. Living phallus; dead man.

The idea is certainly present in accounts of the erections of hanged criminals, as in Robert James's *A Medicinal Dictionary* (1745): "that in Criminals which hang long after Death, this Part becomes erected, the Blood in that Position of the Body falling to the inferior Parts" (3: s.v. "Penis"). The eery image of an erectile motion in the dead man is not confined to technical writing. Popular narratives likewise served as vehicles for the concept of the autonomous yard severed from the conscious mind. An anonymous poem of the period provides a comical non-medical counterpart to De Graaf's dead man/personified erection:

> Within this coffin, sinew-shrunk and dead,
> Lies Doll's delight, and she no tear hath shed.
> Not that she wants affection to lament
> Th' entombing of so sweet an instrument
> Of her content, but that her power is such
> That she can raise it up, and with her touch
> Make it so speak that he which understands
> The language must confess her active hands
> Have strength, though not the chain of fate to break,
> Yet sure to raise the dead and make it speak.
> And if you be impatient of delay
> To know the mystery, then bid her play.[111]

In these personifying gestures, it is as though a male identity or masculine character has been transferred from the dead man to his now independent and detachable genital member which has become the only important site of signification. But what exactly is being signified, and what does this radical separation of brain/mind from the sexual member imply for notions of a masculine identity?

That the phallus can be mechanically created *outside* the man, detached completely from mind and body, has problematic implications for mind-yard equations. In the hands of De Graaf or Doll the enigmatic yard evinces an impressive independence incommensurate with a male will formerly present in the dead man. The erection in these contexts signifies a loss of power and identity for the man, whose now dead body and irrelevant selfhood are dismissed from the scene. And yet there remains an apparently autonomous masculine power in the

(Erect) penis as Supplement to masculinity

artificial erection that becomes the subject of dramatic treatment, mysteriously able to rise over and in spite of the lifeless carcass. But the personified agency and enigmatic life projected onto this amputated phallus includes an interesting appropriation: it is, after all, only through the sexual "power" of Doll's "active hands" or through the mechanical means of De Graafian techniques that the personified yard can be raised and made to "speak." Indeed, the manual ministrations of a Doll or a De Graaf transform the privy member into a commodity whose erigibility signifies the loss of male selfhood, power, and identity. Dependent on the dexterity and control of others for its enigmatic turgidity, the hard penis—detached, separate, commodified—becomes an item which now can be made, owned, and exchanged quite independent of the male self and character to which it was attached.

De Graaf's *Tractatus* offers a memorable instance of this constellation of ideas. Reminiscent of the ritualistic display of the victorious Ethiopian warriors who cut off the penises of the vanquished, dried them, and then spat them out at the feet of their king who then returned them so they could be sewed together as necklaces for proud wives (*Tractatus*, 45–46), De Graaf has his own collection of dried out erections and reproductive parts used to show off his medical stature and proudly display his authority as anatomist:

> if they do not trust my words and if they have no human subject at hand, I ask them to come to our house and at any time we shall demonstrate . . . that the vasa deferentia have very considerable communication with the seminal vesicles. We shall demonstrate this not in the organs of brutes but in those of various human males which we always keep inflated and dried out in our museum. (34)

De Graaf's "museum" of inflated male genital "items" is of course part of a growing trend in the period for the organized display of collections, cabinets of curiosities from the natural world, and the obsessive gathering of unusual items by the frequently satirized virtuosi. But his macabre museum is also a remarkably apt emblem of a discourse in which the man is usurped by his own detachable phallus which in turn circulates variously as a thing to be owned by others. Paradoxically, the man is, but is not, defined by his privy member: commodified as his amputated phallus, he is also replaced by it in these examples. The enigmatic yard—engorged thing of maleness itself—thus becomes a threat to the individual male will and masculine character in these figurations, sign of an unruly power controlled only by others, and guarantor of an absent male identity.

Many of the narratives about dildoes function precisely in this way. Just as Doll does not need a living man for "so sweet an instrument" to respond, the dildo is independent of male body and mind and always available for use. Like the artificial erections used in anatomical study, the dildo is free of the biological and temporal contexts of living men and their penises. Most often made of glass, leather, or ivory in this period, the hand-made phallus is a simulacrum which defies a particularized masculine self or character even while it is intended to represent an essential maleness. As such, these sexual instruments are a concrete extension of ideas we have just examined, and many male-authored poems and stories about women and dildoes register a misogynistic uneasiness about this detached phallus which paradoxically emblematizes maleness while replacing the man and his penis. Carrying a mixture of male sexual fantasy and comic anxiety, dildo narratives are largely about who controls the economy within which maleness has been reduced to a phallic commodity. These surrogate objects are another instance of the penis-phallus differentiation, except that here the phallus has been symbolically castrated, separating individual men from the male power associated with the erect member. The second speaker in Butler's *Dildoides* understands this threat perfectly:

> Are we among
> Heathens, or Divells to let Scape us
> The Image of this lewd Priapus?
> Green Sicknesse Girles will soon adore him,
> And wickedly Fall down before him.
> For him each Superstitious Hussy,
> Will Temple make of Tussy Mussy.
> Idolatry will fill the Land,
> And all True Pricks forget to Stand.
> Curs'd be the wretch that found these Arts
> Of Loosing us the womens hearts:
> For Pray henceforth, who'l not refuse one
> When she hath All, that she hath use on?
> For how shall I make her to Pitty me
> Who Injoys Man in this Epitome? (7)

"To Epitomise," says Johnson, is "To abstract; to contract into a narrow space," and Butler's speaker recognizes that such reduction of "Man" has dire consequences in the realm of personal identity: the "True Pricks" of actual men will no longer have meaning or function, and a masculine character defined and given status in part by one's yard will be diminished, irrelevant, or forgotten. However comic the poem is meant to be, its articulation of the autonomous and detached erection has links to other more serious treatments we have been examining.

Epitomized in this fashion, the symbolic value of the phallus be-comes a transferable thing, owned and controlled not necessarily by men with penises, but by whomever has possession of the now com-modified figure, whether anatomist, Doll, or the randy female intent on pleasing herself or another woman. The consequences for men are clear enough, but this aspect of the discourse has interesting implica-tions for the socio-sexual and political hierarchy upon which patriar-chal structures depended. Jill Campbell has written persuasively about Fielding's racy *The Female Husband* (1746), which was based on real-life lesbian male impersonator Mary Hamilton, who allegedly married sev-eral women in the guise of a man, penetrating her wives with a dildo. Campbell argues that Hamilton's phallic impersonation was for Field-ing an instance of "the thorough appropriability of a masculine iden-tity" and "the failure of the phallus to guarantee a masculine authority based on the possession of an inalienable natural part."[112]

There was for the man and his penis a difficult metaphorical frame-work in these examples: the symbolically-laden bodily part of mas-culinity and male dominance could be appropriated, stolen, and acted by women; attached to and intimately informing and being informed by the man, the yard could be the uncanny signifier of something powerfully masculine which was lost or out of reach. In short, the arti-ficial phallus further complicated newer models of a physically-based masculine symbolism. Enigmatic not only in the sense that it could be wayward and outside a man's conscious control, the yard also hinted at another kind of enigma for masculinity as a sexualized interiority: in some contexts a marker of male power, mental capacity, or stature of character, the detached and turgid yard could also represent a self-alienating part.

In summary, the very different strands of this section can certainly be understood on their own terms as isolated contexts not obviously related. But taken together it seems to me they reflect a larger dis-course which, in its most general sense, threatened the hierarchy of mind over body. The examples are various, but they are also related by the possibility that the meaning of the yard is precariously and enigmatically outside male prerogative even as it somehow defines him: monarchy led by a prick; man as mouthpiece for underlying genital drive; yard as irrational, ungovernable Other, or as autono-mous and detached from male brain; the erection as unconscious in origin and not subject to will; erections created in cadavers and amputated members; the stiffening tarse of hanged criminal; a liv-ing dynamic lifted from dead man and bestowed on personified phal-lus; man commodified as and replaced by detachable phallus or dildo which circulates as commodity. These images and structures resonate together as an important cultural subset about the relationship of male mind and yard as a site profoundly characterized by paradox and ambiguity.

Impotence Trials

That "man" and "manliness" were constituted somehow by male genitalia is the underlying assumption shared by all the examples above. That the head-groin equations were also differential and sometimes contradictory is clear, suggesting the extent to which the semiotics of men's crotches were a problem of cultural perception. Having a penis and testicles meant you were a man, so it would seem; but in some cases, the testimony of one's privy members made even this identification far from clear. Indeed, impotence trials constituted a remarkable instance of gender trouble in which even the stiffened pintle was no guarantee of virility, and where the synecdochic yard in the courtroom was so fetishized as a symbolic commodity that individual male defendants often appeared to vanish from the textual records. Having a penis sometimes meant nothing at all until it had been re-invented as detached phallus, as simulacrum which replaced the complex living realities of men. In this discursive scenario, masculinity as interiorized sexuality became a fractured matter, with the yard simultaneously the sign of manliness and of the problematic relationship of men to the site where masculinity was defined.

The subjects of impotence and "imperfect enjoyment" traditions have received their due from scholars, but the history of impotence trials deserves far more attention than it has received, because printed records of these divorce suits brought against husbands by their wives represent a rich encoding of attitudes and ideological substructures, not only about the socio-politics of sex and gender, but also about the vexed cultural meanings of the penis.[113] Moreover, these notorious accounts—eagerly published by Edmund Curll and his ilk for a readership fascinated by the sex-lives of aristocrats—constitute a rich historical context in which legal, medical, conjugal, and erotic interests converged in public debate about the yard. Legal initiatives for divorce or annulment on the grounds of impotence had the effect of bringing the yard and its various discourses into the limelight of an official cultural adjudication in which institutional definitions relied on the proofs and rules of evidence advanced by spokespersons for wife and husband. At stake was the discursive and evidential logic that would prevail in the court's definition of a man's virility. What semiotic logic, in other words, would finally be applied to the relationship of the husband and his privy member as this might define his masculinity? The

situation and satisfaction of wives in these trials are important historical matters, as well, but what interests me here is the revealing manner in which the penis was taken to court, not only as the defendant
but also as one of the key witnesses.

   Proof of virility in a court of law was not a simple matter.[114] Summa-
rizing the background of French and English law, Ephraim Chambers's *Cyclopaedia: Or, An Universal Dictionary of Arts and Sciences* (2nd
ed., 1738) explained that there were three tests of a man's potency:
"To evince a man's virility, in a court of justice, where he is accused of
impotency, it is required he give evidence of erection, intromission,
and *ejaculation*. . . . CONGRESS is also used in an obscene sense, for
an essay, or trial, made by appointment of a lay or a spiritual judge, in
the presence of chirurgeons and matrons, to prove whether or no a
man be impotent; in order for the dissolving of a marriage."[115] This
tripartite test by erection, entry, and emission involved a two-step sequence. In the first instance, the court appointed up to six examiners
(usually male physicians) who sought visual evidence of the husband's
ability to get an erection and then ejaculate by masturbating. The defendant was allowed several tries and his own choice of place and
time. In some cases, the husband was obliged to proceed to an incredi-
ble second demonstration called "trial by congress," or public intercourse with a prostitute in front of court-appointed witnesses; this test,
Lawrence Stone writes, was "urged by plaintiff wives, who were rightly
confident that most men would fail under such conditions" (135). I
am not aware of any court-ordered public copulations in the English
divorce cases of the seventeenth or eighteenth centuries, and such
proofs were abolished in France in 1677 when the ex-husband in a notorious annulment case—one M. Roger—remarried and sired seven
children. But the memory of public congress played an important
rhetorical part in courtroom arguments and trial reports. No one has
so far provided comprehensive statistical evidence which would settle
the question of how successful such divorce suits were in France and
England at this time, but if the most popular published accounts of
these scandals are any indication, it appears the courts sided more
often with the husband than the wife, suggesting the extent to which
the ideological implications of family structures and larger socio-political
orders were embedded in such trials. As Jeffrey Merrick puts it, "Impotence cases took place . . . against the background of the gendered
structures of authority and subordination, ostensibly dictated by nature and sanctified by religion, that regulated the household and the
state" (192–93). The dissolution of marriage on any grounds, in other
words, represented a complex threat to the social order and thus, in a
systemic sense, all-male courts might have been disposed to take the
husband's side in passing judgement.[116] But within the context of in-

dividual males and particular divorce cases, the charge of impotence guaranteed prolonged discussion of the man's penis in courtrooms jammed with prurient crowds, followed by a flood of publications offering the most intimate sexual facts and scandalous allegations to a readership only too eager to get at the dirt. At the center of this interest, both official and unofficial, was the significance of the yard.

The popularity of these court cases in Pope's day should not be underestimated, as Peter Wagner and Judith Mueller have pointed out. In 1714, the ever-diligent and opportunistic Curll published a two-volume account of a sensational French impotence trial of 1712, *The Case of Impotency Debated in the Late Famous Tryal at Paris*. . . . Interest in Curll's rendition—complete with appendix which translated the racier Latin passages in the French original—was remarkable. Shrewdly knowing a good thing, Curll quickly followed up with two other titles aimed to satisfy prurient interest in sex-lives, genitalia, and the broken marriages of the rich. Other exploiters followed suit, cashing in on the public fascination for disputes about the status of the privy parts of plaintiff and defendant.

Not surprisingly, the impotence trial became part of a collective vocabulary of ideas and imaginative possibilities, showing up in diverse places such as Jean Barrin's pornographic *Venus in the Cloister* (1725), in which Sister Angelica explains to the younger Sister Agnes that her blunt description of sexual matters ought to be seen as the vehicle for truth, just as "in the spiritual Courts the Gravity of my Lords the venerable Bishops, [is not] ruffled by hearing, in Matters of Divorce Things mentioned in Terms most plain and open: And Actions too which the unthinking Vulgar would think lewd and lascivious, have been ordered by their Reverend Paternities, as Inspections of Bodies in Cases of Impotency."[117] *The Humours of the Court: Or, Modern Gallantry. A New Ballad Opera* (1732) likewise included in one of its subplots the story of Impotentio, who is finally "cured of my fatal Indisposition" by doctors who confidently assert that "if the Lady [his wife] will complain for want of *due benevolence*, by my Consent the Gentleman shall *Consummate* with her in open Court, till every-body is fully satisfied."[118] Taking one other literary example: it is seldom recognized that *Tristram Shandy* ends with a direct reference to impotence trials, the incapable Shandy bull "who is as good a Bull as ever p-ss'd, and might have done for *Europa* herself in purer times—had he but two legs less, might have been driven into Doctors Commons [where divorces were transacted] and lost his character—which to a Town Bull, brother *Toby*, is the very same thing as his life." The allusion gives a particularly literal dimension to Yorick's answer to Mrs. Shandy's query, "what is all this story about?—A COCK and a BULL, said *Yorick*" (9: 33, 496).

That ordinary people were deeply interested in courtroom stories about cocks is amusingly evident in Horace Walpole's epistolary account of the court battle between the Duke of Beaufort and his adulterous Duchess in the early 1740s. The Duchess's suit for annulment on grounds of impotence had been rejected but then upheld on appeal in December 1742. In March 1743 the Duke took the risky step of volunteering to demonstrate his ability to have an erection and ejaculate before court-appointed examiners. In Walpole's words,

I have no victories to tell you, but the Duke of Beaufort's; you have heard all that story of his wife and Lord Talbot: when they had got such proofs of her gallantries, she took a bold step, and swore impotence to his Grace. He, with more than mortal courage, stood the trial. T'other night was appointed for the action; the lists were at Dr Meade's house: he, another physician, three surgeons and the Dean of the Arches, all very matron-like personages, were inspectors. I should never have been potent again!—well, but he was. They offered to wait upon his Grace to any place of public resort—"No, no he would only go behind the screen, and when he knocked, they were to come to him, but come that moment." He was some time behind the scenes: at last he knocked, and the good old folks saw what amazed them—what they had not seen many a day! Cibber says "His Grace's ——— is in everybody's mouth." He is now upon his mettle, and will sue Lord Talbot [the adulterer with his wife] for fourscore thousand pounds damages.[119]

Facetious though it may be, Walpole's oral-genital image of the Duke's yard and its status as public conversation piece testify to the imaginative hold which legal debates about individual penises had on a diverse population. Turning now to a close analysis of the most famous of these accounts, we will see that part of the public fascination was sustained by the semiotic instability of the male sex-organs.

What is particularly significant in Curll's account of the de Gesvres dispute in *The Case of Impotency Debated* (1714) is that each of the three proofs of virility—erection, entry, ejaculation—was contested as a sign, with the result that customary physical evidence of a competent phallicism was not, according to the disputants, necessarily proof of a man's virility. Such apparently paradoxical reasoning did not exist in a vacuum. Treatments of impotence in other discourses, the imperfect enjoyment poems for example, had often been informed by a contradictory sense that an excess of phallic passion was itself the cause of unwanted limpness.[120]

What distinguishes Curll's two-volume presentation of the famous de Gesvres affair is the startling proposition that the erected yard is *not* the sign of male virility. Arguing on the wife's behalf, the advocate suggests that the healthy appearance of the Marquis's reproductive parts is insufficient for establishing virility. Explaining "the Difference between able Womens Men, and those that are frigid," the advocate for Lady de Gesvres asserts that

In the former, the Penis is contracted and shrunk up, during the Time that it does not actually stand; so that it is impossible to judge of its Length and Thickness, unless it is erect and stiff. Whereas 'tis quite the contrary in those that are frigid, as in the Carcass of a dead Man. For such indeed have a Pizzle, but it's never contracted or shrunk up; it has a continual Length and Thickness, (as in other men when it stands) but then it always hangs its Head, and is uncapable of a perfect or consistent Erection. (1: Appendix 1v)

Following from this line of argument, the raised yard itself ought not to be accepted as a reliable sign of a man's sexual competence:

our Searchers warn us not to trust to the Stiffness of the virile Organ; there being in many an erective Force, but not effective, because not solid, sober, and strong enough to hold to the End. . . . For tho' he appears to be a Man, he is not presently to be concluded such, because there are some whose Ensign of Manhood is a mere Cheat, gives mighty Hopes, but performs nothing. Again, tho' he does not appear a Man, it does not follow, that he's not a Man; because the Tokens of Manhood do sometimes lye hid, and some times pop out. And therefore, by inspecting the Husband, no certain Judgment can be made either for or against Virility; but by inspecting the Wife, both Doubts are remov'd. (1: Appendix 2v)

This argument is a complex addition to the discursive contexts we have examined earlier. Here, the question of masculinity as it inheres in and is proven by the phallus is thrown into doubt: having an erection does *not* prove one's manhood; possessing an unpromising-looking flaccidity is *not* evidence that one is not a man. The "Tokens of Manhood" are in this account semiotically opaque, making phallus/virility, masculinity/yard equations hopelessly entangled. The turgid pego, it seems, can also be a false sign. In this logic, the stiff prick is a symbol not of potent maleness but of an inherent dissembling which hides a man's reproductive and erotic failure.

Of course the legal advocate is emphasizing function and performance as the key signs of male virility, relocating the site of evidence from the yard to the wife's vagina. In turn, the Marquis's counsel would advance a common-place about the equally problematic signs of female chastity and the hymen, stating that the "Physicians, the Canonists, hold for a Rule, that in Nature, there is no certain Sign of Virginity; that some are Virgins, and yet don't appear so, while others may appear so, and yet are not so" (2: 57–58). That the signs of virility are as vexed as the signs of virginity speaks volumes about the respective value placed by this culture on male and female sexual economies, but for the immediate subject at hand the semiotic ambiguity claimed on behalf of the plaintiff heralds a more complicated question about where and how a masculine identity or male status is to be found. Spokespersons for the Marquis likewise problematize the evidence that might be gleaned from the defendant's penis, but the overall result is the same: putting up a good defense of the man's sex-organs by concentrating on the questionable status of court-appointed examinations, his lawyers nonetheless destabilize a notion of masculine sensibility or identity in relation to male genitalia. The problem with a committee of searchers assigned to find proof of erection and ejaculation, they say, is that the court wrongly supposes a man's yard is controlled by his will:

But let us suppose, that in a first Visit, in a Second, in a Third, a young Man, the best constituted in the World, even, in his Chamber, in his Bed, who should have Tidings brought him of the Arrival of four old Dotards, capable of suppressing that desired Token, that Gift of Fancy and Nature, rather than to provoke it. . . . I would fain know what they could honestly conclude or pronounce against him? These Parts of his well form'd in their Consistence, Number, Length, &c. have not produc'd in our Sight, the Tokens, which our Curiosity desired; is he therefore incapable of those Tokens? We have not found him in this Condition; does it therefore follow, he never can be in it? We have not seen him *erectum*; is he therefore *inerigible*? We have seen the Causes of Ability, but not the Effects; is he therefore unable; and must his Marriage be dissolv'd? . . . All that passes in the Congress, is at least the Effect of a lawful Embracing, between a Wife and a Husband; but how can People dare to maintain, that it is lawful, out of the Action of Marriage, either to the Party to use Friction himself, or to the Searchers to provoke him to it?

And indeed, to speak here only of the first Sign (without stretching our Thoughts to the filthiness of the second [ejaculation]) this first Sign must be either natural or procured.

The natural depends upon a Caprice of the Fancy, which the Will has no Command over.

The procured, out of the Action of Marriage, is a Crime. (2: 46–48)

The argument's rhetorical questions represent a solid retort, perhaps, combining physical impracticality with moral repugnance. At the center is a question about the relationship of tumescence and the male character: if the man has no willed power over his yard, how then can he be usefully commanded to prove he is not impotent in circumstances completely uncongenial to the erotic imagination? Suggesting that the primary evidential site of sexual potency is psychological—a question of de Gesvres's fancy titillating the yard into stiffness—is a skillful enough rejoinder because erection, entry, and emission are made the "natural" results of an imaginative "Caprice" and erotic desire impossible to control. Virility is thus "a Donation of the Fancy; there's no commanding the Fancy" (2: 249). This counter-argument insinuates that the court's very attempt to secure evidence proving the defendant can get it up, insert his yard into the vagina, and ejaculate is guaranteed to produce a false impotence, unfairly suppressing the mysterious well-springs of carnal responsiveness which might otherwise prove his phallic prowess. The pleasure-giving erection, reproductively potent and conjugally obliged, cannot be forced in such crude fashion, however official the order. But in defending the potential competence of de Gesvres's privy member in this way, his lawyers also sustain the complex disjunction of male mind and enigmatic yard we have already seen in other contexts, here making virility and its connotations for masculine status something outside the man's character or control.

These disputes about engorged or floppy yards as evidence of a man's potency had real (and sometimes devastating) consequences for the husbands and wives involved. As a symptom of cultural semiotics, however, these public legal debates also made it clear that it was the meaning of the penis which was pre-eminently on trial, descriptions and reports of the accused privy member at times all but replacing the man to whom it was attached. In another example of the yard symbolizing and then replacing the man altogether, lawyers for de Gesvres used six previous impotence cases to establish precedents useful to their defense. In each case the physical medical evidence derived from examination of the husband's genitals had been somehow less than reassuring, as the sampling below makes clear:

We have found the exterior of his person [one Joseph le Page] to be like other Mens, the P-ck of a good Conformation . . . the Cod of an unexceptionable Thickness and Extent, and in it are Vessels of a good Conformation and Size, but terminating unequally; on the Right Side they end in a small flabby Substance, instead [of] a true Testicle. . . . We have proceeded to inspect *Peter Damour*, Master-Sadler at *Paris*; [his genitalia seem normal in appearance but] the said *Danmour* . . . told us, that when he embraces his Wife his Instrument will just stand, but no more. . . . We find the String of the Fore-skin [of one Anthony de Bret] is shorter than it should be for giving the Nut free Scope to extend it self when it swells. . . . [T]he Spermatick Vessels likewise seem'd to us to be lank, weak and fall'n away. (2: 184–86, 188)

And in each case the wife's petition has been rejected, evidence of the court's willingness to give benefit of the doubt to husbandly competence however feeble it might be. Noteworthy, however, is how the penis replaces the man in these reports, as it does spectacularly in the following deposition provided to the court by two physicians and two chirurgeons: "We have, they say, proceeded to visit the *Penis* of the said *Claude Grenet*" (2: 188). The matter-of-fact "visit" underscores the bizarre separation of man from his tarse, as though the inspection could bypass Grenet's mind, character, or corporeal wholeness and proceed instantly to the true site of their masculine origins. The husband was at the center of these official examinations, of course, his legal status as a sexually potent man dependent on the ability of his yard, whose capacity in turn held larger implications for his psychological and sociopolitical stature. But in a metaphorical gesture we have already seen, a tendency of the impotence trials was to separate the man's character or mind from the yard while simultaneously equating male identity or power with the raised rod. We do not know how M. Grenet felt about the public charge of impotence, or what were his thoughts about the examination, or his sense of what it meant to have a penis, hard or soft; we only know that his pintle received an official visit from the court appointees charged with providing evidence. " 'Tis visible in *Grenet*'s Report," de Gesvres's lawyer concludes, "that they who inspected him, did, as one may say, make an Anatomy of his Genitals in Terms capable of putting Modesty to the Squeak" (2: 251). Privy member is visited by court-appointed examiners; pintle is the official object of legal scrutiny; inspection of pego will be part of the state's definition of virility. In this almost surrealistic legal approach to the yard as commodity of maleness itself, the actual man all but disappears except for his name.

These public tribunals had the effect of putting the penis on trial, with accused yard both notorious defendant and star witness. That the pintle had an owner with a complex mental and experiential history is also very important, even if those realities are lost to us. But what the legal arguments and unofficial reports accentuated—and what was so eagerly consumed by a prurient public—were inspections, assessments, and descriptions of the husband's yard and its history of stands. The accused's prick had everything to do with being a man, it would seem, but these official public wranglings provided no secure definition by which the relationship could be unequivocally understood. Instead, legal questions about the penis/phallus paradoxically accentuated a gap between the sexually-embodied site of masculinity and the male mind, identity, and character of man-with-penis. The impotence trials are an especially dramatic example of a cultural logic we have seen earlier in this chapter: that is, a tendency to separate men from the symbolic physical site that had also become the key marker of maleness itself.

Detectable in these early modern formations is the separation of literal from symbolic genitalia which Lacanian and feminist psychoanalysis has inherited and upon which the postmodern phallus depends. But in the eighteenth century the relationship of the symbolic to the real had not yet been so completely severed, and the literal male body was still the important newer site where masculinity was to be found. There are other well-known features of the history of the male body which testify to this: the nervous sensibility of the new Man of Feeling whose very physicality would define his psychological, moral, and fashionable worth; the heterosexual, middle-class *homo economicus* of reproductive potency versus the effete or depraved bodies of aristocrats and the new-style sodomite; the reformation of male manners which explains the historical transformation of masculine physical types from libertines such as Rochester or Wycherley's Horner or Richardson's Lovelace, to Fielding's good-natured but promiscuous Tom Jones, to Mackenzie's desexualized man of feeling in Harley, to Burney's sexually desirable aristocrat of delicacy in Lord Orville.[121] Each of these somatic fields was clearly informed by notions of masculinity-as-sexual-embodiment, even though male sexuality was also being absorbed by changing codes of politeness and models of the self-controlled gentleman of sensibility.[122] But the new phallus-as-commodity created a significant gap between the cultural imaginary and the lived experience of real men. Although attached to a man's psychological and biological systems, yards had also been assigned a variety of symbolic functions against which individual male experience might or might not agree. Inverse models, enigmatic yards, penises not subject to male will or desire, propositions that the erect member might *not* be a sign of sexual competence, the legal reification of prick over its owner—these diverse head-groin configurations collectively problematized the very connection which was the object of clarification. And such discourses were bound to have an imperfect relationship to the lived realities of men.

One result of this gap was that the yard was simultaneously about power and loss. The new location of definitional power for manliness was the groin, but some cultural equations removed men and their conscious will from the site of defining power. In this sense, the yard could be a curiously self-alienating part, attached to but not necessarily owned or controlled by the man. Moreover, the idea of the symbolic phallus could be put into public circulation where other men, the state, public opinion, and even women might lay claim to it. The separation of brain/mind from the sexual member which was *the* physical marker of maleness represents an important historical shift. To be defined by a body part which is also symbolically detached from you and transformed into a public item of potential value over which you do not necessarily have ownership or control is the very process by which the literal part becomes synecdoche *and* a commodity in circulation. I am suggesting that this process informs the larger historical implication of the newer links of masculinity to sexual embodment. The discourses I have set forth in this chapter together point to a reorganization of the collective meaning of the male body and manliness, both of which came to be represented by the yard itself—emblem of the "manly," a cultural shorthand for head-groin associations, and the symbolic commodity of a new kind of traffic in maleness. As we will see now, male literary commentary captured some sense of this gap, of how individual males encountered the cultural commodification of their selfhood as sexualized parts.

Chapter 3

The Sexual Traffic in Male Creativity

The category "male creativity" contained its own versions of the larger cultural uneasiness about what genitalia meant for the male character. The discourses I have described intensified the perceived links between the reproductive system and an essentialized maleness, and these associations permeated changing notions about the poetical character in a rapidly commercialized literary world. Never before had the male body become so elaborate a literal and figurative topography for describing creativity. Of course there are other well-known metaphors that enter the scene of eighteenth-century literary professionalization: the author as proprietor and the text as real estate; the elitist figure of the inspired prophet-Bard magically in touch with a god-like imagination and capable of a divine optics. But it is the male body—its somatic and sexual characteristics—which so often informed the collective vocabulary concerning the nature of creativity and its public status. Like the phallus-as-commodity, male creativity too became marketable, an item of commercial traffic.

Let me clarify what I mean by "traffic" and "commodity," both of which are clearly defined in Samuel Johnson's *Dictionary* (1755). "TRAFFICK": "1. Commerce; merchandising; large trade; exchange of commodities. 2. Commodities; subject of traffick." "COMMODITY": "1. Interest; advantage; profit 3. Wares; merchandise; goods for traffick." Quoting first Locke and then Arbuthnot, Johnson's gloss on "commodity" is especially relevant to this chapter: "*Commodities* are moveables, valuable by money, the common measure. *Locke*. Of money in the commerce and traffick of mankind, the principal use is that of saving the commutation of more bulky commodities. *Arbuthnot on Coins*." The key ideas defining a traffic in commodities are symbolic value (as in coins or paper credit), ease of exchange, and the common measure by which value- and exchange-protocols are assigned. By "traffic in male creativity" I will mean these Johnsonian senses, the buying and selling a thing—whether literal or symbolic—of market value. But I want to go beyond currently accepted notions that the new eighteenth-century commercialism created an economic traffic in books and authors; I am suggesting that there also emerged a traffic in the new rhetoric of masculinity/creativity-as-male-embodiment. That is, the literal and figurative connections of heads and groins became marketable tropes, rhetorical commodities whose sexual redefinitions of male authorship also helped to sell books in a capitalist print-culture. Johnson could not have predicted that toward the end of the eighteenth century his very name, "Doctor Johnson," would become slang for the male organ itself.[1] In this remarkable rhetorical conflation of famous male author with yard we are seeing a deeper cultural traffic: the ways a sexualized male creativity had been put into circulation with a commodity value in the new marketplace of letters.

The male body was used literally and figuratively to identify three aspects of a man's literary labor: the inner site of creativity; the process of writing and generating the text; the public entry of author and his works into a world of homosocial and economic status. Each aspect was informed by some version of the head-groin connection, either a literal transaction between male mind and male genitalia or a figurative condition linking male brain to an eroticized female reproductivity. The first of these—the interior site of writerly inspiration—was variously associated with the copulatory pleasure and power of the erection or with some enigmatic conception and embryonic formation. This symbolic inner scene might be about the chaste or erotic relationship with one's female Muse, or about a priapic and masturbatory state; it could also be the place where male author was impregnated by another male. The second context—writing and the production of the text itself—might be represented as birthing the fully-formed Athena, the prolonged gestation and labor pains of book-child, abortions and monstrous offspring, or an anal birthing of book-turd; writing and ink could be figured as the copulatory pen-as-penis, semen (or urine, venereal pus), or offensive testicles requiring castration. The entry of author into the literary marketplace was likewise subject to related tropes, from male writer as female virgin Muse who becomes a whore to other men, to writer as would-be fornicator either successful or impotent, to writer as the penis itself measured against competing male writers. These sexual constructions served as rhetorical signposts marking the position of male author and his perceived literary value somewhere in the marketplace of letters. From immaculate patriarchal begettings to anal births, from powerful Priapus to Pope's penis-for-sale in graphic lampoons, these various formations reflect the history of how authors and their works entered the world of other commodities.

By far the most vexed relationship was between the interior origins of creative energies and the public place of printers, booksellers, and readers. My last chapter tried to describe the gap that opened as individual males encountered the cultural commodification of their self-hood as sexualized parts; one result was that the yard was paradoxically about power and loss, with individual men-with-penises sometimes removed from the site of defining power. A similar gap is reflected in the literary realm, where the traffic in male creativity caused a disjunction between concepts of the inner site and public status of creativity. Most typically, the private energies of inspiration were characterized as an interior creative power linked somehow to a sexual condition; but the public circulation of the literary—whether published work or author himself—functioned as a sexualized commodity in a marketplace. The result was a complex representation of male creativity as simultaneously about sexual power *and* loss. The transgendered versions of this ambiguity are evident in Swift's quip that "A Copy of Verses kept in the Cabinet, and only shewn to a few Friends, is like a Virgin, much sought after and admired; but when printed and published, is like a common Whore, whom any body may purchase for Half a Crown."[2] The contradictory senses of erotic power and depletion are present, too, in yard-wit tropes, where a man's creative interiority could be imaged as potent priapic creator or prodigious fornicator, and where the public status of an author and his works could be presented as a pathetic masturbation, laughable impotence, or as a yard to be owned and sold by others. Male writers were particularly conscious that there was a "cost" to their sexualized wit, first in the obvious sense that one's creative power was lost as soon as it entered the public domain, as in Pope's compact rendition in *An Essay on Criticism* where the power of a sexualized creative ownership slips out of one's hands to become a public erotic commodity: "What is this *Wit* which must our Cares employ? / The *Owner's Wife*, that *other Men* enjoy" (*TE* 1: 294, ll. 500–1). But there was a deeper psychological concern, too, that a man's wit might be inversely related to his erotic capacities, that there might be a literal head-groin exchange in which one's creativity came with a sexual "cost." The erotic power of male wit—impregnating brain-wombs, spilling inspired ink-semen—was sometimes figured also as a sexual loss or phallic removal.

Male writers also tried to attenuate the disjunction between representations of the interior site of male creativity and its public status, and the historical record suggests that they modified the collective vocabulary so as to maintain an imagery of the power of their creativity while at the same time improving and dignifying representations of their position within a tawdry commercialism. At stake was the changing value of literary "labor," and writers of Pope's generation and the new one that followed were eager to influence public views of their own professionalization, or at least, according to J. S. Peters, "to uphold the dignity of letters" and authorship at a time when both had come to be seen increasingly as property to be owned.[3] Aspects of the history of notions of literary labor and its relationship to profit have already been sketched by scholars, most notably by Linda Zionkowski, who has convincingly demonstrated that the century-long shift (beginning in the late seventeenth century) from the model of author as gentleman amateur to the figure of the professional writer (like Pope) whose commercial success was associated with the author's masculinity and cultural power, also entailed a new conceptualization of creative labor. By the time we get to Samuel Johnson, she argues, the "*Lives* proposes labor as a defining characteristic of a poet's career. . . . [A]ristocrats whose writing, according to Johnson, takes the form of self-indulgent play, are subordinated to poets by profession, whose writing represents the prolonged labor of genius that is tested and confirmed in a competitive marketplace."[4] Relevant to this chapter is that a part of these developments included a changing set of metaphors about male physicality and work. That history, briefly, is as follows. Earlier in the period, privileged gentlemanly or aristocratic authorial ease was seen to depend on mental inspiration derived from the judgment/invention model of classical systems, the kind of invisible "labor" that required genius and whose execution was seemingly without effort.[5] Hacks and writers unrelated to court influence were often dubbed mere "mechanicks," akin to common laborers who used their hands. As the professional writer emerged in greater numbers in the first third of the eighteenth century, one's literary labor was sometimes idealized within a hierarchy of labor, hands, and brains which presented the poet's work as sacred, morally committed, and vigilantly aloof from common domains of sweat and money, even though matters had already changed by this time, and literary labor was variously assigned a commercial value along with other commodities. With Edward Young and Samuel Johnson came a new kind of embodiment with literary labor now associated with an enigmatic, hands-on organic formation or growth set against notions of a debased mechanical or manual replication. I introduce this strand of historical investigation here because what these various accounts of literary labor have not recognized is that *reproductive* labor as a trope for male writing is also an important feature of the professionalization of the male author.

In the newer capitalist milieu where the status of literary labor was in transition, and where authors quite self-consciously tried to define their own worth when questions of value were no longer straightforward issues of aesthetics, male creativity as reproductive brain-womb also helped to salvage the dignity of authorship and literary commodities. As we will see below, the shift in embryological theory from preformationist to epigenetic models was absorbed into the vocabulary of male creativity, where it was perfectly suited to the new cult of original genius and the related fashion for literary labor as an enigmatic organic process. Tropes of lengthy gestation and mysterious embryological development thus claimed a heightened value for certain kinds of male creativity in the marketplace. The discourse of reproductive labor, that is, could in some ways serve to redeem authorship from the lower-order materiality of money, objects, and traffic. Writers transformed their figurative status as sexual commodities in other ways as well, as for instance in ideas of male creativity as an eroticized female Muse. Tropes of this order were certainly used to capture the power-loss sense of the male writer's relationship to the literary market as a prostitution, but in other deployments the author as sexy Muse could dramatize his positive relationship to other men within homosocial contexts of patrons, male friends, and the male publishing industry. Throughout this chapter, then, I will also be tracking the various ways in which male writers themselves actively negotiated a sense of their professional self-identification which influenced how the cultural imaginary would come at questions of literary value. The first two sections explore these possibilities in uses of brain-womb and female Muse tropes.

Not surprisingly, the creative mind-yard discourses contained the most provocative forms of ambiguity and instability. So often representing the desire for independence from a material realm of market values, the yard of wit entered the world of commodities and economic arrangements sometimes threatening a dangerous excess of the male body. Linked to impolite and powerful energies of the libido and brute physiology, male imagination and yard were also harbingers of a lawless and unruly manifestation not always subject to the will, and as such represented a potentially disruptive energy whose dangerous play and mysterious condition threatened to escape polite confinement. The historical reasons for this collective anxiety are difficult to come at, but appear to be a product of the uneasy intersection of the "literary" and the "manly" as both came to be commodified as aspects of male sexuality. Sections three through five consider the ways that the genital essence and origins of male creativity were part of the new economic order, items and images of traffic that came with a "cost"; but in some cases they could also be dangerous commodities.

Brain-Wombs and Birthing Hierarchies

How would traditional procreativity/creativity tropes be refitted for the new economy? The origins of the Enlightenment male brain-womb can be traced to a conjunction of classical mythology and new embryological models used to create a value-laden hierarchy of *kinds* of poetic birthing. Images of reproductive labor reflected something about literary labor, either the male writer's relationship to his own creative process or the status of his work in the public realm. Situated somewhere on a spectrum between instantaneous birthing and anal-birth labors, the author's creativity was imaged as either independent of or mired in the material realities of print.

There were four analogies in this hierarchy. In the position of first importance was an immaculate patriarchal birth whose motherless, bodiless head-birthing was the supreme act of male genius: instantaneous, already completely formed, springing into life out of the sheer creative will of the male mind. This model highlighted the dramatic sense of enigmatic conception and wondrous birth as male prerogatives which transcended (or simply ignored) the material demands of the market. Not quite as good as these acts of creation were the laborious body-births which gave the male poet all the physical accoutrements of gestation, maternal confinement, care, and pain, thus emphasizing the rigorous temporal dimension of creative process, aesthetic growth, and finally entry and status within a literary public. These metaphors accompanied the professionalization of the eighteenth-century author in the new print economy, and they served to sustain or even heighten the value of the author's literary commodity. If head-births represented a superior figurative begetting and birthing to the prolonged body-births of male poets, both of these structures were better than any involvement of a *female* mother. Female-mothered birth from an ordinary heterosexual begetting was always close to the bottom of the hierarchy because, as a metaphor, it could be associated with a female realm of fleshy matter and laboring animal processes unredeemed by any mental creativity. At the very bottom was male creativity as an anal birth, the most debased version of both the inner site and public status of an author's literary labor. Lending themselves to genuine defenses of men and their quills, and to sometimes vicious satirical assaults on literary enemies, these metaphors reveal a great deal about male authors' responses to their own professionalization.

Let me briefly establish the context of typical use and then take up the matter of classical myth and modern embryology. The idea of pregnant male brain-wombs does not need a cumbersome inventory.[6] When Daniel Defoe remarks that "A Book is . . . the Child of his Inventions, the Brat of his Brain" (*Review . . .* , 2 February 1710), or, when Fielding's narrator comments in *Tom Jones* that the reader should "consider a Book as the Author's Offspring, and indeed as the Child of his Brain,"[7] or, when old Wycherley writes that "ill Authors, like indulgent Parents, are most fond of their weakest Offsprings; and therefore all are fondest of those begotten in their Age"[8]—we can quickly acknowledge a shared set of metaphorical assumptions. Features of the analogy are readily available in the literary record of the period, as for instance in Smollett's *The Adventures of Peregrine Pickle*, in which the colorful Pallet angrily defends his works as "the children of my fancy, conceived by the glowing imagination, and formed by the art of my own hands."[9] Not surprisingly, the idea of the pregnant male mind yields a host of related metaphors which constitute a widespread currency of phrases such as "The genuine Issue of the Poet's Brain,"[10] or "Your *Fancy's Offspring.* . . . [and] *Embryo Thoughts.*"[11] And, if male writers and artists could conceive and be big with embryo, then ultimately they had books or children/offspring to contend with, as Colley Cibber would make shamelessly clear in the Dedication of his *An Apology for the Life of Colley Cibber* (1740): "the brat is now born, and rather than see it starve upon the bare parish provision, I chuse thus clandestinely to drop it at your door, that it may exercise one of your many virtues, your charity, in supporting it."[12] Books were often imaged as the children of poet-parents, and the implications of the analogy were frequently extended to include several aspects of the book trade, literary reputation, or the difficult-to-please taste of readers. In this metaphorical world of creative endeavor, the male poet was a father to his literary child; but sometimes he was the pregnant female who had been impregnated by his female Muse or by some male principle (Apollo, for example, or the inspiration of other men); at other times he was the female Muse himself, about to give birth. These analogies are abundant in the literary and critical record of Pope's world, and will be familiar to experienced readers of the period.

More important are backgrounds. In Pope's day, the two discourses which had given rise to and then reinforced ideas of male creative pregnancy and birth were classical mythology, particularly the tradition of the female Muse(s), and early modern physiology, particularly embryological commentary. (The male Christian God, whose word creates life in the Old Testament, is a related version of the idea of male creativity, but seems not to have had the same impact on this figurative lexicon.) Allegories and myths of origin appear to have been present in the earliest Greek representations of creative inspiration, the three most common being the birth of Athena (later Minerva), the birth of the nine Muses, and a sexual relationship (varying in its specific details) between male poet and female Muse. To recapitulate these three structures briefly: the most widely known account of Athena's birth is that she springs forth fully formed out of Zeus's (later Jupiter's) head, and this motherless birthing becomes a common feature in Enlightenment allegorizations of the creative act and the products of the male poet's brain. As for the birth of the Muses, Hesiod's rendition (*Theogony*, 1–104) was perhaps the most influential source, and the story is well known: Zeus and Mnemosyne copulate for nine successive nights, giving rise to the nine female Muses who in turn, through a quasi-sexual conjunction with Apollo, create or bring into being the figure of the male poet who is himself (in subsequent versions of the poet/Muse relationship) frequently subject to quasi-sexual impregnation by either of his parents in order that he might give birth to poetic utterance. Some sense of the transmission of these structures into the Enlightenment is suggested by the obvious connections between George Sandys's account of the genealogy of the male poet in his influential *Ovid's Metamorphosis Englished, Mythologized, and Represented in Figures* (1621–26)—"*Jupiter* the divine mind inspires *Apollo*; *Apollo* the Muses; and they their legitimate issue"[13]—and Pope's use of the same mythology a century later in the illustrated headpiece to the Preface of his 1717 *Works*, in which Apollo, sun-god and god of poetry, sits in glory with his heavenly lyre among the adoring nine Muses who assist in their own specialized ways (Figure 5). It is under the auspices of this conjunction of Apollo and the Muses—who together give birth to poetry and to male poets—that the twenty-nine-year-old Pope would offer his first collection of poetry to the republic of letters.[14]

Out of these three often interrelated stories about origins and birth emerged a variety of analogies for male creativity, the most striking of which was the pregnant male whose begetting and birthing of poetry mimic female reproduction while remaining essentially motherless. Although different sexual features such as copulation, impregnation, birthing, or parenthood might be singled out for emphasis in any version of these stories, in each case the male brain was imagined as the sexually receptive and fertile womb, and the poet as a parent, child, or lover (either active or passive, male or female) within an eroticized reproductive narrative.

These classical analogues of motherless birthing, Apollo and the Muses, and pregnant male poets continued to be used long after any literal belief in them, becoming mere clichés for many writers at this time. However, some of the most typical literary-critical and forward-looking anthropological treatises of the period continued to recognize the heuristic value of these myths even as they distanced their own modern culture from the primitive and superstitious practices of Greek and Roman records. By the late seventeenth century the elaborately allegorized religious, political, moral, and philosophical interpretations of earlier mythographers had been replaced largely by increasingly psychological readings,[15] reflecting the new attention to the brain and its hidden creative processes as the loci for accounts of the poetical character.[16] At the middle of the eighteenth century John Ogilvie's psycho-anthropological analysis of myth, "An Essay on the Lyric Poetry of the Ancients" (1762), would reject the vulgar primitivism of the past while retaining its metaphors: "Hesiod introduces his work with recounting the genealogy of the Muses. . . . Some tale of

S. Gribelin in:et:fcu

Figure 5. Headpiece to the Preface of Alexander Pope's 1717 *Works*, representing Apollo and the nine Muses. Courtesy of the William Ready Division of Archives and Research Collections, McMaster University Library, Hamilton, Canada.

this kind it was usual with the Poets to invent, that the vulgar in those ages of fiction and ignorance might consider their persons as sacred, and that the *offspring of their imaginations* might be regarded as *the children of Truth*."[17] Given the perennial difficulties of describing the creative process, it is not surprising that these psychological approaches to classical accounts of poetic births and origins proved popular, thus maintaining the narrative utility of the myths themselves despite the overall waning of classical authority. Moreover, these classical stories about origins embodied convenient narratives for two aspects of how the creative process was experienced: as an enigmatic act in the male brain which seemed like a visitation of something Other from outside himself; and as a knowable, intentional act of the creative will which confirmed his mental prowess and the power of his own creativity. One or the other side of this complex experience tended to be emphasized, depending on which version of which classical stories a male writer used, and often the two ideas appeared together.

A second feature of a history of pregnant male poets and their female Muses is the embryological tradition which viewed the brain and uterus as similar in form and function. The most spectacular of these mind/womb connections was to appear in William Harvey's *De Generatione Animalium* (1651), whose final chapter, "Of Conception," would propose that "the conception, therefore of the egg or of the uterus will be, at least in some manner, similar to the conception of the brain"[18]:

First the uterus appears thicker and more fleshy, and then, in so far as the inner surface is concerned, that is, the place of the future conception, it becomes more tender and corresponds in smoothness to the inner parts of the ventricles of the brain. . . . [S]eeing that the substance of the uterus that has been made ready for conception is so very like the constitution of the brain, why may we not justly surmise that the function of each of them is also alike, and that what imagination and appetite are to the brain, that same thing, or at least something analogous to it, is awakened in the uterus by coitus and from this proceeds the generation or procreation of the egg? . . . And just as appetite or desire springs from the conception of the brain . . . , so also from the male as being the more perfect animal . . . the natural conception arises in the uterus of a woman, even as the animal conception is made in the brain. . . . Thus the painter expresses a likeness through the intermediary of the conception and gives it actuality by imitating the conception that is internal to the brain. . . . So that what instruction effects in the brain, namely Art, its analogue is bestowed on the uterus by coitus with the male.[19]

Indeed, as Elizabeth Sacks has pointed out in her study of Shakespeare, the very language of neurophysiological terminology had for a long time blended the brain and uterus as visually or functionally similar: "Mediaeval physicians had followed classical Arabic writers in generally calling the cavities of the brain 'ventricles,' a diminutive term which could mean either 'little belly' or 'little womb.' . . . The two protective membranes sheltering the brain from the cranium were called *pia mater* and *dura mater* ('tender mother' and 'hard mother')."[20] The metaphorical interchangeability of the two physiologies is carried over into eighteenth-century scientific writing, as is evident in La Mettrie's materialist *L'Homme machine* (1748): "Without learning, the best constructed brain would be at a complete loss. . . . For what fruit could the most excellent school produce without a womb wide open to the entry and conception of ideas?"[21] By the time of Samuel Johnson's monumental *A Dictionary of the English Language* (1755) the conjunction of mental and procreative processes is embedded in the very language of conception itself: "To CONCEIVE: 1. To admit into the womb. 2. To form in the mind; to imagine." "WOMB: 1. The place of the faetus in the mother. 2. The place whence any thing is produced." Of course, neither Johnson nor Enlightenment science actually believed that the brain *was* the uterus, or that their respective physiological functions were identical, but the medical analogy situated the mysteries of male creativity within a gendered body where the poet's brain became the mysterious female Other—specifically, a female reduced to her body and reproductive organs—upon which the male principle (sperm, authorial fiat)—purposeful, inspiring, generative— could prod and push the conception into life.

Together, the classical and medical conceptualizations provided a metapoetic language about male creativity in literary and non-literary writing. An example of the conflation of these two backgrounds is evident in the frontispiece to Harvey's *De Generatione Animalium* (Figure 6), in which Zeus is portrayed liberating living beings from an egg. In this instance, the female egg awaits the powerful male god whose creative will gives instant birth to all life-forms. The words written on the egg— "*Ex ovo omnia*"—certainly reflect the central insight of Harvey's embryological system, but what is most telling is that conception and procreation—both physiological and mental—are presided over by an act of male creativity which transforms the female principle into art, organized being, life-form itself. What happens to the egg in Zeus's hands is a lower-order example of Athena springing forth fully-armed from the head of Zeus. There is clearly an element of misogyny and patriarchal gesturing in the brain/uterus analogy and in the classical stories,[22] but I would like to examine more carefully the *kinds* of pregnant male brains which created a hierarchy in this symbolic landscape.

The most significant historical shift is that Zeus-Athena (Jupiter-Minerva) models of motherless and bodiless delivery appear to decrease as the period wears on, and writers rely more frequently on metaphors of the difficult and prolonged process of embryogenetic formation, gestation, labor pains, and birth travail. The reasons for this are clear: while the former encouraged fictions of authorial power,

Figure 6. Frontispiece to William Harvey's *Exercitationes De Generatione Animalium* (1651), in which Zeus is portrayed liberating living beings from an egg. Courtesy of History and Special Collections Division, Louise M. Darling Biomedical Library, University of California, Los Angeles.

autonomy, or removal from material contingencies, they were unsuited as metaphors describing the sometimes difficult entry of author and his book-child into the public scrutiny of readers and critics. The latter tropes not only better captured this transition from interior site to public status, but also advertized a new kind of value for the "literary" in the marketplace.

A few examples of both types will provide a sense of typical usage. In a flattering dedication "To the Earl of Roscommon, on his Excellent Essay on Translated Verse," one J. Amherst relies on the former scenario for his compliment: "The Dear *Minerva*'s form'd without the Pain, / And nothing less, could spring from such a Brain."[23] If brilliance could be imagined as a birth without pain, it was also presented as an offspring completely formed, as it is in John Hippisley's *An Essay On Wit* (1748): "When one is thoroughly struck with an Idea, when a Man of Sense, fill'd with Warmth, is in full Possession of his Thought, it comes from him all ornamented with suitable Expressions, as *Minerva* sprang out, compleatly arm'd, from the Head of *Jupiter*."[24] In a variation of this idea, William Congreve's Preface to his novel, *Incognita . . .* (1692), would distinguish drama over other genres as a more vital form of wit on the grounds that "*Drama . . .* 'tis the Midwife to Industry, and brings forth alive the Conceptions of the Brain. Minerva walks upon the Stage before us, and we are more assured of the real presence of Wit when it is delivered *viva voce*."[25] Edward Young's distinction between types of genius in *Conjectures on Original Composition . . .* (1759) is almost a carbon-copy: "An Adult Genius comes out of Nature's hand, as *Pallas* out of *Jove*'s head, at full growth, and mature."[26] The Zeus-Athena (Jupiter-Minerva) model avoided the notion of an embryo laboriously developing toward form and completion, and instead dramatized successful creativity as procreation and birth by quasi-divine authorial fiat. The metaphorical structure here is largely autogenetic, a self-contained act within the male brain-womb in which femaleness exists only as a by-product, as feminized literary object. Motherless, bodiless brain-births dramatized the power and self-sufficiency of the creative male mind.

This model extended beyond the literary domain, and was not always attended by Zeus-Athena allusions. For example, the 1653 English translation of *De Generatione* included a dedicatory poem by Martin Llewellyn which used the same metaphorical logic to celebrate Harvey's scientific creativity:

> Live *Modern Wonder*, and be read alone,
> Thy *Brain* hath *Issue*, though thy *Loins* have none.
> Let fraile *Succession* be the Vulgar care;
> Great *Generation's* selfe is now *thy Heire*.[27]

According to the poet, what distinguishes Harvey's accomplishment as the acme of male brain-birthing is that his "Issue" avoids the "Vulgar" realm of female bodies concerned with "fraile Succession," and gives birth to Reproduction itself, a conceptual birthing which at once explains the inner structure of the body's fleshy processes in generation and yet transcends those material, temporal realms of embodiment. Notwithstanding Harvey's epigenetic stance in embryological theory, both the frontispiece and the dedicatory poem of *De Generatione* are preformationist in their underlying construction of male creativity, depending on a symbolic structure frequently found in the literary sphere as well.[28] That is, models of motherless and bodiless creativity were represented as an enigmatic unfolding or instantaneous revealing of inherent form or preformed material rather than as the earthier, messier matters of reproductive labor and the slow process of pre-natal development: Zeus wills the opening of the egg, instantly generating all life-form; Harvey's brain gives birth to "Great *Generation's* selfe," by-passing a vulgar descent into matter.

These effortless head-births maximized male creative power and independence.[29] But the second kind of pregnant male birthing—lengthy gestation, lying-in, confinement, labor pain—became increasingly common, suggesting the extent to which male writers were just as likely to emphasize deliberate process and the ever-present frustrations of their craft over the fictions of transcendent acts of creation. These well-known analogies require no lengthy contextualization. Preparing to work on the second volume of the *Iliad*, Pope would say to his friend, Martha Blount: "Pitty me, Madam, who am to lye in of a Poetical Child for at least two Months. As Soon as I am up again I'll wait upon you" (*Corr.* 1: 293, 3 June 1715). Ideas of difficult conception, lengthy pre-natal care, and painstaking delivery allowed a writer to suggest something of the prolonged and difficult effort required in his art, a creative dynamic as much interested in the potentially disrupted organic process as in the finished product. Defending *Tom Jones* from the attacks of malicious critics who do not appreciate that a novel is "the Child of his Brain," Fielding employed a notion of male creativity as birth-travail:

The Reader who hath suffered his Muse to continue hitherto in a Virgin State, can have but a very inadequate Idea of this Kind of paternal Fondness. . . . But the Author whose Muse hath brought forth, will feel the pathetic Strain, perhaps will accompany me with Tears (especially if his Darling be already no more) while I mention the Uneasiness with which the big Muse bears about her Burden, the painful Labour with which she produces it, and lastly, the Care, the Fondness, with which the tender Father nourishes his Favourite, till it be brought to Maturity, and produced into the World. (Bk. 11, ch. 1, 568–69)

Writing to a friend about volumes nine and ten of *Tristram Shandy*, Sterne would likewise use this second type of pregnant male birthing to reflect on the sometimes difficult processes of male creativity: "I miscarried of my tenth volume by the violence of a fever, I have just got thro'—I have however gone on to my reckoning with the ninth, of which I am all this week in Labour pains; and if to Day's Advertiser is to be depended upon shall be safely deliver'd by tuesday."[30]

Dramatists also used the trope (although the usage is frequently comical), especially in dramatic prologues and epilogues where an apparent diffidence was used to gain laughs and to strut one's wit about theatrical marketplaces. John Vanbrugh's First Prologue to *The Relapse* (1696) is typical of such ironic play: "Ladies, this play in too much haste was writ, / To be o'ercharged with either plot or wit; / 'Twas got, conceived, and born in six weeks' space, / And wit, you know, 's as slow in growth as grace. / Sure it can ne'er be ripened to your taste; / I doubt 'twill prove, our author bred too fast: / For mark 'em well, who with the Muses marry, / They rarely do conceive, but they miscarry. / 'Tis the hard fate of those wh' are big with rhyme, / Still to be brought to bed before their time."[31] Nearly a century later, the Prologue to Richard Cumberland's *The Fashionable Lover* (1772) carries the conceit even further:

> If any author of prolific brains,
> In this good company, feels labour-pains;
> If any gentle-poet, big with rhime,
> Has run his reck'ning out and gone his time;
> . . . .
> Know such, that at our Hospital of Muses
> He may lye in, in private, if he chuses;
> We've single lodgings there for secret sinners,
> With good encouragement for young beginners.
> Here's one now that is free enough in reason;
> This bard breeds regularly once a season.[32]

A collective imagery of prolonged reproductive labor can be found throughout the period, in all genres, and I am arguing that these tropes became a more popular image for authors and their book-children when market pressures began to affect the literary scene in a large-scale manner, which happened earlier for the stage—note the date of the Vanbrugh example—than for poetry and fiction. This is not to say that one cannot find earlier instances of the laborious gestation and body-births of pregnant male authors, but rather to note that their frequency appears to be tied to an emergent literary capitalism and the professionalization of authors.

But I want to emphasize that the increased use of these analogies also constituted a type of rhetorical traffic which helped to shape the perceived value of books for sale *and* the men who wrote them. The tone of the examples I have used is light and comical, a reflection perhaps of the self-conscious sense authors must have had of their redefined position. Less often imaged as powerful birth-givers and Zeus-figures remote from mundane material concerns, male writers often reflected their compromised and contingent role in the marketplace of letters as a comical gestation, subject to possible failure or miscarriage.[33] But there was another side to the traffic in male creativity as embodied birth-travail. I have already mentioned that recent histories of literary professionalization have excluded reproductive labor from their accounts of metaphors of manual labor. Indeed, both metaphorical economies were simultaneously present in the newer capitalist literary milieu, and writers adapted these labor tropes strategically for purposes of self-definition. Occasionally the two figurative systems would appear together, as they do in a very early letter from the eighteen year-old Pope to older friend Wycherley, whose poems the young man was editing:

for the great dealers in Wit [Wycherley himself], like those in Trade, take least Pains to set off their Goods; while the Haberdashers of small Wit, spare for no Decorations or Ornaments. You have commission'd me to paint your Shop, and I have done my best to brush you up like your Neighbours. But I can no more pretend to the Merit of the Production, than a Midwife to the Virtues and good Qualities of the Child she helps into the Light. (*Corr.* 1: 16, 10 April 1706)

Combining both ideas of market labor and reproductive labor, young Pope inadvertently pointed to the future of the professional author, whose *corpus*, that poetic body issuing from the figurative reproductive act, and whose *works*, the product of time and effort, would necessarily have to find a position in the marketplace of printers, readers, and book-sales. In 1706, Pope's language of trade, advertising, and economic traffic was still largely metaphorical for Restoration court wits such as Wycherley, and even for Pope himself, who was three years away from his first deal with Jacob Tonson, the publisher who had grown rich off the backs of Shakespeare, Milton, and Dryden, the copyrights to whose works he owned.[34] But a decade later, such language was very real indeed, especially for authors like Pope, who shrewdly fashioned an economic arrangement around his Homer translations which left him comparatively rich. The point is that writers became acutely conscious of the traffic in their wares and book-children, and they too had to play the market in which they were often items bought and owned by publishers and booksellers. Tough deal-makers like Pope gained considerable control of their own com-modification; many others remained wholly dependent on Grubstreet pay, writing "Hackney for Bread."[35] But part of this history also had to do with the language of public imaging and contests over who would shape the perceived value of men and their literary works.

As an uncoordinated but collective exercise in public relations, the very different kind of "labor" represented by the male poet's pregnant brain offered a positive construction of what authorship was about. Analogies of embryogenetic formation, prolonged gestation, lying-in, confinement, and labor pain proved ultimately to be a more empow-ering metaphor to characterize the creative activities of the profes-sional writer, because they accommodated, in ways the Zeus-Athena model and the metaphor of literary production as manual "work" did not, the material and temporal realms of creative (re)production and print culture without giving up the idea of an illustrious male birth-giver. The image of the pregnant male writer laboring to give birth to his book-child was a powerful public myth deployed to gain sanction for the modern writer at a time when, increasingly, the literary arts and the talented men who produced them had to negotiate their de-scent into the economic world of other items-for-sale. Henry Fielding reflected comically on this profound historical transition in *Tom Jones*, acknowledging in 1749 the necessity of presenting one's "work" to two different symbolic literary dames—the older Muse of classical mythol-ogy who inspired the generative male writer, and the newer, "much plumper Dame" of the marketplace, "the fat Ufrow Gelt." Wondering which one of "this ill-yoked Pair, this lean Shadow and this fat Sub-stance . . . shall I invoke to direct my Pen?" and wanting the benefits of both, Fielding's narrator hopes that "my Labours, may one Time be amply rewarded" (Bk. 13, ch. 1, 683–85). Fielding was well aware of the symbolic and material differences between classical Muses oversee-ing the inner moment of inspiration and the public price-tags which accompanied the new literary order, and like Pope, his writing occa-sionally ponders the complex merging of Ancients and Moderns in this way.

Certainly the tropes of lengthy reproductive labor emphasized the unreliable material and commercial realities of invention and produc-tion; at first glance they appear to fall far short of the impressive crea-tivity which inhered in the model of Zeus-Athena head-births. But metaphors of laborious gestation and body-births are also linked his-torically to the ideas of enigmatic growth and organic development which dominated aesthetic theory in the second half of the eighteenth century, as well as to the direction of embryological debate, with its re-newed interest in epigenetic views.[36] Just as preformationist theories gave way to more complex embryological views of fetal development and sequential growth from apparently unorganized material, tropes of the pregnant male brain turned increasingly to ideas of enigmatic but purposeful growth within the creative mind. I am suggesting that these two conceptual fields are historically related, not necessarily in a causal sense, but rather as part of the larger cultural revisions in the life sciences and aesthetics which combined a renewed interest in the mysteries of life-essences with more sophisticated techniques of measurement and description. Tropes of reproductive embodiment presented a creative male genius which acknowledged painstaking intentionality and craft—that is, the "labor" of literary invention—but now emphasized mysterious inner process and a privileged organicism as a kind of value-added rhetorical tax on the literary commodity.

The history of manual labor tropes reveals a similar attempt to transform lower-order material processes—mechanical labor—into a potentially heightened creative work now associated with the subtle mysteries of organic growth. Edward Young's mid-century *Conjectures on Original Composition* reflected this metaphorical shift in aesthetic debates by setting an inferior mechanical labor against an organic growth whose labor is unperceived. Metaphorizing primary genius (what he calls "original") and secondary genius (imitative) in precisely this way, Young's quite unoriginal essay reiterated what was already widely agreed by 1759: "An *Original* may be said to be of a *vegetable* nature; it rises spontaneously from the vital root of Genius; it *grows*, it is not *made*: *Imitations* are often a sort of *Manufacture* wrought up by those *Mechanics, Art,* and *Labour,* out of pre-existent materials not their own."[37] The temporal efforts of genius are acknowledged by Young, but the work of male creativity—its "labor"—is registered as enigmatic growth, something beyond vulgar application or mechanical mimicry. A similar conceptualization of the creative male brain can be found in Samuel Johnson's life of Pope, where a differentiation of kinds of labor would distinguish ineffective creative toil from the mysterious process of successful genius:

for it will not always happen that the success of a poet is proportionate to his labour. The same observation may be extended to all works of imagination, which are often influenced by causes wholly out of the performer's power, by hints of which he perceives not the origin, by sudden elevations of mind which he cannot produce in himself, and which sometimes rise when he expects them least.[38]

Young's and Johnson's positive model of literary labor as organic growth and enigmatic inspiration is part of the same cultural milieu in which pregnant male brains were linked to epigenetic models of embryological formation.

The use of these two labor tropes runs a parallel course through the second half of the eighteenth century, occasionally merging, and extending well beyond Young and Johnson into the nineteenth century, where they show up together in Shelley's "Defence of Poetry" (1821): "A great statue or picture grows under the power of the artist as a child in the mother's womb; and the very mind which directs the hands in formation is incapable of accounting to itself for the origin, the gradations, or the media of the process."[39] By linking the authorial process to the slower rhythms and mysterious developmental sequences of gestation and childbirth, eighteenth-century writers laid claim to the importance of their creative output, using the apparently lower order of material labor and reproductive embodiment to reflect the contingent world of literary markets while still preserving the idea of enigmatic male creativity. Shelley's "mind which directs the hands in formation" is a paradigmatic fusion of these two eighteenth-century tropes, including ideas of manual labor and work as well as the mysterious but still purposeful creative power of the pregnant male mind. The male poet as birth-giver was an ancient idea, but for Pope's generation and the one to follow, the conjunction of "labor" and inspired conceptualization served in part to acknowledge but also protest the potential devaluation of book-commodities which the new literary commercialism represented. The tropes also constituted an amelioration of the difficult transition from the inner site of creativity to its public status, and thus played a positive role in the reorganization of the perceived value of the literary commodity and of male authorship.

A very different sort of sexual traffic attended the two analogies at the bottom of the reproductive hierarchy—female-mothered birth, anal birth—and these two can be dealt with briefly since they had a straightforward satirical purpose. Geared to literary assault upon one's enemy, these lower-order misbegettings were obviously a strategy of devaluation, reducing the man and his writing to an inherently defective female procreativity or male defecation. The first of these relied on two misogynistic assumptions about female mental capacity which were then applied to male creativity. One was the notion that female brain labor itself was already a lesser order mental operation than its male counterpart. Part of a larger cultural perception of the more limited intellectual abilities of women, this idea needs little proof. As early as 1701, Mary, Lady Chudleigh's *The Ladies Defence: Or, a Dialogue Between Sir John Bute, Sir William Loveall, Melissa, and a Parson* would give to the Parson the prevailing view about women who might want to be creative writers: "Your shallow Minds can nothing else contain [i.e., than "the little Arts to please"], / You were not made for Labours of the Brain; / Those are the Manly Toils which we sustain."[40] Despite the many Enlightenment women like Chudleigh whose accomplishments we now study, brain labor was for men, it seemed, and reproductive labor for women. And yet, perversely paradoxical as it may seem to us now, for the literary culture of this period male creativity was seen to be more suited to procreative metaphors than female creativity, whose lesser mental capacity was so often associated with a lower-order physicality. Thus, the application of an inferior female (pro)creativity—physical and mental—to the male brain-womb was exclusively reserved for satire, where notions of male creativity would be converted downward into a base female embodiment. The most startling extension of this analogy can be found in John Oldham's "Upon the Author of the Play call'd *Sodom*" (1677/78), a mock-libertine response to the Rochesterian pornographic drama:

> Thy Muse has got the Flowers [menses], and they ascend
> As in some greensick Girl, at upper End.
> Sure Nature made, or meant at least 't have don't,
> Thy Tongue a Clitoris, thy Mouth a Cunt.
> How well a Dildoe would that place become,
> To gag it up, and make 't for ever dumb![41]

The initial image of Rochester's mouth as the menstruating, obscenely speaking vagina of the sexually-starved girl is meant to be an unflattering version of male creativity as female sexuality, certainly, but by associating the male writer's head and inner creativity with the outer sexual parts of female reproductivity rather than the hidden female womb, Oldham also drags Rochester's poetry down into the physical domain of a potentially threatening female sexuality or disgusting menses, equations reserved for satirical treatment and, in this case, phallic reprisal. The metaphor of male brain-womb became a contaminated image as soon as it was linked directly to female creativity, an actual mothered birth, or female genitalia—each presented as a debased form of male creativity and figurative birth-giving.

There was a second reason why male creativity imaged as female-mothered birth was low on the hierarchy of metaphors, and this too had to do with the female brain—this time of the pregnant woman—which was seen as capable of transferring traumatic experience or obsessional longing to the fetus through the mother's imagination, leaving either an unsightly birthmark or a cluster of harmful psychological tendencies in the child.[42] Together, these two aspects of female brain labors represented a stark contrast to the pregnant male brain at its autogenetic best. As opposed to the male writer as Zeus, head-birthing Athena in an instant creation which required no mother at all, male creativity as (pro)creative female brain was satirically located in the lower realm of laboring matter and flesh, a feminine gut giving birth to some monstrous deformation. As I will suggest in chapter four, Pope's put-down of his male literary enemies in *The Dunciad* would rely heavily on these forms of devaluation.

At the very bottom of the hierarchy was male creativity as an anal birth, the most satirically pungent inversion of high-order conceptions and creative execution. Psychoanalytical accounts of this idea, while insufficiently historicized to explain Enlightenment satirical usage, are still worth mentioning. Briefly, Freud proposed that children's

ignorance of the vagina also makes it possible for children to believe in the second of their sexual theories. If the baby grows in the mother's body and is then removed from it, this can only happen along the one possible pathway— the anal aperture. *The baby must be evacuated like a piece of excrement, like a stool....* If babies are born through the anus, then a man can give birth just as well as a woman. It is therefore possible for a boy to imagine that he, too, has children of his own, without there being any need to accuse him on that account of having feminine inclinations. He is merely giving evidence in this of the anal erotism which is still alive in him.[43]

But as Carolyn Williams has suggested, we must remember that, unlike Freud's naive children, Pope and his contemporaries used anal materials self-consciously, and "understood the impulses behind their own behaviour far more clearly than later generations of psychoanalysts would have us believe."[44] Every student of the period will recall Dryden's scatalogical jibe at Shadwell in *MacFlecknoe*—"But loads of *Sh*— almost choakt the way" (l. 103)—or Pope's shot at Ambrose Philips in *An Epistle to Dr. Arbuthnot*—"Just writes to make his barrenness appear, / And strains from hard-bound brains eight lines a-year" (*TE* 4: 109, ll. 181–2)—and readers may well be familiar with common satirical constructions such as "excrements of wit."[45] Within the collective imagination of late seventeenth- and eighteenth-century writers and readers, male brains could be made analogous to the body's nether regions in various fashion: as wombs issuing book-children (or deformed offspring), as male genitalia, and as arseholes shitting words and paper. But in relocating the internal site of male creativity from the brain to the abdomen, an interesting association was also put into play, not only the creative brain as anus—with poetry as shit and books as toilet paper or "Bum-Fodder"[46]—but also, by a simple extension, the brain-anus as a type of brain-womb engaged in acts of excremental birthing. The most debased form of the reproductive male body, anal births were a disgustingly complete antithesis to immaculate head-births of the Zeus-Athena order. Here, creative male oracle was turned into impolite orifice—an anal womb—with powerful inner place of creative energy transformed into a surrealistic abdominal realm squeezing forth book-turds.

In *The Secret History of Clubs* (1709), Edward Ward combined the anal-birth motif with ideas of birth deformity in his satirical portrayal, "Of the Scatter-Wit Club":

A few years since a parcel of young Gentlemen, who were pretenders to Wit, and great adorers of the Muses, form'd themselves into a Society. . . . When such a merry Piece of Drollery, as the foregoing Whim, had been lug'd out and Read to the satisfaction of the Company, it commonly put the rest upon producing some Deform'd Off-spring or other, lest one above the rest, should plead a Title to the Bays, which they had the Equity to think ought not to be ingros'd, but shared among the Society: So that no sooner had the former been Conn'd over with applause; but it was seconded by the following Rapture, which was Compos'd by one of the Members, as he was colling his In-trails upon a Close-Stool, after he had taken Physick, *viz.* . . . .

> II.
> *Some Night-man's Doxy would I dub my Muse,*
> *She should my Guts, instead of Brains, inspire.*
> *A Painter's Pencil for a Pen I'd chuse,*
> *And dawb whole Fools-Cap Reams with T—d and Mire.*
> III.
> *My Tail Prophetick Poems should excrete;*
> *I'd Rise Arse upwards e'ery Day by-times;*
> *On Boghouse Walls I'd digitize my Wit,*
> *And shitten luck should wait upon my Rhimes.*[47]

Moving from narratives of the classical female Muse to cloacal allegory, Ward's scatter-wit poet exchanges the possibility of inspired impregnation and brain-birthing for inspired guts which will issue poetry-as-excrement and ink-as-turd. No Muse oversees the conception of male brain-womb in this surrealistic scenario; rather, brain-womb becomes brain-arse on the close-stool, and creative offspring becomes uncreative ordure. The male writer can here digitize his wit as a completely self-contained, self-absorbed defecatory act whose embodiment mimics a birthing while remaining utterly unredeemable.[48] Ward's birthing scene carried the head-groin connection to its lowest and most unsavory depths, reducing creativity to a gastrointestinal event. The gross materiality of the literary commodity—valueless, offensive, without life—was offered up in anal birth imagery with a satirical vengeance.

These four tropes represented the spectrum of possibilities which informed the hierarchy of male creativity as figurative birth. From mental inspiration and figurative begetting to the gross matter of defecation; from brain to womb to anus; from idea to excrement; from effortless creative execution to abdominal grunts and groanings; from motherless and bodiless head-births to the lyings-in of male writers and the laboring bodies of women in the act of birth; from quill and ink to the smell of turd written with bare finger on boghouse wall—variations of these birthing ideas often attended representations of the author's cultural and economic positioning. Whether it was the moment of inspiration itself or the public terrain in which literary objects and labor were given value, the metaphors of brain-wombs were part of a larger traffic in revised ideas of male creativity which reflected the pressures of the new literary economy and functioned as a sometimes strategic public imaging by writers themselves who tried to preserve the dignity of authorship.

Virgins, Whores, and Other Commodities: Male Writer as Female Muse

There was another important narrative which sexualized the realities of male creativity in the literary marketplace, namely, an image of the young female Muse entering a male sexual economy. The use of the female Muse(s) as invocatory creative principle was a clichéd remnant from classical myth, but it was also perfectly suited to representing the vexed status of a man's creativity: some aspect of his inventive mind was imagined as female (i.e., as virgin, wife, mistress, or whore) and then, typically, projected as the Other with whom the author (or his usually male readers) had a relationship. The result was two common tropes: the inner site of his invention as the sometimes chaste or far more often eroticized female Muse, and his authorial status in a public print culture as a compromised female sexuality or prostitution. These images constituted a well-known traffic between friends and enemies, who used them either to characterize the origins of male creativity or to foreground matters of homosocial connection or competition. As well, the two different kinds of Muses—one internal, the other public—together reflected some of the collective uneasiness about the connections between creative inspiration and public consumerism.[49]

The inspirational site within the writer's head was typically presented as an erotic one where successful creativity was imaged as passionate intimacy with one's Muse. There were some who saw it the other way—i.e., that there was an inverse relationship between sexuality and creativity, that mental ability depended on a literal chastity, that the Muse within ought to be figuratively chaste. But such views were minority ones.[50] Throughout the period, the impulses of creativity and sexuality were commonly viewed as interchangeable: if one was endowed with wit, one was also likely to have a powerful libido. In his "An Essay Upon Wit," Sir Richard Blackmore had warned that "The same swiftness of Thought, and sprightliness of Imagination, that qualifies them for ingenious Conversation, Sports of Fancy and Comick Writing, do likewise give them an exquisite Taste of sensual

Pleasures, and expose them to the prevailing Power of Tempting, to forbidden Enjoyments."[51] Joseph Warton later repeated this general perception that "If the imagination be lively, the passions will be strong. . . .
The same temperament, and the same sensibility that makes a poet or a
painter, will be apt to make a man a lover and a debauchee."[52] Not surprisingly, then, when it came to discourses about literary labor and the
female Muses the prevailing view likened the mental energies of literary invention to some copulatory act with one's Muse. Sometimes this
was represented as a heightened sexuality outside a quotidian world
of politics, money, and marriage, as in J. Amherst's "To the Earl of
Roscommon":

> Happy the Man, when no concern is nigh,
> But Nature's wanton, and his Blood runs high,
> Who free from Cares enjoys without controul
> His Muse, the darling Mistress of his Soul;
> No tedious Court his Appetite destroys,
> Nor thoughts of Gain pollute the rapturous Joys.[53]

Amherst's fantasy is of the creative spark as some prelapsarian erotic
joy with one's mistress—not a wife—before mundane relational arrangements arrived on the scene. Joseph Trapp, too, would reiterate the
eighteenth-century cliché of the poet-Muse relationship as an exclusive sexual encounter, but in this case one in which the female carefully selects her writers only if they are worthy lovers: "it [Poetry] is a
Mistress, to whom all [poets] by natural Impulse, as it were, pay their
Addresses, tho' there are so few, upon whom she bestows her Favours."[54]
In these deployments, the analogy emphasizes a pleasing erotic removal from the world, focusing on the inner delights of a sexualized
creativity.

Sometimes the less savory temporal aspects of private literary labor
became a disappointing transformation of Muse from mistress to wife.
Writing to Martha Blount while hard at work on volume two of his *Iliad* translation, Pope would present himself as the husbandly drudge
in the dull round of conjugal duty: "I am to be entertain'd only with
that Jade whom every body thinks I love, as a Mistress, but whom in
reality I hate as a Wife, my Muse. Pitty me, Madam, who am to lye in
of a Poetical Child for at least two Months" (*Corr.* 1: 293, 3 June 1715).
In this figuration, Pope's labor is not about the Muse-mistress who
embraces the creative thrusts of her chosen lover-poet, but rather the
irritating marital routines and the pains of extended confinement that
may or may not produce the poetical brat.[55] My point here is that the
inner site of male wit was, in its preferred metaphorical mode, an
erotic one, a creativity which depended on rapturous lovemaking, on

ravishing or being ravished by one's Muse-mistress (even if the labors of writing sometimes threatened to devolve into marital drudgery).

However, a very different Muse-figure was used when the writer's creativity entered the public realm of commodities. Just as the entry of the vulnerable young woman into the "world" defined her erotic availability and thus meant a host of dangers, rituals, and temptations, so the entry of the male poet into the literary public was seen to entail a similar risk and instability in which one was valued only as a commodity to be used by others, or subjected to unfair treatment, undeserved abuse, or betrayal. Johnson's *Dictionary* had been too polite to mention that "commodity" was also slang for female genitalia, sign of a traffic in women whose pudenda represented their chief symbolic value within a male sexual economy. But most writers were familiar with this synecdoche, and many presented themselves as the young Muse-virgin to suggest a parallel between the commodification of female sexuality and the traffic in male creativity.

The best known trope for this precarious entry was the male writer as whore-Muse who had allowed herself to be compromised sexually or who had used her attractiveness for gain. The writer as female prostitute used to be considered a cultural rubber-stamping only of the female author, especially in the late seventeenth and early eighteenth centuries.[56] But recent scholarship makes clear that this trope was not exclusive to women writers who braved publication. As Linda Zionkowski has argued, "the image of the wanton muse" can be found "in descriptions of [male] writers' entry into print and called attention to their feminization through that process. . . . writers who lived upon the sale of their work faced the charge of debasing their talents, often being stigmatized as hacks or prostitutes who exchanged their abilities for maintenance by a patron, bookseller, political party, or combination of the three."[57] In fact, the male poet or his Muse as whore is a very common figure, and runs through the entire period I have been examining.

The metaphorical logic was straightforward. The young author's first publication was equivalent to the young virgin's entry into a world of male admirers or predators where sexual compromise of some sort was almost certain to happen. Like the vulnerable virgin, the poet's sexualized entry into print would depend on the character of the men who assisted that entry—men who might either serve as protector-patrons or as the metaphorically sly pimp with his eye on sex-trade lucre. William Congreve's elitist dedication to the Earl of Montague in *The Way of the World* (1700) is an example of the former: because the very name "poet" has been prostituted by a large, common, lower order of writers, "It is only by the countenance of your Lordship, and the *few* so qualified, that such who write with care and pains can hope to be distinguished; for the prostituted name of *poet* promiscuously levels all that bear it."[58] But homosocial protection had its other dimension in which friends or male publishers were bawds seeking a handsome fee for the first-time favors of this young virgin. In these analogies, the male writer entered the world of commodities where books and young female bodies were bought, sold, and appraised. In one of his prologues, Dryden used the trope in blunt and cynical fashion, suggesting that the eroticized female must simply make the best of her inevitable commodification by a demanding audience: "Gallants, a bashful young Poet bids me say / He's come to lose his Maidenhead to day."[59] In these sexualized allegories, the writer's public offering of his creativity put him in a vulnerable position. He might fare well with the right friends or booksellers behind him, but he also risked a loss of reputation, as in Robert Lloyd's "To George Colman, Esq." (1761): "Authors, like maids at fifteen years, / Are full of wishes, full of fears. / One night by pleasant thoughts be led, / To lose a trifling maiden-head; / But 'tis a terrible vexation / To give up with it reputation."[60] Attempting to please his readership, and hoping to do well by it both economically and in terms of fame, the male author brought the reproductive issue of his eroticized creativity to market, where he and his literary labor were re-metaphorized, re-sexualized, as the young female Muse whose hymen, modesty, reputation, and bargaining-power were dependent on being able to please a public reader, who was in turn represented as a male who might idolize her or protect her, but who would more likely pay for her beauties and then debauch, abuse, and abandon her.

Chronology is important here. Tropes of writer as whore can be found readily in Restoration court culture where the image could be understood as wanting to please one's patron, audience, or political master by writing the witty line, or it could be seen as a penchant for writing scandal, libel, or a racy dramatic content that would satisfy the prurient gossip but offend a Jeremy Collier. Rochester used a version of the image when constructions of the male writer had not yet become defined by the economic contexts of professional authorial labor: "And wit was his vain, frivolous pretense / Of pleasing others at his own expense. / For wits are treated just like common whores; / First they're enjoyed and then kicked out of doors."[61] Trading on the popularity of invective and personal satire was metaphorized as an unseemly prostitution, as was anything that pandered to the lowest common denominator of readerly interest:"Who *bundle* up the *Scandals* of the *Town*, / And in *lewd Couplets* make it all their *own*: / *Just Shame* be *theirs* who thus *debauch* a *Muse*, / To vile *Lampoons* a *noble Art* abuse."[62]

In the late seventeenth century when sophisticated authors were supposed to be gentlemen who disdained a crass materiality, those men who wrote only for money or who hired out their talents were seen as whores: "I pity, from my Soul, Unhappy Men, / Compell'd by *Want* to *prostitute* their *Pen.*"[63] But the Muse-whore as an economic and professional symbol—as opposed to court sycophant, political hireling—did not emerge until a bit later in the more ferociously capitalist climate of the early and mid eighteenth century. "Others there are," Edward Ward had written in 1729, "who prostitute their Brains."[64] This more modern version of the Grubstreet author/female Muse as whore was used not only to disparage a writer's false wit but to call attention to a whole system of literary economics which compromised authorial integrity and diluted aesthetic values.

What we are seeing here are two very different female Muses. One's inner Muse was ideally an erotic female Other, a mistress to be fucked, an encounter where one's powerful sexual energy would produce the brilliant book. But one's public Muse was the sweet young thing who nervously entered a world where she had everything to lose, where she already had a price-tag, and in which the traffic in her own commodified sexuality was encouraged. These versions of the eroticized male writer as female are in one sense easily decoded. Metaphorized as an erotic female energy or condition of some kind, the value of male creativity as a thing of potential pleasure or use by others—like potentially eroticized female bodies—was both a gift and a liability, both an internal erotic power and a public loss of control, both a mistress and a whore. The author as female Muse dramatized the traffic in male creativity as a sex trade, as cash for a woman's genitals.

But there was another sense to these metaphors: the sexual cross-dressing also had the effect of turning the male writer into an object of erotic attention to other men, not literally, but as a literary commodity whose value would be defined by a language of sexual purchase. Men-as-Muses were of course not really about women at all but about men—circles of friends and patrons, other writers, enemies, booksellers. The male author as female Muse called attention to the homosocial realities of the literary marketplace in striking fashion by metaphorizing him as an item of sexual traffic for a predominantly male readership. The circulation of a female principle between men has been examined by Eve Kosofsky Sedgwick, who helped to precipitate literary-critical studies of how male-male relationships foregrounded a "schism in women's status, between being ostensibly the objects of men's heterosexual desire and being more functionally the conduits of their homosocial desire toward other men." Relying on Gayle Rubin's influential argument "that patriarchal heterosexuality" is really about "the use of women as exchangeable, perhaps symbolic, property for the primary purpose of cementing the bonds of men with men," Sedgwick's specific interpretations are focused particularly on the "traffic in women"[65]; she is less interested than I am in how such exchange principles could also create a traffic in men. Male creativity in the late seventeenth and eighteenth centuries was men's business, depending on the social, commercial, and political relationships and arrangements among men. This, too, was replayed in the eroticized female Muse tropes, where a writer's exchange value in the public literary scene could be fashioned as a sexual traffic.

A related version of such realities was also present in images of the birthing of male creativity (or of the male writer himself) in which one male played man midwife to the figurative birth-process of another male author. The tradition goes back to Plato's *Theaetetus* (150c, 151a, c) and was a commonplace in the Enlightenment, where man midwife assisted male thinker or writer to a symbolic birthing of ideas.[66] The function of the metaphor is of course related in part to the increasing prominence of the male midwife, who was gaining ascendancy in the medical realm during the eighteenth century, and whose new obstetrical techniques were gradually eroding the ground traditionally held by midwives. As Roy Porter points out, "When, for example, Joseph Reed referred to David Garrick as 'the greatest theatrical Man midwife that ever assisted at the labours of the Stage,' the conceit was self-conscious, almost jokingly grotesque."[67] But the history of midwifery and its professional battles does not wholly account for the function of the man midwife figure in the literary scene, where he underlined the gendered power of an all-male publishing world as well as a male-male homoerotics as metaphor for the new commercialism. Moreover, the figure of the man midwife was one of brokerage, an analogy which—like male pimp or bawd to another man's creativity—captured a sense of traffic, in this case between inner site and public status.

Like literary man midwives, the male author as female Muse also suited gestures of homosocial hierarchy, friendship, competition, and obligation. Such usage often created triangular arrangements in which the Muse was sexually shared by the writer and his male friend. These figurative *ménages à trois* were less obviously about entering the literary marketplace as a commodity, but they did sexualize male creativity as a use-object with potential value, as well as providing eroticized tropes for affectionate expressions of one's appreciation of the friend's talents. In this sense, the sexual traffic in male creativity was likened to a threesome where the pleasure of reading was akin to a shared woman. Writing to Dryden, John Dennis employed an elaborate analogy in which the female Muses of less brilliant writers were seen as a lesser sexual satisfaction than what Dryden's Muse could offer:

Suckling, Cowley and Denham, who formerly Ravish'd me in ev'ry part of them, now appear tastless to me in most, and Waller himself with all his Gallantry, and all that Admirable Art of his turns, appears three quarters Prose to me. Thus 'tis plain that your Muse has done me an injury; but she has made me amends for it. For she is like those Extraordinary Women, who, besides the Regularity of their Charming Features, besides their engaging Wit, have Secret, Unaccountable, Enchanting Graces, which thô they have been long and often Enjoy'd, make them always new and always desirable.[68]

What distinguishes Dryden's Muse for the obsequious Dennis is that she can ravish the friend-reader without producing subsequent sexual *ennui*—the extraordinary female who continues to please without satiety, who can be enjoyed or owned by other male readers. Although the trope allowed a complex positioning of an eroticized element between men as one focus of their bond, the sexualized gesture here is not about same-sex genital desire, functioning rather as personal testimony to the perceived public status of the author as friend. But in these scenarios, the traffic in figurative women or exchange of female principles is also about the male author and his text as having a potential cultural capital as commodity, an object eliciting deference or condescension or appraisal in ways analogous to how female sexuality might be assessed as a male erotic pleasure. Man-as-Muse was something to be had, enjoyed, shared, or owned.

Sometimes the sexual triangulation was put more directly. In a flattering letter to Wycherley, Dennis again used the trope of the male author-friend whose pleasing female Muse can be the object of both men's sexual attention—a shared mistress:

Immortal Company still attends you, and the Virtues, the Graces, and the Charming Nine who love the Groves, and are fond of you, follow you to remotest Retirements. The comick Muse is more particularly yours; and it is your peculiar praise to allure the most ravishing of all the Sisters after you into Retirement. To make that Goddess forsake the crowd with you, who loves it most of the Nine. You have been constantly her Darling, her best belov'd. Thus in Retirement with her and you, I should have the Conversation of Mankind; I should enjoy it with all its Advantages, without its least inconveniencies.[69]

In this metaphorized threesome, Wycherley's relations with his inner Muse issue in impressive literary output, which in turn becomes the public Muse who now provides sexual pleasure to the reader-friend. In the shift from inner site to public location, his eroticized creativity enters the value-realm of other sexual commodities, which in this case requires no real economic exchange since it can be shared intimately with the friend. But the letter's trope nevertheless models the traffic of male creativity as a symbolic value. Dennis's metaphorical pleasure as co-lover of the dramatist's sexy female Muse might have been testament to Wycherley's high status within the male literary community, but it also pointed to the homosocial structures within which literary value was most often located. In these allegories, men copulated with the same female, or became voyeurs to the sexuality of other men, or made available their internalized female Muse to the erotic attentions of male friends. But in every case, the narrative was about the *value* of the author and his literary labor as it was considered as a thing of pleasure for others, like a woman.

Taken together, the two Muses replayed the complexities that informed perceptions of the transition from the inner site of creativity to its public status, with the first Muse often situated in a fiction of erotic authorial independence or sexual power, and the second presenting the sexual compromises of a public print culture or the male contexts of friendship and competition. Representing forms of power and loss, the male writer as female Muse registered some sense of the "cost" of one's imaginative abilities as they were located in the capitalist republic of letters. But these transgendered tropes were also about the poetical character as forms of male embodiment and sexuality. It is important that we can go beyond our current academic obsession with the female body to see how much these transvestite gestures are about the male physicality of wit. That is, the use of a feminized self ought not to obscure the fact that what was being written about as the object of a newer commercial traffic was the male sexual body as the origin of creativity. By this I do not mean to ignore the very real historical senses in which women were a crass sexual "commodity." But the female Muse figures also served to call attention to the male author's sexuality as a symbolic commodity critically important to definitions of his status as a writer. Both a copulator with his Muse and a body of potential phallic use by other men, male writer as erotic Muse dramatically foregrounded sex and the body in a homosocial traffic of creativity.

No Muses Here! Priapus, Autogenesis, Autoeroticism

The yard of wit also reflected these ambiguities. Male-brain/male-genitalia connections were easily transferred to the literary scene, where creativity-as-yard (or stones, or seed) became a rhetorical commodity characterizing male authorship either as a powerful creativity or a material item of traffic. But the yard of wit contained other tensions, too. The poetical character was sometimes represented as functioning like the unruly erection, an anti-authoritarian Priapus-like energy which refused to be contained by polite social order. Notions of quill-as-yard, writing as intercourse or masturbation, censorship as castration, and ink as seminal flow reflected a cultural nervousness about the sexualized connection of male body and mind even while these tropes helped to sustain the newer constructions of masculinity as a sexualized interiority. And for individual men, this imagery of head-groin associations sometimes functioned to psychologize their commodification as a profound loss, as the disturbing possibility that one could have wit or the phallus but not both at the same time. The next three sections examine these anxieties, both as cultural manifestations and as concerns for the writer.

Earlier sections on Zeus-Athena birthings and men-as-Muses have suggested the extent to which notions of the homocentric origins of male creativity were part of the collective rhetoric even in heterosexual and transvestite allegories about the poetical character. Sometimes female Muses were simply removed from the scene altogether and replaced by tropes of male-male begetting. In literary usage, same-sex reproduction reflected a desire to view male creativity as somehow self-generated within male sexuality itself. In these formations, a heterosexual reproductive model was transferred to two men, one of whom was figuratively impregnated by the inspiration of the other. Specific usage could be a relatively simple affair, as in Samuel Wesley's compliment to Richard Blackmore in *An Epistle to a Friend Concerning Poetry* (1700) in which the history of male creativity was imaged as a sexualized traffic between older and younger men: "Each page [of Blackmore's *Prince Arthur*] is big with Virgil's Manly Thought."[70] Or it might assume more complex dimensions, as in James Boswell's apology to the reader "for the imperfect manner in which I am obliged to exhibit Johnson's conversation at this [early] period. . . . In progress of time, when my mind was, as it were, *strongly impregnated with the Johnsonian aether*, I could, with much more facility and exactness, carry in my memory and commit to paper the exuberant variety of his wisdom and wit."[71] The notion that the fertility of one's own imagination depended on a figurative impregnation by another male poet is a common trope in the period, serving as an abbreviated gesture by which male literary hierarchies or the importance of male friendship could be signaled. Pope's "On lying in the Earl of Rochester's Bed at Atterbury" (1739), for example, imagines the begetting of poetry as a choice between Rochester, the former owner of Atterbury, and its current owner and friendly host, the Duke of Argyle:

> With no poetick ardors fir'd,
>   I press the bed where *Wilmot* lay:
> That here he lov'd, or here expir'd,
>   Begets no numbers grave or gay.
> But 'neath thy roof, *Argyle*, are bred
>   Such thoughts . . . (*TE* 6: 380, ll. 1–6)

Pope's conceit that friend Argyle's bed will yield better imaginative breeding than will Rochester's, accomplishes several things, being at once friendly flattery to his host as well as a distancing of his own poetic moment from symbolic influence by the libertine Wilmot. But Pope is also acknowledging and participating in the metaphorization of sexualized male relationships collectively used to speak of the poetical character within the larger community and history of male writing; in this sense, of course, the symbolic community between Pope and Rochester is unmistakable.

But there was a second kind of creative autogenesis—a counter-tradition to the Muses, as it were—which represented the primal scene of male writing as a self-generating erection or priapic state. Predictably, there were classical precedents. Roman writers in particular recognized with considerable humor that these two accounts of origins were oppositional, with very different implications for both the figure of the poet and notions of an acceptable subject-matter. Catullus, for example, frames the antagonism around the personified yard-poet's unsuccessful attempt to scale the Olympian heights: "Mentula conatur Pipleium scandere montem: / Musae furcillis praecipitem eiciunt" ("TOOL tries to scale the Mount of Pipla: / Muses with pitchforks throw him down").[72] As Amy Richlin has commented, "the Priapic figure opposes the Muses, and in this case is ignominiously rejected by them; as the Muses eject the would-be poet, so their *furcillae* push out the *Mentula*."[73] But the Muses, too, could be excluded from a male poetic enterprise that might deal in impolite truths or a satirically sexualized subject. Thus, Ovid's opening lines to book one of *The Art of Love* simply reject the politer implications of Apollo and the Muses as a traditional allegory of creative inspiration:

> . . . . Nor shall I falsely ascribe my arts to Apollo:
> No airy bird comes twittering advice
> Into *my* ear, *I* never had a vision of the Muses
> Herding sheep in Ascra's valleys. This work is based
> On experience: what I write, believe me, I have practised.[74]

That Ovid wants to separate his poetic subject from the Apollo/Muses tradition is part of a classical literary subset that organizes its symbolic gestures around male sexuality itself, which is sometimes marked off as having its own kind of literary character.

The bluntest classical version of a male creativity which excludes the Apollo/Muses tradition is to be found in the *Priapea*, a collection of eighty Latin poems which takes Priapus as its creative foundation.[75] In the first of these poems, "A warning to the reader," the poet offers a simple choice between the chaste mythology of poetic reproduction and the rude power of the visible phallus:

These verses here are full of rudery,
So lay aside your Roman prudery:
Dian' and Vesta dwell not in this fane,
Nor goddess [Athena] who from head of father came,
But ruddy orchard guard with tool that's blessed
With immense size, and hidden by no vest.
So cover up his shameful member—or,
Gazing on it, with those same eyes read more.[76]

In subsequent poems, the personified "tool" that is Priapus functions variously to protect the male poet in the orchard, to satirize or rape/ sodomize any would-be intruder, and to supply the symbolic generative energy which will issue in the fruits of male creativity. In the second introductory poem, for example, in which "The author dedicates his verses to Priapus," the Apollo/Muses tradition is perfunctorily replaced by the unchaste, unholy space of the ithyphallic god whose heated privy member will be associated with male creativity, whose garden will be the terrain of poetry, and whose sometimes comical status as god-figure will be linked to the male poet:

You've seen, Priapus, these fruits of my wit:
More for a garden than a book they're fit,
And without too much trouble I've them writ.
Although 'tis poets' custom, I have not
Summoned the Muses to this unchaste spot.
For the heart and the will I haven't got
To bring such chaste sisters—the Pierian lot—
So close to the member of Priapus hot.
And so, whatever in my idle scrawl
You find I've written on your temple wall,
Please be so good as to accept it all. (69)

Impolite, obscene, humorous, satirical—and rejecting the symbolic reproductions of the Apollo/Muses variety—the *Priapea* was rediscovered in the Renaissance and, as a supplement to Petronius's *Satyricon*, was printed throughout the seventeenth and eighteenth centuries.[77]

The question of transmission is an important one, and yet it is hard to gauge the impact of the *Priapea* on the male literary culture contemporary with Pope. As I have noted earlier, the function of the Priapic deity before the middle of the eighteenth century seems typically limited to the comic scarecrow figure with the grotesquely over-sized tarse; it is not until mid-century excavation at Herculaneum and the anthropological annotations of Richard Payne Knight that older ideas of the ithyphallic deity and his generative symbolism appear to be resuscitated. Nonetheless, aspects of this classical context are still evident in the period, as they are in Charles Sackville's "Another Letter from

Lord Buckhurst to Mr. Etherege" (ca. 1663–64). In libertine fashion, Sackville links the stirring of wit to a phallic response, suggesting that just as the lowest forms of poetry are inspired by genitalia—as in Rochester's "I . . . never rhymed but for my pintle's sake"[78]—so too the most august expressions of creative endeavor are linked to Priapus, whose comic scarecrow function ought not to blind one to his underlying symbolic importance:

> If I can guess the Devil choke me
> What horrid fury could provoke thee
> To use thy railing, scurrilous wit
> Gainst prick and cunt, the source of it:
> For what but prick and cunt does raise
> Our thoughts to songs and roundelays,
> Enables us to anagrams
> And other amorous flim flams?
> Then we write plays and so proceed
> To bays, the poet's sacred weed.
> Hast no respect for God Priapus?
> That ancient story should not scape us:
> Priapus was a Roman God,
> (But in plain English, prick and cod)
> Who pleased their sisters, wives, and daughters,
> Guarded their pippins and pomwaters,
> For at the orchard's utmost entry
> This mighty Deity stood sentry,
> Invested in a tattered blanket,
> To scare the magpies from their banquet.[79]

Between libertine friends, the very "source" of wit—"the poet's sacred weed"—is to be located in a comically sexualized Chain of Being, rising from "prick and cunt" up to god Priapus.

Alexis Piron's *Ode à Priape* (1710) is an even more outrageous adaptation of the idea of Priapus as the male poet's symbolic life-force, the sign under which the writer will seek his creative inspiration:

> F. . . . . des neuf garces du Pinde,
> F. . . . . de l'amant de Daphné,
> Dont le flasque v.. ne se guinde,
> Qu'à force d'être patiné :
> C'est toi que j'invoque à mon aide,
> Toi qui dans les c . . . d'un v.. roide,
> Lances le f. . . . . à gros bouillons ;
> Priape soutiens mon haleine,
> Et pour un moment dans ma veine
> Porte le feu de tes c. . . . .
> [Fuck the nine whores of Pindos,
> Fuck Daphne's lover [Apollo],

Whose limp prick can go stiff
Only by dint of being caressed;
You are the one whose help I invoke,
You, who with stiff prick, send hurtling into cunts
Big foaming bubbles of semen;
Priapus, sustain my [poetic] breath,
And send for the nonce into my inspiration
The fire of your balls.][80]

Direct invocations such as this are uncommon in the materials I have examined, but they point to the cluster of ideas which characterized male creativity as a self-contained sexual dynamic whose emphasis is on erotic pleasure and power. The Priapus who is invoked in this mode is seldom the procreative source of figurative children-as-art or immaculate birthings, but rather it is the aggressive turgidity of the personified phallic god itself which represents inspiration, creative act, and written text. It remains now to explore the most typical manifestations of this phallocentrism in which no Muses are required.

If Priapus was not a common figure in the meta-commentaries of the male literary culture ca. 1650–1750, then how did this kind of autogenesis figure itself in male writing? The most striking visual example is the frontispiece to the notorious pornographic French novel, *Histoire de Dom B* (1741; see Figure 7), whose caption reads "the author full of his subject."[81] With right hand writing and left hand clutching distended pego, the smiling author represents the symbolic scene of male writing—not only the act, but also the subject—which is here linked directly to the phallus. In this interior space of male creativity, quill and yard are almost interchangeable, overseen by a grinning satyr whose stiffened tarse and intimate closeness signal Dionysian approval and Priapic heritage. Priapus is not actually present in the scene, but the frontispiece captures a male discourse whose visual logic neatly presents the phallus as the central energy, both the source and the object of male wit. In this tableau, the imaginative act is an engorged privy member *and* a pen. The male author's imagination is both masturbated and written under the protection and encouragement of smiling satyr, whose swollen member is the inspirational agent behind authorial endeavor as well as its visible token. At the center of this tableau is the author's head, framed by the half-circle of directional cues (quill, author's yard, satyr's yard, satyr's head) which point to the attentive gaze of the author. In turn, his line of vision (reinforced by the satyr's) directs us to hand, quill, page, the act of writing. Does the author require an erection in order to write, or does he write to acquire an erection? "L'AUTEUR Remplie de son Sujet" suggests that writing and erection are coeval and coincident, that they are also

L'Auteur
Rempli de
son Sujet

Figure 7. The frontispiece to Jacques Charles Gervaise de La Touche's *Histoire de Dom B* (1790). By permission of the British Library. Shelfmark PC 13 H. 19.

interdependent and somehow interchangeable. There are no Muses here, no quasi-reproductive allegories. The poetical character is the pleasurable, stiffened, masturbated prick-quill under the approving watch of a potentially transgressive, partly bestial virility.

The emphasis of this discourse is not on a Priapic begetting of life or the ithyphallic origin of procreation itself. Rather, the image here is non-procreative, a self-contained autoerotic capacity associated with symbolic power and pleasure. Another version of the idea can be found in juxtapositions of phallus and poet's head. The earliest instance, of course, is the classical herm, that phallic column (of stone or wood) featuring a carved head and an erect penis; in Augustan Rome, according to Leo Braudy, the idea of genius was sometimes represented by such columns.[82] The best-known modern example is Wilkes's clever parody in his *An Essay on Woman* (1763) of the title page of William Warburton's 1751 edition of Pope's *An Essay on Man*. The Warburtonian original presented the title of the poem in capitals at the top of the page, and then "BY / ALEXANDER POPE, Esq. / Enlarged and Improved by the AUTHOR. / Together with his MS. Additions and Variations / as in the Last Edition of his Works. / With the NOTES of / William, Lord Bishop of Gloucester." Just below this was a medallion of Pope's head, followed by publication information. Wilkes parodied as follows: "AN / Essay on Woman; / By Pego Borewell, Esq; / WITH NOTES / By Roger Cunaeus, Vigerus Mutoniatus, &c. / AND / A Commentary by the Rev. Dr. Warburton. / INSCRIBED TO / Miss Fanny Murray [a well-known courtesan of the 1750s]." Occupying the position where the medallion had been was a copper engraving of a phallus bearing the Greek phrase "Creator of the world." Other features followed, satirically directed towards George Stone. Wilkes's title page is complex in its intent, using Pope's eloquent poem as a vehicle for attacking Warburton and other political enemies.[83] And of course the parody also included Pope as part of the satirical object, playfully implicating him in blunt sexual topoi from which he was likely excluded in real life. What interests me here is Wilkes's visual equation of the famous poet's head and the prevailing erection, as though they are somehow equivalent or interchangeable. Not unlike the Greek herms in which head and yard were symbolically linked, Wilkes juxtaposed the head of male poetic genius with rampant privy member and a phallic subject-matter. Irreverent it may be, but the Wilkesean coupling was part of a larger discursive practice dramatizing a mythos about the poetical character.

If the poet's head could be figured as an erect yard, so too could the poet and the subject of male poetry. I have already mentioned the amazing metonymic gesture recorded by Eric Partridge in which "Doctor Johnson" was slang for the male organ itself.[84] By using the name and idea of the influential Johnson in this way, the yard was personified as dominant poet. Powerful literary figure became powerful genital tool, one standing in for the other as a sign of rank and stature. As a remnant of sexual slang, it is perhaps passingly amusing, the idea of the poet's power now to be found between one's legs. But in the collective vocabulary which explains the self-fashioning of male literary communities, a "Dr. Johnson" is a marvelously fortuitous artefact testifying to the cultural reach of the poet-yard connection even outside the literary realm. A similar transfer of poetry, poet, and the poetic into the penis is evident in Charles Hanbury Williams's "An Ode to Lord Lincoln" (1744), in which the prodigious Lincoln was transformed into his phallus, which in turn became the inspirational power and subject of the friend's ode:

> O Linc-ln! joy of womankind,
> To you this humble ode's design'd;
> Let —— [yard, cock] inspire my song:
> Gods! with what pow'rs are you endu'd,
> Tiberius was not half so lewd,
> Nor Hercules so strong.
> 'Tis —— now my pen employs,
> And since I sing of heav'nly joys,
> From heav'n my notes I'll bring;
> And tho' the lyric strain I chuse,
> I'll open like the Mantuan muse
> ——, and the man I sing.[85]

Echoing Dryden's translation of the first line of Virgil's *Aeneid*—"Arms, and the Man I sing"—Lincoln's large phallus becomes the Virgilian subject, the occasion of poetry itself. Not only will this epic phallicism "inspire my song" and "now my pen employ[]," it will of its own powerful essence be associated with the acme of literary kinds in a heritage of famous epic poets.

Poet/poetry-as-yard could also be used aggressively to combat the literary enemy. In an indignant response to Pope's *Sober Advice from Horace*, in which Richard Bentley had been savagely satirized in footnotes, nephew Thomas Bentley came to the rescue, giving Pope a taste of his own medicine in a sarcastic footnote: "Can there be a more odd Sight, than to see this Sermonizer, Mr. POPE . . . come forth all naked and bloody, with his *Testes & Cauda salax* [testicles and yard] in his Hands? . . . What an *Erection* of Wit, what a *Tentigo* [lustful tension] of Parts in his Note! How he triumphs, and dashes his Sp[erm] about him!"[86] The almost surreal image of male wit as the erect penis ejaculating semen-as-writing was at the center of quill-yard equations, as we will see next section, but Bentley's satiric tactic is to use the yard-poet discourse maliciously, as he does again in his last paragraph: "Enough for you, sure, to be called as HORACE was by AUGUSTUS, *Putissi-mum penem, the purest Wag-prick*; and *Lepidissimum homuncionem, the cleverest parted little Fellow in the World*" (18). Having a little prick, or being one, would also be a conventional accusation in tussles between literary opponents, as it is here in Bentley's clever collapsing of classical precedent and current insult.

The very idea of the male poet—his head, wit, status, and even his poetry—was imaged in these various ways as a penis: pleasurably hard, priapically powerful, or masturbated and about to ejaculate; the yard-poet was curiously non-procreative, needing no female principle to impregnate, but vitally creative nonetheless. There are several reasons for such literary emphasis, but we need to contextualize them within the wider cultural applications of male-yard equations previously examined, especially enigmatic yard versus mind. Of particular importance is the way that sexual responsiveness or arousal was viewed not simply as a biological given but, importantly, as the result of the imagination. We have already seen physiological theorists such as Haller, Whytt, and Boerhaave locate the causes of the erection not in the will but in the imagination, and this concept would circulate widely in popularized accounts of how the fancy was itself *the* sexual site, an adjunct or agent which made erigibility possible.

The step from physiological to literary accounts of erections and imagination was a short one, where the more specialized connections between the *poetic* imagination and the privy member represented an integrated subset of culturally-current thought rather than merely the stuff of outdated myths or quaint poeticisms. The imagination-yard nexus was most famously figured in *Tristram Shandy*'s comic nose-penis trope:

that the size and jollity of every individual nose, and by which one nose ranks above another, and bears a higher price, is owing to the cartilagenous and muscular parts of it, into whose ducts and sinuses the blood and animal spirits being impell'd, and driven by the warmth and force of the imagination, which is but a step from it. . . . "That so far was *Prignitz* from the truth, in affirming that the fancy begat the nose, that on the contrary,—the nose begat the fancy." (3: 38, 174–75)

In his adaptation of physiological theory about the causes of the erection, Sterne frames the phallicism of wit as a mutually dependent relationship, a two-way begetting in which nose/penis and fancy give rise to one another. The question of which is the begetter of the other is not so important for Sterne as is their interchangeability. Presented here as directly proportionate, erection and imagination are somehow homologous conditions, existing in a state of symbiosis. For Sterne and the physiologists, wit and erections issue enigmatically from the same cranial wellspring, and are therefore seen as interdependent. In addition, both are located at that mysterious inner site of mind which is beyond the will or conscious control, linked in their capacity to override the higher orders of mental capacity and thus potentially lawless. In this sense, the phallus and imagination were sometimes seen as disorderly and dangerous threats to the internal hierarchy of mind and body, which required subordinating such unruly energies to the authoritative categories of reason or judgement. However, the physiologists realized that the process of tumescence was enigmatic, frequently at odds with intentionality, and that the erection also had features of otherness with a "mind" of its own. Sterne makes much of this idea, dramatizing the phallicized imagination's power to disrupt the linear train of ideas associated with reason. In a well-known passage riddled with sexual suggestiveness, narrator Tristram playfully proposes what Sterne's novel has dramatized all along, namely, that the wit-yard persistently penetrates and overthrows the sternest Lockean categories of mind:

—But softly—for in these sportive plains, and under this genial sun, where at this instant all flesh is running out piping, fiddling, and dancing to the vintage, and every step that's taken, the judgment is surprised by the imagination, I defy, notwithstanding all that has been said upon *straight lines** in sundry pages of my book—I defy the best cabbage planter that ever existed, whether he plants backwards or forwards, it makes little difference in the account (except that he will have more to answer for in the one case than in the other)—I defy him to go on cooly, critically, and canonically, planting his cabbages one by one, in straight lines, and stoical distances, especially if slits in petticoats are unsew'd up—without ever and anon straddling out, or sliding into some bastardly digression. (8: 1, 415)

In this provocative interlude, imagination functions like the unruly erection, desirously "straddling" and "sliding into" the many "slits" which all the armaments of judgement are powerless to prevent. Opposed to this sexualized energy of mind are the representatives of philosophy, State, and Church—"the great *Locke*," "great wigs," "your graver gentry," "your reverences" (3: 20, 149–50), "your Worships" (3: 40, 177)—whose censorious and orthodox presence fails to restrain these potentially disorderly energies emanating from the yard-fancy. Indeed, a good deal of the novel's reading pleasures can be explained by the threat which bastardly (hence sexually transgressive, illegitimate) digression poses to official decorum.

Sterne knows he is risking offence and charges of obscenity with such associations, but his determination to link mind and imagination with penis—whether Walter's or Uncle Toby's, whether impotent or sound, whether well-hung or circumcised by window-sash—is unmistakable, illustrating the extent to which male writers relied on this particular discursive trope in their meta-commentaries about the poetical character as a sexualized terrain. Spoofing the pseudo-mathematical calculations of earlier theologians to enumerate how many souls could fit into a mile, and comically predicting that the shrunken modern soul may soon make Christianity itself a thing of the past, Sterne's Tristram offers up the prospect of a return to a pagan classicism whose prevailing deity will be nothing less than the phallic god himself:

> Blessed *Jupiter*! and blessed every other heathen god and goddess! for now ye will all come into play again, and with *Priapus* at your tails—what jovial times!—but where am I? and into what a delicious riot of things am I rushing? I—I who must be cut short in the midst of my days, and taste no more of 'em than what I borrow from my imagination. . . . (7: 14, 377)

Even with illness and death lurking in the near future—archly hinted as a castration in "cut short"—his phallicized imagination is still symbolically connected to Priapus, the orchard god whose rude, ruddy tool promises a transgressive creativity. What we are seeing here is a typical feature in characterizations of the self-generating priapic imagination: an anti-authoritarian energy of a potentially transgressive order. Rampant, aggressive, and powerfully linked to a figurative priapism, this discourse reflected a need by male writers to assert a sense of their creative autonomy. The self-contained creativity-as-phallus was a gesture by which the writer could fictionalize his own authorial independence and self-generated creative sway, holding forth an eroticized intentionality or act of genital bravado lawlessly at odds with more conventional notions of the conscious will as storehouse of social norms and moral censors.[87] Like Priapus, the self-erecting will of the phallus-wit depended on nothing but itself while subordinating everything else to its own presence and pleasure.

Figurative autogenesis often nurtured the fiction that male creativity could transcend the baser attributes of a literary market-place. In *Conjectures on Original Composition* (1759), for example, Edward Young used the autogenetic trope to fashion his hierarchy of genius, originality, and levels of literary production:

> Though *Pope's* noble Muse may boast her illustrious descent from *Homer*, *Virgil*, *Horace*, yet is an *Original* author more nobly born. . . . an *Original* author is born of himself, is his own progenitor, and will probably propagate a numerous offspring of Imitators, to eternize his glory; while mule-like Imitators, die without issue.[88]

Adopting familiar metaphors to frame his critique of Pope, Young places autogenetic acts at the top of his hierarchy, offering an ideal of the male poet who, although quite capable of propagating offspring, is more properly concerned with his own self-begetting. This self-created "Original author" is also presented quite implausibly as being above questions of profitable poetic simulacra and independent of literary tradition itself. Lesser authors and more contingent forms of male creativity are presented in a descending scale of reproductive value: Pope's female Muse as offspring of famous poet-fathers; the lesser heterosexual reproduction of imitators; an abject heterosexual barrenness. Implicit in this hierarchy was the literary desire for creative independence from a mundane relational world.

But literary independence was available to few in this period, and even the great Pope—made comparatively rich by his translations of Homer—would be unable to ignore the material and economic dependency thrust upon the day-to-day realities of authorship by the new print culture he had so successfully exploited. In this capitalist and legalistic milieu—of writerly competition, the changing tastes of a paying public, the purchase of copyright from authors, the sometimes deleterious effects on authorial success by a burgeoning literary-review industry—the figure of the writer could easily be imaged as hireling, hack, mechanic, or as literary prostitute selling her body. In this environment, the figure of the male writer as self-originating phallus offered a counter-thrust which fitfully asserted the dignity and importance of male creativity.

But there was a negative side to the self-generating yard-wit. The fantasy of a self-sufficient male creativity was also linked to cultural fears about the imagination as cause of sexual and psychological disorder. That is, tropes of patriarchal autogenesis functioned uneasily and occupied an ambiguous position, capable as they were of shifting from ideas of creative autonomy to narcissistic excess. Part of the problem with the cluster of priapic, autogenetic, and autoerotic imagery was that however much it might have captured a notion of the private, interior site of male creativity, the recurring idea of an exclusive solitariness and self-sufficiency was nearly impossible to adapt as a positive metaphor for one's public status as a writer. This alone does much to explain why such tropes do not dominate the collective self-fashioning in the larger community of writers. One side of the coin might have figured male creativity as a pleasurable and independent priapism; but on the other side was the image of the deviant onanist, perversely alienated from public norms.

In the discursive space of Priapus where male writers could do without Muses and heterosexual reproductive allegories altogether, the self-generating male was sometimes imaged as a masturbator whose autoerotic scene of writing might contain a positive or, more likely, a negative capacity. On one hand, the self-stimulated yard could repre-

sent an autonomous authorial inspiration transcending the venal structures of a consumerist print culture. Such is the case in the frontispiece
to *Histoire de Dom B*, with its masturbating author happily writing his
own inspired yard-wit in a creative space far from the madding crowd
of booksellers and readers who paid for their pleasures. Far more
often, however, the writer's solitary act of masturbatory self-absorption
was used metaphorically to illustrate a perverse authorial self-regard,
a solipsistic vice whose figurative literary results were disastrously out
of touch with communal norms. Thomas Bentley's retaliation against
Pope adopts this more prevalent cultural conception of the onanist,
portraying the famous poet as the pathetic little masturbator dashing
his sperm-ink about him. The writer as masturbator was a small but
significant trope in the discourse of male writing as priapic condition,
signaling the possibility of a pathology of the literary imagination itself.

The debilitating results of the link between masturbation and the
imagination were well-established physiological concepts in eighteenth
century medical commentary. Tissot had drawn attention to the fact
that masturbatory desires were prompted not by nature but by the
imagination, which "having great influence upon these [genital] parts,
it may, by being occupied with desires, put them into such a situation
as serves reciprocally to excite them; and desire leads to the act, which
is the more pernicious in proportion as it is unnecessary."[89] D. T. De
Bienville's *Nymphomania, or, a Dissertation Concerning the Furor Uterinus*
(English translation, 1775) concluded with a thirty-page chapter of
"Observations on the Imagination, As connected with the Nymphomania," whose case-history of the teenaged Julia similarly warned
against "this fatal rage of *Masturbation*, of which the imagination is the
artisan."[90] Already associated with the causes of the enigmatic erection, the imagination was also linked to the enervating obsession of
the delusional masturbator, whose self-seeking desires were seen as a
dangerous narcotic, producing compulsive behavior pathologically di-
vorced from reproductive normalcy, virtue, health, and sanity. Despite
the fashionable "pleasures of the imagination" as a new leisure commodity of a population keen to confirm its own taste,[91] there was also a
concern throughout the period with "the dangerous prevalence of
imagination" (to use one of Johnson's chapter-headings in *Rasselas*)
which could lead to delusional self-consideration or masturbatory in-
sanity. As a solitary practice, masturbation was inevitably connected to
other isolated imaginative acts, such as reading or writing, which
threatened an unhealthy alienation.[92] Anti-masturbation advice thus
had much to say about the dangers of reading, particularly by youth
and women, whose imaginations were considered more susceptible
and whose autoerotic proclivities were more easily provoked by the
erotic hints in novels.

But masturbation and writing were also linked, and male authors with already heightened imaginative abilities were sometimes included within the pathological definition. Indeed, in *Onanism* . . . Tissot had remarked on what he believed was a precise physiological analogy between the onanist and the man of letters, although the passage has received scant attention:[93]

The masturbator, entirely devoted to his filthy meditations, is subject to the same disorders as the man of letters, who fixes his attention upon a single question; and this excess is almost constantly prejudicial. That part of the brain, which is then occupied, makes an effort similar to that of a muscle, which has been for a long time greatly extended; the consequences of which are such a continued motion in the part as cannot be stopt, or such a fixed attention, that the idea cannot be changed: this is the case with masturbators. (75)

The negative idea of the writer-masturbator included some major figures: Rousseau confessed to "This vice, which shame and timidity find so convenient, has a particular attraction for lively imaginations";[94] Thomas Beddoes insinuated in his *Hygeia* (1802) that masturbation had caused Swift's mental decline into madness and misanthropy.[95] Already constructed as an eroticized interior site, the male writer's imagination was also subject to libidinal disorder and deviance—doubly susceptible, it would seem, to physical and mental self-pollutions.

Pope, too, was included in the negative domain of masturbatory failure in the anonymous *The Poet Finish'd in Prose* (1735), a satirical dialogue between speakers A and B in which the poet's sexuality is the target. Speculating on why Pope had attacked Lady Mary Wortley Montagu so savagely in *The First Satire of the Second Book of Horace Imitated* (1733)—"P-x'd by her Love, or libell'd by her Hate" (*TE* 4: 13, l. 84)—they conclude that, being a "Gentleman who has not the least Passion for the Sex," Pope was fearful of being raped by Lady Mary. Comparing their own heterosexual inclinations to the poet's curious disinterest, the speakers hint none-too-subtly that Pope prefers to masturbate:

Why, you love a pretty Girl now, and so do I. Very well, Sir, let us follow our Inclinations, I dare say Mr. *Pope* will not interefere with us. Perhaps *He* does not; what is that to us? . . . 'Tis possible his Fondness for Retirement may have given him this Disrelish for the Sex; but no doubt he has found out some other Amusement, equally entertaining to him in his Solitude.[96]

Turning away from heterosexual pursuits to autoerotic solitude, Pope is lampooned as the failed cocksman whose masturbatory habits are linked to an ineffective phallicism and a wretched poetry of slanderous assault. John Armstrong's *The Oeconomy of Love* had described masturbation as "Th' ungenerous, selfish, solitary Joy," warning the obsessional offender to "Hold, Parricide, thy hand! For thee alone / Did Nature form thee? For thy narrow self / Grant thee the means of Pleasure? Dreamst thou so?"[97] Pope's attackers and Armstrong both spurn the onanist in these two examples, whose genital self-gropings are signs of a dangerously sick imagination and an infertile selfhood.

Masturbation as a metaphor for male writing in the period was usually linked to these pathological contexts, although there are surprisingly few studies of the trope. Christopher Fox has considered Swift's use of narcissism in *Gulliver's Travels*, suggesting that "masturbation becomes a metaphor for writing that finds its sole basis in self."[98] Hugh Ormsby-Lennon's more elaborate investigation has shown how *A Discourse Concerning the Mechanical Operation of the Spirit* (1710) "begins, proceeds, and ends in masturbatory *double entendre*," presenting the Grubstreet Hack as compulsive masturbator whose mechanical writing "is onanistic, not coital."[99] The negative construction of certain kinds of writers and writing as a figurative onanism dominated the use of the metaphor well into the next century, and Romantics specialists will be aware of Byron's notorious criticism of Keats: "why his is the *Onanism* of Poetry. . . . such writing is a sort of mental masturbation— he is always f—gg—g his *Imagination*."[100] In these configurations the trope captures the idea of a dangerously compulsive, narcissistic creativity of a false or mechanical nature, the literary products of which are perversely idiosyncratic and inaccessible.

With these contexts in mind, one can see the related cluster of priapic, autogenetic, and autoerotic tropes for male creative power as double-sided: while such figures might have offered collective fictions of the creative power and autonomy of the author, they were also easily linked to cultural paranoia about a perverse imaginative self-indulgence. The result is that in metacommentaries about the male writer, the related figures of self-sufficiency—priapic writer, authorial autogenesis—seldom received extended textual treatment without sharing the contextual space with other tropes we have already seen. While ideas of priapic or masturbatory autonomy could be used to oppose the newer market forces which were preoccupied with the commercial value of books, the figure of the isolated yard-wit also imaged a perverse and impossible removal from the now inescapable material demands of booksellers, contracts, and the buying public. In part what we are seeing is a clash between representations of the interior site of male creativity and of the public status of the writer and his output. The double-sidedness of these tropes reflected the collective difficulty within the larger male literary community to control an image of authorial dignity and power, or to negotiate ideas of creative independence with the relational character and material contingencies of the marketplace.

But at another level these ambiguous tropes also contained a cultural nervousness about newer definitions of masculinity defined by an interiorized sexuality. In a milieu where male identity and mental creativity were increasingly linked to the body and the deeper influences of one's genitalia, the solitary figure of the wanker poet or priapic wit—turgid symbol of creative self-sufficiency and powerful self-generation—threatened too many cultural codes. An imagery of poets, their heads, and male writing as the enigmatically autonomous yard—whose swelling blood-surges originated deep in the fancy in opposition to will, reason, and judgement—was not only anti-authoritarian, anti-social, and pathological, but also a threatening violation of reproductive and erotic norms. The fiction of a phallic self-sufficiency, in other words, was ultimately too transgressive as a metaphor in literary self-fashioning because it was non-procreative, lawless, and antagonistic toward official structures. Moreover, as an idea of successful authorial genius the trope too dangerously emphasized pleasurable self-stimulation and ejaculatory readiness, both threatening images of a powerfully eroticized male creativity isolated from the public world of letters, contracts, money, and reputation. This metaphorical terrain featured no wombs or fetching female Muses or reproductive processes which could be linked to familiar heterosexual frameworks or to economic realms of literary birth-products; instead, there lurked the possibility of a monstrous yard of wit, symbol of masculine essence, identity, and creativity—subject to no other defining power or hierarchy, and capable of overturning established cultural categories. Magnifying the head-groin associations in this way, these versions of the author/male-creativity-as-yard were typically attenuated by pathological aspects or by other rhetorical gestures whose sexual tropes and allegories more clearly located the author's public status. Indeed, male writers themselves tended to assign such figures to the realm of the comical (as, for example, in *Tristram Shandy*), the pornographic (Wilkes), or the satirical attack on one's enemy (Bentley). Far more prevalent than the author-as-phallus in powerful isolation was the image of the male writer as fornicator, as dynamic cocksman whose copulatory power resided in the quill-yard and ink-semen, tokens of his creative sway. To this better-known metaphor we now turn.

Quill-Yards, Castration, and Flow

In 1979 Gilbert and Gubar asked what was then an impolite (and for some, an unsettling) question: "Is a pen a metaphorical penis?"[101] Since then the trope has been used as a feminist shorthand—often as the clever coinage, "pen(is)"—to indicate both a patriarchal dominance in the canon as well as the presumed phallogocentric character of language itself. One cannot deny the gender-implications of discourses in which male writing was so frequently imagined as a quintessentially sexual act inscribed onto feminized pages by masculinist representatives of patriarchy. But pens-as-penises are rather more involved than these clichés suggest, and feminist equations of male author with "aesthetic patriarch whose pen is an instrument of generative power like his penis"[102] tell only part of the story. The metaphorical logic of quill-yards also included ink-as-semen, which in turn prompted the cause-and-effect implication that male writing, like a man's seed, originated in the testicles. A curious cultural tension emerged in figurative uses of this head-groin proposition: despite the fact that seed was so often viewed as an etherial life-force, the precious essence of maleness itself, the metaphorical framework of quill-yards often made penile discharge a potentially dangerous fluid. Why? And in what ways were these underlying fears about male embodiment-as-creativity connected to castration-expurgation tropes?

Writers sometimes used the figurative equivalence of pen and penis, just as they sometimes metaphorized the quill as a lash or sword directed aggressively toward the opponent. As we have already seen, the connection between male sexual passion and notions of successful genius were common, and thus the inspired male poet as prolific fornicator followed easily as a metapoetic gesture. Playing the young rake with Cromwell, for example, the nearly twenty-one year-old Pope fantasized the friend's assignations with some "Sapho" as a conflation of poetic and phallic power: "I hope you will have a fair opportunity of ravishing her:—I mean only (as Oldfox in ye Plaindealer says) of ravishing her thro' the Ear with your well-penn'd Verses" (*Corr.* 1: 57, 7 May 1709). The idea of the writer-as-copulator also informed Pope's Chaucerian allusion in a letter to Gay: "He who is forc'd to live wholly upon those Ladies favours [the Muses], is indeed in as precarious a condition as any He who does what *Chaucer* says for Sustenance" (*Corr.* 1: 24, 24 December 1712). "The Cook's Tale" had concluded with "a wyf that heeld for contenance / A shoppe, and swyved for hir sustenance," lines which Pope transposes here onto the sexualized idea of male poet and his writing, both cleverly presented to Gay as copulating for a living.[103]

A predictable extension of the writing-as-swiving metaphor was the quill as erect yard spilling ink-semen. No lengthy inventory is required for this well-known analogy, but a few examples will suggest the range of usage. In "To the most famous University of London-Courtezans"—the Epistle Dedicatory of *The Whore's Rhetoric* (1683)— "Philo-Puttanus" explains that "You have at this instant got the Maiden-head of my officious scribbling Instrument, as you have some years since, the Virginity of another Quill. The ink of this is black and smutty, but that of the other was of a more innocent and pleasing colour."[104] The quill as surrogate instrument of ejaculatory power found its way into some unusual applications, as in the Pamela-esque letter which Wilkes received from his friend Charles Churchill, who writes, it appears, while sexually engaged with a mistress: "In my right hand is the Pen—what is in my left? She says—by Christ she can't say."[105] Reminiscent of the frontispiece to *Histoire de Dom B*, in which pen and distended yard are equivalent, this pornographic writing-to-the-moment offers a curiously triangular interplay in which the phallic quill is supported by male friendship and (presumably?) fellatio. But the pen-penis/ink-semen trope was not confined to libertine correspondence or the emerging genre of pornography, and sometimes entered ostensibly politer domains, as it does in two of Pope's letters—the first to Teresa Blount and the second to Lady Mary, who was at the time still on her European travels with her husband:

considering how often & how openly I have declared Love to you, I am astonished (and a little affronted) that you have not forbid my correspondence, & directly said, *See my face no more*. It is not enough, Madam, for your reputation, that you keep your hands pure, from the Stain of Such Ink as might be shed to gratify a male Correspondent; Alas! while your heart consents to encourage him in this lewd liberty of writing, you are not (indeed you are not) what you would so fain have me think you, a Prude! I am vain enough to conclude (like most young fellows) that a fine Lady's Silence is Consent, and so I write on. (*Corr.* 1: 350, 7 August [1716])

After having dream'd of you severall nights, besides a hundred Reveries by day, I find it necessary to relieve myself by writing. (*Corr.* 1: 363, October 1716)

The sexual insinuation lurking within Pope's gallantry is unmistakable, and depends on the figurative logic of ink as sperm and writing as coitus: the "lewd" liberties which fine ladies silently encourage by reading his letters lead to the "Stain" of ink-semen which will finally "gratify" and "relieve" the male correspondent.[106]

Coital writing and venereal pens were related to another metaphorical extension: textual expurgation as castration. Johnson's *Dictionary* makes clear that such convergence was common: "Castrate" included both "1. To geld. 2. To take away the obscene parts of a writing." If writing was copulating, with ejaculatory ink filling the page, then to expurgate, cancel, or excise one's text was a castration, a testicular loss which stopped or removed the seminal flow of writing. Carried out against the writer's will, the figurative castration could represent either the conscientious removal of an unacceptable breach of propriety or a ruthless censorship. This cluster of ideas is certainly not new, and can be discovered as early as Martial's *Epigrams*.[107] The contest between individual expression and censorship informed a variety of works in the seventeenth and eighteenth centuries in which the castration of texts was protested and then "restored."[108] The other side of the trope was a virtuous policing of the tribe of writers whose smutty expressions shamelessly posed as wit. At the middle of the seventeenth century, John Cleveland's "The Hecatomb to his Mistress" reprimanded authorial riff-raff in this way: "Be dumb ye beggers of the rhiming trade, / Geld your loose wits."[109] In either case—offensive text or unfair censorship—the passage in question was metaphorized as testicles which might be cut out by force, retroactively cancelling the semen-ink trace and the sexualized text which offended.

Detectable in this symbolic mutilation is an underlying fear that the genital site of male creativity produced some unwanted truth, whether political, psychological, or social. As much as the poetical character was informed by the wit-phallus connection, there was also a palpable anxiety about its ambivalent character, at once the source of creative power and of a potentially unthinkable transgression. The intricacies of this ambivalence can be seen more clearly when the literal and figurative senses of castration met, as in a passage from Boswell's *Life of Johnson* in which the question of editing Rochester's poems comes up: "Talking of Rochester's Poems, he said, he had given them to Mr. Steevens to castrate for the edition of the poets, to which he was to write Prefaces. Dr. Taylor (the only time I ever heard him say any thing witty) observed, that 'if Rochester had been castrated himself, his exceptionable poems would not have been written.' "[110] Taylor's humor relies on the direct mind-genitalia correspondence, figuring the author's reservoir of wit as semen-producing testicles. A literal castration would have made Rochester a poet-eunuch, one whose poetical character had been purged of its libidinal nature by severing the intimate flow between mind and testes. The more unruly truths of these testicular visions could be cancelled through a literal gelding, removing the very source of male creativity. Potentially transgressive, sexualized male wit was linked in these formulations to a dangerous excess requiring collective surveillance and even harsh intervention. Those writers unable to transform their imaginative energies into polite forms acceptable to a self-policing literary community risked these castration gestures.

But what kinds of cultural anxieties resided in these tropes? Was it simply a nervousness about impolite sexual expression, the sort of outrageous erotic depths to which a mind like Rochester's could sink? Or was it a nervousness about the sexually-embodied origins of the male mind? Did some truth lay hidden in a man's stones, awaiting physiological transubstantiation into creativity of mind, or was it rather a fear of the male body? I am speculative here, because these questions cannot be answered with certainty, but they are worth asking. The uneasy function of the poet-as-yard, likewise, may be related to the reactionary and aggressive energies revealed in these castration tropes, and one wonders whether the ambiguities associated with the male creativity-genitalia links registered an underlying worry about the implications of sexualized embodiment as the defining agent of maleness. Was spirit-as-semen an unthinkable reduction of "man"—his character, essence, mind, soul—to the leaky fluids of brute matter? Or, in their most threatening aspect, were the testicles imagined to be the symbolic location of *all* cultural transgression, the covered and very private place where everything unthinkable originated? If some of these speculations are plausible, then castration as censorship was perhaps a predictable reaction.

These various figures—writer-copulator, pen-penis, ink-semen, expurgation-castration—occurred often in satirical formulations, and the mostly comical tone which accompanied their deployment suggests that humor was one strategy for dealing with these underlying ambiguities. Charging one's literary opponent with a failure of wit or unsuccessful writing meant simple conversions of these figures into their most contemptible forms. Lousy writer, little quill, little penis: the conjunction informed the attack on Pope in *Sawney and Colley* (1742)—one of many satires after Cibber's published letter about young Pope's alleged visit to a whorehouse—in which Sawney-Pope trades barbs with Colley:

> SAW. 'Tis well, you'll see me draw my *Quill.*
> COL. Oh! Sir, I've seen your *Quill* before,
> So did your *Lord*, and eke your *Whore*;
> But 'twas so *very, very small*,
> I trust it holds but little *Gall*. (7)

Likewise, the writer as copulator was often satirically inverted to produce the writer as eunuch, as in Leonard Welsted's swipe at Pope—whose "unabating thirst, to scribble still, / Giv'n at thy birth! the Poetaster's gust, / False and unsated as the Eunuch's lust!"[111]—or in French-influenced writing metaphorized as "A smooth, emasculate, tun'd, Eunuch-breed."[112] The pen-yard/ink-semen conjunction, similarly, was deployed negatively in comments about the impotent man who "had no Ink in his Pen," or the castrato's status as "a pen without ink."[113] And of course one could project a literal castration onto one's enemy in more directly aggressive ways, as in *An Epistle to Dr. Arbuthnot* and Pope's famous conversion of Lord Hervey into Sporus, the young man castrated by Nero so as to become catamite-wife to the depraved emperor's tastes.[114]

Pen-penis and ink-semen tropes underwent other satirical revisions, as well. One of the more complex gestures was derived from myths of writing as "flow," usually associated with the sacred streams of classical myth—Castalia, Hippocrene, or Aganippe—flowing from the tops of mountains—Helicon, Parnassus—which were in turn sacred to Apollo and the Muses. Whether produced by the metamorphosis of the sexually-pursued Castalia or Pegasus's foot striking against the rock, these mythical streams were used widely in English literary history to image a timeless idea of poetic creativity as a fountainhead whose sacred waters—symbolic of harmony, successful versification, inventive brilliance, aural refinement—were reserved exclusively for writers of genius. The result was a rhetorical shorthand containing both a mythos of sacred male creativity—transcendent, transhistorical—and an elitist history of lineage and transmission which defined the canon of great writers from Homer, Virgil, and Ovid down through Chaucer, Spenser, and Milton, and into the eighteenth century. One could claim an association with these symbolic waters by climbing the sacred mountain and tasting the Heliconian stream which would inspire the creative language that would then "flow" from one's pen or tongue. In *The Progress of Poesy* (1757), for instance, Thomas Gray relied on these allusive clichés, combining Apollonian lyre and sacred waters to produce an image of the origins of poetic genius flowing through time and informing different poetic genres:

> Awake, Æolian lyre, awake,
> And give to rapture all thy trembling strings.
> From Helicon's harmonious springs
> A thousand rills their mazy progress take:
> . . . .
> Now the rich stream of music winds along
> Deep, majestic, smooth, and strong.[115]

The important thing was to taste: if one was not worthy to drink of the sacred stream, one's writing would not "flow" with inspiration. In his translation of *The First Satire of Persius* (1693), Dryden captured the mock-anxiety of the rough-and-tumble satirist whose "rugged numbers" will "claim no part in all the mighty nine":

> I never did on cleft Parnassus dream
> Nor taste the sacred Heliconian stream;
> Nor can remember when my brain, inspired,
> Was by the muses into madness fired.[116]

Drinking from the fountainhead—source of poetic creativity itself—created an internal "flow" within the writer which issued in mellifluous speech or brilliantly inked poetry.

Pope and his contemporaries frequently updated these myths so that classical allusions about writing as "flow" could be transplanted to the modern scene of living English poets. Thus, the Thames and Cooper's Hill replaced classical rivers and mountains, and myths about the sacred streams of poetic inspiration could be replayed on local ground.[117] For the purposes of my argument, however, one feature of this cluster of mythological associations would be linked to pen-penis and ink-semen tropes, namely, that inspired poet would emulate sacred rivers, producing a poetry which had its own liquid "flow." The most famous expression of this idea comes from Denham's "Cooper's Hill":

> O could I flow like thee, and make thy streame
> My great example, as it is my theme!
> Though deep, yet cleare, though Gentle, yet not dull,
> Strong without rage, without ore-flowing full. (ll. 189–92)[118]

By a simple extension, this trope lent itself to writing as a "flow" of other liquids besides water or inky inspiration.

There existed, then, a formal or polite allusiveness used to characterize male writing as a flow of fluids, and an informal deployment which impolitely connected itself to the ink-semen conjunction. Whether writers were aware that "pego" came from the Greek πηγή, a spring or fountain,[119] is difficult to know, but the sense of writing as a flow from the penis was also used satirically. Most typically, the creative potential of semen—embodied sign of male will and pleasure—was replaced comically by urine, as in Pope's hilarious put-down of Leonard Welsted in *The Dunciad*:

> Flow Welsted, flow! Like thine inspirer, Beer,
> Tho' stale, not ripe; tho' thin, yet never clear;
> So sweetly mawkish, and so smoothly dull;
> Heady, not strong; o'erflowing, tho' not full. (*TE* 5: 328, bk. 3: 169–72)

Already anticipated by the pissing contest between Osborne and Curll in the second book, the conceit here depends on a witty parody of Denham's lines from "Cooper's Hill" (above) in which the poetic genius, inspired by sacred waters to write brilliantly flowing verse, becomes—in Pope's outrageous reduction—the dunce-poetaster inspired by beer, ineffectively urinating his own cloudy, dull lines. Some satirical usage went beyond the ink-urine reduction to even more off-putting images of flow, as in John Oldham's scabrous "Upon the Author of the Play call'd *Sodom*," a mock-attack on Rochester: "Vile Sot! Who clapt with Poetry art sick, / And voidst Corruption like a Shanker'd Prick."[120] In this case, ineffective or offensive male writing becomes a flow of infected, venereal pus. Satirical approaches to the flow of ethereal liquids, whether inspired ink or generative sperm, typically transformed the symbolic liquids of creative inspiration into prosaic bodily elimination, messy leakage, or impolite oozings.

Although it is rarely used, a variation of this trope was writing as a flow of menses. Whether writers were aware that "flowers," a term for menstrual discharge, was etymologically suggestive of "flow" or "flux" (from Old French *flueurs* and Latin *fluor*),[121] is also difficult to know, but the metaphor is used sarcastically to figure male writing as an impolite, bloody flow, as in Buckingham's "A Familiar Epistle to Mr. Julian, Secretary to the Muses" (1677):

> Such is our charming Strephon's [Rochester's] outward man;
> His inward parts let those describe who can.
> But, by his monthly flow'rs discharg'd abroad,
> 'Tis full, brim-full, of pastoral and ode.[122]

More properly a subset of the brain-womb procreative metaphors than an instance of yard-wit associations, the male writer and his writing as feminized menstrual flow was a wholly negative association, equating authorial effort with an imperfect female realm of messy flux and fleshy matter.[123]

Returning to the yard-wit examples, however, one can detect a range of values for "flow" which writers used variously to comment on myths of creative inspiration or bathetic failure. Sacred stream, potent semen, humdrum urine, sickly oozings of venereal disease: the hierarchy was clear. After mythological rivers and potent ink-semen, the lower order embodiments of male writing as flow were about mundane or disgusting liquids reflecting the mediocrity or pretension of one's literary opponent. But these satirical modifications captured more than lousy poets and bad writing. "Shanker'd Prick[s]" and urinating pegos were dangerously embodied variations of writing-flow which harbored a destructive energy of larger proportions. As with Pope's Dulness—feminized symbol of writerly hacks and dunces—these figures also represented threats of cultural entropy, the bathetic dissolution of form, and the breakdown of aesthetic distinctions. If pens could be metaphorical penises, male writing was also sometimes associated with a potentially dangerous excess of the body which violated polite forms and social decorum.[124] But whether used positively or satirically, the quill or male writing figured as an ejaculating, urinating, or infected yard also contained a cultural nervousness about the sexualized connection between male body and mind—an uncertainty we have already seen in other contexts. Always lurking near the discursive conjunction of male genitalia, wit, and writing was the possibility of a transgression, here represented as a potentially disruptive "flow" requiring drastic censorship or transformation through some figurative stoppage or castration. Whether flow, overflow, or putrid

flow, the image of penile discharge was also part of the fear of male
genitalia as unwanted truth or dangerous excess

Pego for Poetry: Exchange and Compensation

Despite these hesitations, traffic in images of the yard of wit permeated the literary culture of the period, both as a rhetorical shorthand
for masculinity as male genitalia and as a tactic for assigning public
value to authors and their works. The directly proportionate head-
groin interrelationships were dominant, if not somewhat impolite,
verbal presences in literary and non-literary contexts. But deployments of the inverse model were also in circulation, suggesting that
a man's artistry or intellectual energy could also be constructed as
an exchange of male sexuality for creativity—that one's genitals were
somehow transformed and traded in for art: pego for poetry. The exchange principle here may strike some readers as Freudian, and I
should clarify my position in advance. That male wit might depend
upon a transformed phallicism or a sexual denial was an important
strand in the discursive logic surrounding the conjunction of mind
and genitalia, but Freud's concept of sublimation provides a rather
limited model for what to make of Enlightenment structures. Never
very clearly described by Freud himself, his idea of art as a making
"sublime" of deep-seated libidinal drives lends itself too simplistically
to assumptions of art as neurotic symptom; moreover, the idea does
not account for the historically specific features of male creativity as
it was sexualized in the Enlightenment.[125] Physiologists such as De
Graaf and Willis are a more helpful starting point here.

Both had posited an inverse hydraulic relationship between brain
and testicles in their competing needs for vital matter from the blood
in the production of animal spirits and semen. Ideally, one sought a
healthy balance of fluid use, which usually meant avoiding prolonged
semen retention or mental preoccupation, and achieving periodic
ejaculations and mental rest. This either-or conceptualization led to
notions that genital capacity entailed mental depletion or weakness,
and vice versa. The inverse model was informed by two principles: exchange and compensation. In their simplest literal articulations this
meant a pretty straightforward tit-for-tat, and I have already used
popular equations of idiot (or Irishmen) with over-sized privy member and castrato with gifted voice to illustrate this trade-off or "cost."
In the literary realm, however, the inverse mind-yard nexus included
both a literal and figurative dimension, with the physiology of inverse
hydraulics combining with metaphorical literary usage. In its literal
manifestation, a writer might enjoy a successful phallicism or the tal-

ent of genius but not both at the same time. Or, writing poetry might compensate a dismal sex life. But in its figurative function, the inverse model also had a complex psychological aspect, both at a cultural level and for individual writers. Inverse equations presented the movement from the inner site to its public location as an erotic exchange, removal, or metamorphosis, although the transaction was more a symbolic than an economic one. But for male writers themselves the cost was often psychologized as a loss. Men sometimes wrote bluntly about the implications of such exchange principles, dramatizing trade-offs between heads and groins or voicing their doubts about whether a successful creativity was adequate compensation for some phallic absence or genital deficiency. At the heart of the matter was a deep uncertainty about the symbolic cost to individual writers which resulted from the commodification of male selfhood as sexualized body parts. The exchange and compensation principles of the inverse model certainly called attention to the Johnsonian senses of "traffic" and "commodity," emphasizing the cultural value of male creativity as an eroticized trade in the marketplace of letters. But they also encouraged dramatizations of the exchange as a loss to the author himself, who traded pego for wit only to be traded again as an economic literary item. One result was that writers sometimes psychologized the contradictory connections of their yards to their creative energies by using direct *and* inverse models together in the same work. Another result was that male writers represented the poetical character as simultaneously about sexual power and loss.

The two most obvious examples of inverse formulations were the transformation of male sexual aggression into the feminized art object, and the exchange of creativity for the cut-off penis. Both narratives had a history. In the first instance, classical fables of male creativity as transformed sexuality were available in the Apollo-Daphne story, as well as in Pan-Syrinx and Apollo-Castalia narratives. In each case, sexual pursuit and near-rape undergo a last-second transformation in which phallic aggression and female victim are simultaneously metamorphosed into male creativity and feminized male art-object: thus, Daphne becomes the laurel tree, sacred to Apollo and emblematic of poetic merit; Syrinx becomes the reeds which are associated with the pan-pipe, the shepherd's pastoral flute invented by Pan; Castalia becomes a spring atop Parnassus, whose stream is sacred to Apollo and the Muses. Orpheus is a unique instance of violent sex-into-art, although he is more often associated with a poetic power that subdues and harmonizes all nature. But if one attends to the end of the Orpheus story, another important feature of his symbolic function as poet emerges: following the death of Eurydice, the now homosexual

Orpheus abjures female company and is dismembered by a group of women angered by his sexual rejection of them; at the end, he exists as the bodiless, decapitated, singing poet's head floating down the Hebrus, an unusual example of the displacement of sexuality to a world of art, and an image Pope would use in the epigraph to *The Dunciad in Four Books*. Direct or indirect references to Apollo, Pan, and Orpheus were common in the highly self-conscious poetic world of pastoral poetry, since they functioned variously as figures of the inspired poet, of the harmony of song, and of poetic merit, and as such were predictable patron deities in a pastoral milieu where the singer-poet is omnipresent and the task of mellifluous delivery is frequently the subject itself.[126] But as classical emblems of the origins of poetic inspiration and utterance, these three figures also constituted a fable of male poetic creativity as some sudden metamorphosis of the yard, sexual pursuit, or the male body.

In its most typical enactment, male lust or phallic enterprise became male art or knowledge. To take one example before Pope, Cowley's "Ode Upon Doctor Harvey" (1657) commemorated the recently deceased physiologist with specific reference to the Apollo-Daphne story:

> Coy Nature, (which remain'd though aged grown,
> A beauteous Virgin still, injoy'd by none,
> Nor seen unveil'd by any one)
> When *Harvey*'s violent passion she did see,
> Began to tremble and to flee,
> Took sanctuary, like *Daphne*, in a Tree:
> There *Daphne*'s Lover stopt, and thought it much
> The very Leaves of her to touch:
> But *Harvey* our *Apollo*, stopt not so,
> Into the Bark and Root he after her did go:
> . . . .
> *Harvey* pursues, and keeps her still in sight.
> But as the Deer long hunted, takes a Flood,
> She leap'd at last into the Winding-streams of Blood;[127]

The result is not a physical rape so much as a transformation of "Harvey's" lust into the anatomist's knowledge of the action of the heart and blood.[128] A similar structure is present in Pope's *Windsor-Forest*, especially in the Pan-Lodona episode:

> It chanc'd, as eager of the Chace the Maid
> Beyond the Forest's verdant Limits stray'd,
> *Pan* saw and lov'd, and burning with Desire
> Pursu'd her Flight; her Flight increas'd his Fire.
> . . . .
> And now his shorter Breath with sultry Air
> Pants on her Neck, and fans her parting Hair.

In vain on Father *Thames* she calls for Aid,
Nor could *Diana* help her injur'd Maid.
Faint, breathless, thus she pray'd, nor pray'd in vain;
"Ah *Cynthia*! ah—tho' banish'd from thy Train,
Let me, O let me, to the Shades repair,
My native Shades—there weep, and murmur there."
She said, and melting as in Tears she lay,
In a soft, silver Stream dissolv'd away.

. . . .

In her chast Current oft the Goddess laves,
And with Celestial Tears augments the Waves.
Oft in her Glass the musing Shepherd spies
The headlong Mountains and the downward Skies,
The watry Landskip of the pendant Woods,
And absent Trees that tremble in the Floods; (*TE* 1: 166–69,
ll. 181–84, 195–204, 209–14)

Although part of the larger set of transformations which help to frame
the central concept of *concordia discors* in the poem, Pan's orgasmic desire and potential discharge of semen are converted here through
Lodona's metamorphosis—"In a soft, silver Stream dissolv'd away"—
into the contemplative pastoral world where feminized river is now a
passive mirror of life. As with Harvey-Apollo's "violent passion," Pan's
priapic desire and pursuit modulate suddenly into the sequestered
sylvan world where art (or male intellectual accomplishment) becomes
possible.

Other examples from early in Pope's career show a similar interest
in the inverse model. Written in his early twenties, the seldom-read
"On the Statue of Cleopatra, made into a Fountain by Leo the Tenth"
presents the already-erected statue of the dead Cleopatra as the art
object by which Octavius replaces the sexual possession and subjuga-
tion he desired, and the justly more famous *The Rape of the Lock* comically articulates a similar transformation of the Baron's "rape" by
removing the lock into a world of art—"sudden Star, it shot thro' Air"
(*TE* 2: 205, l. 127)—where it can be commemorated by "quick Poetic
Eyes" (*TE* 2: 204, l. 124). Certainly one can appeal to the fact of Pope's
impoverished sex life and find an understandable inclination in the
young poet to deal with sexual rejection through narratives in which
libidinal drives are displaced into successful art. Or one can emphasize
Pope's specific literary use of Ovid and suggest, as Ronald Paulson
has, that the "Ovidian metamorphoses that Pope evokes are the fables
of the artist (or of art): the initial transformation is at the wish of the
pursued (Lodona, Arabella Fermor, or Lord Petre), the second by the
pursuer himself, who turns Daphne or Syrinx or Arabella into an instrument or product of his art."[129] But these transformations also

resonate within wider cultural domains about the sexualized nature of male wit, which in these examples undergoes a process of displacement and exchange.

An even more striking instance of inverse formulation was the exchange of art or creativity for the cut-off penis. The originary myth is found in Hesiod's story of the castration of Ouranos by Kronos, and the subsequent creation of Aphrodite from the foaming privy members.[130] One aspect of the myth is of course the son's sexual aggression toward the father, but an equally important feature is the birth of love-goddess Aphrodite, representing the creation of the feminized art object from male genitalia. For Pope and his contemporaries, literal castrations were mostly about violent aggression: the castration of Abelard which is remembered in *Eloisa to Abelard*; Pope's own use of the gelded Sporus to attack Hervey, a gesture which much later caused Joseph Warton to say that Pope "has armed his muse with a scalping knife";[131] or shocking accounts of prostitutes severing the penises of johns in red-light areas.[132] The more complex cultural uses of the exchange between cut-off yards or testicles and the creation of wit, love, desire, or art were mainly to be found in responses to the castrato, whose genital deficiency was understood either in terms of a simple exchange in return for the exquisite musical voice, or else as a resonant symbol of social, material, or political power. In a study of the cultural positioning of Farinelli, Thomas A. King has explained in detail how "the missing testicular potency, Farinelli's private power of familial reproduction, has been replaced by the productive power of his music, bringing him fame and political power."[133] As public spectacle, the more successful Italian castrati were visible emblems of the material wealth, social sway, and powerful notoriety that accompanied the inverse traffic of genitalia-for-art.

Indeed, castration or genital deficiency were sometimes linked in these senses to a compensatory talent, despite the fact that such conditions were also attended by a cultural shame and derision. In *A Treatise of All the Degrees and Symptoms of the Venereal Disease* (6th ed., 1708), the ever-colorful John Marten produced an anecdote about castration as a desirable, strategic action in which the pintle was exchanged quite specifically for political prestige:

This kind of *Eunuchism* was, in old Times, a Fashion in *Persia*, and all parts of the *Levant*, being then a Custom there to geld their *Male* Children, and cut off their *Yards* when they were young, to make them capable of Places of Trust and Preferment in Princes Courts, they being by that means often advanc'd, none being held so trusty as they, to look to their Women. Those *Eunuchs* as they grow up, were [sic] a Quill in their Hats, in a way of jolly Ostentation, that it may be known what they are, and think they have made a good Bargain in exchanging the natural Conduit of their Urine for that artificial one, they always placing in the Quill to discharge their Urine, as they have occasion. (358–59)

The yard-mind connection is commodified here in dramatic visual fashion, with substitute penis resting symbolically on the head, compact public emblem of the exchange itself. As a sign both of power and the missing penis, as well as literal prosthesis to piss through, the eunuch's proud quill advertizes the advantages which might accrue to men without yards.[134] Of course, having seen the material advantages of the Italian castrati, or having read accounts such as Marten's, male contemporaries of Pope did not dash out looking to exchange yard or stones for power or cash: eunuchs, limp fumblers, men with little pricks were also still objects of a collective cultural sneer. Nonetheless, a "jolly Ostentation" over the absent tarse—however implausible or unhistorical the account—is an outlandish instance of inverse relationships.

While these either-or structures did not dominate numerically as discourses, their presence called attention to notions of compensation. Johnson's *Dictionary* had defined "To COMPENSATE" as "To recompense; to be equivalent to; to counterballance; to countervail; to make amends for." Certainly a notion of equivalency or equal weight and value is evident in yard-wit formulations such as Sterne's and the frontispiece to *Histoire de Dom B*, where nose and fancy beget one another, or male writing and turgid tarse are interdependent and interchangeable. The examples above would appear to replay these ideas of equivalency, offering narratives in which poetic creativity, art and knowledge, or stature would adequately compensate a frustrated sexual desiring or a missing phallicism. Concepts of compensation and equivalency were used in both serious and comical contexts. Writing to the Blount sisters from a friend's in Windsor forest, the twenty-nine year-old Pope sentimentalized the concept of art as recompense for sexual rejection, hinting decorously that his passions must be relocated in a compensatory world of poetry:

I . . . past the rest of the day in those Woods where I have so often enjoyd—an Author & a Book; and begot such Sons upon the Muses, as I hope will live to see their father what he never was yet, an old and a good Man. I made a Hymn as I past thro' these Groves; it ended with a deep Sigh, which I will not tell you the meaning of.

All hail! once pleasing, once inspiring Shade,
   Scene of my youthful Loves, and happier hours!
Where the kind Muses met me as I stray'd,
   And gently pressd my hand, and said, Be Ours.

> Take all thou e're shalt have, a constant Muse:
>   At Court thou may'st be lik'd, but nothing gain;
> Stocks thou may'st buy & sell, but always lose;
> And love the brightest eyes, but love in vain!
> (*Corr.* 1: 428–29, 13 September 1717)

However much he might desire otherwise, Pope's amorous energies would not be met by the bodies of women such as the Blounts, but rather discharged in the displaced creative space represented by his female Muse. Or, as Sterne's yard-plagued Tristram would put it in a moment of sad reflection: "Oh *Tristram*! *Tristram*! . . . the credit, which will attend thee as an author, shall counterbalance the many evils which have befallen thee as a man" (4: 32, 255). Frustrated sexual desire, impotence, emasculation—all appear to be equivalent to, and can be compensated or counterbalanced, it seems, by wit and the successful creative act.

Not surprisingly, these issues had their comical, ironic, and pornographic versions as well. Readers of Sterne's *Tristram Shandy* will recall the hilarious stop-and-go anecdote of the hot, testicle-shaped chestnut which rolls into the open codpiece of the significantly-named Phutatorious, or "fucker." As the heat moves into his privy parts, "the soul of *Phutatorious*, together with all his ideas, his thoughts, his attention, his imagination, his judgment, resolution, deliberation, ratiocination, memory, fancy, with ten battalions of animal spirits, all tumultuously crouded down, through different defiles and circuits, to the place in danger, leaving all his upper regions, as you may imagine, as empty as my purse" (4: 27, 243). That "purse" was a slang term for scrotum is part of the fun here, but it is in the suggested treatment of this chestnut burn that notions of exchange and compensation are conveniently thrown into relief. Phutatorious's friends advise him to "send to the next printer, and trust your cure to such a simple thing as a soft sheet of paper just come off the press—you need do nothing more than twist it around—The damp paper, quoth *Yorick* . . . has a refreshing coolness in it—yet I presume is no more than the vehicle—and that the oil and lamp-black with which the paper is so strongly impregnated, does the business—Right, said *Eugenius*, and is of any outward application I would venture to recommend the most anodyne and safe" (4: 28, 246). In this now curiously physical application of damp words, text, print to the injured groin of Phutatorius, one can see a sophisticated inverse relationship in which male creativity now compensates in a comically literal way for genital deficiency or some emblematic phallic loss. Funnier yet is that the damp page which will provide comfort and relief to poor Phutatorious's scalded stones or overheated privy member will come from the ninth chapter of his own book which "is at this instant in the press." That the chapter's Latin title means "On the Keeping of Concubines" comically sharpens the point that male creativity—itself so often obsessed with sexual subject matter—can act as direct compensation for male sexual incompetence, injury, or failure. There is an equivalency of genitalia and male art in Sterne's amusing deployment of the inverse model, although it functions in a somewhat different manner than the examples above: here, the absent or blocked phallic energies and desires of the already accomplished male author have been relocated in the sexualized content of his writing, now potentially a form of reparation, consolation, or even treatment. If pintle is the ultimate source of male writing, then written text can come to the rescue of pintle.

The comic literalism of a compensatory logic also informed Oldham's "Upon the Author of the Play call'd *Sodom*," in which male writing becomes a physical sex-aid, a fricatory device whose application to the tarse will help to get it up:

> Thou Moorfields Author! fit for Bawds to quote
> (If Bawds themselves with Honour safe may do't)
> When Suburb-Prentice comes to hire Delight,
> And wants Incentives to dull Appetite,
> There Punk, perhaps, may thy brave works rehearse,
> Frigging the senseless thing with Hand and Verse;
> Which after shall (prefer'd to Dressing-Box)
> Hold Turpentine, and Med'cines for the Pox:
> Or (if I may ordain a Fate more fit
> For such foul, nasty Excrements of Wit)
> May they, condemn'd, to th' publick Jakes be lent,
> (For me, I'd fear the Piles in Vengeance sent
> Should I with them profane my Fundament)
> There bugger wiping Porters when they shite,
> And so thy Book itself turn Sodomite. (*Poems*, ll. 39–53)

Here, the pages of male poetry can be rubbed on "the senseless thing" to achieve tumescence, soothe the venereally infected pintle, or—in an aggressive metaphorical shift—serve as surrogate sodomitical tool. In Oldham's outrageous literalism (as in Sterne's), compensation involves a physically direct exchange: deficient genital condition is relieved by the creativity/text which has replaced the yard; or, the sexual content of the text is now a stand-in or substitute for male genitalia. Equivalent to the penis in these examples, male writing has displaced and now compensates the limp, injured, or absent yard.

However, dramatizations of equivalency and compensation also foregrounded questions about commensurability. As much as wit might compensate a denied sexual desiring or missing phallicism, it was also clear that wit was an inadequate exchange and incommensurate with desiring or male sexual need. Inverse models seemed to promise an equivalency, but were Muses-for-women and poetry-for-pego adequate compensations? One might seek relief by applying pages of damp male writing directly to the yard and stones, but such comical dramatizations also harbored the suspicion that where wit resided the yard would not be found. And it was precisely this fear which haunted the inverse model: wit and yard were interchangeable and interdependent, yes, but could not really be simultaneous. That is, erection and imagination were understood as interdependent and somehow homologous conditions, but they both competed for completion—either an orgasm or the creative act. Like the body's blood as reservoir of raw ingredients for either animal spirits or sperm, sexualized creative energy could issue either in ejaculations or poetry. So often imagined as necessary to male creativity, the yard, cods, and seed were also presented as somehow at odds with a successful wit, related in an either-or tension that also carried with it a cost or some depletion to the male writer. One of the prologues to the Rochesterian *Sodom* is a case in point. Initially similar to the closeted writer-as-masturbator in the *Histoire de Dom B* frontispiece, the author-figure here suggests that, while phallicism generates wit, the erigible yard also threatens to rob or steal from wit, too:

> Our scenes are drawn to th' life in every shape:
> They'll make all pricks to stand, cunts to gape.
> And all young persons, they at such command,
> They'll make both theirs, and old men's pricks to stand.
> The author's prick was so unruly grown
> Whilst writing this, he could not keep it down.
> But thinking on the postures of the play,
> Was forced at last to take his strength away
> And make him sick, by frigging til he spews,
> A sweet revenge, 'cause he disturbs his Muse.
> This prologue certainly had ne'er been made
> Had not the little spirit been allayed.[135]

As in the direct mind-genitalia constructions, the stiffened pego is initially presented as both the source and result of male wit, erection and creativity begetting one another in a happy reciprocity. But then enters the curious contradictory sense that turgid tarse simultaneously interferes with male creativity and must be obviated, removed, transformed, dealt with in some way, if only "by frigging til he spews." Typical of so many inverse equations, there is the suggestion here that yard and writing somehow take away from one another, even as they are symbolically or physiologically related in mutual necessity.

This Rochesterian example predates the commercialized print culture which Pope and his contemporaries learned to navigate, but it testifies to the ambiguous ground upon which male mind-body structures were being built from the late seventeenth century onward. When the newer economic pressures entered and overwhelmed the eighteenth-century literary scene, the uncertainties and ambivalence of inverse models were easily adapted to expressions of concern by men who responded to their vexed cultural status as creators and things of traffic. But these either-or equations were also related to other kinds of contradictory tendencies, particularly in dramatizations of successful wit and writing as simultaneously dependent on both direct *and* inverse connections to male privy members. Indeed, one of the tell-tale features of exchange and compensation contexts was their contrariness, presenting male creativity as the result of both the conjunction *and* separation of mind and genitalia. These either-or/both-and gestures pointed to a kind of collective alienation among male authors who struggled to define the problematic implications of being both a yard of wit and the new wit-phallus-as-commodity.

Contradictory responses manifested themselves variously. The *Sodom* example above captured one sense of the either-or dilemma in which the erect penis simultaneously caused, yet interfered with, wit. Another was the question of whether the yard-wit connection was figuratively chaste or erotic, an issue also rehearsed in tropes of male writer as female Muse. Sometimes it was presented as both at the same time: wit and writing required a mental chastity, and yet the rampant privy member was also the true source of imagination and the poetical character. In a related construction, poetry issued from sexual completion and fulfilment, and yet writing was also the result of erotic frustration and denial. Three brief examples will help make the point. In "Sapho to Phaon" and the *Pastorals*, the young Pope sometimes suggests that poetic creativity is linked to a fulfilled sexuality, but elsewhere in the same poems it seems clear that wit issues from sexual denial and frustration. The pastoral shepherd and poet-figure in "Summer," for instance, who is pointedly named Alexis, complains that his poetic voice is silenced because his sexual passion has been spurned by Daphne: "But now the Reeds shall hang on yonder Tree, / For ever silent, since despis'd by thee" (*TE* 1: 75, ll. 43–44). In "Sapho to Phaon," likewise, Phaon's sexual rejection of Sapho, another of Pope's self-projected poet figures, results in poetic loss and silencing: "Absent from thee, the Poet's Flame expires" (*TE* 1: 404, l. 240). Of course, in these highly stylized and imitative poems, Pope's figure of the pastoral singer whose song cannot be sung at all is something of a generic pose, the *topos* of the spurned shepherd-lover who laments his inability to sing while doing it all the same. The point is that although the poetical character is sometimes associated with phallic mastery or sexual completion— Alexis and Sapho needing the sexual Other to enable poetic creativity, even while uttering a poetry of loss—it is sometimes presented, too, as the result of erotic absence or a frustrated sexual desiring. The result either of carnal impulse or its denial, the poetical character in these cases occupied ambiguous ground, uncertainly positioned as equivalent both to male sexual power and loss.

A third example—in this case of chaste poet amid poetically sexual or phallic contexts—is to be found in the first triad of William Collins's "Ode on the Poetical Character" (1747), where poetic vision is given only to the chosen few, and then only to those whose imagination and genitals have been symbolically dissociated by the girdle of poetry:

> Young *Fancy* thus, to me Divinest Name,
>   To whom, prepar'd and bath'd in Heav'n,
>   The Cest of amplest Pow'r is giv'n:
>   To few the God-like Gift assigns,
>   To gird their blest prophetic Loins,
> And gaze her Visions wild, and feel unmix'd her Flame![136]

And yet, notwithstanding this requirement of chastity, the next triad quickly embraces an allegory of the poetical character now as the result of copulation by "He" (l. 25) and "the lov'd *Enthusiast*" (l. 29), or feminized Fancy, whose sexual congress will produce both the male poet and poetry itself: "And Thou, Thou rich-hair'd Youth of Morn, / And all thy subject Life was born!" (ll. 39–40). Collins did not draw particular attention to the contrariness of these competing accounts of poetic origins, and Pope certainly left his erotic fulfilment/rejection contradiction plain to see. Clearly some sort of cultural tension or paradox is at work in these examples.

Why did authors need to have it both ways? It may well be that the erotic/chaste opposition reflected a larger cultural desire to keep lower-order physical urges in check, transforming the potentially phallic energies of the unruly imagination into politer aesthetic expression. And clearly the possibility that yard and writing somehow took away from one another—in competition, as it were, for ejaculation or the creative act—can be linked to the popularized medical model of an inverse hydraulic relationship between brain and testicles. But simultaneously deployed notions of the poetical character as equivalent to both male sexual power *and* loss—or to the conjunction *and* separation of mind and genitalia—also reflected the deeper concerns of authors themselves. As we have seen, perceptions of manliness were increasingly constructed as vitally informed by the sexual parts. In the literary realm, too, male authors, their poetry, and the poetical character were doubly commodified as the eroticized results of male genitalia and as economic items in the marketplace of letters. We have also seen how the traffic in sexualized male creativity caused a disjunction between concepts of the inner site and public status of creativity. Inverse yard-wit equations and contradictory discursive codes reflected this troubled gap, the sense that male creative power emanated from the privy member only to be repositioned, relinquished, or lost as a sexualized trope in a public traffic. For the male author this constituted an unsatisfying metaphorical logic: having given up pego for creativity, his yard of wit then entered the world of other commodities where it was exchanged for money, reputation, status. Worse yet, the implications of inverse models contained the unsettling proposition that where wit or poetry existed there could not be the distended tarse or a phallic competence. Of course, this was not true in its literal sense, but notions of "cost" or "loss" were another sign of the commercialization of the yard of wit, and a symptom, perhaps, of the self-alienating consequences for male authors as their sexually embodied creativity became a rhetorical commodity.

To summarize: the sexual traffic in male creativity was recorded in a diverse and sometimes unstable set of discourses in which the cultural value of men and their writing was defined. That value had several aspects: as a commercial value in the new marketplace of letters; as a homosocial value defined by one's designated or earned position in a male hierarchy of friends (or foes); as a figurative procreative value; as a phallic value in relation to an eroticized masculinity. Brain-wombs, Muses, quill-yards, and related figures reflected the history of male creativity as it became an item of traffic related to the sexualized male body. The most complex function of these collective tropes was evident in ambiguous representations of the relationship of the interior mind-body origins of creativity to the public location and status of male writing. But underneath was a cultural nervousness about the sexualized connection of male body and mind. Transgressive erections, solitary onanists, dangerous fluids, and castration tropes also pointed to the uneasy implications of the commodification of male selfhood as sexualized body parts. Whether this new somatic system threatened the traditional superiority of mind over body, or harbored an unthinkable democratization of masculinity, or led to impolite locutions in a gathering world of politeness and sensibility, the record of literary usage suggests that the male body was sometimes a dangerous commodity, a not completely governable physical terrain which informed a newer cultural symbolism about masculinity.

Perhaps these discourses also signalled the historical advent of a new Priapus—not quite the invisible phallus of Lacanian and feminist psychoanalysis, and no longer the scarecrow figure from Roman humor— but the new Priapus of the marketplace. Symbolic genitalia were now items of traffic in a capitalist world in which men were the biological evidence of cultural symbols they did not necessarily own and over which they had no certain power. In this early modern separation of

literal and symbolic genitalia we are certainly witnessing the historical origins of our postmodern Phallus, but the gap between individual male bodies and totemic genitalia also explains some of the ambiguity and contradiction informing the examples of this chapter. The yard of wit was not only a literary cliché but part of a public traffic in male bodies where men's creativity and written pages were sent into the world as privy members for sale. In this fracturing of man and his groin, notions of power-loss and doubts about the value of male creativity were predictable. These issues would prove to be spectacularly true in the case of Pope's penis.

this fracturing of man, which is — for (in Thomas A. King's terms) the gendering of man.

Chapter 4

Pope and Male Literary Communities

Alexander Pope dominated his literary world like no one else, and his life and writing—as well as his reputation—were richly imbued with the discourses I have described. Not only did he use both metaphorical economies widely—brain-wombs/Muses, the yard of wit—but he became the most famous public example of the sexual traffic in male creativity. More dramatically than any other writer of the period, Pope's head and groin were put up for sale, a commercial testimony to the newer definition of masculinity as sexualized interiority. And, in an astonishing sequence of texts and illustrations near the end of his life, Pope's penis became a cultural emblem of the conjunction of male bodies, creativity, and market forces.

Many features of Pope's life drew particular attention to the collective idiom I have been describing, especially to the transaction between the inner place of creativity and its public value. At a time when discourses about male mind-genitalia interrelationships were entering the cultural scene, Pope presented an intriguing cluster of characteristics and questions: how was his creative genius linked to his anatomical condition as a hunchback, or to his woeful sex life? Was his talent explained by inverse models in which his authorial skills were compensation for phallic deficiency? For Alexander the Little, questions about the erotically embodied poetical character or the genital origins of creativity were not simply rhetorical matters, and he must have been excruciatingly self-conscious about their personal implications. The various possibilities of the head-groin association were certainly not lost on his enemies, who used them time and again to portray the poet's interior site of creativity in unflattering sexual terms. The shift from inner site to public status was likewise not simply a metaphorical matter in Pope's case. His publishing successes and advantageous deals with booksellers and printers made him one of the bright stars of the new marketplace. Although he pretended a genteel aloofness from the literary capitalism which made him relatively rich—a hypocrisy not lost on his critics, who sometimes painted his Muse as a whore— Pope had greater control over the economic value of his work than perhaps any other writer in the first half of the century. He was thus an exemplary instance of the successful transition from private inspiration to public value. And Pope himself was almost obsessive about the subject, with a good deal of his satire concerned with the entry of male creativity into a public print culture. In these assessments of the new literary economics, Pope's satire of what he deemed the debased value of authors and their books frequently used the reproductive tropes and eroticized allegories I have described. As well, public circulation of the idea of Pope the famous writer—whether as illustrations, lampoons, satirical attacks—made him the most striking modern example of the traffic in male creativity as a commodity and, as we will see, the rhetoric of that circulation was often about creativity and sexualized embodiment. What I am saying is that Pope not only knew and used these discourses, he was also the object of them in the comments of others, and often symbolic of their underlying issues.

This chapter investigates the function of a variety of these collective tropes as they were used by Pope and others to characterize features of his life and career. In his teens and twenties we find him trying to sort out where he fit in relation to older and newer ideas of masculinity and of authors. As his early correspondence with Wycherley makes clear, the social and reputational dimensions of masculinity were immensely important to the young Pope, whose acceptance into the homosocial fold constituted a confirmation of his masculinity *and* his creativity. His double entry into the worlds of manhood and public print was tied together by the affection and condescension of older friends. Correspondents such as Wycherley eroticized Pope's precocious wit in ways that reflected his status and dependency as a younger man. Sometimes Wycherley's tropes were about the yard of wit—affectionately imagining little Alexander as prodigious cocksman—but more often they turned him into a homosocial whore, the sexy young female Muse whose erotic status metaphorically signaled the poet's relative position in the masculine ranks of other men. But during this same period we also find Pope deeply anxious about the creativity-genitalia connection as that might reveal his masculinity as a sexualized interiority. These concerns showed up in competing uses of direct and inverse models, with the poet fantasizing his own powers of imagination variously as randy phallic exploits or an erotic condition plagued by a doubtful reciprocity. Poems such as "Sapho to Phaon" (written when he was nineteen) and "Eloisa to Abelard" (in his late twenties) articulated exchange principles in which letters and poetry were unsatisfactory compensation for missing yards and absent sexual partners. As a young adult, Pope was also considering the "cost" of his creativity as some sexual loss, a sad either-or contest between wit and masculinity. A similar ambiguity informed Pope's early representations of himself and his works in relation to older notions of male creative independence on one hand, and to the economic and professional realities of the newer print culture on the other. Pope was happy enough to have a symbolic commodity value among male friends such as Wycherley, but he was less certain about becoming an item of traffic in the realm of literary commodities. His ambivalence is dramatically present in the differences between the draft and final versions of the preface to his 1717 *Works*, his first major public presentation of himself and collected writings. Draft passages contained images of Pope-the-new-poet as onanist and as whore, tropes which were finally deleted in favor of an image of polite gentleman-author removed from lower-order material realms. From his early teens to his late twenties the gifted young writer's use of the collective discourses focused on matters of public entry and self-dramatization, and on deeper questions about the relationship of his poetry and his sexual embodiment. The first section of this chapter examines Pope's early handling of these central issues.

By his forties, Pope's use of the discourses of creativity-as-sexual-embodiment comprised a much more sophisticated commentary on the new literary commercialism, especially in his *Dunciad*s (1728, 1729, 1742, 1743), which represent one of the period's most elaborate responses to the perceived shift from an elite literary culture to a market apparently less concerned with traditional notions of aesthetic and moral values. The second section of this chapter assesses Pope's deployment of brain-womb and other birthing tropes as they were used to transform Cibber into a reproductive symbol of the new capitalism. As befits the son of Dulness—Queen of poet-dunces, mother of leaden bathos and materialist obsession—Laureate Cibber's (pro)creative head is made the frenzied birthing place where questions of value—aesthetic, moral, social, economic, political—are dramatized as the site of monstrous begetting or oozing misbirth. Against Colley's symbolic crack-brained head, Pope contrasts the troubled cultural position of the true wit (Pope himself) in his compact Ovidian motto which served as doorway into the poem. A rich allusion to poet Orpheus's singing head saved by Apollo from the jaws of a serpent, the motto brilliantly captured what were for Pope the negative aspects of male creativity under the sway of the Moderns: the personal "cost" to the poet, whose voice came at the expense of his sexualized body, with Orphic power exchanged for phallic loss; and the bravely singing voice of the decapitated poet's head trying to survive the unstoppable wave of dull commodities such as Cibber. The brazen brain-womb of Laureate Colley, reproductive symbol of national mediocrity, ironically contrasted the isolated head of the true poet, saved by Apollo—that phallic god of male poetry—only to suffer the indignities of the literary marketplace. In bygone literary cultures the heads of poets might have been

dramatized as the enigmatic sites of gentlemanly removal and powerful creativity, but the heads of male writers were now for sale. The
Dunciad's spoof of Laureate brain-wombs reflected Pope's sense of the
failure of literary value in the new commercialism, but such noble
protests would not exempt him from the sphere which Cibber occupied. Enemies such as Edmund Curll would make money in the traffic
of Pope's literal and symbolic head, and so would friends and execu-
tors such as William Warburton. Perhaps it was ironically right, historically appropriate, that Pope, too, would profit from the very system
he derided, underhandedly exploiting the always-exploitative Curll so
as to publish his carefully selected and edited correspondence in 1737.
Well aware of the new literary traffic, Pope included a medallion of his
own head on the title page.

At forty-six, Pope published his most self-conscious poem about the
yard, although he never openly acknowledged it and the work seldom
features as a significant part of Pope scholarship. *Sober Advice from Ho-*
race, to the Young Gentlemen about Town (1734) featured nothing less than
the talking pego whose soliloquy drew attention to the curious doubleness in a man's experience of what his yard might mean. Comically
obscene, this Horatian imitation was also Pope's most complex reflection on how yard-as-man equations might have been understood by
real men with real penises. The new cultural symbolism for mind-
genitalia connections had powerful influence on how masculinity was
being redefined, but what about masculine subjectivity: how did individual men experience their relationship to such discourses? *Sober Ad-*
vice was one of the few poems—along with John Wilkes's pornographic
Pope-parody, *An Essay on Woman*—to explore such questions from this
perspective. Invoking the enigmatic yard versus mind contexts, both
writers offered a critique of the simpler cultural equations, suggesting
that men were related ambiguously to their own privy members by
the over-reaching imagination. It was not the yard that was enigmatic,
but male desiring. *Sober Advice* presented another version of the yard
of wit, an important historical record of how head-groin relations were
experienced as an inner strife, psychological divisiveness, or some self-
alienating quality.

The final section tells the story of Pope's penis. It was unfortunate
for him that the urinary stricture that began to trouble him by his
early fifties became public knowledge.[1] For literary opponents intent
on satirizing him, or settling scores, or simply cashing in on his notoriety, rumors of the great poet's strangury offered a convenient tidbit
for his enemies and played directly into yard-creativity discourses. In
this case, literal genitals and figurative yard converged, with Pope's
physiological condition perfectly suited to various of the cultural symbolisms we have been examining. Pope had figured in literary yard-

wars well before this time, the object of satirical belittlement in which his creative talents were figured as the tiny penis, impotent fumbler, premature ejaculator, pathetic masturbator, or the spurned lover. And Pope was not above using the same tropes to attack his enemies, as in the memorable Hervey-castrate figure of *An Epistle to Dr. Arbuthnot*, written in his mid-forties. The tradition of literary yard-attacks was a well-recognized strategy, a common cultural language which was part of the genitalia-creativity associations. But of the 158 published attacks on Pope listed in J. V. Guerinot's survey,[2] it was Colley Cibber's 1742 *A Letter from Mr. Cibber to Mr. Pope, Inquiring into the Motives that might induce him in his Satyrical Works, to be so frequently fond of Mr. Cibber's Name* that was perhaps the most devastating and embarrassing reference to the poet's penis. Protesting Pope's references to him in *The New Dunciad* of 1742, the now seventy year-old Cibber used three pages of his *Letter* to recall a sexual adventure of 1714 or 1715 in which he, Pope (then in his mid-twenties), the young Lord Warwick, and another unnamed male visited a whorehouse. According to Cibber, prankster Warwick was keen to see what sort of cocksman the diminutive poet would turn out to be. At the critical moment, little Alexander's frail lust is interrupted when Cibber rushes into the room and pulls Pope off the belly of a prostitute. The anecdote presented the poet as sexually incompetent, physically disproportionate to the task, and utterly laughable as a man. Within days, four engravings and a half-dozen other pamphlets were in circulation, all capitalizing on the whorehouse story. Whether Cibber was telling the truth is not particularly important to my argument, but Pope's reaction is: pained, humiliated, and no doubt infuriated by this public attack on his virility, Pope retaliated quickly by making Cibber the chief dunce in his 1743 *The Dunciad in Four Books*.[3]

The value of Cibber's *Letter* for the kind of discursive history I am recounting here is that it contained the intersecting assumptions of several discourses we have already examined. Indeed, if one searched the period for a paradigmatic cultural moment which publicly set forth both literal and figurative implications of the juncture of male creativity and sexuality—of heads and groins—Cibber's scandalous anecdote stands out. Here, poet-yard equations moved out of figurative domains and into the seedy closets of brothels where real bodies and pintles became vehicles of a complex literary symbolism. Cibber's *Letter* and the texts and illustrations which followed together focused the cultural intersection of male sexuality, creativity, marketplace competition, and questions of literary value. Pope's penis and his wit were put in circulation as interchangeable commodities, as a profitable traffic in images and discourses about the genital origins of the "manly" and the "literary." However hurtful it must have been to Pope, this public attention to his groin was also an historical confirmation of sorts: the new Priapus of the literary marketplace had indeed arrived. Not Alexander Pope, the great poet of Twickenham, but the yard of wit, that commercial symbol of men's bodies and their imaginations. Alexander the Little proved to be its first modern embodiment.

The Early Pope:
Homosocial Whore, Phallic Ambiguity, Onanism

From his teens to his late twenties when he offered his 1717 *Works* to the world, we see the young Pope defining his relationship to these discourses in three important contexts: (1) how his entry into the adult world of male friends and other writers would be valued; (2) how he and others might understand the troubled connection of his writing and his sexual body; (3) how he would manipulate his self-image as a literary commodity. The earliest appearances of the sexualized tropes for male creativity were focused on these questions. This section examines, in turn, the important homosocial milieu into which the precocious Alexander was admitted as a serious poet, early poems and letters which register his psychological sense of the "cost" of wit in sexual terms, and his artful revisions of the preface to his 1717 *Works* as he adopted the elitist pose of the autonomous gentleman-author. Above all, young Pope wanted to be accepted by older men, and I examine first the creativity-sexuality discourses used by his male friends.

Male friendship as it was experienced and understood by Pope's contemporaries was an important reality commonly present at the conjunction of rank, literary stature, politics, sexuality, and male hierarchy. The central role of older male friends in Pope's life is well known, and his correspondence testifies in all sorts of ways to the deep emotional loyalty to the men he loved, friends who helped anchor the personal and public identities to which he aspired. From about 1704 to his majority in 1709 (that is, from early puberty to his later teens and early adulthood), Alexander was drawn to adult male authority figures who, besides providing him encouragement as a writer, represented a positive range of adult male competence in various realms: literary, physical, political, social, and sexual. Some gave father-like approval, some corrected his verses, others opened doors to social and literary networks, and still others enabled him to relocate his interests from a rural world of pious parental governance to the sophisticated urban environment of Will's coffee house and the male enclave of wit.

These men—John Caryll, William Wycherley, William Walsh, Sir William Trumbull, Henry Cromwell—represented a homosocial elite to the precocious but deferential young Alexander, who was only too happy to be invited to enter an adult male world. These older friends influenced how he experienced his poetic aspirations as an essential aspect of his masculinity and, predictably, Pope's sense of a sexualized poetical character was also informed by these contacts as an adolescent and young adult. Of particular significance are the ways that Pope's eroticized creativity was located in the context of male friends, and I want briefly to examine evidence from the Pope-Wycherley correspondence that calls attention to the convergence of homosocial affection, dependency, hierarchy, and the discourses of a sexualized creativity as they defined Pope's auspicious beginnings as a writer.

Their friendship included a kind of hero-worship by the diminutive sixteen year-old: after all, "Wycherley was Mr. Pope's first poet-friend,"[4] and striking up a relationship with a masculine literary figure as noteworthy as Wycherley was surely a dazzling and satisfying experience for the younger poet. As he confessed to Cromwell, "my Dog . . . follows me about as constantly here in the Country, as I was us'd to do Mr W. in the Towne" (*Corr.* 1: 73, 19 October 1709). The epistolary faces the young Pope and the senior Wycherley prepared for one another in the early eighteenth century were characterized by mutual flattery, polite diffidence, much witty posturing and whipping-up of the *bon mot*, bawdy quips from the old *roué* to the young would-be chaser-of-maidenheads, and a good deal of talk about their poetic abilities, especially Pope's. The verbal tokens of epicoene friendship were frequent, relying on equations of friend-as-mistress or friendship as sexual love. Especially noteworthy, however, was the extent to which discussions of Pope's poetic abilities were wittily positioned by Wycherley in such a way as to present the teenager as the sexually willing female or as the adolescent male whose sexuality depended on the older male. In every case where an eroticized exchange was present, the senior Wycherley cleverly confirmed his status as the dominant masculinity, graciously flattering the up-and-coming young genius, but consistently appropriating the young man's sexualized creativity in ways designed to emphasize their relative differences in rank, social power, and age.

Such is the case in a letter in which Alexander's talents were presented as a copulatory pleasure with his female Muse. This discourse informed an early letter from the old dramatist to the sixteen-year-old poet in which the young poet-as-yard is located in an erotic triangle overseen by Wycherley, who finally sponsors and facilitates the adolescent's metaphorical phallic abilities:

As to my enquiry after your Intrigues with the *Muses*, you may allow me to make it, since no old Man can give so young, so great, and able a Favourite of theirs, Jealousy. I am, in my Enquiry, like old Sir *Bernard Gascoign*, who us'd to say, That when he was grown too old to have his Visits admitted alone by the Ladies, he always took along with him a young Man, to ensure his Welcome to them; who, had he come alone had been rejected, only because his Visits were not scandalous to them. So I am (like an old Rook, who is ruin'd by Gaming) forc'd to live on the good Fortune of the pushing young Men, whose Fancies are so vigorous, that they ensure their Success in their Adventures with the Muses, by their Strength of Imagination. (*Corr.* 1: 6–7, 29 March 1705)

Wycherley's recurrent pose as one of those "old Impotent Fumblers" (*Corr.* 1: 62, Wycherley to Pope, 23 May 1709) who approaches the women-Muses voyeuristically through the phallic imagination of the "pushing" young stud, certainly emphasizes Pope's male wit as the potent and "vigorous" yard. But the witty role-playing also insinuates that the younger man will function as a surrogate cock old Wycherley would use to fuck the ladies. That is, the solicitous over-the-hill rake can participate in a fantasized erotic triangle which allows him a vicarious share of the female Muse and a certain erotic claim over his phallic surrogate, the lusty young friend. However much Wycherley's analogy was meant as flattery, what lingers is his patronizing appropriation of the young Pope's promising poetic abilities, which are metaphorized as a potential form of male sexual energy in turn used to define the young writer's status as the dependent younger male.

Wycherley's flattery throws into relief the structures that so influenced the poet's early sense of his own creativity: that the acceptance and approval of his writing by male friends would be characterized as a kind of sexual dependency; that his creative energies would be typically eroticized so as to reflect his complex and contradictory status as a man—younger but prodigiously talented, physically limited but homosocially accepted, little Alexander but manly writer; in short, that the poetical character was an articulation of his masculinity, just as the eroticized tropes about his creativity were used to define his reputation and social position as a man. Pope certainly benefitted from his patronized entry into adult male circles where his wit and personal worth conferred upon him a symbolic commodity value among friends. But his homosocial value was also linked, however subtly, to the literary capitalism which was emerging, and so were the creativity-sexuality discourses. This is evident in a letter from Wycherley to Pope in which both are presented as female Muses—one an old bawd, the other a fetching country lass—together seeking to outdo their female counterparts at court. The biographical context of the letter is Pope's *Pastorals*, which were to come out in Tonson's *Miscellany* of 1709:

Your Pastoral Muse outshines, in her modest and natural dress, all *Apollo*'s Court-Ladies, in their more artful, labour'd, and costly Finery; therefore I am glad to find by your Letter, you design your Country-beauty of a Muse shall appear at Court and in Publick; to outshine all the farded, lewd, confident, affected, Town-dowdies, who aim at being honour'd only to their Shame: But her artful Innocence (on the contrary) will gain more Honour as she becomes more Publick; and in spite of Custom will bring Modesty again into Fashion, or at least make her Sister-rivals of this Age, blush for Spite, if not for Shame. . . . So that let your Country-gentlewoman appear when she will in the World, my old worn-out Jade of a lost Reputation, shall be her attendant into it, to procure her Admirers; as an old Whore who can get no more Friends of her own, bawds for others, to make Sport or Pleasure yet, one way or other, for Mankind. I approve of your making *Tonson* your Muse's Introductor into the World, or Master of the Ceremonies, who has been so long a Pimp, or Gentleman-Usher to the Muses. (*Corr.* 1: 49–50, 13 May 1708)

Wycherley is making clear the affectionate protection the new writer can count on from his older male friend, but the letter also hints at the connection between the homosocial traffic in creativity—however friendly and symbolic—and the economic value of male wit. The young poet's foray into public print is likened to the entry of the innocent but sexually-attractive and available young woman into the world. And, in this precarious urban place where country modesty will be overtaken sooner or later, the "artful Innocence" of Pope's "Country-beauty" is best left to bawd Wycherley, it seems, who will introduce her, protect her, show her off, and broker her favor with the town for "Sport or Pleasure." The inclusion of Tonson as "Pimp" extends the question of value from the hierarchy of male friends, where one's sexual attractions privately please, to the public realm of booksellers and printers where one's fetching Muse entered the world of commodities in which books and young female bodies alike were bought and sold. Young Pope had both a homosocial and an economic value as a wit, in both cases imaged here as an entry into whoredom. Interestingly, Pope downplayed this second sense of the idea—Muse-prostitute in the market—preferring to be the homosocial whore.

In replies to Wycherley, Pope did not protest this metaphorical role, and in fact participated willingly in the sexual discourses. One example in particular captures the younger poet's deferential sense of his own place within both the friendship and the larger context of a homosocial hierarchy. A day before his twenty-first birthday Pope responded to Wycherley's congratulations on the successful publication and reception of the *Pastorals*, using two revealing images of dependency, one patronal and the other sexual:

As to the success which you say my part [publication of the *Pastorals* in Tonson's *Miscellany*] has met with, it is to be attributed to what you were pleas'd to say of me to the World; which you do well to call your *Prophecy*, since whatever is said in my favour, must be a Prediction of things that are not yet; you, like a true Godfather, engage on my part for much more than ever I can perform. My Pastoral Muse, like other Country Girls, is but out of Countenance, by what you Courtiers say to her; yet I hope you would not deceive me too far, as knowing that a young Scribler's vanity needs no Recruits from abroad. (*Corr.* 1: 60, 20 May 1709)

The young scribbler first imagines himself as the dependent godson whose identity is authorized by the loving adult father-figure; and then, in an epicoene projection, Pope takes on the role of the naive country girl (not unlike Wycherley's Margery Pinchwife) whose head is turned by the strategic sweet-talk of urban rakes. Pope did not pursue the economic implication of the sexual analogy here—predatory courtiers who will ultimately determine her fate and her market-value—but there is a quiet acknowledgment that his entry into the social world of men *and* into print shared an eroticized metaphorical protocol. Young Pope was content to be Wycherley's homosocial whore in these flattering exchanges where power relations and hierarchy were signaled because friendly correspondence of this sort offered him the social and psychological acceptance he so dearly needed in his teens. Images of the prostituted female Muse in the public realm of literary economics lurked in the background of these epistolary exchanges, but for up-and-coming Alexander it was the homosocial erotics of his creativity that he was happy to emphasize. Moreover, his commodity value as younger poet-friend was an important authentication of his masculinity at a time when the effects of his spinal tuberculosis were already placing him outside the boundaries of a normal physicality.

While the young Pope happily earned his entry into the world of adult males—his poetic talents a marker of his status as a man—he was also pondering the connections of his sexuality and body to the inner site of his wit. The relationship of a masculine self to an interiorized sexuality was of considerable concern to him, with direct and inverse models together suggesting Alexander's doubts and anxiety about how to characterize the head-groin association in his own case. There are instances of Pope playing the rake, writing bluntly about the equivalency of creativity and intercourse. In a letter to friend Cromwell, for example, the twenty-two year-old explains that he is sexually aroused in the presence of Teresa and Martha Blount:

and that every moment my Eyes are employed upon this paper, they are taken off from Two of the finest faces in the Universe: For I am at this instant placd betwixt Two such Ladies that in good faith 'tis all I'm able to do, to keep my self in my [fore]Skin. *He! Monsieur Cromvell! Entendez-vous bien?*. . . . How gladly wou'd I give all I am worth, that is to say, my *Pastorals* for *one* of their *Maidenheads*, & my *Essay* for the other? I wou'd lay out all my *Poetry* in *Love*; an *Original* for a *Lady*, & a *Translation* for a *Waiting Maid*! And now (since you find what a blessed disposition I am in)

> Tell me, by all the melting joys of Love,
> By the warm Transports & entrancing Langours,
> By the soft Fannings of the wafting sheets,
> By the dear Tremblings of the Bed of Bliss;
> By all these tender Adjurations tell me,
> —Am I not fit to write a Tragedy? (*Corr.* 1: 137–38, 21 December 1711)

Interesting here is the association of his genital arousal and poetry. Not only are "the dear Tremblings" of erotic stimulation the signs and symptoms of the poetic itch, but poems themselves become the equivalent of maidenheads and sexual satisfaction in a crude inter- changeability. Pope is assuming a libertine posture, certainly—the ex- aggerated sexual swagger he sometimes used in letters to Cromwell and Wycherley[5]—but the comical equation of erection with creative spark, or the simple transaction of writing for intercourse, also sug- gests that for Pope the creative imagination and phallic urges were di- rectly linked, originating in the same enigmatic region where mind and body met. The letter hinted, too, that he would gladly trade his wit for use of the sexual female body.

This lingering desire for a straight exchange—poems for maidenheads—draws attention to the obvious fact that Pope was not always so confident in his use of the direct mode, and this is also true in his figurative representations of the yard of wit. We have seen how the male author's brain could be portrayed as an erotic site where he copulated with his female Muse to engender art, and where the im- plied phallicism and willingness of the sexy Muse were guarantors of a successful creativity. The twenty-three year-old Alexander used this trope in a letter to Cromwell in which he fantasizes his erotic desire and pursuit of the female Muse:

I take up with the Muses for want of your better Company: the Muses, *Quae nobiscum pernoctant, peregrinantur, rusticantur* [from Cicero's *Pro Archia*, 7: 16: "Through the night-watches, on all our journeying, and in our hours of coun- try ease, it is our unfailing companion"]. Those Aeriall Ladies just discover to me enough of their Beauties to urge my Pursuit, and draw me on in a wan- dring Maze of Thought, still in hopes (& only in hopes) of attaining those fa- vors from 'em, which they confer on their more happy admirers elsewhere. We grasp some more beautiful Idea in our Brain, than our Endeavors to ex- press it can set to the view of others; & still do but labour to fall short of our first Imagination. The gay Colouring which Fancy gave to our Design at the first transient glance we had of it, goes off in the Execution; like those various Figures in the gilded Clouds, which while we gaze long upon, to separate the Parts of each imaginary Image, the whole faints before the Eye, & decays into Confusion. (*Corr.* 1: 135, 12 November 1711)

Pope pursues the sexually alluring Muses who coyly express their erotic interest. But while he is thus teased into eager chase, he doubts any successful conclusion, imagining instead that the Muses will pro- voke his desire but then fade away as he tries to possess them. Pope concludes the paragraph by shifting away from the erotic analogy to a version of problematic "labour" in which the brain's sexualized concep- tion is ruined by a faulty and frustrated execution: no copulatory crea- tivity with female Muses here; no immaculate patriarchal conception and Athena birth; but rather a shape-shifting confusion. In Pope's fantasy of transformed sexuality in the displaced world of art, the eroticized Muses turn out to be as ineffable or hard to come by as objects of desire in the real world. Even the compensatory site of creativity seems to contain a principle of sexual loss, with coy but provocative Muses urging the poet's sexual pursuit without yielding the final favor. Although Pope's analogy is primarily about the difficulties of transforming creative conception into successful execution, the passage nevertheless participates in the direct yard-wit mode, demonstrating young Pope's familiarity with the discourses as well as his own anxieties about the connection of his poetry to his penis.

These deployments of the direct mode were not the only expressions of Pope's phallic ambiguities. I have already pointed out his early use of direct and inverse wit-genitalia equations in the same work ("Sapho to Phaon," *Pastorals*) in which poetry and creative inspiration depended on both phallic satisfaction *and* sexual denial. His contradictory dramatizations of how the poetical character is the product of his sexually embodied maleness owes something to the larger cultural vocabulary we examined at the end of last chapter, but it is symptomatic as well of his unhappy anatomical condition. As is well known, the onset of Pott's disease arrested his growth at four feet six inches and gradually turned him into a hunchback. The initial attacks occurred when he was about twelve and lasted at least four years. Although we have no record of how far his spinal curvature had advanced during this severe illness from about 1700 to 1704, it would seem that by his late teens Pope's physical appearance had been affected by the tubercular infection, and that he had entered into the realm of periodic ill health whose worst moments would reduce him almost to complete invalidism. The heterosexual consequences of his disability have been put plainly by Maynard Mack: "no one knew better than he did that women either pitied him or patronized him. They were not standing in line to marry him or go to bed with him."[6] With damage to his body, self-image, and sense of his own developing masculinity, young Alexander would be confronted with the inevitable recognition that the consequences of his diminutive stature and deformed body entailed a life of erotic unfulfillment. These biographical dimensions of Pope's heterosexual disappointments are well known, with the figure of the sexually-spurned Pope a scholarly commonplace. Sexually attracted to the Blount sisters Teresa and Martha from his late teens, and then to the clever and worldly Lady Mary Wortley Montagu in his twenties, Pope's come-ons and sexual teases were politely refused. His playing the rake in letters to Wycherley and Cromwell would sadly contrast his doubts in other letters about his masculine presence, physical abilities, and sexual attractiveness to women.

But these anxieties also found a ready-made vehicle in head-groin discourses in which Pope's phallic insecurities were played out in dramas of problematic exchange and compensation. Ambiguities about the yard-creativity nexus are particularly evident in Pope's early treatments of the idea of art-for-sex or poetry-for-penis, as in his two ventriloquized poems, "Sapho to Phaon" and "Eloisa to Abelard"—fantasies of sexually-desirous female speakers seeking the absent male or yard. In the first, written when Pope was in his late teens, poet Sapho articulates the power of the imagination as compensation: "When Fancy gives what Absence takes away" (*TE* 1: 400, l. 146). And a decade later, in almost identical words, Pope's Eloisa mournfully balances letters and imaginative worlds against the absent Abelard and his castrated penis: "Fancy restores what vengeance snatch'd away" (*TE* 2: 317, l. 226). In both cases, Pope's impersonation of transgressive female desire for the absent male body is so heightened that its compensatory value for sexual denial is obvious. John Hughes's *Letters of Abelard and Heloise*, which Pope knew and used, had already provided an epistolary dramatization of language and art as compensation for missing penises and love partners. In a letter to a male friend, Abelard complains that "in short, without losing my Life, I lost my Manhood. I was punished indeed in the offending Part; the Desire was left me, but not the Possibility of satisfying the Passion." For Heloise and Abelard both, their letters—like other art forms—will compensate their separation and the missing yard:

If a Picture, which is but a mute Representation of an Object, can give such Pleasure, what cannot Letters inspire? They have Souls, they can Speak. . . . In spite of your Misfortunes, you may be what you please in your Letter. Letters were first invented for comforting such solitary Wretches as myself. Having lost the substantial Pleasures of seeing and possessing you, I shall in some Measure compensate this Loss, by the Satisfaction I shall find in your Writing.[7]

While not exactly a restoration of the missing phallic partner, language itself and its imaginative resources have the power to counterbalance or make amends for the absent yard, as Pope's Eloisa also recognizes:

Come! with thy looks, thy words, relieve my woe;
Those still at least are left thee to bestow.
. . . .
Give all thou canst—and let me dream the rest. (*TE* 2: 309, ll. 119–20, 124)

However, as I have already suggested, these dramatizations of equivalency and compensation also come with hesitation about commensurability. As much as wit might compensate a denied sexual desiring or missing phallicism, there is a suspicion that wit is also an

inadequate exchange. A fundamental thematic issue in "Eloisa to
Abelard" turns around Eloisa's frustrated dependence on words, language, poetry as substitute for the absent Abelard and his castrated
penis. Fancy might replace lover and phallus with "Desires compos'd"
(*TE* 2: 316, l. 213)—Pope's clever pun describing the "blameless
Vestal's lot" (*TE* 2: 315, l. 207)—but only momentarily. Despite night-
dreams filled with sexual promise, the imagined Abelard slips away
with wakefulness: "I wake—no more I hear, no more I view, . . . / I
stretch my empty arms; it glides away" (*TE* 2: 318, ll. 235–38). These
anxieties are transferred more specifically to questions of poetic compensation at the end of the poem, where the entry of "some future
Bard" who will poeticize their story catapults the reader out of the fic-
tional realm of dramatic monologue onto another level—historical,
autobiographical—where Pope's own unrequited passion for Lady Mary
Wortley Montagu or Teresa Blount, or both, is now made equivalent
to Eloisa's situation:

> And sure if fate some future Bard shall join
> In sad similitude of griefs to mine,
> Condemn'd whole years in absence to deplore,
> And image charms he must behold no more,
> Such if there be, who loves so long, so well;
> Let him our sad, our tender story tell; (*TE* 2: 327, ll. 359–64)

By ending the poem with a thinly-disguised gesture toward his own
life, Pope draws his persona and reader into the non-fictional, real
world where poet and poem must confront their own acts of desire
and sexual longing. Despite Eloisa's final fantasy of poetic memorialization, the poem's closure draws attention to the problematic exchange which poetry might offer in an historical world of sexual and
emotional uncertainty. In this revealing moment, where ideals of the
sustaining language of poetry and the enduring works of poets are
pressed uncomfortably against the erotic disappointments of real life,
the twenty-eight-year-old poet also intimates that the exchange is inadequate, a cold comfort for lingering desire. Certainly we ought not
to underestimate the importance, for Pope, of skilled poetic accomplishment as compensation for phallic denial, but neither can we ignore or minimize the passionately felt sexual losses which this poem
and its ending throw into relief. Pope's female impersonations—not
only of Eloisa but also of Sapho—in which a woman-as-poet figure
searches in vain for the yard or a male sexuality which is already absent, reflect his sense of the inadequacy of pen and poetry as substi-
tutes for the phallus and a male body of fleshly desire. Poems such as
these suggest the poet's combined fears that wit's power of language
does not counterbalance or make amends for Abelard's cut off yard or

Pope's unmet libidinal energies, and that he will fail to generate a poetic language that is commensurate with his physical desiring. Moreover, his narrative transvestism links these doubts about the potency
and efficacy of poetic language to the plight of female speech, which
in the cases of Eloisa and Sapho is a paradoxically silent and unheeded language internalized as tears or sexual frustration. For Pope,
the exchange of male genitalia for the poetical character was not always understood as equivalent, and, despite the rakish jocularity of his
earlier letter to Cromwell, in which Pope desired the trade of "my *Pastorals* for *one* of their *Maidenheads*, & my *Essay* for the other," there was
also a somber recognition that the yard-wit traffic was not likely to be
reversed. The movement from the sexual male body to the compensatory creative space was often framed as an irreversible one, with an
accompanying anxiety about his poetry as stifled virility, dysfunctional
penis, or the missing yard.

Pope's anxieties about the sexualized embodiment of his creativity
ran deep in "Eloisa to Abelard," especially in his almost perverse use
of the testicles-text-castration trope. After 1720, Pope's published versions of the poem expurgated a couplet that had formerly stood between lines 258 and 259 of the text we now read:

> Come *Abelard*! for what hast thou to dread?
> The torch of *Venus* burns not for the dead;
> [Cut from the root my perish'd joys I see,
> And love's warm tyde for ever stopt in thee.]
> Nature stands check'd; Religion disapproves;
> Ev'n thou art cold—yet *Eloisa* loves. (*TE* 2: 319, ll. 257–60)

Editor Geoffrey Tillotson is likely correct to suggest that "Pope may
have withdrawn this couplet because of Concanen's citing it [in his
1728 *Supplement to the Profound* in response to Pope's *Peri Bathous*] as an
instance of his pruriency" (*TE* 2: 319). But the self-censoring also represents a curious double gelding: not only does Pope engage in a figurative self-castration by removing the couplet from post-1720 publications
of the poem, he also cuts out lines that most closely acknowledge the
impolite scene of Abelard's literal castration. The flowing "warm tyde"
of sperm-ink—fond traces of Eloisa's coital memories and Pope's own
sexual desires for Lady Mary and Teresa Blount—is removed in this
editorial castration, "cut from the root" in the interests of Pope's passionate but polite self-imaging. That Pope would expurgate his own
lines about castration reflects not only an uneasiness about direct reference to male genitalia as source of creative pleasure, but also an uneasiness about revealing too openly the site where his writing could be
"check'd" or "Cut." Always sensitive to criticism, Pope was willing to
mutilate his own poem, placing the intimate convergence of testicles,

yard-quill, and ink-semen off stage. In a remarkable retreat from his own subject—linked to larger cultural fears about a transgressive penile discharge—Pope's hesitation here is part of several gestures in his teens and twenties in which his doubts and anxieties about his masculinity as a sexualized interiority showed up in poems as an ambiguity at the genital site where his creativity was problematically located. For Alexander the Little, yard-wit reciprocities were troubled by worries of loss, incommensurability, and physical vulnerability.

The most striking example of young Pope's problematic use of the discourses—direct versus inverse modes, either-or ambiguities—is found in an epigram written in his own hand on the verso of the autograph manuscript of "Sapho to Phaon." The poet was in his late teens; the obscene lines were apparently intended for the eyes of his womanizing friend, Henry Cromwell:

> Poor Gellius keeps or rather starves two Maids,
> Seldome he feeds, but often f[uck]s ye Jades.
> He stops one Mouth that tother may not mutter
> So what they want in Bread, they have in Butter.[8]

The misogynistic hint of forced fellatio—effected through the not-so-subtle equivalence of upper and nether mouths—might have been intended as a clever locker-room gesture. But this salacious epigram is also significant for the tension it creates with the poem's subject matter, which together are emblematic of the phallic ambiguity haunting the early Pope. While teenaged Alexander uses poet Sapho's monologue to mourn the loss of an absent male sexuality and the inefficacy of poetry as compensation, his epigram enfolds the poem's doubts within a male graffiti of phallic mastery to be shared with Cromwell. This paradoxical gesture shares in the larger cultural uncertainty about the status of male creativity, but its main significance here is autobiographical. In this example, Pope's doubts about exchange and compensation are situated within the inner frame of the poem's subject matter, where Sapho articulates the uncertain relationship of absent pintle and erotic satisfaction to the inner site of poetic creativity. Against this, and positioned on the outer frame, the bawdy epigraph confidently offers a public phallicism as the poet's friendly signature of his talents. Although this boghouse witticism was not intended for public circulation beyond Cromwell, its very presence is emblematic of the phallic ambiguity I have been describing: at the content level of desirous poet Sapho and missing lover, the implications of yard-wit equations leave the disturbing possibility that male creativity may also be the site of erotic loss, impotence, emasculation; at the outer frame of the epigraph, which serves as threshold commentary for a reader's entrance to the poem, successful poet and master cocksman are linked interdependently as interchangeable states. Together, poem and epi-gram capture young Pope's deep anxieties about his yard and wit, with the poetical character simultaneously juxtaposed with notions of male sexual aggression and failure, of power and loss.

As the various examples of this section suggest, many aspects of Pope's early career were perfectly suited to the use of the creativity-sexuality discourses, both privately as a young male seeking admission into powerful homosocial circles, and professionally as he received greater attention as the promising new poet. The collective tropes linked his budding wit to issues of his masculinity, both as a reputational mat-ter of stature among other men and as an interiorized question about his genitalia. Interestingly, these two aspects would converge around Pope's uncertain sense of how to present himself as a literary com-modity. Published in 1717 when he was twenty-nine, the first collected edition of his *Works* also contained his first public self-representation as a writer in his carefully revised and polished preface.[9] Comparis-ons of Pope's draft and final versions of the preface reveal his uneasi-ness about how to shape an image of himself as participant in the commercialized republic of letters. The draft preface draws on tropes of writer as onanist to capture a sense of the young poet's inspired and isolated inner creativity, and also of the writer as prostitute in the mar-ketplace of other commodities. But Pope's careful revisions removed these discursive fingerprints from the scene, replacing them with an artfully contrived image as gentleman-poet happily removed from ve-nal and venereal realms to a homosocial world of approving male friends.

Let's look first at his final version. Kept is the headpiece of Apollo and the nine Muses (see Figure 5), introducing Pope's creative ener-gies within a familiar reproductive allegory of the origins of the prom-ising son-poet. The private site of male creativity is mythologized in this visual conceit, tastefully positioned within a cliché about super-natural lineage. Also kept in the final text are the well-known lines on the relationship of poetic undertaking to a hard-to-please public: "The life of a Wit is a warfare upon earth; and the present spirit of the learned world is such, that to attempt to serve it (any way) one must have the constancy of a martyr, and a resolution to suffer for its sake" (*TE* 1: 6). Together, the visual and textual images emphasize the idea of dignified distance and forbearance rather than self as literary com-modity: poet-son inspired within a fanciful place of heavenly removal and etherial begetting; patiently suffering author-genius who humbly submits to the slings and arrows of a demanding public. Against the latter image, Pope presents his own preferred model of public ap-proval as a question of being "commended by the best and most know-ing," of "the privilege of being admitted into the best company" (*TE* 1:

5–6). Blending ideas of an elite male readership and friendship, Pope says "I publish'd because I was told I might please such as it was a credit to please" (*TE* 1: 6). And for Pope, "credit" will not be allowed to tilt here toward ideas of capitalist competition and economic value, but rather toward a friendly acceptance into the homosocial community at large, and especially into the smaller circle of knowing men.

Deletions reveal a completely different side to how Pope first approached his self-imaging. His use of sexual and genital tropes—both autoerotic and autogenetic—suggest that his initial strategy was to characterize his creativity as removed from the world of others, pleasurably isolated within the inner site of his imagination. Originally appearing in the same paragraph as the images of the wit as warfare and martyr, a cancelled passage portrays young Pope's writerly enthusiasm with language recalling the masturbatory contexts I examined earlier: "But I was too young to resist temptations & I was very innocently in love with myself wn I began to write & my first productions were the children of Self-Love upon Innocence. . . . I had then too much fondness to judge of my productions and had too much judgmt to be pleased" (Mack, 104, note 11). Although he stresses youthful innocence and lack of judgement, Pope's "children of Self-Love" conflates ideas of self-generation and solo eroticism in relatively direct fashion. In another deleted passage one paragraph further on, the autogenetic and autoerotic ideas are developed further: "Tis a SERIOUS 'vast' happiness to HAVE 'possess' the pleasures of the Head, the only pleasures 'in wch' a Man is sufficient to himself, & the only Part of him wch he can employ 'to his satisfaction' all day long. It was this tht made me a writer" (Mack, 104, note 15). Solitary and self-sufficient, the poet's early creativity here carries the trappings of the onanist whose narcissism is both a powerful temptation and the ultimate source of private pleasure.

These tropes of authorial autonomy and sexualized self-regard would be replaced in the final text by significantly muted gestures: "Poetry and Criticism being by no means the universal concern of the world, but only the affair of idle men who write in their closets, and of idle men who read there" (*TE* 1: 3). While certainly not a replication of the masturbatory/writerly closet in the frontispiece to *Histoire de Dom B*, Pope's toned-down image of private male pleasure—closeted and harmlessly aloof from the world's concerns—still resonates with the onanistic possibilities of a secretive narcissism. But while the structure and setting of the self-pollutor are there, the direct implications have been cautiously removed. Appreciating the difficulty in deploying an image of libidinal self-sufficiency to define one's relation to a reading public, Pope deleted these passages, opting for the vaguely religious metaphor of the martyr: "The only plea I shall use for the favour of the publick, is . . . that I have sacrificed much of my own self-love for its sake" (*TE* 1: 8). Poet-Pope as solitary wanker was an image potentially damaging to his masculine profile, and was much better replaced by the approving "idle" gentlemen he so wished to please.

In this clever self-dramatization, Pope takes the high road, polishing his strategic picture of the humble genius seeking an honest fame among like-minded gentlemen, pretending to a dignified removal from market forces. But other cancelled passages tell a different story, with Pope considering the use of poet-whore tropes to acknowledge the tawdry realities and material contingencies of his entry into the print world: "THE MUSES ARE MISTRESSES WITHOUT POR-TIONS, & / WHOEVER HAS ONCE MADE <HIS> COURT TO THEM, CAN / HARDLY SETT UP <AFTERWARDS> FOR A FOR-TUNE: FOR ONCE / A POET & ALWAYS A POET, IS THOUGHT AS UN / DOUBTED A MAXIME, AS ONCE A WHORE AND / AL-WAYS A WHORE. . . . But <I fear> tis far otherwise with modern Po-ets; THEY We / must bring THEIR <our> Wit to the Press, as Gardiners / do their Flowers to the market, which if they / cannot vend in the morning are sure to die be- / fore night" (Mack, 98, 101). Why did Pope cut these sexual and economic tropes? Mack astutely points out that the metaphor of Pope the female Muse-whore "may have been thought too undignified for the translator of Homer" and the Muses-without-portions lines a reason to "bring down laughter on a poet who was at this very instant receiving an excellent monetary return" from his "shrewd subscription arrangements for the *Iliad*" (92). Mack's point needs to be underlined. Pope's preface and 1717 *Works* were published the same year as volume three of his Homer translation, the project which would ultimately make him richer than any other professional writer of his day. Pope was well aware of the new commercialism, was a shrewd bargainer, and understood economic realities, whether they were metaphorized as gardeners selling flowers in a farmer's market or prostitutes who sold their bodies over and over. And yet when it came to his use of the creativity-sexuality discourses as they might represent his status as literary commodity, Pope's public pronouncements es-chewed tropes of whores-for-money even while his private correspon-dence candidly—and sometimes lasciviously—acknowledged whores, privy members, maidenheads, and copulating for a living as figurative estimates of his poetic activities.[10] Why?

To say that Pope sought maximum dignity in his self-portrait, that he wanted to minimize the inaugural presentation of himself as meanly dependent on the public-as-marketplace is one reasonable an-swer. But matters were more complex than this for the little cripple whose real-life erotic forays were being forever blotted not by Muses but by the casual rejection of real women. As the cancellations make clear, Pope knew very well the discourses that would sexualize his value as a literary commodity, but in this public presentation of himself Little Alexander would delete tropes pointing to head-groin associations because they led too uncomfortably toward deeper anxieties about the erotic power or sexual value of his creativity. Instead, his value as trendy market item in the literary scene of 1717 and beyond would depend on a retro imaging of the older Restoration gentleman-author, one of those "idle men who write in their closets," seeking only a self-satisfied aesthetic autonomy or a privileged homosocial acceptance. Pope's revised preface was a brilliant traffic in public relations imaging, dodging any mention of money, contracts, material compromises, or anything that might draw attention to his sexual or physical being. Safer by far was the image of an elitist homosocial acceptance which apparently aligned him with power brokers in the literary scene at the same time as it silently acknowledged the elision of his bodily infirmities and sexual doubts. Pope would maintain this image of his commodity value as a man and poet all his life, painfully aware of how fitting the creativity-sexuality discourses were to his own case, but not willing to use them publicly if they came anywhere near his own sexual insecurities. From a psychological perspective, Pope's 1717 self-dramatization was completely understandable: the network of approving older men had conferred upon him the symbolic phallic authority he worried over. Being the homosocial whore had its rewards for Pope's sense of his masculinity, and the marketplace implications of head-groin links in his own case could be made invisible, saved for the likes of Lewis Theobald and Colley Cibber, symbols for Pope of the commercialism by which he had already profited.

Self-preoccupied with his masculinity and sexual body, young Pope's relationship to the creativity-sexuality discourses had deeply-felt personal implications, and while his use of figurative equations was part of his early self-definitions, the literal connections of his sexualized embodiment as a man and his debut as poet weighed more heavily. For this reason, he was cautious in his use of the collective tropes and analogies, sometimes suppressing them in his own case even though they were perfectly suited to expressions of his value as male and professional author. Pope's enemies, as we will see, would quite happily fill in the blanks for him, using the shared lingo in ways certain to focus the literal associations he wished to ignore. After 1717, the maturing Alexander would seldom use the head-groin associations to describe his own situation, preferring instead to deploy them in satires of other men who could be made to represent the worst versions of a sexualized traffic in the literary marketplace.

Poets' Heads: Cibber, Orpheus, and *The Dunciad*

With his first *Dunciad* in 1728, and then refined considerably by the time he finished with *The Dunciad in Four Books* (1743), Pope had pursued the implications of the powerful new links of writing and money, suggesting that the explosion of would-be writers "setting up in this sad and sorry merchandice" threatened a pervasive cultural mediocrity: "We shall next declare the occasion and the cause which moved our poet to this particular work. He lived in those days, when (after Providence had permitted the invention of Printing as a scourge for the sins of the learned) Paper also became so cheap, and Printers so numerous, that a deluge of Authors covered the land: Whereby not only the peace of the honest unwriting subject was daily molested, but unmerciful demands were made of his applause, yea of his money, by such as would neither earn the one, nor deserve the other."[11] Cibber's Laureateship in 1730 was not only ludicrous given the range of alternate choices, but a sign for Pope that a material vulgarity had invaded the arts. Together, the ill-placed honor and the aging dramatist's lousy poetry were a confirmation of the debased literary value now officially accepted as public norm. And Cibber was no less shy about calling a spade a spade, pointing out that Pope knew very well the commercial value of his satire, relying on personal invective for his own profit:

that satyr shall have a thousand readers where panegyric has one. When I therefore find my name at length in the satyrical works of our most celebrated living author, I never look upon those lines as malice meant to me (for he knows I never provok'd it) but profit to himself. One of his points must be, to have many readers: he considers that my face and name are more known than those of many thousands of more consequence in the kingdom: that therefore, right or wrong, a lick at the Laureate will always be a sure bait.[12]

If Pope knew how to profit from an active literary traffic in the faces and names of dunces like Cibber, Laureate Colley also symbolized the literary commercialism of the day. *The Dunciad in Four Books* is emblematic of the sexual traffic in male creativity, with Cibber's head as icon of the new order and poet Alexander's satire exemplary of the new trafficking.

When it came to the inverted world of Dulness and her dunces, where anti-form, eroded standards, books-as-money, and laughable Laureates cluttered the landscape, one might have expected Pope to use the figure of male author as female Muse-whore, with mock-hero Cibber imaged as prostitute. Instead, he drew on two other ideas, linking the origins of Cibber the poet-son to a lower-order heterosexual begetting, and then making his pregnant skull the chief symbolic site of a reproductive malaise.[13] Together, these two tropes presented

Cibber as the dunce-version of the inner site of male creativity and its public status in the new economic order.

The begetting and birth of the male writer was often mythologized, and mimicked the metaphorical structures of the birthing hierarchies I examined earlier. The most typical narrative was that he was brought into being through some quasi-sexual conjunction of Apollo and the nine female Muses, producing not only the writer but also his proper creative attributes. These heightened begettings had their lower-order satirical versions, too, which—as in the hierarchies described in chapter three—involved ordinary mothers or a tainted conception. In female-mothered births of the poetaster, the wayward imagination of the pregnant earthly mother could affect the poet-fetus directly, later causing him, in turn, to produce deformed poem-children or literary abortion. Cibber's lineage is made a travesty, with Pope attributing to him the satirical markings of lower-order heterosexual origins, and an inverted father-son line meant to recall Dryden's *MacFlecknoe*. In fact, Pope offers a series of reproductive origins, beginning with his creation of Dulness—daughter, Queen, and mother-figure—whose genesis and function are centrally informed by discourses we have examined.

From the beginning of the poem, Pope ushers in the birthing analogies which will characterize Dulness the perverse Muse figure, as well as her dunce-poet son and false procreator, Cibber. Following the mock-epic invocation which opens *The Dunciad in Four Books*, Pope commences with a direct allusion to the Zeus-Athena myth:

> In eldest time, e'er mortals writ or read,
> E'er Pallas [Athena] issu'd from the Thund'rer's head,
> Dulness o'er all possess'd her ancient right,
> Daughter of Chaos and eternal Night:
> Fate in their dotage this fair Ideot gave,
> Gross as her sire, and as her mother grave,
> Laborious, heavy, busy, bold, and blind,
> She rul'd, in native Anarchy, the mind. (98–99, Bk. 1: 9–16)

In this initial allegory of primal birth and origins, a significant juxtaposition awaited the eighteenth-century reader. Against the head-birth of Athena—and somehow prior to it—is the birth of Dulness, daughter of Chaos (the sire) and eternal Night (the mother). The differences are crucial in the symbolic order of the poem: not only is an immaculate patriarchal birth contrasted with some dark and dirty heterosexual begetting, but the female-mothered birth of "Laborious" Dulness signals the inferior material and bodily realm of the dunce and his mental procreations. In this symbolic space, male creativity will be laborious in both its reproductive and manual senses, unredeemed by an autogenetic transcendence or successful epigenetic growth.

Cibber's parentage likewise mimics this fallen heterosexual mode. Despite the mock-autogenetic prefatory comment that, "For, his lineage he bringeth into his life as an Anecdote, and is sensible he had it in his power *to be thought no body's son at all*" ("Ricardus Aristarchus of the Hero of the Poem," 85), the reproductive origins of dunce-Cibber are mother Dulness and father Settle, both guarantors of embryonic formlessness or perverted formation in their misbegotten poet-son. Pope cannot resist adding to this lower-order heterosexual source the idea of male-male lineage and father-son transmission, although (following Dryden's model) this masculine reproductive line is a case of "Dunce the second reigns like Dunce the first" (98, Bk. 1: 6). Taken together, the result is a perfect genetic replication of the parents: "In each [of the duly surveyed by Dulness] she marks her Image full exprest, / But chief in BAYS'S monster-breeding breast" (114, Bk. 1: 107–8); "She saw, with joy, the line immortal run, / Each sire imprest and glaring in his son" (110, Bk. 1: 99–100). Cibber's placement as the chosen son is in the satirically fallen world of monstrous breeding and a homosocially-imprest dulness, informed by laborious mother and vapid father. Predictably, the son's own reproductive literary labors will continue this fallen state. As Cibber says in momentary despair to his literary offspring: "O born in sin, and forth in folly brought! / Works damn'd, or to be damn'd! (your father's fault)" (128, Bk. 1: 225–26).

Given the position of Dulness and her tribe within this inaugural differentiation of reproductive symbols, it is not surprising that she will preside over a male literary family whose figurative copulations, gestations, and childbirths will go terribly (and comically) wrong, spoiled by the unnatural couplings and perverse brain-womb of the dunce. Mindful of the various avenues offered by the tradition of pregnant male poets, Pope centers the action of Book 1 around the uterine "Cave of Poverty and Poetry" (102, Bk. 1: 34), the symbolic matrix out of which will issue a mock poetical character of chaotic pregnancies and deformed poetic offspring. One of the chief functions of Dulness is to inspire and then supervise a grotesque reproductive ambition in her devotees:

> Here she beholds the Chaos dark and deep,
> Where nameless Somethings in their causes sleep,
> 'Till genial Jacob, or a warm Third day,
> Call forth each mass, a Poem, or a Play:
> How hints, like spawn, scarce quick in embryo lie,
> How new-born nonsense first is taught to cry,

Maggots [grubs; whimsies, odd fancies] half-form'd in rhyme exactly meet,
And learn to crawl upon poetic feet. (106–7, Bk. 1: 55–62)

In this parody of conception and birth, the ill-conceived poetic proj-
ects of untalented hacks will earn a satirical notoriety, the dunce's
uterus/brain being capable only of spawning deformity or—what is
just as bad—a grub-like formlessness. Within this metaphorical terrain, Pope insinuates a logic of cause and effect in which deformity in
the conceiving mind necessarily entails deformity in birthing. Like the
potentially disastrous effect of the female imagination on the fetus, the
pregnant brain-womb of the dunce will labor in vain, or breed monsters, or issue in new-born nonsense. In turn, these failures will be
dramatized misogynistically as the direct result of Dulness, female
mother to the dunce-son and negative symbol of a debased reproductive process.

Having provided the origins of Cibber and his (pro)creative head,
Pope turns directly to the Laureate's brain-womb as symbol of a literary commercialism, making it the surrealistic setting for his critique of
widespread cultural decay. Indeed, Pope's interest in the male poet's
head reverberates throughout the *Dunciad*, encountered first in the
Ovidian epigraph in which Phoebus comes to the aid of the still-
singing head of Orpheus—a complex allegory, as we will see, of Pope's
own embattled status among a host of belligerent dunces and critics—
and then in the prefatory section "Ricardus Aristarchus of the Hero of
the Poem," in which Cibber's head is offered up as a brasslike impu-
dence: "And whose *Os sublime* is not simply an *erect face*, but a Brazen
head" (81). Throughout the poem, the Dunce's head and brain are
variously characterized as brazen, block-headed, or spectacularly empty:
"Great Cibber's brazen, brainless brothers stand" (102, Bk. 1: 32); "Cibberian forehead, and Cibberian brain" (127, Bk. 1: 218); "With pert flat
eyes she window'd well its head; / A brain of feathers, and a heart of
lead; / And empty words she gave, and sounding strain, / But senseless, lifeless! idol void and vain! / Never was dash'd out, at one lucky
hit, / A fool, so just a copy of a wit" (152, Bk. 2: 43–48). The unredeemed thickness or brazen surface of the Laureate's head is an amusing satirical stroke, but Pope's most significant treatment of the
Cibberian head is as a cracked brain-womb oozing dangerous fluids or
birthing disorder.

In perhaps the most memorable passage of Book 1, Laureate Cibber
is assigned the unenviable narrative task of a parodic Zeus-Athena birth
that brilliantly and grotesquely inverts the creational norms residing
in the original myth. Frustrated, lacking inspiration, and despairing
of any redeeming conceptual idea, Cibber nevertheless continues to
write:

Yet wrote and flounder'd on, in mere despair.
Round him much Embryo, much Abortion lay,
Much future Ode, and abdicated Play;
Nonsense precipitate, like running Lead,
That slip'd thro' Cracks and Zig-zags of the Head;
All that on Folly Frenzy could beget,
Fruits of dull Heat, and Sooterkins [Johnson: "a kind of false birth fabled to
be produced by the Dutch women from sitting over their stoves"] of Wit.
(116, Bk. 1: 120–26)

In this compact imaging of the inner place of male creativity, the laureate's head and emblematic brain-womb are literally opened up by Pope, whose imaginative audacity represents Cibber's mundane but deviant creativity as a messy and preposterous reproductive failure. This highly visualized scenario presents the Laureate of the new marketplace in "labor," with images of Cibber surrounded grotesquely by embryo and abortion—the results of previous literary efforts—and his current authorial pretensions figured as a deviant case of mental Frenzy impregnating Folly. Predictably, the offspring are Nonsense and Sooterkins, which slip out of Cibber's cracked-open head-womb like heated lead—a lifeless precipitate descending in fluid but heavy state. As it turns out, Cibber's wit—just like his mother Dulness—is "Laborious, heavy, busy, bold, and blind," and it is also abortive, false and deformed. No Minerva or Athena issues from the birth-pangs of Cibber's foolish and frenzied head; rather, the outline of a mock Zeus-Jupiter ludicrously placed in a surreal natal setting of discarded embryo, aborted fetus, and oozing misbirth. In this tableau of the cracked brain straining forth its own reproductive failure, Pope cannot resist one final misogynistic touch linking Cibber's head to the debased female realm of mother-Dulness and an unredeemable maternal body: the warmed pudenda of Dutch women squatting over stoves and false births.

Cibber's zig-zag head is about reproductive and creative deviance— "Sooterkins of Wit"—just as the world which has chosen him Laureate is about the devaluation of literary labor. But the Cibberian cranium appears again in the account of the relationship of the Laureate's head to mother Dulness that begins Book 3. The position of Cibber's head on Dulness's lap is rich in implication, and Pope merges ideas of birth, madness, and incest:

But in her Temple's last recess inclos'd,
On Dulness' lap th' Anointed head repos'd.
Him close she curtains round with Vapours blue,
And soft besprinkles with Cimmerian dew.
Then raptures high the seat of Sense o'erflow,
Which only heads refin'd from Reason know.

> Hence, from the straw where Bedlam's Prophet nods,
> He hears loud Oracles, and talks with Gods:
> Hence the Fool's Paradise, the Statesman's Scheme,
> The air-built Castle, and the golden Dream,
> The Maid's romantic wish, the Chemist's flame,
> And Poet's vision of eternal Fame. (220–21, Bk. 3: 1–12)

The juxtaposition of male head/brain and female vagina/womb recalls in a concrete and strangely allegorized manner not only the comments of physiologists on the brain/uterus analogy, but also the classical tradition which frequently imagined the origin of the male poet as the son issuing from some primal reproductive act. The proximity of Cibber's slumbering head and Dulness's lap certainly suggests a sexually regressive fetal position and thus an archetypal scenario of the female-mothered birthing of the male poet-dunce. As well, there is a hint of slippery birthing in the idea of anointed head and dark dew. But lurking, too, is an incestuous sexuality in which the passive, grotesquely fertile brain of Cibber is rapt by this perverse Muse-mother figure, engendering the sleeping "Poet's vision" (221, Bk. 3: 12). Of course, in a positive use of the trope about the poet and his lover-Muse, the sexual exchange yielded real poetic vision, as it does in Pope's *Windsor-Forest*: "Ye sacred Nine! that all my Soul possess, / Whose Raptures fire me, and whose Visions bless" (*TE* 1: 173, ll. 259–60). In this case, however, the ambiguously placed head of Cibber will be inspired with the vision of father Settle, lumpen City Poet of mediocre commendatory verse, who in turn prophesies to the still-sleeping son the coming of the Cibberian age. When Settle's visionary tableaux of theatrical history under the tutelage of Dulness climax with the messianic Cibber, the reproductive metaphors reach their highest pitch of grotesque incredulity: "Another Aeschylus [Cibber] appears! prepare / For new abortions, all ye pregnant fair!" (258, Bk. 3: 313–14). Pope's own footnote to the couplet focuses the idea of violent misbirth: "It is reported of Aeschylus, that when his Tragedy of the Furies was acted, the audience were so terrify'd that the children fell into fits, and the big-bellied women miscarried." But Cibber is no Aeschylus: his theatrical misconceptions will represent a general reproductive malaise threatening to spill over from the figurative space of pregnant male poet into the literal domain of the pregnant female body.

Cibber's head is a travesty of procreative cause and effect. Pope has satirically rearranged the hierarchy of metaphors we examined earlier (patriarchal head-birth, pregnant male body-birth, female-mothered birth) to dramatize the utter perversity of the dunce's creative transgressions: female mother gives birth to the poet-son, whose brain in turn is figuratively impregnated by its closeness to the maternal womb, and who then gives birth to his visionary offspring, the father, whose own brain-vision confirms the future cycle of unnatural begettings and birthing chaos. As part of the satire, this sequence of engenderings reverses the reproductive hierarchy by making the male poet's creative conceptions and births a seemingly endless by-product of Dulness's female sexuality and bodily womb, and therefore unstable, inferior, and threatening.[14]

By making the brazen and deviantly reproductive head of Cibber a symbol of the inherent threat which the forces of modernism represented, Pope engaged the collective head-groin discourses and participated in the very literary traffic he also protested. Cibber was right: "a lick at the Laureate will always be a sure bait." But Pope's satire was much more than a timely exploitation geared to profit, and he wanted to call attention to his own clever creativity which towered above its victims. The unstated but clearly implied point of this contrast was that there is no room in the new order for a poet such as Pope, or, that in the world of Dulness the life and career of such a poet will be a constant embattlement. The prefatory machinery and appendices commemorated Pope's sometimes bitter contest with the dunces, but it was the Ovidian motto of the title page—Orpheus's decapitated but still singing head—which offered his most self-conscious assessment of the new professional climate where poets' heads were a rhetorical part of the sexual traffic in male creativity.

The epigraph comes from near the end of the Orpheus story in *Metamorphoses*. Having been torn apart by the angry Ciconian women who have been sexually rejected, Orpheus now exists only as the still murmuring head and singing lyre which float down the Hebrus and wash up on the shore of Lesbos. What happens next in Ovid's story clearly struck Pope as a symbolically apt prefatory image for what his own *Dunciad* was about: on the Lesbian shore, the Orphic head is saved from the jaws of a snake by Phoebus Apollo, god of poetry, who petrifies the attacking mouth. Pope's epigraph uses two lines: "Tandem *Phoebus* adest, morsusque inferre parantem / Congelat, et patulos, ut erant, indurat hiatus" (XI. 58, 60).[15] The most common scholarly answers to why Pope thought of his narrator as an Orphic figure, or why he associated his poem with this Ovidian detail, are summarized concisely by Valerie Rumbold, the poem's most recent editor: "This implies an identification between Orpheus, the Apollonian poet-priest whose song brought order and peace and continued even after his death, and the author of the *Dunciad*, suggesting that Pope's adversaries will find a similarly unwelcome immortality through their representation in the *Dunciad*."[16] As a signpost to the satire that follows, the epigraph can be interpreted as a witty reminder of the various dangers that beset the true wit in a world of dunces, or as the poet's fierce rejoinder to an antagonistic republic of letters that his Orphic poet-figure will not be silenced. But this allusive framing device is metapoetically self-conscious in other ways as well, epitomizing Pope's sense of the contradictory cultural status of the author, whose creativity could be understood as both a sexual power and a loss.

More specifically, the motto associates Pope's poetic enterprise with both Apollo and Orpheus. The Apollonian Pope is the god-poet whose *Dunciad* will publicly champion worthy male poets and their creativity, rendering ineffectual the shafts and barbs of malicious critics and foes through a witty commemoration of their threat. Phoebus Apollo is also about male sexual power as poetry—the fully-sexed priapic lover-rapist whose phallic desires can be transformed into male art without removing the yard or canceling erotic impulse. In contrast, the Orphic Pope is about the poet under public attack, but this aspect of the allusion is also about male creativity as sexual loss of a drastic order, not just at the beginning of the myth with the twice-lost Eurydice, but more importantly later on when the male body is violently dismembered and separated from the poet's still-singing head. The epigraph isolates an Orpheus whose head and wit have been literally separated from libidinal power in a horrific exchange where creativity remains, but at the expense of the sexualized male body. Together, the Apollo and Orpheus projections are miniatures of the contradictory attitudes about inverse models of exchange and the ambiguous sexual nature of the poetical character. Gesturing simultaneously toward both the inner site of male creativity as well as the difficult public treatment one's wit might receive in the literary community, the epigraph portrays the poetical character as both a powerfully assertive male sexuality-as-art (Pope as Apollo) and as an exchange whose cost is the yard, sexuality, the male body itself (Pope as Orpheus).

The dominant image of the epigraph is an idealized one—a fantasy of the singing head of brave and worthy poet rescued by Apollo. But it also represents a contrast to the Cibberian head in the poem proper. As a threshold to a satire of public literary values and quarrels, the motto has something to say about what happens when male poet and his inner creativity march into the rough-and-tumble world of publishers, readers, profits, critics, and reputation. The true wit in isolated integrity—Orpheus-Pope's singing head—will come with a personal cost, either unheeded in its isolation or attacked as a false and unprofitable integrity. Against this is Colley Cibber—false wit and champion of the materialist world—whose head has birthed an array of misbegotten literary commodities for sale, prompting even a traffic in images of his own head. Pope's motto is compact and subtle in its implications, requiring the sort of readerly work for which the Age of Colley has presumably neither time nor taste. A private triumph, perhaps, Pope's allusion contained both a psychological gesture about the ambiguous creativity-sexuality nexus, and a cultural critique of a literary commercialism that happily traded in Colleys at the expense of true wits such as Pope.

While *The Dunciad* retailed the Cibberian head in brilliant satire, Pope knew only too well that images of his own head were part of the commercial scene, not just as portraits for sale but also as a commodity symbolic of the marketplace itself. In the summer of 1735 when Edmund Curll moved his printing shop to Rose Street in Covent Garden, his new shop sign was "Pope's Head"[17] (see Figure 8). In this sarcastic business gesture, the wily Curll had his own use for the heads of Orphic poets such as the famous Pope, whose function on Curll's shop sign was now symbolic of all that Pope despised in the marketplace of letters, but also emblematic of the commercial realities from which both men benefitted. Catherine Ingrassia has argued that "Curll's appropriation of Pope's physical image materially manifests the symbolic medium of their exchange. They [Curll and Pope] were competing for control over Pope's persona and literary commodities, and the economic rewards of both. By using Pope's image to mark the site of commercial activity, Curll literally merged the tenuous oppositions that characterize this period: the literary and the commercial, the classic and the carnivalesque."[18] To this persuasive analysis I would add a double irony: while Curll was changing his shop sign to "Pope's Head" in 1735, the sneaky Pope was tricking him into publishing an unauthorized edition of Pope's letters, the occasion that would allow the poet to realize his own financial gains through his authorized edition in 1737; and, when the official *Letters of Mr. Alexander Pope, and Several of his Friends* came out, Pope did not hesitate to include on his title page a medallion of his own head (see Figure 9), prepared by Jonathan Richardson senior, under which was another Latin motto, "Amicitiae Causa," tribute to male friends and an idealized homosocial world of dignified rural retreat. In the public realm where the heads (and yards) of male authors existed as potential property—as items of economic value, images to be traded and fought over—the commercialized head-trophy on Rose Street might have signaled Curll's ownership of Pope, whose head would also sing for Curll's profit. But Pope knew very well the currency of this imagery, disingenuously setting up Curll's traffic-in-Pope in order to promote an image of his own worthy head.

In another kind of irony, friends also used Pope's head as a pictorial emblem of the power (or potential gain) conferred on them by virtue of their friendship with the famous writer. In 1751, William Warburton—Pope's handpicked literary executor and editor—would use the dead poet's head as well as his own in the frontispiece to *The Works of Alexander*

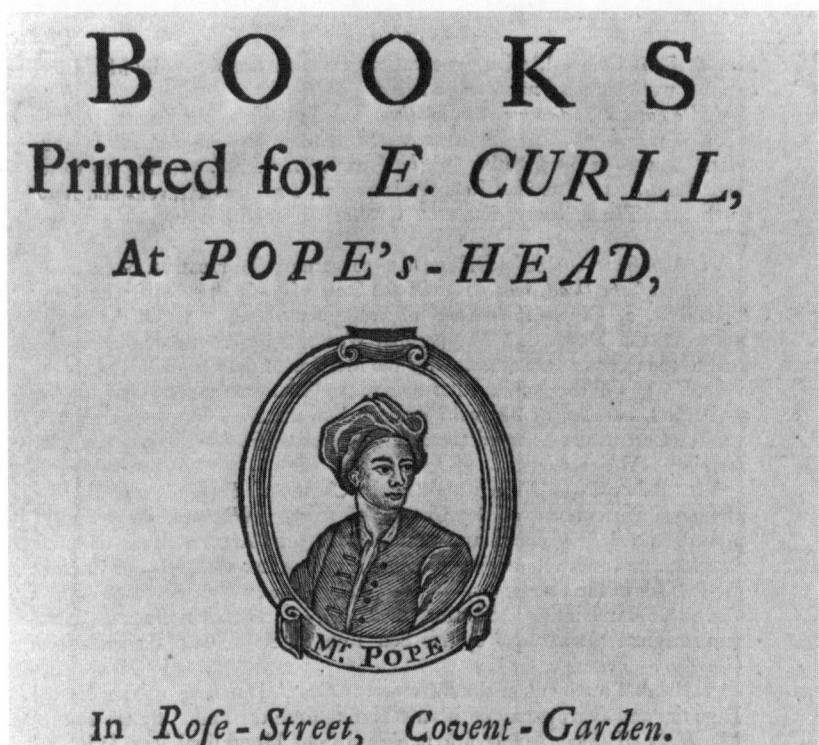

BOOKS
Printed for *E. CURLL*,
At *POPE's-HEAD*,

Mr POPE

In *Rofe-Street*, *Covent-Garden*.

Figure 8. Shop sign for Edmund Curll, *Books Printed for E. CURLL, At Pope's-Head, In Rose-Street, Covent-Garden* (1735). Courtesy of the William Ready Division of Archives and Research Collections, McMaster University Library, Hamilton, Canada.

Pope Esq. In Nine Volumes Complete (see Figure 10). The medallions reveal much about the latter's inflated sense of his importance to Pope's work, published editions of which made Warburton a handsome profit. As Donald W. Nichol has shrewdly observed, "Pope might have been taken aback by a frontispiece which placed Warburton in the central point and made the editor the source of creative light while the poet appeared distinctly shaded."[19] Their relative worth linked by a putto, the two heads together are an iconic symbol of the editor's material sway and literal ownership of Pope's oeuvre, here figured as the lesser, shaded head.

As a coda to these examples of the traffic in poets' heads, I bring forward an anecdote which comes from near the end of Pope's life, when he was bed ridden and only two weeks away from death. According to Owen Ruffhead, David Mallet was visiting the ailing poet, who was now slipping in and out of consciousness:

LETTERS

O F

Mr. *ALEXANDER POPE*,

And Several of his FRIENDS.

LONDON:

Printed by J. WRIGHT for J. KNAPTON in *Ludgateſtreet,*
L. GILLIVER in *Fleetſtreet,* J. BRINDLEY in *New Bond
ſtreet,* and R. DODSLEY in *Pall-mall,* MDCCXXXVII.

Figure 9. Jonathan Richardson senior, medallion of Pope's head, title page, *Letters of Mr. Alexander Pope, and Several of his Friends* (1737). Courtesy of the William Ready Division of Archives and Research Collections, McMaster University Library, Hamilton, Canada.

I was sitting one day, said he, with Mr. Pope, in his last illness, who coming suddenly out of a reverie, which you know he frequently fell into at that time, and fixing his eyes steadfastly on me, Mr. M—, said he, I have had an odd kind of vision: methought I saw my own head open, and *Apollo* come out of it; I then saw your head open, and *Apollo* went into it; after which our heads closed up again.[20]

One must be careful not to misuse this kind of anecdote, which is, after all, a rather touching story about a dying man whose mind was playing tricks on him in his final days. But it is an exemplary story nonetheless, revealing Pope's psychological pull toward older notions of literary creativity as gentlemanly removal. Taking its source from the Zeus-Athena head birth—bodiless and motherless—which characterized the purest form of literary autogenesis, the exaggerations of this hallucination throw into relief Pope's final fantasy of his own creativity, here offered as an idyllic homosocial removal from markets and all traffic except that between friends. There are no female Muses here, no wombs, no birth-travail, and there are no buyers and sellers, no unspeakable Curlls or shameless Cibbers—only like-minded men sharing in male conception and the symbolic exchange of creative intimacies. Emerging from Pope's opening head, fully formed, Apollo, male god of poetry, is in turn transferred into the waiting, receptive head of friend Mallet. A nostalgic desire for simpler times, perhaps, or a deep vanity about his own talents, dying Alexander's odd vision imagined male creativity as a head containing both Apollonian inspiration and the friendly community of other men. The sexual traffic in male creativity—in which Pope had been both user and used—was gone, buried, or forgotten in this last recorded comment about literary men.

Talking Yards: *Sober Advice from Horace* and Wilkes's *Essay on Woman*

Aged forty six, Pope produced his most self-conscious thematizing of the yard, tackling the difficult implications for masculine subjectivity as it might be affected by yard-as-man equations. *Sober Advice from Horace* (1734) presented the reader with the startling and comical figure of the talking penis which chastised the perverse desires of its owner in favor of the unpretentious needs of the "honest" (*TE* 4: 83, l. 87) prick which understood only too well that there is no point "In errant Pride [to] continue stiff, and burn" (*TE* 4: 87, l. 152) when there is "a tight, neat Girl, [to] serve the Turn" (*TE* 4: 87, l. 151). Pope never openly claimed the poem, although everyone knew it was his. This Horatian imitation is seldom discussed by scholars, who are perhaps surprised to find (or embarrassed to acknowledge) the great poet's

Plate I.

Vol. I. facing the general Title.

Blakey del.

Major Sculp.

Figure 10. Frontispiece to William Warburton's edition of *The Works of Alexander Pope Esq. In Nine Volumes Complete* (1751). Courtesy of the William Ready Division of Archives and Research Collections, McMaster University Library, Hamilton, Canada.

personification of the penis.[21] But it would not have been so surprising a poetic offering within a culture where male genitalia were increasingly associated with an essentialized male interiority. And it is understandable that as the nature of that inwardness was elaborated, questions of how male experience might be grounded by reference to the yard would receive self-conscious treatment. Yet the curious literary tradition of the personified penis is all but neglected in the history of sexuality for this period.

Poems and essays which addressed the privy member as a sentient Other self-consciously brought into focus the experiential issues for men as they were objects and agents of the widespread cultural revision of the connections of male body and masculinity. In Chapter 2 I described how the new phallus-as-commodity created a gap between discourses of the cultural imaginary and the lived experience of real men. Impotence trials and enigmatic yard models suggested that a man's pintle could be something of a self-alienating part, attached to but not necessarily owned or controlled by the man. That writers such as Pope, his admirer Wilkes (and before them, Rochester), would personify the penis—throwing their voices into the dummy body-part—is a telling sign that they wished to explore the subjective implications of the yard-man synecdoche. How did these men read their own rising, falling, urinating, ejaculating pegos against the symbolic values in the collective head-groin vocabulary? Pope's *Sober Advice* and Wilkes's Popean *Essay on Woman* comically foregrounded this kind of question.

As always, there were classical precedents. Amy Richlin has noted the relatively small tradition in which Priapus appears as "a talking, deified phallus," as well as the more dramatic "address to the impotent phallus" which is "something of a topos in Latin literature."[22] Some of the seventeenth- and eighteenth-century examples glance backwards at these earlier models, but the important differentiating mark is that the classical topos does not occur in contexts which equate or commodify the man as penis. Classical usage relies either on the older myth of Priapus as symbolic life-force or comic wooden guardian of orchards, or on the potentially comic figure of the impotent male. Although several ancient writers—notably Horace, Petronius, Martial—represent men self-consciously responding to the meaning of their yards, these works are concerned with the present moment of phallic failure or sexual desire rather than the implications for a sexually-based male subjectivity. The personified-yard poems written by the moderns, on the other hand, more typically register the man-penis dialogue as an epistemological dilemma for men in which the physical basis or sexual origins of a masculine identity are problematic.

There are three discernible treatments of the personified yard in the seventeenth and eighteenth centuries, the first two representing discursive tactics we have already seen: the privy member as symbolic male power; the yard as a second self at odds with the man to whose body and mind it is attached. The third is a much more complex handling of the penis-identity nexus in which individual male experience of his own symbolized pego is self-consciously dramatized, as it is in Pope and Wilkes. The first and simplest literary version relies on an older classical mythology of the idolized Priapus-figure who symbolizes generation and a deified male life-force. Thus in *The Members to their Soveraign* (1726), supposedly written by Matthew Prior (with Hildebrand Jacob the second most likely author), the superficial political metaphor of the title opens immediately to reveal dutifully obedient male members glorifying the personified phallus as symbolic leader and inspirational force to be emulated:

> O Thou design'd by Nature to controul.
> And in the Center plaic'd to guide the *Whole*,
> What praise to suit thy Merit shall we bring
> Or how great Limb thy nervous glory Sing?
> . . . .
> By Day by Night, thro' Heat, thro' Winters Snow,
> Fatigue and Danger scorn'd, we'll Boldly go,
> Not coldly Asking why, when you Command,
> For you in Reasons place, Triumphant Stand. (1–2)

Holding sway over mind and reason, this sovereign cock rules men and women both, democratically "Partial to no Condition or Degree," "visit[ing] both the Wealthy and the Poor" (1). As the members contemplate the inevitable demise of their aging sovereign through a debilitating clap, they are hopeful that in this final phase "A *Priapism* all your Labours Crown, / And may you prove a *Dildo* of the Town" (2). Hardly sophisticated, the poem nonetheless mirrors the unstable wish for the ever-ready phallus (and not the limp penis) as definitive and pervasive maleness. This version of the personified yard is rare in the period, and is to be found in only one other poem that I know of, Wilkes's "Veni Creator; Or, the Maid's Prayer":

> Creator Pego, by whose Aid,
> Thy humble Suppliant was made;
> O Source of Bliss and God of Love,
> Shed thy Influence from above;
> . . . .
> Immortal Honour, endless Fame,
> Almighty Pego! to thy Name;
> And equal Adoration be
> Paid to the neighbouring Pair with Thee,
> Thrice blessed Glorious Trinity.[23]

Wilkes's "Creator Pego" and sacrilegious trinity hearken back to classical models of the god Priapus, but this form of personification is less frequent in the period than a persistent doubtfulness about the ability of the humanized yard to signify a symbolic male prowess.

This uncertainty informs the second type of personified penis poem which is indebted partly to classical models and is concerned with the disobedient penis and impotence.[24] In the section on the enigmatic yard we saw the most typical discursive features of the unruly tarse and its unpredictable relationship to the male mind. What distinguishes the personified-yard version of these ideas is that now an individual male's subjective experience of the man-yard disjunction becomes the subject proper, opening up a new dramatic context in which the meaning of the yard is explored in its relationship to the man's erotic yearnings and imagination. The perceived Other-ness of the uncooperative member remains, but a psycho-sexual terrain of failed or frustrated male desire is foregrounded, throwing into relief the contours of a masculine subjectivity as somehow inherently split or chaotic. The best-known rendition by the moderns is Rochester's *The Imperfect Enjoyment* (1680), in which the premature ejaculator curses his now unresponsive, "unmoving lump":

> Thou treacherous, base deserter of my flame,
> False to my passion, fatal to my fame,
> By what mistaken magic dost thou prove
> So true to lewdness, so untrue to Love?
> What oyster, cinder, beggar, common whore
> Didst thou e'er fail in all thy life before?
> When vice, disease, and scandal lead the way,
> With what officious haste dost thou obey?
> Like a rude, roaring hector in the streets
> That scuffles, cuffs, and justles all he meets,
> But if his king or country claim his aid,
> The rakehell villain shrinks and hides his head;
> Ev'n so thy brutal valor is displayed,
> Breaks every stew, does each small whore invade,
> But if great Love the onset does command,
> Base recreant to thy prince, thou dar'st not stand.[25]

Noteworthy here are the contexts of personification, all of them associated with an illicit attraction to a rough-and-tumble street-anarchy which threatens established social order and political hierarchy. Only too happy to engage in every low-life, red-light area debauchery, the now recalcitrant yard refuses to cooperate in the normative realm of the speaker's heterosexual passion, which is linked metaphorically to the cultural glue of class and rank holding the socio-economic fabric together, a patriotic duty to king and country, and the psychological prerogatives of love over lewdness. The obstinate penis—personified as "rakehell villain," "Base recreant," and "roaring hector"—represents a principle of treachery and rebellion, but in the end such contest between speaker and yard signifies a potentially uncontrolled desiring within the man, a subjectivity whose sexually-defined essence is marked by strife or an alarming gap between the desired and the acted-upon. Accentuated here is the idea of an inherent alterity or doubleness as a feature of maleness itself. Implicit in Rochester's treatment is more than the comical or frustrated scene of the penis-with-a-mind-of-it-own; the imperfectly enjoyed genital lump also signals the vexed collision of wayward physiology and cultural symbolism, of the tension between erotic imagination and culturally expected phallic function.

But what would the personified privy member say about the mind-yard relationship if given the chance to speak? Such is the dramatic focus of the third kind of personification, which is represented so notoriously in the eighteenth century by Pope's *Sober Advice from Horace*. There were two famous precedents for Pope's treatment of the talking yard: Horace's *Satire* 1: 2, which provided the immediate occasion for the imitation; and Montaigne's late sixteenth-century essay, "On the power of the imagination." The object of Horace's satire is the man whose overweening sexual desires move outside the reasonable opportunities provided by Nature, seeking the wives of other men or otherwise problematic sex-partners rather than copulating contentedly with an available male or female servant. Protesting the unreasonableness of such exotic lusting by one Villius, the personified yard presents its own argument through the mind, both of which are somehow separated from Villius's unrealistic carnal desires:

Now suppose, speaking for the prick, who saw the whole mess, Villius's mind had asked their owner, "What do you want? Did I ever ask you for a fancy cunt, born to a great consul, swathed in a long dress, even when I was at my hottest?" What would he [Villius] have answered? "The girl has a famous father." But nature, who has a special store of riches, will guide you better and in quite another way, if only you would choose to be a wiser manager and not confuse desirable goods with those you should avoid. . . . So when your member swells, if you have a serving girl convenient, or a serving boy, to satisfy the impulse on the spot, why endure a prick about to blow? Not me. It's the available I like and getting an easy lay.[26]

Horace's moral is simple: to follow Nature in sexual matters means cooperation between reason and phallic impulse; be sensible and eschew perverse refinements of erotic desire. What attracts Pope to this satire, I think, is its striking reversal of the more common formulation which locates the problem within a wayward penis. Here, the yard is associated with the reasonable currents and balancing energies of Nature, which are evident in the observable world and available to men within

themselves, if only they would seek it. The simple desires of the unpretentious prick are unduly problematized by Villius's unpredictable
or irrational desiring, and Horace satirizes the man who fails to harmonize his unrealistic libidinal attractions with the most practical op-
tions within reach. As we will see in a moment, what Pope develops
and expands in his imitation is the idea that it is not the yard which
is the recalcitrant Other—perverse betrayer of male will and sexual
desire—but rather the imagination and psychological idiosyncrasy of a
masculine subjectivity which precipitates this inner strife or divisiveness.

Montaigne's essay "On the Power of the Imagination" also anticipates Pope's refitted use of the yard as a simple part and process of
nature, with the most problematic features of the mind-yard relationship resituated within the male imagination. Montaigne's handling of
the humanized penis-as-Other is clever, recalling the impotence trials:
acknowledging the apparent intractability of the male member, the
narrator imagines himself as legal counsel for the unjustly accused
yard. The advocate points out that there are a variety of bodily organs
which operate independently of the will, and thus there is no good
reason for the privy member to be singled out for such attack:

We have reason to remark the untractable liberties taken by this member,
which intrudes so tiresomely when we do not require it and fails us so annoy-
ingly when we need it most, imperiously pitting its authority against that of
the will, and most proudly and obstinately refusing our solicitations both
mental and manual. Yet if on being rebuked for rebellion and condemned on
that score he were to engage me to plead his cause, I might perhaps cast some
suspicion on our other members, his fellows, of having framed this fictitious
case against him out of pure envy of the importance and pleasure attached to
his functions. I might arraign them for plotting to make the world his enemy
by maliciously blaming him alone for their common fault. For I ask you to
consider whether there is a single part of our bodies that does not often refuse
to work at our will, and does not often operate in defiance of it.[27]

Having established the apparent whimsy of the uncooperative yard as
one of many physical processes which, while often outside the mind's
control, is nevertheless a perfectly normal aspect of nature, Montaigne's narrator goes on to pose in more sophisticated fashion the
question inherent in Horace's satire:

But let us take our will, on whose behalf we are preferring this charge. How
much more justifiably can we brand it with rebellion and sedition, on account
of its constant irregularities and disobedience! Does it always desire what we
wish it to desire? Does it not often desire, to our obvious disadvantage, what
we forbid it to? Does it let itself be guided, either, by the conclusions of our
reason?
In short, I ask you on behalf of my noble client kindly to reflect that, although his case in this matter is inseparably and indistinguishably joined with
that of an accomplice, nevertheless he alone is attacked, and with such argu-

ments and accusations as, seeing the condition of the parties, cannot possibly appertain to or concern the said accomplice. (43–44).

Having aligned the apparently unruly yard with the normal functions of nature, the counsel for the yard locates the trouble in an aberrant male mind whose irregular and irrational energies betray the confusion of male desiring itself. It is not the penis but the man who causes the disjunction between mind and yard.

What Pope sees in the example of Horace and Montaigne is precisely this sense of the yard as a testimony or witness to an inner confusion or instability. In *Sober Advice* the meaning of the penis/phallus is finally about its failure to square itself with a man's erotic imagination or the complex projection of male desire onto the real. Having considered the extremes of sexual inclination in which

> diff'rent Taste in diff'rent Men prevails,
> And one is fired by Heads, and one by Tails;
> Some feel no Flames but at the *Court* or *Ball*,
> And others hunt white Aprons in the *Mall* (*TE* 4: 79, ll. 35–38)

Pope's speaker asks "Has Nature set no bounds to wild Desire? / No Sense to guide, no Reason to enquire" (*TE* 4: 87, ll. 143–44)? Why is it that the yard's own simple needs—aligned with Nature and Reason in the poem—are never exactly equivalent to or representative of the man's erotic desires? Pope's talking penis asks its owner about this apparent disjunction between simple phallic impulse and idiosyncratic libidinal desire, framing the larger question about literal and symbolic meanings of the penis/phallus. As the yard's oration commences, Pope cannot resist a moment of political satire in which first Minister Walpole is chastised by his privy member:

> Suppose that honest Part that rules us all,
> Should rise, and say—"Sir *Robert* [Walpole]! or Sir *Paul* [Methuen]!
> "Did I demand, in my most vig'rous hour,
> "A Thing descended from the Conqueror?
> "Or when my pulse beat highest, ask for any
> "Such Nicety, as Lady or Lord *Fanny*?—
> What would you answer? Could you have the Face,
> When the poor Suff'rer humbly mourn'd his Case,
> To cry "You weep the Favours of her GRACE?
> Hath not indulgent Nature spread a Feast,
> And giv'n enough for Man, enough for Beast?
> But Man corrupt, perverse in all his ways,
> In search of vanities from Nature strays:
> Yea, tho' the Blessing's more than he can use,
> Shuns the permitted, the forbid pursues!
> Weigh well the Cause from whence these Evils spring,
> 'Tis in thyself, and not in God's good Thing: (*TE* 4: 83, ll. 87–103)

The personified penis—complainant in a fractured mind-body arrangement—speaks to the futile meaning of its function when faced with the irrational erotic imagination of its owner. The indignant "honest Part"—"God's good Thing"—asks why the man's sexual imagination is unable to harmonize itself reasonably or simply with Nature, here presented as a thoughtful cornucopia of sexual convenience.

Pope's "sober advice" is ironic, however. In the first stage of resolution, the poem's closure would appear to offer a pragmatic strategy by which highfalutin lusts can be subordinated to the simpler ejaculatory needs of the no-nonsense prick:

> If neither Gems adorn, nor Silver tip
> The flowing Bowl, will you not wet your Lip?
> When sharp with Hunger, scorn you to be fed,
> Except on *Pea-Chicks*, at the *Bedford-head*?
> Or, when a tight, neat Girl, will serve the Turn,
> In errant Pride continue stiff, and burn?
> I'm a plain Man, whose Maxim is profest,
> "The Thing at hand is of all Things the *best*." (*TE* 4: 87, ll. 147–54)

But having eschewed the inconvenient and often downright dangerous refinements of "wild Desire," the speaker's conclusion plays the very game he has just disowned, dramatizing the recuperative strains of the erotic imagination as it attempts to transform mere physiological lust into an agreeable symbolic imaging:

> Give me a willing Nymph! 'tis all I care,
> Extremely clean, and tolerably fair,
> Her Shape her own, whatever Shape she have,
> And just that White and Red which Nature gave.
> Her I transported touch, transported view,
> And call her *Angel! Goddess! Montague!* (*TE* 4: 89, ll. 161–66)

Not content with simple phallic release, male erotic fantasy is here forced into proximity with the real. The "willing Nymph" of domestic convenience (in Horace it is serving girl or boy) becomes the sexual meat onto which fantasy-faces, persons (even enemy Lady Mary Wortley Montagu), or scenarios can be affixed. Pope's "sober advice" about men and their penises is less assured than Horace's, and strikingly vulnerable in its final posture: most men—even the moralistic speaker—will fail to follow Nature or pragmatic common sense, ultimately giving themselves over to a typical imaginative supplement, a fantasy projection to enhance reality. The yard may well be "that honest Part that rules us all," but Pope's Horatian imitation presents it as a long-suffering witness to the imaginative over-reachings of the man, whose experience of his privy member's meaningfulness or function in relation to his sexual desirings is characterized by some differential. According to the complaining pego, erotic imagination and idiosyncratic desire will always exceed the simple disposition of swollen privy member.

This complex disjunction is ironically contrasted in Pope's mock-Bentley figure, whose blockheaded attention to literal meanings contrasts the more sophisticated queries of the poet. "Bentley" is comically obsessed with literally correct translations, naively believing that the cultural formation of meaning around genitalia is a simple matter of correcting the imitator's mistaken reading of "Magno prognatum deposco consule CUNNUM" (*TE* 4: 82, l. 70 in the facing latin original), which Pope has cleverly rendered as "A Thing descended from the Conqueror?" (*TE* 4: 83, l. 90): "*why* Thing?" "Bentley" asks; "*the Poet has it* Cunnum; *which, therefore, boldly place here.* BENT." But of course "things" are not quite so simple a matter. For Pope, the literal and symbolic function of "God's good thing" is a vexed issue, involving a fracture of yard and desire which is always being supplemented by the imagination. While he recognizes the powerful drive of erections and their capacity to lead and define the man, Pope also registers a highly nuanced sense of how the man is related ambiguously to the yard through an act of imagination. In this configuration, masculine desiring and male interiority are the important but enigmatic terrain, with the phallus now a somewhat simple affair of risings, emissions, and detumescence. What Pope foregrounds about the cultural meaning of the yard is how the very gap or slippage between male desire and erection is filled imaginatively through some individual symbolic imaging of the out-of-reach, the forbidden, the exotic, or the fetish. And, while the privy member is stiffened by these provisional (and apparently incessant) inventions of the male imagination, the now rampant yard testifies *not* to its own symbolic status but rather to the erotic gambits of the symbolizing mind as it chases "flying Game" (*TE* 4: 87, l. 139). Pope's speaking pintle bemoans its function as mere repository and physical receptacle of male desiring, and in so doing calls attention to difficulties which individual men might have had in experiencing the symbolic values which diverse cultural contexts had assigned to their tumescent penises. Although the yard was commonly figured as the "honest Part that rules us all," talking-penis poems such as Pope's offered a significant oppositional construct to such cultural discourses and metaphorizations, providing a more intimate archaeological record of how male mind-genitalia connections might have been lived. In this case, the erection is a sign of the inherently unstable connection of the imagination to the real—of the problematic, obsessive, fetishistic bridgings of libidinal desires to a resistant material world of moral laws, social custom, forbidden bodies, and irrational human behavior. Pope's treatment of male experience of the yard in this poem foregrounded ambiguity and erotic frustration for the man, whose stiffened tarse was a label of his uncontainable desiring, a condition symbolic of his imagination itself.

Wilkes's *An Essay on Woman*, a pornographic parody of Pope's *An Essay on Man*, does not feature a speaking penis, but its lengthy apostrophe to the personified yard contains an epistemological ambiguity humorously related to Pope's questions about how the penis/phallus comes by its symbolic content and is experienced by men. In his "Advertisement by the Editor" Wilkes deploys a familiar discourse about how the man-yard equation was often symbolized: "We see the *Pride* and *Glory* of Man well represented in *that* stately Pillar" (Wilkes, 204). As the nature of this relationship is playfully pursued, however, matters quickly become more difficult, especially when the mischievous Wilkes parodies lines 35 and following from the first epistle of the original. As readers will recall, Pope's famous lines challenge universal man—proud, blind, insolent, and infinitesimal—to comprehend the meaning of his relative position within the larger cosmic context of Godly dispensations and designs: "Presumptuous Man! the Reason wouldst thou find, / Why form'd so weak, so little, and so blind?" (*TE* 3, i: 17–18, ll. 35–36). In the Wilkesian metamorphosis, Pope's universal man becomes the personified genital organ: "Presumptuous Prick! the reason wou'dst thou find, / Why form'd so weak, so little, and so blind?" (221, ll. 35–36). Wilkes's parody of the tortured egotistical and epistemological search for the meaning of one's position in the vast scale of being is here applied to the problematic penis, whose symbolic function is comically held forth. Wilkes's personified pego is itself the sign of a cultural confusion, both an exaggerated abstraction of masculinity—the phallus as synecdoche and commodity—and an unpredictable and wayward bit of gristle whose larger purposes are uneven, variable, or perhaps simply unfathomable. Laughable though it may be, there is a revealing cultural tension in Wilkes's use of Pope's famous poem to make the "positions" of both man *and* his penis—their symbolic function, relative importance, epistemological and hierarchical perch—equivalent and interchangeable questions. Like Pope, Wilkes poses the question of the relativity of symbolic systems themselves, acknowledging that the framework of signification will determine the symbolic economy and its metaphorical logic. However, given the problematic varieties and potential oppositions of such economies, the penis is also an emblem of a fundamental uncertainty about maleness: on the one hand, this "stately Pillar" is "the *Pride* and *Glory* of Man," but on the other—to use more famous lines from Pope's second epistle—the presuming pego joins its owner as "The Glory, Jest, and Riddle, of the World!" (*TE* 3, i: 56, l. 18). There is, in other words, a curious doubleness in the man's experience of what his yard will mean, and *An Essay on Woman* comically points to this shifting contextual terrain.

Interested in how the yard is made meaningful as a symbol, sign, and bodily part, Wilkes's parody addresses some of the ways the "Presumptuous Prick" enters and occupies the symbolic economies of rank, hierarchy, and gradations of male power. Recalling Pope's *Sober Advice*, Wilkes musters his own political jibe, aiming squarely at his enemy Lord Bute (rumored by opponents to owe his political prominence to a sexual liaison with the King's mother, the Princess Dowager):

> Of Pego's possible, if 'tis confess'd
> That Wisdom infinite must form some best,
> Where all must rise, or not coherent be,
> And all that rise must rise in due Degree;
> Then in the scale of various Pricks, 'tis plain,
> Godlike erect, BUTE stands the foremost Man,
> And all the Question (wrangle e'er so long)
> Is only This, if Heaven plac'd him wrong. (223, ll. 43–50)

Two familiar discourses are at work here: pego and cocksmanship as differentiator of male rank, with "Godlike" erection and copulatory vigor the markers of power or political might (as we have seen earlier in the examples of Charles II, Bolingbroke, Bathurst, Lincoln, Boswell, Captain Cock in *A Voyage to Lethe*); against this "scale" of man-as-pego is the inverse formula comically suggesting that the "foremost" man is also—in its insulting sense—the biggest prick of all, who has been dangerously misplaced near the seat of political power. In these clever and outrageous lines, the initial implications of the direct equation—ostensibly positive and flattering—satirically open upon the insult of the inverse model.

As it turns out, knowing the meaning of the yard is as difficult in Wilkes's poem as knowledge of man's cosmic position in Pope's *Essay*:

> When the proud Stallion knows whence every Vein
> Now throbs with Lust, and now is shrunk again;
> The lusty Bull, why now he breaks the Clod,
> Now wears a Garland, fair Europa's God:
> Then shall Man's Pride and Pego comprehend
> His Actions and Erections, Use and End. (225, ll. 61–66)

In this epistemological opacity there is only a frustrating doubleness for "Man's Pride and Pego." What makes both Wilkes and Pope so important in any historical consideration of discourses about the yard is the kind of self-consciousness their two poems represented, offering (in transgressive, impolite treatments) some sense of the disjunction for individual men of the experiencing self and the experience of self-as-commodity. While the array of equations and symbolic associations we have examined certainly must have affected men's perceptions, the experience of having a yard was not necessarily identical with or wholly explained by them. These self-conscious works by Pope, Wilkes, and others captured some sense of this gap, of how individual males encountered the cultural commodification of their selfhood as defined by their pintles, and how the experience of their own crotches could be rife with confusion. Wilkes's obscene parody astutely recognized the possibility that individual man-with-penis could never completely or perfectly inhabit the newer discourses of the phallus-as-commodity—that the self as biology and symbol would always be experienced as unresolvable tension or ambiguity. And for Pope's talking tarse, the mind-genitalia connection would be a mutually alienating one, with enigmatic imagination never necessarily in service of the yard, and yard not always any true indication of mind.

Yard-Wars: Cibber et al. Versus Little Alexander

For male authors the mind-genitalia equations could be especially problematic. Head-groin associations meant that creativity could be figured as the yard of wit, and the new wit/phallus-as-commodity circulated as a rhetoric anyone might appropriate and own. In this fracturing of the man's relationship to the defining site of his own creativity, the yard of wit was simultaneously about masculine power and loss, figured variously as an erotic sway or depletion. But literary men also had real penises, and occasionally the literal groins of writers spectacularized the cultural discourses about the phallus-as-commodity. Pope's penis had been attacked in a variety of satires, but rumors of his urinary stricture and Colley Cibber's *A Letter from Mr. Cibber to Mr. Pope, Inquiring into the Motives that might induce him in his Satyrical Works, to be so frequently fond of Mr. Cibber's Name* (1742) removed the all-important line separating literal and figurative pintles. The result was that the genitals of England's most famous living poet were comically hauled up into the public limelight where their literal condition was made to testify to little Alexander's status as man and writer. This amazing traffic in men, yards, and male creativity was humiliating to Pope, but to others it meant money.

There is a significant prehistory to Cibber's *Letter*, however, which contextualizes his attack on Pope's penis. I want briefly to examine other yard-attacks which pre-date Cibber's humiliation of Pope, suggesting that the 1742 *Letter* needs to be read as part of a common cultural language. As we have seen, the sexualized body of the male poet had been anatomized into a variety of stereotypes by which poets' heads and genitals could be used as ornaments in metapoetic self-dramatization or armaments in satirical battles. Tropes of poet-as-pintle or wit-as-yard were used not only as key metaphors to describe the private, internal site of male inspiration, but also as rhetorical items which circulated within the increasingly commercialized male writerly community. As in the impotence trials, where a man's pintle and personality could be unceremoniously separated as part of a process by which the status of his virility could be established, so too in the public literary tribunal a poet's pego could be figuratively detached from its owner and brought before peers and a prurient readership there to be adjudicated as emblem of his creative power. Attacks ranged from casual deployment of metaphor and allusion to extended analogies and full-blown narratives in which stories about a man's tarse were transparently equivalent to assessments of literary worth or public stature. Commodified as his privy member, and then made mock of, the poet either ignored the attack in silence or retaliated.

Like Cibber, Pope, too, was not above attacking the yards of others, making imaginative but also sometimes hackneyed use of the mind-genitalia inventory. He would draw upon the collective rhetoric of genital assault as early as 1716, where in his *A Further Account of the Most Deplorable Condition of Mr. Edmund Curll, Bookseller. . .* the loss of *"one Testicle"* at School by the bite of a black Boar"[28] was added to crude scatological satire. Years later, in "A Strange but True Relation how Edmund Curll . . . Out of an Extraordinary Desire of Lucre, went into Change-Alley, and was converted from the Christian Religion by certain Eminent Jews: And how he was circumcis'd and initiated into their mysteries,"[29] Pope delivered another low blow, turning Curll's fictionalized circumcision-for-gain into accidental castration.

Pope worked in other less malicious veins, too, as is evident in a letter to Lady Mary while she was abroad with her husband and soon to visit Turkey. Although Pope allowed neither passage to stand unrevised in editions of his correspondence published during his lifetime, the original text reveals a different strategy—here the coy but unbuttoned poet clearly comfortable with insinuations about yards and stones, even if to polite fashionable women: "I shall look upon you no longer as a Christian, when you pass from that charitable Court to the Land of Jealousy, where the unhappy Women converse with none but Eunuchs, and where the very Cucumbers are brought to them Cutt"; "I shall hear at Belgrade, how the good Basha receivd the fair Convert with tears of joy, how he was charm'd with her pretty manner of pronouncing the words Allah, and Muhammed, and how earnestly you joind with him in exhorting Mr Wortley to be circumcised" (*Corr.* 1: 368, 369, 10 November 1716). Hardly worthy of elaborate analysis, these teasings are still useful in suggesting the extent to which male privy members represented an available inventory of imaginative play even in Pope's long-distance courtship. For her part, Lady Mary was too smart to respond to her friend's sexual banter, but its jealous gallantry and the sly insinuation of Pope's own phallus as desirable over deficient cucumbers and husbands would have been entirely transparent to the sophisticated traveler. Although this epistolary cheek was not intended for public consumption, it embodies another side of the rhetorical traffic in male genitalia, an intimate and somewhat more friendly version of the phallic pride-of-place which informed the public yard-attacks.

Minor poems such as "A Roman Catholick Version of the First Psalm" (1716, published piratically) and "The Six Maidens" (written 1732, unpublished until the twentieth century) likewise testify to Pope's considerable interest in the risings and fallings of the male member, its status as a bodily "thing," and its multiplicity of cultural implications. But none of these poems formed part of a literary quarrel. For the most memorable of his yard-attacks we must turn to Pope's famous Sporus-Hervey portrait in 1735, a passage so often explicated that the originality of the sexual context of Pope's attack is easily underestimated. Other instances of Hervey-bashing typically aimed at two features: his effeminate appearance (sign of his sodomitical tendencies) and his political function within Robert Walpole's court.[30] Although nicknames for Hervey called attention to his effeminacy by invoking female genitalia (either "Lord Fanny" or "Miss Fanny"), satirical attacks on Hervey's genitals are surprisingly rare. One of the very few examples is *The Countess's Speech to her Son Roderigo . . .* (1731), an uninspired, anonymous squib recounting Hervey's duel with William Pulteney,[31] the title-page motto of which was "Ne'er was a harder Case, pray let me tell you, / To have a Small Prick at Bottom of the Belly." Compared to these clumsy satires, Pope's is the only attack which cleverly synthesized all three contexts—Hervey's effeminate sexuality, his Walpolean politics, and his yard—through the brilliant stroke of turning Hervey into Sporus, Nero's castrated boy-wife. Aspects of the assault on Hervey's sodomitical character and political sycophancy have received proper critical attention,[32] but what remains unremarked is Pope's unique use of the yard-man equation. By presenting courtier Hervey as the castrated and sexually-passive Sporus, the entire political milieu of Walpole's regime was cast as an unnatural, sycophantic sodomy, with pathick Hervey the corrupted and despicable receptacle for sodomite Walpole-as-Nero. Moreover, Pope makes clear that, in the public scale where a man's worth may be seen to be informed somehow by the status of his crotch, Hervey's "thing"—slang for penis—is no thing at all, or rather, "that Thing of silk" (*TE* 4: 117, l. 305); at best, an "Amphibious Thing"(*TE* 4: 119, l. 326), a male body whose "Parts . . . none will trust" (*TE* 4: 120, l. 332). Pope leaves an image of a Hervey whose politics, court connections, masculinity, personal integrity, and body are to be understood together as equivalent to a man deprived of his penis, conveniently available to the yard of his master. Nasty and clever, the passage positions Hervey's masculinity in opposition to Pope's, who writes of himself immediately following the Sporus passage, "That, if he pleas'd, he pleas'd by manly ways" (*TE* 4: 120, l. 337). In the public forum where a contest of privy members could produce phallic winners and emasculated losers, this scathing and memorable portrayal of Lord Hervey suggests that Pope could give as good as he got.

And take it he did. As we fill out the pre-Cibber contexts in which Pope's penis was placed at the forefront of satirical attacks (or in which he was comically juxtaposed to the phallic superiority of male antagonists), it is important to remember his own aggression in the examples above, because the satirical bile of his enemies makes it easy to feel sorry for Pope.[33] Edward Ward's seldom discussed *Apollo's Maggot in his Cups: or, the Whimsical Creation of a Little Satyrical Poet* (1729) is a case in point.[34] This twenty-eight page lampoon embodies a revealing combination of the two metaphorical economies: male creativity dramatized both as a birthing scenario attended by Apollo and the Muses, and as a direct result of the yard or some transformation of masculine genital energy. Part of the backlash against Pope after his 1728 *Dunciad* and *Peri Bathous*, the poem begins with a drunken feast in the heavens til gods and goddesses alike are "in their Cups . . . And left the Care of this low'r World, / At sixes and at sevens."[35] Slipping down to Parnassus to sober up, Apollo approaches the idle Muses, suggesting that "We'll form a little snarling Wit, / And call the thing a POET. / Not that we'll be so bold or vain / To give him human Stature, / But 'twixt a Monkey and a Man, / Just hammer out the Creature" (8). Taking upon themselves the task of forming the poet's body, the Muses combine rubbish, dirt, their own urine and feces, and chopped laurel. Then, using an imperfectly shaped hog-trough to mould the trunk of the poet's body, they attach their handcrafted limbs, "Some crooked and some straighter, / Which made the Muses blush to find / Their Workmanship no better" (18). The birth of this monstrously formed poet-figure now awaits the divine breath of Apollo, who summons Vulcan to put his bellows into the "backward Vent" until "With Air, had fill'd each Organ, / Which kind suppository Puff / Gave Life to little *Durgen* [dwarf]" (22). Of course, Ward is working ironically here with a familiar discourse: the glorious birthing of the male poet from some quasi-sexual conjunction of Apollo and the Muses becomes an anal birth-giving to a Frankenstein-like monstrosity. "Pope" is the deformed offspring whose placement in symbolic terrains will not be near holy streams atop mountains of sacred inspiration; instead, *"Fleet-ditch* shall be his *Helicon,* / And *Bridewel* his *Parnassus"* (28).

Having mustered his best satirical reduction of the poet-birthing tropes, Ward cannot resist adding the yard-wit discourse to complete his assault on Pope. Surveying the work of the Muses, Apollo points out that they have forgotten to provide their misformed poet a "thing":

> Besides, my Dames, in this your Work,
>   There's one Neglect that vexes,
> You've quite forgot the middle Mark
>   That should distinguish Sexes.
> For what Anatomist can tell,
>   By this poor thingless Body,
> Whether you mean it for a Male,
>   Or for a Female Dowdy.
> 'Tis strange you Mistresses of Art,
>   With Love so well acquainted,
> Should quite forget that noble Part,
>   For your delight appointed.
> The Muses blush'd at this Reproof,
>   B'ing modest, young and tender,
> So dab'd on just an Inch of Stuff,
>   Enough to shew the Gender. (18–19)

That the poet's "poor thingless Body" is minimally transformed into maleness, with barely a "thing" at all, is an added insult to the parodic function of the reproductive trope: not only misbegotten and deformed, the grotesquely-fashioned male poet also has a minuscule prick, emblem of his creative status. Ward pretends that this is as it should be, comically invoking the inverse yard-wit equation:

> For Wits are very rarely blest
>   With an extensive Label,
> The am'rous Fool is always best
>   Adorn'd below the Navel. (18–19)

Positioned below fools in the penis-as-man inventory, and excluded from the elitist mythology of the chosen male poet born of Apollo and the Muses, "Pope" is given symbolic sexual embodiment: monstrous "pigmy Son" (23) born of Muses' piss and shit and the flatulent inspiration of a drunken Apollo, "Pope" is also nearly "thingless," placed in an unnatural and contemptible state where a masculine sexuality is almost undetectable. In Ward's satirical logic, "an Inch of Stuff" is a cruel but cunning stroke capturing Pope's size, character, and satire as an unredeemable littleness and deficient materiality.

Alexander's littleness would be folded into a very different phallic attack in *Ingratitude: to Mr. Pope* (1733), a brief anonymous pamphlet charging Pope with mean-spirited ingratitude to the Duke of Chandos and Addison. Complaining of his duplicity and slanderous poetry written against upstanding men of rank, the author warns that

The great Personages whom you therein most falsely calumniate, if you are really the Author, have a Design, as I am inform'd, to truss you by turns under one of their Arms, and then, by lowering your Worship, to *piss* upon you as an Insect beneath their Resentment any other way: Nor can you deny that you deserve such Treatment.[36]

But it is the frontispiece (see Figure 11) which interests me here, in particular the bottom panel depicting the diminutive and childish looking "Pope" being pissed on. Three things are noteworthy in this visual head-groin conceit: (1) the size of the urinating gentleman's yard, which seems to require both hands; (2) the obvious function of Pope's infantilization compared to the robust adult stature and hearty laughter of three of the four men; and (3) the ironic contrast of Pope's threat of satirical memorialization (the bubble reads: "Damn me if I don't put you all in the Dunciad!") with his graphically depicted humiliation. Size *is* of consequence in this illustration. Pope's comical helplessness (note the ineffectual waving of delicate hands) is emphasized by his exaggerated littleness, especially of the head and face, whose juvenile character contrasts with the broad manly faces of the three men we can see. The man's yard is also exaggerated in size, looking more like a large phallus than a limp, urinating penis. Indeed, this impressive two-fisted pego is at least as long as the poet's head and easily longer than the width of his face. Part of the sexual humiliation here turns upon the juxtaposition of little Alexander—puny and physically inferior—with the large phallus of the adult male body, but it also depends on his infantilization as well. The flailing "Pope" is the little boy excluded from the realm of adult masculine power and authority. That he is also urinated on is a denigrating reinforcement of his laughable position low in the hierarchy of maleness. And finally, for Pope's satirical writing—referred to in the bubble—to be comically outmatched by the large and erect privy member of the aggressor constitutes an additional insult. In the iconographic implications of the frontispiece, Pope's writing—even his most aggressive work against other men—is, like his body, unmanly by comparison to the masculine energies of his male opponents. At best, his *Dunciad* will be the ungrateful work of the subordinate boy who, having raised the ire of his superiors, will be publicly humiliated and put in his proper place by the power of the adult yard.

Considerably more sophisticated use of discourses about male genitalia is evident in Lady Mary's and Lord Hervey's *To the Imitator of the*

Figure 11. Frontispiece to *Ingratitude: to Mr. Pope* (1733). This item is reproduced by permission of *The Huntington Library, San Marino, California*.

Satire of the Second Book of Horace (1733). Having back at Pope's satirical references to them, their six page poem links Pope's satirical temperament and poetic practice negatively to both direct and inverse models. Predictably, Pope's sexualized male body becomes the vehicle and emblem of his poetry and moral character. The first of three such equations curiously associates Pope's satirical nastiness with a blind libertinism:

> Thine [Pope's satire] is an Oyster-Knife, that hacks and hews;
> The Rage, but not the Talent of Abuse;
> And is in *Hate*, what *Love* is in the Stews.
> 'Tis the gross *Lust* of Hate, that stil annoys,
> Without distinction, as gross Love enjoys:[37]

Reminiscent of the speaker's undiscriminating red-light area erections in Rochester's *The Imperfect Enjoyment*, Pope's blind satirical rage is imaged, however unlikely in reality, as an undiscriminating phallicism in brothels. In Lady Mary's and Hervey's construction, the lines serve up an image of the man who, "Without distinction," satirizes/fucks all who come within his reach. The inverse equation here—phallic competency producing worthless satire—is then replaced by the direct mode in which Pope the despised hunchback is incapable of being erotically moved or reformed by beauty:

> But how should'st thou by Beauty's Force be mov'd,
> No more for loving made, than to be lov'd?
> It was the Equity of righteous heav'n,
> That such a Soul to such a Form was giv'n;
> And shews the Uniformity of Fate,
> That one so odious, should be born to hate. (5)

His body an outer sign of his inner deformity, Pope-the-libertine now becomes crippled Pope-the-spurned, the odious poet whose sexual rejection and erotic unattractiveness together account for an unsavory poetry and character. In the logic of this equation, sexual acceptance and "for loving made" become requisite to poetic competence. The final strike comes with a challenge to the effectiveness of Pope's satirical attack: comparing his assaults first to the "fretful *Porcupine*" who "shoot[s] forth a harmless Quill" (6), the lines then use one of Pope's own couplets to convert him into the ineffectual insect (a common metaphor in Pope-bashing), before coming to the sarcastic sexual joke on Pope's "thing":

> Thus 'tis with thee:—whilst impotently safe,
> You strike unwounding, we unhurt can laugh.
> *Who but must laugh, this Bully when he sees,*
> *A little Insect shiv'ring at a Breeze?*

> One over-match'd by ev'ry Blast of Wind,
> Insulting and provoking all Mankind.
>   Is this the *Thing* to keep Mankind in awe . . . ? (7)

If "Pope" was earlier condemned for an undiscriminating phallicism, he is now given a *"Thing"* of insect proportion as metaphor for his "impotently safe" satire. Poets Lady Mary and Hervey cannot forbear a final bit of yard-traffic in the conclusion of this verse paragraph:

> Is this the *Thing* to keep Mankind in awe,
> *To make those tremble who escape the Law?*
> Is this *the Ridicule* to live so long,
> *The deathless Satire*, and *immortal Song?*
> No: like thy self-blown Praise, thy Scandal flies;
> And, as we're told of Wasps, it stings and dies. (7)

Using his own lines against him, and returning to the trope of Pope's insect-like aggression, the last couplet makes even the tiny wasp's phallic sting a self-destructive act. In this accomplished satire, Pope's enemies associate his satirical output with the yard in various ways, all of them negative: blind genital lust, erotic deprivation, tiny insect penis, suicidal phallic aggression. A reasonable surmise is that the poem hurt Pope, especially given his former passion for Lady Mary. And she, for her part, with Hervey's assistance, drew upon aspects of the collective inventory certain to embarrass and give pain.

In this literary milieu of attack and counter-attack, with fictionalized pintles and stones of enemies used freely as public targets for contemptuous put-downs, rumors of Pope's urinary stricture surfaced in the early 1740s. His first mention of the problem is in August 1739 in a letter to William Fortescue, but the most detailed information we have comes a year later in a letter to Hugh Bethel, Pope's confidante on these matters before and after the operation by the well-known surgeon, William Cheselden. The date of the operation appears to be 2 August 1740; Pope was fifty-two:

I am at last *resolvd* (tho perhaps *compelld* were the truer word) to submit to the Operation of Mr Cheselden; he comes to me to morrow for that End . . . and it is arrived of late to that point that I am waked five or six times in a night with a Pressure to make water, whatever Diet or Liquids I can use. You shall know how it goes with me; but it shall be upon this Bribe, that you first tell me how you do? . . . I kept this till another post that I might just tell you how I under go this operation. It is with a good deal of pain. the Stoppage is found by the Probe, and lies within an inch of the Os Pubis; it must be often repeated in hopes to wear the passage wider. The worst is the Pain upon every making water after it, for six or seven hours, the Salts of the Urine stimulating the Sore places; which must continue till by Use it grow more open & callous. The

Remedy is (at present) worse than the Disease, for that gives me no pain, but Uneasiness. (*Corr.* 4: 255–56, 2 August 1740)

Some idea of what this condition and procedure meant for the ailing poet can be gathered from Jean Astruc's *A Treatise of the Venereal Disease* (trans. 1737), whose description represents the standard view of these matters in Pope's day:

An obstinate Strangury frequently attends persons that have been troubled with frequent virulent *Gonorrhoea*'s, in which the urine is discharged, not in a full, even, continued stream; but like a slender thread, frequently interrupted and divided; it is not thrown to a good distance with an easy motion, but is scarcely pressed out with the most violent straining; it cannot be retained long in the bladder without giving great uneasiness, but is continually stimulating it, and solliciting a discharge.[38]

Pope's reference to the "Probe" which will "wear the passage wider" reflects a common (and highly uncomfortable) procedure by which the urethral blockage could be flattened or worn away. Astruc's preferred method of treating a strangury offers a graphic image of what Pope suffered at the hands of Cheselden:

it seemed proper to attempt those remedies only, which by an easy mechanism might dilate the straitened passage, and by dilating it repress the obstacles that were formed in it. For this end a strait, hollow, silver pipe was prepared, open at both ends, which could conveniently enough be introduced up the *urethra* as far as the beginning of the obstacles. . . . During the whole course of the cure, the Patient is to abstain from wine, venery, and exercise; to use a sober, moistening, cooling diet; to drink by way of ptisan, an infusion of Linseeds and Mallow flowers; lastly the *perinaeum* should be relaxed by an emollient fomentation. (336, 355)

A month and a half after the urethral dilatation by Cheselden, in a follow-up letter to Bethel, Pope's progress-report is an unhappy one:

I was willing to delay my answer a while to your very kind letter, in a view of giving you the fuller account of the Effect of my progress in the Operation for the Strangury. But I cannot do it in a way that will be satisfactory; for indeed the Severity of it, & the present Consequences from the Soreness of the Parts, made it too much for me to repeat often enough to obtain any effectual remedy. I find much will depend upon Diet & drink, and if that will not do to palliate I shall never be able to remove, the Complaint entirely. When one arrives to a certain Time of Life, stepping into Age, so many Maladies come upon us, that the only question seems to be, Which of them one had best die of? . . . So I must compound with the Piles, and Indigestion, and suffer them to get ground, in hopes to defeat the pains of the Strangury. Vegetable diet & cool liquors, with frequent purges, &c. (*Corr.* 4: 268–69, 26 September 1740)

How the word got out about Pope's urinary woes is unclear, and whether Cheselden or Bethel unwisely leaked the word to a gossip is beside the point now. Suffice it to say that the rumor circulated, and Pope had the experience of reading squibs not only about his fictionalized yard but also about the factual condition of his urethra and the sexual implications of his condition.

Significant here are the likely causes of the strangury as they were then understood. Although urinary strictures can be caused by nonvenereal infections, an enlarged prostate gland, or trauma such as horseback riding (something in which the younger Pope had indulged), a strangury was typically thought to be the result of an earlier gonorrhea, as the Astruc passage above suggests. While it is not at all certain that Pope ever experienced sexual intercourse—a possibility not lost on some satirists, who emphasized his sexlessness or erotic unattractiveness—public knowledge of his strangury allowed opponents to make links between an ill-fated copulation which left Pope with a clap and subsequent urinary stricture. Cibber's *Another Occasional Letter from Mr. Cibber to Mr. Pope* (1744)—a follow-up to his 1742 *A Letter from Mr. Cibber* and to Pope's 1743 *The Dunciad in Four Books*—would take this satirical direction. Claiming that Pope has been a greater "Martyr" to Love than he has, Cibber makes snide reference to the venereal causes of Pope's strangury: "for by the inadvertent Commiseration of thy Health which lately escap'd from a Person of Honour in my Hearing we are afraid, that if the earthen Receiver on thy Night-table could speak, it might tell us, by how slow a Distilment of Drop, by Drop (passing through the *Strainers* of a Stricture) thy Tears of Penitence, to this Hour, fall from thee!"[39] Conflating head and penis, so that tears and urine become equivalent signs of his earlier carnality and its punishment, Cibber presents the ailing poet in a genital tableau of pathetic discharge and Catholic mock-martyrdom, the sexual penitent revealed by indiscreet friends and personified bedpan.

What did these various references to his penis and urinary condition mean to Pope? We have only the most limited record of how he felt about these uses of the facts about his blockage and treatment, or the fictionalized accounts of his yard. Nevertheless, the impact on Pope surely must have been huge in its psychological toll. To be the great poet of Twickenham and watch the enemy publish insulting images of one's privy members was bad enough, although, as we have already seen, Pope knew how to return the favor in his own "manly ways," capable of brilliant satire flowing from a virile quill as well as crude counter-punches below the belt. But to have one's literal genitalia and urinary woes dragged into the print world was insult of another, more insidious, kind, perhaps—a devastating move from a collective inventory of tropes to the private, individual case which appeared to be based on blunt anatomical fact. As we return now to Cibber's first *A Letter from Mr. Cibber* in 1742, we need to recognize that its power to wound and embarrass—far more deeply than the other satires of Pope's sexual status—depended on the convenient collapsing of shared discourse and private condition which the whorehouse anecdote and Pope's strangury both afforded. Previous satires of his yard and sexuality could always be dismissed—however painful to Pope personally—as malicious exaggeration or downright lies effectively countered by his "manly" poetry. But here were two apparently accurate claims about his actual body which dismantled what Eric V. Chandler has called Pope's "state of corporeal denial,"[40] drawing direct attention for the first time in Pope's life, in public, to the factual, literal site of his penis. For someone as sensitive about his physicality as Pope, these public rumors must have been shattering. G. S. Rousseau has recently argued (in the context of Pope's response to opera and castrati) that the poet "*must* have been conscious of his symbolic phallic incongruity" and "of his own symbolic castration" given his physical deformity, lack of sexual outlets, bachelorhood, dependence on other men, decades of attack on his size and physical characteristics, the feud with Lady Mary, and so forth.[41] What Cibber's published attacks of 1742 and 1744 offered a prurient reading public was the possibility of finding out the truth about the famous poet's yard and fumbling attempts as a fornicator. For little Alexander, public exposure of this kind cut through to one of his deepest insecurities as a man, and by extension, as a male poet. In Cibber's anecdote, Pope's poetic accomplishment would be juxtaposed ignominiously to the performance of his yard. As humiliating as any impotence trial, Cibber's phallic tribunal brought Pope's penis into the public glare where it would testify—comically, laughably—to his manly and poetic stature.

   The alleged whorehouse episode in *A Letter from Mr. Cibber to Mr. Pope* is narrated with some skill by Cibber, who proceeds with the joke-teller's dramatic sense of how to generate humor even while setting up circumstantial description for an effective punch line:

He must excuse me, then, if in what I am going to relate, I am reduced to make bold with a little private Conversation. . . . He may remember, then (or if he won't I will) when *Button*'s Coffee-house was in vogue, and so long ago, as when he had not translated above two or three Books of *Homer*; there was a late young Nobleman (as much his *Lord* as mine) who had a good deal of wicked Humour, and who, though he was fond of having Wits in his Company, was not so restrained by his Conscience, but that he lov'd to laugh at any merry Mischief he could do them: This noble Wag, I say, in his usual *Gayetè de Cœur*, with another Gentleman still in Being, one Evening slily seduced the celebrated Mr. *Pope* as a Wit, and myself as a Laugher, to a certain House of Carnal Recreation, near the *Hay-Market*; where his Lordship's Frolick propos'd was to slip his little *Homer*, as he call'd him, at a Girl of the Game, that he might see what sort of Figure a Man of his Size, Sobriety, and Vigour (in Verse) would make, when the frail Fit of Love had got into him; in which he so far succeeded, that the smirking Damsel, who serv'd us with Tea, happen'd to have Charms sufficient to tempt the little-tiny Manhood of Mr. *Pope* into the next Room with her: at which you may imagine, his Lordship was in as much Joy, at what might happen within, as our small Friend could probably be in Possession of it: But I (forgive me all ye mortified Mortals whom his fell Satyr has since fallen upon) observing he had staid as long as without hazard of his Health he might, I, *Prick'd to it by foolish Honesty and Love*, As *Shakespear* says, without Ceremony, threw open the Door upon him, where I found this little hasty Hero, like a terrible *Tom Tit*, pertly perching upon the Mount of Love! But such was my Surprize, that I fairly laid hold of his Heels, and actually drew him down safe and sound from his Danger. My Lord, who staid tittering without, in hopes the sweet Mischief he came for would have been com-pleated, upon my giving an Account of the Action within, began to curse, and call me an hundred silly Puppies, for my impertinently spoiling the Sport; to which with great Gravity I reply'd; pray, my Lord, consider what I have done was, in regard to the Honour of our Nation! For would you have had so glori-ous a Work as that of making *Homer* speak elegant *English*, cut short by laying up our little Gentleman of a Malady, which his thin Body might never have been cured of? No, my Lord! *Homer* would have been too serious a Sacrifice to our Evening Merriment. Now as his *Homer* has since been so happily com-pleated, who can say, that the World may not have been obliged to the kindly Care of *Colley* that so great a Work ever came to Perfection?[42]

Warwick's prank stages the fundamental question: will "a Man of his Size, Sobriety, and Vigour (in Verse)" register a comparable phallicism in the arms of "the smirking Damsel"? Of course, the outcome is known in advance, given "the little-tiny Manhood of Mr. *Pope*," and thus the dwarfish poet is assigned a ridiculous role in an inverse sce-nario where poetic might and virility are accompanied not by potent yard and copulatory vigor—as in direct formulations—but rather by phallic littleness and erotic laughability. Cibber exaggerates the comic disproportion of Pope, whom he presents as the "little hasty Hero, like a terrible *Tom Tit*, pertly perching upon the Mount of Love." There is no revered genius here in Cibber's image, no beloved poet-son of Apollo and the Muses, atop sacred Parnassus, the elite mount of the chosen few among writers; but rather, a different Mount altogether, with hasty little bird-poet precariously perched on the whore's pubis, comically lubricious in intent and yet in danger of falling off, or into, the Damsel's "commodity." While Cibber acknowledges Pope's superior poetic capacity throughout his *Letter*, he contextualizes the poet's tal-ents alongside indignant claims about the malice of the *Dunciad* or, more spectacularly in the whorehouse story, as somehow related to Pope's pathetic cocksmanship.

But Cibber saves the best for last, ending the anecdote not with Pope's sexual puniness but with his own mock-heroic action in "sav-ing" the poet, "*Prick'd to it*," he says punningly, "*by foolish Honesty and*

Love." Relying now on a direct equation of poetic and phallic ability—
a poxed yard would prevent Pope's translation of Homer—Cibber
turns from puns on "cut short" and "our little Gentleman" to an erotic
triangulation of a comical order: engaged dangerously with "a Girl of
the Game" (47), Pope's groin and poetic career are obliged, he boasts,
"to the kindly Care of *Colley*," who has entered in a mock-flourish to
replace the whore, save the poet's penis, and guarantee the text. In
this travesty of sex/genitalia exchanged for art, Cibber makes himself
the real sexual agent in contrast to the poet's "little-tiny Manhood"—
the adult male of normal stature who forcibly transforms Pope's yard
into poetry, and without whose presence Pope's penis would be a worthless "thing," both as male anatomy and as symbolic creative repository.
In making Pope's literal and figurative yard so comically dependent
on his pretended good-nature, Cibber scored a brilliant hit, using the
double commodification of man-as-penis and male creativity-as-genitalia
to pin the ailing and famous poet in a discursive crossfire sure to wound.
But, as in Curll's devilishly renamed "Pope's-Head," Cibber propels
the poet's literary and sexual commodification into the public domain
of print culture and marketplace rivalry where Pope and his pintle
can now be owned and circulated as public items helpful to sales. As
Laura J. Rosenthal has noted, Cibber's anecdote of Pope and the prostitute also satirized "Pope's claim of superiority to market-driven professionals" by making Cibber the production-manager who has saved
the poet's " 'Homer' from infection by the market-driven prostitute,"
thus enabling Pope's translation to enter the market where he would
profit handsomely.[43] Eric V. Chandler has gone one step further in
suggesting that the figure of the prostitute herself is a means by which
Cibber can bracket Pope in "the growing commercialization of literary
and publishing practice," insinuating that "behind the scenes and in
his own way, Pope himself is every bit the whore and ultimately no different from anyone else, except perhaps in his inability, his feebleness
or impotence, in admitting his actual role in the marketplace."[44] To
these astute observations I would add that the whore's "commodity"—
her genitals-for-sale in the market of sex-for-money—is a version of
Pope's commodified "thing" in the marketplace of literary labor where
poets' heads and genitalia had potential economic value. "Pope," too,
had been turned into a "commodity," a "thing" of commercial traffic.
However brilliantly Pope's verse had tried to differentiate and distance his economically successful career from the crass materiality of
his Dunces and their Grub Street literary production, Cibber's *Letter*
of 1742 comically ignored such distinctions, making questions of
Pope's literary and pecuniary worth, masculine creativity, and public
stature as author dependent on Pope's yard. The *Letter* may have been
Cibber's most triumphant moment as Poet Laureate.

Cibber's *Letter* came out in late July 1742 and, as Norman Ault has noted, the fall-out was spectacular: in under two weeks four engravings were published which offered pictorial caricatures of Cibber's story; the August issue of *The Gentleman's Magazine* listed no less than six pamphlets relating to the *Letter*.[45] One of these, the anonymous *Sawney and Colley, a Poetical Dialogue: Occasioned by a Late Letter from the Laureat of St. James's, to the Homer of Twickenham* (1742), made fun of both Cibber and Sawney/Alexander, shrewdly noting that a voyeuristic public keen to watch their print-battle (as well as prurient interest in the whorehouse anecdote), was actually to their mutual advantage, and, with proper stage management, could increase sales for both of them:

So, Thee and I may make a Pother,
And closely press, in *Print*, each other;
The more we rail, the more bespatter,
'Twill make our *Pamphlets* sell the better;
Write *Satire*, then, for *Daily*-bread;
By G—d, you'll not by * *Prayer* [Pope's "The Universal Prayer," 1738] be fed.
Do you *Dunce* me, I'll *Tom-Tit* you—[46]

But the anonymous author took aim at Pope in particular, cashing in on Cibber's clever tom-tit image and bluntly suggesting that, no matter how sexually desirous little Sawney might be, only the lowest and most desperate of whores would ever consider letting him pay her for sex:

> For who, except a venal *Punkey*,
> That car'd not whether Man or *Monkey*,
> But set to Sale her *Titillation*,
> For Bread, not carnal Recreation,
> Would suffer Thee, *small* Friend, to come
> Within ten Foot of her *Fore-bum*?
> . . . .
> SAWNEY, I know thy *ruling Passion*
> Is *Love of Women*; but the Fashion
> Of that warpt Carcase, and sad Grace,
> Which hangs upon thy *Wezel* Face,
> Could only cold Contempt procure,
> And 'gainst thee barr'd the *fringed* Door:
> Hence all thy Libels on the *Fair*,
> Born not of *Hatred*, but *Despair*; (11–12)

Although rough and obscene, the satirical tactics in *Sawney and Colley* capture the kind of Pope-bashing which characterized the aftermath of Cibber's anecdote: the laughably horny Alexander Pope, lascivious little insect or weasel or monkey, pathetically equipped between his legs, dwarfed and deformed, spurned, frustrated, exposed with his breeches down in public before male peers and smirking Damsels, and yet still the most famous poet in England. Cibber's attack and the follow-up by other satirists brought together sex, masculinity, the author's wit, competition in the marketplace of letters, and, most remarkably, these interrelationships were foregrounded in the public coupling of Pope's wit and his penis, through the simple but scandalous image of the poet as would-be fornicator. A dramatic sexual traffic in male creativity, these pamphlets and engravings traded in head-groin associations at little Alexander's expense.

In this literary yard-tribunal Pope was in something of a trap: to publicly protest these stories of his carnality was to yield to charges of his sexlessness and phallic incompetence; to acknowledge some version of his having been a young rake—as in the libertine figure he liked to strut about in letters to Cromwell—was to yield to charges such as Curll's that Pope was in fact an immoral and lascivious hypocrite, capable of writing scurrilous poems such as "A Roman Catholick Version of the First Psalm" (1716)—which included a transparent reference to a "Maid's" giving her husband an erection using her hand (*TE* 6: 164, ll. 9–12)—but too cowardly to own up to his obscene authorship and personal immorality. Indeed, Pope privately denied Cibber's claim:

The story published by Cibber, as to the main point, is an absolute lie. I do remember that I was invited by Lord Warwick to pass an evening with him. He carried me and Cibber in his coach to a bawdy-house. There was a woman there, but I had nothing to do with her of the kind that Cibber mentions, to the best of my memory—and I had so few things of that kind ever on my hands that I could scarce have forgot it, especially so circumstanced as he pretends. . . . Pope 26–28 August 1742.[47]

Three months after Pope's death in 1744, Cheselden confirmed Pope's counter-claim, although his insinuations about the poet's earlier sexual activities make the gonorrhea-strangury connection ambiguous: "I could give a more particular account of his health than perhaps any man. Cibber's slander of a carnosity [is] false. [He] had been gay, but left it on his acquaintance with Mrs. Blount. [He] had been in fear of a c[lap], but even that [was] without grounds. . . . Cheselden August 1744."[48] I dwell on the public and private evidence surrounding Pope's strangury and Cibber's allegations to suggest how important these matters were at this moment to Pope and his contemporaries. No major writer before this had experienced the widespread public imaging of his privy members as direct signs of his literary stature. The diminutive poet, genitally insecure for much of his life, had been turned into the yard of wit, emblem of the creativity-sexuality discourses that had become rhetorical stock-in-trade, a language sure to garner profits.

Pope's penis had been made literal *and* literary; his poetry had been made flesh, a sordid matter about his "thing."

The magnitude for Pope of this public interest in his genitals ought not to be under-estimated, and Johnson's anecdote about his response speaks volumes:

I have heard Mr. Richardson relate that he attended his father the painter on a visit when one of Cibber's pamphlets came into the hands of Pope, who said: "These things are my diversion." They sat by him while he perused it, and saw his features writhen with anguish, and young Richardson said to his father, when they returned, that he hoped to be preserved from such diversion as had been that day the lot of Pope.[49]

Cibber, too, in his follow-up attack in 1744, *Another Occasional letter from Mr. Cibber to Mr. Pope*, sensed the powerful affront which his earlier pamphlet represented:

For, if I am rightly inform'd, the ridiculous Light which his Letter . . . has laid thee in, has hurt thee more, and lain deeper in thy Mind, than all the severer Attacks he has made upon thy Character. Now, there, I must own, thou seemest to me, to have been quite uneasy, in the wrong Place! For, sure, to have been expos'd, as a *bad Man*, ought to have given thee thrice the Concern, of being shewn a *ridiculous Lover*! . . . Thy taking it, then, so bitterly to heart, to have been compared to so pretty a little Creature, as a TOM TIT is a Weakness, I am asham'd to think thou wert capable of! Yet this, I am told is the unpardonable Provocation, which has once more, and so particularly, inflam'd thee! (51)

That Pope responded in 1743 by making Cibber the new mock-hero of *The Dunciad in Four Books*—the Laureate-buffoon incestuously asleep "On Dulness' lap" (220, Bk. 3: 2), awaiting the inseminating vision leading to monstrous literary reproduction—needs to be understood in large part as Pope's single, and most elaborate, pay-back for Cibber's assault on his yard.

Few people were interested in whether Pope denied Cibber's story or not. The whorehouse anecdote created a large-scale prurience not unlike the public fascination with testimony about the defendant's virility at impotence trials. And nothing could have whetted a reading public's interest more in the great poet's penis than copies of the four engravings which were displayed for sale in print shop windows within days of the publication of Cibber's *Letter*. The first two appeared on 31 July 1742, and the last two, identical to one another except in small detail, in the second week of August. In their different ways, each portrayed Cibber pulling the tiny Pope (by the heels) off the belly of a large, reclining woman, and a man, presumably Warwick, voyeuristically watching the action through a doorway or a hole in the wall.

Maynard Mack has reproduced the second print of 31 July entitled *An Essay on Woman, by the Author of the Essay on Man: Being Homer Preserv'd, or the Twickenham Squire Caught by the Heels*, with its iconic references to earlier stages of the Pope-Cibber quarrel.[50] But it is the first engraving from 31 July (see Figure 12), and the bawdiest of the four—the whore's breasts are exposed, Pope's breeches are down enough to expose his thigh—that interests me here. Entitled *The Poetical Tom-Titt perch'd upon the Mount of Love. Being the Representation of a Merry Description in Mr. Cibber's Letter to Mr. Pope. Publish'd according to Act of Parliamt, July 31. 1742. Price 6d*, this engraving is a pictorial allusion to one of the engravings illustrating a scene in the notorious *Histoire de Dom B* (see Figure 13), which had been published in French in 1741 and would be translated into English the following year.[51] The narrative moment which the *Dom B* plate illustrates comes early in the novel, with young Silas peering voyeuristically through a hole in the wall, masturbating while he observes the sex-play and intercourse of his stepmother Annette and the proctor of the convent.

Despite the reversal of image direction, the similarities of these two engravings are striking, and the congruence of small details is substantial enough to rule out accidental or coincidental likeness. The intertextual nature of much pictorial representation at this time has been emphasized by both Vincent Carretta, who points out that "verbal and visual political satirists from Pope to Charles Churchill communicated with a shared iconic vocabulary," and by Philip Stewart, who says of eighteenth-century pornographic illustrations "that any plate or set of plates made to accompany a given work are likely to be modeled more on previous ones than on any fresh, untainted reading of the text."[52] Although it was an easy enough matter for a skilled engraver to re-touch, repair, or significantly alter parts of a plate with scrapers, rockers, and burnishers so that new faces or ornamental features could be situated within a plate used earlier for different representational function,[53] the kind of pictorial plagiarism in *The Poetical Tom-Titt* seems not to be a case of the altered plate but rather a copied image whose similarities and modifications constitute a sexual allusion. Whether many viewers would have known that this illustration of Cibber's anecdote was a pictorial allusion to *Dom B* is impossible to know, but it is significant that so many people, in this case the engraver, wanted to provide his or her own imagistic commentary on Cibber's nexus of manliness, sexuality, and male creativity. And not only that, this one intertextual gesture also suggests, as do the earlier examples of this section, the extent to which cultural equations of man-yard/creativity-male sexuality could be satirically fashioned from a common vocabulary of tropes and images.

Figure 12. *The Poetical Tom-Titt perch'd upon the Mount of Love. Being the Representation of a Merry Description in Mr. Cibber's Letter to Mr. Pope. Publish'd according to Act of Parliamt, July 31, 1742.* By permission of the British Library. Shelfmark D.G. 2571 33182/2/4.

Figure 13. Pornographic scene from Jacques Charles Gervaise de La Touche's *Histoire de Dom B* (1741). By permission of the Bibliothèque Nationale de France, Paris.

What, then, does the allusive use of *Dom B* bring to the public circulation of a commodified Pope, available here as the sexualized Tom-Titt at a modest 6d? In this more discreet copy of the pornographic original, there are no erect pintles (although Pope's breeches are clearly open and drawn down), and yet comparative reference to the French plate reveals a variety of phallic replacements and transferences of intriguing symbolic import. Cibber now occupies the position of the monk, and "Pope" of the monk's hardened tarse. But in turning the famous poet—his corporeality, creative abilities, reputation—into *the* yard, the engraving also intimates that this poet-phallus is Colley's, that Pope is merely a kind of yard-prosthesis, an extension of Colley's cock, which is being frigged in readiness for the whore's commodity. And Cibber's left hand: is this a trademark Cibberian flourish, a measure of Pope's "little-tiny Manhood," or a lewd hand symbol for the hired vagina which Colley's Pope-pego is about to enter or be pulled out of? The function of the voyeur is also suggestive. As Robert Darnton has pointed out, the figure of the secret gazer—often masturbating to the scene he or she is witnessing—which is so common in eighteenth-century pornographic illustrations, is a visual trope figuring the reader's own masturbatory relationship to the scene.[54] In these two engravings, however, the voyeur figure mirrors more than the foregrounded sex-scene or the reader's prurient engagement with text; both illustrations emphasize the sense of homosocial and possibly homoerotic witnessing of phallic enterprise, with the added insinuation in *The Poetical Tom-Titt* of a sodomitical aggression: that is, while the relationship of Cibber's and Pope's bodies can be read against *Dom B* so as to situate the poet as the Laureate's readied tarse-in-hand, Colley's leaning toward little Alexander's backside can also be translated as Pope's being buggered by his antagonist. In either case, the diminutive poet is portrayed as pathetically small and ineffectual against the huge woman's body, useful only in reference to the implied yard of Cibber, and poetically able only on condition of his being a sexual laughing stock.

These readings of the pictorial record can be offered only as my own speculation about one engraver's intent, but whatever decoding one might finally prefer, the intertextual and allusive dynamic linking the two engravings is emblematic, as it seems to me, not only of the cultural association of sexuality, creativity, masculine competition, and questions of literary value, but also of the energy and sometimes vicious intensity of the new literary marketplace. Cibber's anecdote resulted in Pope's being bought and sold in ways he could not have predicted and doubtless despised: his head, yard, and creativity had been made laughably interchangeable and hung out for public purchase by the likes of Curll, Cibber, and anonymous engravers and pamphleteers. The yard of wit had entered the newer capitalist realm of writers and writing for profit, a sometimes tawdry economy of letters where the traffic in head-groin images was sure to sell books. In this increasingly commercial domain where, as Richard Savage had said ironically in 1729, there was *An Author to be Lett*, it is a historical irony that Alexander Pope had grown richer than his Dunce-enemies despite, or perhaps partly because of, these attacks on his yard.

The yard of wit, that commercial symbol of men's bodies and their imaginations, is still with us. The historical shift in the eighteenth century which turned the penis into both a synecdoche and a commodity in circulation is our inheritance, although we seldom realize it. To take one example: the variously construed gaps between penis and phallus, between literal and figurative genitalia, are significant historical developments which Lacanian and feminist psychoanalysis has inherited, and yet this history is largely obscured or ignored in versions of the postmodern Phallus. The new Priapus of the eighteenth-century literary marketplace, likewise, is our heritage, persisting in all sorts of ways from clichés about male intellectual accomplishment (or failure) to electronic images of male genitalia informed by stereotypes of head-groin relationships. Trapped as we still are within that cocoon of neo-Freudian forgetfulness, the history of men's bodies easily disappears, and along with it the antecedents of modern and postmodern symbol-making. I cannot here begin to explore in detail the historical connections between then and now—that would require another lengthy study. But historical continuities are also important to this book's subject, and as an end-piece I offer two recent examples to demonstrate how the Enlightenment yard of wit continues to be both a synecdoche and a commodity.

Current analyses and representations of Pope have certainly inherited discourses of the man-yard and creativity-genitalia equations, although not always conscious of this legacy. In 1980, Book-of-the-Month-Club's alternate choice was a lavishly produced ersatz eighteenth-century novel by Erica Jong, complete with sexy cover photo of a woman's leg in stockings and garters. It sold well. *Fanny: Being the True History of the Adventures of Fanny Hackabout-Jones*[55] offered up a clever and playful narrative in which the sexually-curious, seventeen year-old foundling, Fanny, has opportunity to meet "the Divine Dwarf, Mr. Pope" (32). The first-person narrator sets up the encounter by explaining two features of her former naiveté: "It did not then occur to me that Poets perhaps write in order to . . . augment with their Quills the paltry Equipment Nature hath bestow'd upon 'em" (25); and, that "we presume, in our Innocence, that a beauteous Brow contains a beauteous Brain, a handsome Mouth, handsome Words, and a robust manly Form, robust manly Deeds. Alas, my Daughter, 'tis not so" (26).

Following this, Fanny recounts being in bed, imagining herself becoming a poetess, when "Pope" enters and begins taking liberties:

Alarm'd as I was, I could not think of how to interrupt him without insulting an honour'd Guest, and as he suckt upon one Nipple and then the other, firing my Blood and putting all my Thoughts into Disorder, my Resolve grew e'er more befuddl'd. For tho' I found his Person loathsome, his Words were fine and elegant, and despite what he argu'd about the Fair Sex and the Art of Poesy, I was e'er more conquer'd by fine Language than by fine Looks. (41)

Continuing to grope and fondle Fanny, "Pope" then explains that women are not meant to be poets:

Whereupon he loosen'd his Breeches, fumbl'd 'neath his Waistcoat and curious Doublet for his tiny pink Member, threw my Petticoats above my Head, and stood ready to assault my Maidenhead, with the very Weapon made for the Purpose. But my Guardian Angel must have been attending me at that Moment, for just as he drew near my tender Virgin Cunnikin, his own Eagerness brought on the Ultimate Period of his Hot Fit of Lust, of which my firm young Thighs and clean Petticoats receiv'd the egregious Effusion. (42)

What interests me about this portrayal is how completely similar Jong's treatment is to Colley Cibber's satire of Pope in his whorehouse *Letter*. To enable one aspect of her late twentieth-century feminist humor, author Jong replicates the two dominant modes, direct and inverse, which originate in the earlier culture: Fanny's initial assumption that there is a one-to-one correspondence between masculine physicality—beauty, strength, sexuality—and male creativity, and, her revised equation of famous poet/brilliant poetry as genital deficiency or phallic incompetence (here, Pope the premature ejaculator of little pego). Whether Jong—who is no stranger to eighteenth-century studies[56]—was entirely aware that hers was an accurate reconstruction of these discursive elements is not so important as the fact that, like Cibber, she trades in the yard of wit, owning Pope's literal and symbolic dick for humor, insult, and commercial gain. Like Cibber's *Letter* of 1742, Jong's rendition is part of the sexual traffic in male creativity in which the yard of wit is appropriated as a commodity—in this case a "tiny pink member" for sale. Cibber and Jong have different aims, but their tactics are identical and historically related: the genital essence and origins of male creativity are taken for granted, circulated as a common rhetoric, and wittily served up to a literary market which has a taste for such imagery and is willing to pay for it.

We have also inherited the idea of Pope's yard of wit as synecdoche. In 1986, Brean S. Hammond published *Pope*,[57] a smart and accessible book which applied what in the mid-80s were newer critical approaches to questions of political and gender ideology. In a chapter on Pope's poems about women, Hammond argued that

Pope was both a marginal and a castrated figure and it seems likely that Pope's attitudes were not those of the normative eighteenth-century male, and that he was less oppressed than most by the prevailing sexual politics. He had an unusually heightened sense of his physical incapacities and understood how these compromised his gender orientation. . . . If the reader accepts the hypothesis that Pope's marginalised sexuality entails his occupation of an unusual gender position, his experience of physical harassment and discrimination giving him at least some insight into sexual oppression, there is still no reason to accept that this is manifest in the poems. Far from it. Indeed, there is an observable paradox here. For Pope *is* the phallus for the poetry of the age. In the *Epistle to Dr Arbuthnot*, Pope, having devoted some lines to that creature of uncertain gender Sporus, goes on to refer to his own verse as "manly", almost as a way of washing his hands after the distasteful contact with Hervey. (154, 159–60)

Expert in the period, Hammond also replicates aspects of Enlightenment discourses we have examined: here, Pope the figurative castrate whose physical incapacity and sexual starvation are compensated by a brilliant poetry whose "manly" character transforms both the poet and his verse into an honorary yard, an engorged pego symbolically representative of the sexualized character of male creativity itself. Hammond's version of Pope's phallus is also a traffic in the yard of wit—in this case a desktop traffic in abstracted academic ideas—but his "phallus for the poetry of the age" is an invisible phallus, *not* the mixed literal-figurative mode of "a Dr. Johnson" or a Pego Borewell—Wilkes's modern herm applied to Pope's head. We can see in this modern analysis a conceptual shifting toward the already symbolic yard which characterizes the Lacanian/feminist Phallus. Indeed, Hammond's equation wants Pope's literal penis to disappear altogether ("a castrated figure"), replaced by the yard-man synecdoche, and in this sense he is linked historically to late-seventeenth and eighteenth-century juxtapositions of particular-man-with-penis and yard-as-maleness. The origins of his symbolic phallus as academic commodity are clearly rooted in the discursive terrain of the earlier period, but Hammond's gesture is also symptomatic of the historical development precipitated by the Enlightenment commodification and commercialization of the masculinity-genitalia conjunction: the separation of literal from symbolic genitalia. For the likes of Cibber, Pope's penis was both literal and figurative, although Colley shrewdly knew the greater value of Alexander Pope the wit-phallus-as-commodity. Inheriting these eighteenth-century conceptual modes, our modern practice has more fully separated humble yard from symbolic Phallus, which ironically has obscured the history of that separation. No wonder that historical questions about men's bodies and real penises have tended so easily to slip away from academic and scholarly discussion, absorbed or forgotten by a presentist obsession with the timeless and always already symbolic realm. My point is that there is good reason to consider the extent to which our own conceptual vocabulary is dependent on early modern formations, and that our current clichés about the phallus need to be replaced by a more conscientious historicism.

In another sense, Hammond is exactly right about Pope's being the phallus for the poetry of the age, since Alexander the Little was the most prominent (if not the first) sexualized commercial symbol for male creativity in the new marketplace of letters.

Notes

Chapter 1. Introduction: Male Creativity and Its Changing Contexts

1. John Tosh, "The Old Adam and the New Man: Emerging Themes in the History of English Masculinities, 1750–1850," in *English Masculinities 1660–1800*, ed. Tim Hitchcock and Michèle Cohen (London: Longman, 1999), 230–31.

2. Anthony Fletcher, *Gender, Sex, and Subordination in England, 1500–1800* (New Haven, Conn.: Yale University Press, 1995), 322–23. Samuel Johnson's *Dictionary* (1755) does not include "masculinity," instead encompassing the various senses of maleness in eight entries: "Man," "Manful," "Manfully," "Manfulness," "Manhood," "Manlike," "Manliness," "Manly." The dominant Johnsonian definitions include "Human nature," "Virility" (as opposed to womanhood, childhood), "Courage," "Bravery," "Resolution," "Fortitude," "Dignity," "Stoutness," "Becoming a man," "Firm," "Undaunted," "Undismayed."

3. Tosh, "The Old Adam and the New Man," 236.

4. Tim Hitchcock and Michèle Cohen, Introduction, in *English Masculinities 1660–1800*, ed. Hitchcock and Cohen, 21.

5. Randolph Trumbach has refined his paradigm in a handful of essays, the best known of which are "Sodomitical Assaults, Gender Role, and Sexual Development in Eighteenth-Century London," *Journal of Homosexuality* 16 (1989): 407–29; "The Birth of the Queen: Sodomy and the Emergence of Gender Equality in Modern Culture, 1660–1750," in *Hidden from History: Reclaiming the Gay and Lesbian Past*, ed. Martin Bauml Duberman, Martha Vicinus, and George Chauncey, Jr. (New York: New American Library, 1989), 29–40; "Gender and the Homosexual Role in Modern Western Culture: The 18th and 19th Centuries Compared," in *Homosexuality, Which Homosexuality?* ed. Dennis Altman, Carole Vance, et al. (London: GMP Publishers, 1989), 149–69; and "London's Sapphists: From Three Sexes to Four Genders in the Making of Modern Culture," in *Body Guards: The Cultural Politics of Gender Ambiguity*, ed. Julia Epstein and Kristina Straub (New York: Routledge, 1991), 112–41. His recent book, *Sex and the Gender Revolution, Vol. 1, Heterosexuality and the Third Gender in Enlightenment London* (Chicago: University of Chicago Press, 1998), offers considerable evidence for his claim "that by 1730 the majority of men of all social classes had a heterosexual identity" (428).

6. See in particular G. S. Rousseau, "The Pursuit of Homosexuality in the Eighteenth Century: 'Utterly Confused Category' and/or Rich Repository?" *Eighteenth-Century Life* 11 (1986): 132–69; " 'In the House of Madame Van der Tasse': Homosocial Desire and a University Club During the Enlightenment," in *The Pursuit of Sodomy: Male Homosexuality in Renaissance and Enlightenment Europe*, ed. Kent Gerard and Gert Hekma (New York: Harrington Park Press,

1989), 311–48; "Love and Antiquities: Walpole and Gray on the Grand Tour," in his *Perilous Enlightenment: Pre- and Post-Modern Discourses Sexual, Historical* (Manchester: Manchester University Press, 1991), 172–99.

7. Thomas Laqueur, *Making Sex: Body and Gender from the Greeks to Freud* (Cambridge, Mass.: Harvard University Press, 1990).

8. Michael McKeon, "Historicizing Patriarchy: The Emergence of Gender Difference in England, 1660–1760," *Eighteenth-Century Studies* 28 (1995): 295–322.

9. Kristina Straub, *Sexual Suspects: Eighteenth-Century Players and Sexual Ideology* (Princeton, N.J.: Princeton University Press, 1992).

10. Jill Campbell, *Natural Masques: Gender and Identity in Fielding's Plays and Novels* (Stanford, Calif.: Stanford University Press, 1995), 12–3.

11. Raymond Stephanson, " 'Epicoene Friendship': Understanding Male Friendship in the Early Eighteenth Century, With Some Speculations About Pope," *Eighteenth Century: Theory and Interpretation* 38 (1997): 151–70.

12. Shawn Lisa Maurer, *Proposing Men: Dialectics of Gender and Class in the Eighteenth-Century Periodical* (Stanford, Calif.: Stanford University Press, 1998), 3.

13. George Haggerty, *Men In Love: Masculinity and Sexuality in the Eighteenth Century* (New York: Columbia University Press, 1999), 44–5, 143.

14. Philip Carter, "James Boswell's Manliness," in *English Masculinities 1660–1880*, ed. Hitchcock and Cohen, 126, 128, 129. In an important article which precedes Carter's, David M. Weed has explained how Boswell's "position at the nexus of several kinds of masculine identity" reflects the development of "a new relationship between male sexuality and market economics at mid-century" ("Sexual Positions: Men of Pleasure, Economy, and Dignity in Boswell's *London Journal*," *Eighteenth-Century Studies* 31 [1997–98]: 216, 231). Carter's new book, *Men and the Emergence of Polite Society, Britain 1660–1800* (Harlow: Longman, 2001) downplays the importance of sexuality as identity, arguing that the "dominant ideal would have been understood . . . as centred on men's participation in polite society" (209).

15. David M. Halperin, "Forgetting Foucault: Acts, Identities, and the History of Sexuality," *Representations* 63 (1998): 96.

16. Mark Breitenberg, *Anxious Masculinity in Early Modern England* (Cambridge: Cambridge University Press, 1996), 12.

17. Roy Porter, Introduction, in *Rewriting the Self: Histories from the Renaissance to the Present*, ed. Porter (London: Routledge, 1997), 9.

18. R. W. Connell, *Masculinities* (Oxford: Polity Press, 1995), 29.

19. Halperin, 97, 104, 109.

20. E. J. Hundert, "The European Enlightenment and the History of the Self," in *Rewriting the Self: Histories from the Renaissance to the Present*, ed. Porter, 81.

21. In addition to works by Trumbach and Fletcher listed above, see Robert B. Shoemaker, *Gender in English Society, 1650–1850: The Emergence of Separate Spheres?* (London: Longman, 1998), 59–86; two forthcoming studies by Thomas A. King: *Queer Articulations: Enacting Masculinity and Difference* (Madison: University of Wisconsin Press); *The Gendering of Men* (Madison: University of Wisconsin Press). Also see Alan Bray and Michel Rey, "The Body of the Friend: Continuity and Change in Masculine Friendship in the Seventeenth Century," in *English Masculinities 1660–1800*, ed. Hitchcock and Cohen, 65–84; Anita Guerrini, *Obesity and Depression in the Enlightenment: The Life and Times of George Cheyne* (Norman: University of Oklahoma Press, 2000); Lynn Hunt and Margaret Jacob, "The Affective Revolution in 1790s Britain," *Eighteenth-Century Studies* 34 (2001): 491–521; David Stevenson, *The Beggar's*

Bennison: Sex Clubs of Enlightenment Scotland and Their Rituals (East Lothian: Tuckwell Press, 2001); David Kuchta, *The Three-Piece Suit and Modern Masculinity: England, 1550–1850* (Berkeley: University of California Press, 2002). Other pertinent essays are located in endnotes throughout.

22. In their study of *Gout: The Patrician Malady* (New Haven, Conn.: Yale University Press, 1998), Roy Porter and G. S. Rousseau show how the gouty male body in the Enlightenment could serve as symbol of masculine superiority, the sign of the gentleman whose intellectual or creative abilities were manifested in the ailing male body; see especially chapters 6–7. See also Karen Harvey, " 'The Majesty of the Masculine Form': Multiplicity and Male Bodies in Eighteenth-Century Erotica," in *English Masculinities 1660–1800*, ed. Hitchcock and Cohen, who argues that "concerns about masculinity in wider cultural, social, economic and political contexts were projected" onto male genitalia (197).

23. For example, Richard G. Swartz, "Patrimony and the Figuration of Authorship in the Eighteenth-Century Literary Property Debates," *Works and Days* 7 (1989): 29–54; Linda Zionkowski, "Territorial Disputes in the Republic of Letters: Canon Formation and the Literary Profession," *Eighteenth Century: Theory and Interpretation* 31 (1990): 3–22; Catherine Gallagher, *Nobody's Story: The Vanishing Acts of Women Writers in the Marketplace, 1670–1820* (Berkeley: University of California Press, 1994); Laura J. Rosenthal, *Playwrights and Plagiarists in Early Modern England: Gender, Authorship, Literary Property* (Ithaca, N.Y.: Cornell University Press, 1996); Dustin Griffin, *Literary Patronage in England, 1650–1800* (Cambridge: Cambridge University Press, 1996); Brean S. Hammond, *Professional Imaginative Writing in England, 1640–1740: "Hackney for Bread"* (Oxford: Clarendon Press, 1997); Catherine Ingrassia, *Authorship, Commerce, and Gender in Early Eighteenth-Century England: A Culture of Paper Credit* (Cambridge: Cambridge University Press, 1998).

24. Linda Zionkowski, *Men's Work: Gender, Class, and the Professionalization of Poetry, 1660–1784* (New York: Palgrave, 2001).

25. For a fine study of the symbolic body part, see Robert A. Erickson's *The Language of the Heart, 1600–1750* (Philadelphia: University of Pennsylvania Press, 1997).

26. I have already examined one aspect of this cultural metaphor in "The Symbolic Structure of Eighteenth-Century Male Creativity: Pregnant Men, Brain-Wombs, and Female Muses (with some comments on Pope's *Dunciad*)," *Studies in Eighteenth-Century Culture* 27 (1998): 103–30.

27. I will be using the phrase "epicoene friendship" and the adjective "epicoene" to account for three rhetorical gestures of same-sex physical desire between predominantly heterosexual males which were not in themselves viewed as necessarily transgressive of gender codes for men at the turn of the century, and not yet the signs of the newly-defined effeminate adult male or deviant homosexual type: (1) an emotionally-charged language of love, (2) acts of narrative transvestism projecting one or both men as a female of sexual interest, and (3) desire for physical presence or bodily contact expressed in a sensuous language of appetite, grasping, or the fusion of bodies. This psychosexual rhetoric constituted part of a public discourse which encouraged men to imagine their friendship with other men in ways similar to their expressions of affection for wives and female lovers. See my " 'Epicoene Friendship': Understanding Male Friendship in the Early Eighteenth Century, With Some Speculations About Pope," *Eighteenth Century: Theory and Interpretation* 38 (1997): 151–70.

28. *The Correspondence of Alexander Pope*, ed. George Sherburn, 5 vols. (Oxford:

Clarendon Press, 1956), 1: 2, Pope to Wycherley, 26 December 1704. Subsequent references to this edition will be cited parenthetically.

29. Pope's sometimes transgressive gender play within the dominant patriarchal and heterosexual ideology has been recently sketched by Carole Fabricant, "Defining Self and Others: Pope and Eighteenth-Century Gender Ideology," *Criticism* 39 (1997): 503–29. For important studies which consider Pope and sexuality, see Paul-Gabriel Boucé, "The Secret Nexus: Sex and Literature in Eighteenth-Century Britain," in *The Sexual Dimension in Literature*, ed. Alan Bold (London: Vision Press, 1982), 70–89; Maynard Mack, " 'The Least Thing like a Man in England': Some Effects of Pope's Physical Disability on His Life and Literary Career," in *Collected in Himself: Essays Critical, Biographical, and Bibliographical on Pope and Some of His Contemporaries*, ed. Mack (Newark: University of Delaware Press, 1982), 372–92; Brean Hammond, *Pope* (Atlantic Highlands, N.J.: Humanities Press International, 1986); James Grantham Turner, "Pope's Libertine Self-Fashioning," *Eighteenth Century: Theory and Interpretation* 29 (1988): 123–44; G. S. Rousseau, "Scriblerians," in *The Gay and Lesbian Literary Heritage*, ed. Claude J. Summers (New York: H. Holt, 1995), 645–48.

30. Helen Deutsch, *Resemblance and Disgrace: Alexander Pope and the Deformation of Culture* (Cambridge, Mass.: Harvard University Press, 1996), 19, 2, 13.

31. G. S. Rousseau, " '*et in Arcadia homo*': Opera, Gender, and Sexual Politics in *The Dunciad*," in *'More Solid Learning': New Perspectives on Alexander Pope's Dunciad*, ed. Catherine Ingrassia and Claudia N. Thomas (Lewisburg, Pa.: Bucknell University Press, 2000), 43.

Chapter 2. Masculinity as Male Genitalia

1. For the ubiquitous public herms and male genital display of fourth-century Athens, see Eva C. Keuls, *The Reign of the Phallus: Sexual Politics in Ancient Athens* (New York: Harper and Row, 1985). The periodic phallic rituals and fertility rites of early Mediterranean cultures are well known to classicists and historians of sexuality. Early descriptions of the public adoration of the phallus can be found in Herodotus, *The Histories*, trans. A. D. Godley, Loeb Classical Library (New York: Putnam, 1920–25), 2.48–49, Plutarch, *Moralia*, trans. Frank Cole Babbett, Loeb Classical Library (New York: Putnam, 1920–25), 355 e, 358 b, 365 b, and St. Augustine, *De Civitate Dei: The City of God Against the Pagans* (Cambridge, Mass.: Harvard University Press, 1969–88), 7.21.

2. *The Twickenham Edition of the Poems of Alexander Pope*, ed. John Butt et al., 11 vols. (London: Methuen, 1961–1967), 4: 71–89. Subsequent references to this edition will be abbreviated *TE* and cited parenthetically by volume, page, and line numbers.

3. *A Voyage to Lethe; By Capt. Samuel Cock; Sometime Commander of the Good Ship the Charming Sally. Dedicated to the Right Worshipful Adam Cock, Esq; Of Black-Mary's-Hole, Coney-Skin Merchant* (London, 1741).

4. The onomastic punning in *A Voyage to Lethe* has been described briefly in Paul-Gabriel Boucé's "The Secret Nexus: Sex and Literature in Eighteenth-Century Britain," in *The Sexual Dimension in Literature*, ed. Alan Bold (London: Vision Press, 1982), 81–83.

5. Sander L. Gilman's *Sexuality: An Illustrated History Representing the Sexual in Medicine and Culture from the Middle Ages to the Age of AIDS* (New York: John Wiley, 1989); Thomas Laqueur's *Making Sex: Body and Gender from the Greeks to Freud* (Cambridge, Mass.: Harvard University Press, 1990).

6. The emergence of the popular sex manual (what I am calling "low" medical narratives) and its relationship to vernacular medical books ("high" narratives) about the organs of generation are enormously important in understanding the wide transmission of new knowledge among a non-specialist readership. But the pop-sexologies (the most famous were Aristotle's Master-Piece and Venette's Conjugal Love), works on midwifery, the anti-masturbation tracts, and the huge trade of publications on venereal disease also kept alive some of the older myths and nomenclature. The best treatments of these extremely popular sex manuals as vehicles of new medical concepts and older misinformation can be found in Paul-Gabriel Boucé, "Some Sexual Beliefs and Myths in Eighteenth-Century Britain," in Sexuality in Eighteenth-Century Britain, ed. Paul-Gabriel Boucé (Manchester: Manchester University Press, 1982), 28–46; Patricia Crawford, "Sexual Knowledge in England, 1500–1750," in Sexual Knowledge, Sexual Science: The History of Attitudes to Sexuality, ed. Roy Porter and Mikulas Teich (Cambridge, Mass.: Cambridge University Press, 1994), 82–106; and in several studies by Roy Porter: "Spreading Carnal Knowledge or Selling Dirt Cheap? Nicolas Venette's Tableau de l'Amour Conjugal in Eighteenth Century England," Journal of European Studies 14 (1984): 233–55; "The Literature of Sexual Advice Before 1800," in Sexual Knowledge, Sexual Science, ed. Porter and Teich, 134–57; and, with Lesley Hall, The Facts of Life: The Creation of Sexual Knowledge in Britain, 1650–1950 (New Haven, Conn.: Yale University Press, 1995).

7. Regnier De Graaf, Regnier De Graaf on the Human Reproductive Organs: An Annotated Translation of "Tractatus De Virorum Organis Generationi Inservientibus" (1668) and "De Mulierum Organis Generationi Inservientibus Tractatus Novus" (1672), trans. H. D. Jocelyn and B. P. Setchell (Oxford: Blackwell, 1972). As a textual repository of then-current knowledge and previous systems of explanation, the importance of Regnier De Graaf's Tractatus as a history of perceptual models of male parts has been largely ignored. He is much better known for his De Mulierum, the "Graafian follicle," interpretations of pancreatic function, and the development of syringes. Useful studies of De Graaf are few: Charles Singer, "The History of Anatomical Injections," in Studies in the History and Method of Science, ed. Charles Singer (Oxford: Clarendon Press, 1921), 2: 285–342; Julius Friedenwald and Samuel Morrison, "The History of the Enema With Some Notes on Related Procedures (Part 1)," Bulletin of the History of Medicine 8 (1940): 68–114; Hubert R. Catchpole, "Regnier De Graaf 1641–1673," Bulletin of the History of Medicine 8 (1940): 1261–1300; Mark Klein, "Regnier De Graaf," in Dictionary of Scientific Biography, ed. Charles Coulston Gillispie (New York: Charles Scribner's Sons, 1972), 5: 484–85; B. P. Setchell, "The Contributions of Regnier de Graaf to Reproductive Biology," European Journal of Gynecology and Reproductive Biology 4 (1974): 1–13; Jacques Roger, "Two Scientific Discoveries: Their Genesis and Destiny," in On Scientific Discovery, ed. Mirko D. Grmek et al. (Dordrecht: Reidel, 1981), 229–37.

8. De Graaf, On the Human Reproductive Organs, 10.

9. Thomas Gibson, The Anatomy of Humane Bodies Epitomized (London, 1685), 109.

10. Nicholas Venette, Conjugal Love or, The Pleasures of the Marriage Bed (London, 1750), 10.

11. Voltaire, Philosophical Dictionary, trans. Theodore Besterman (Harmondsworth: Penguin, 1971), s.v. "On Ezekiel," 199.

12. John Marten, A Treatise of all the Degrees and Symptoms of the Venereal Disease (6th ed. London, 1708), 357.

13. According to G. S. Rousseau's "The sorrows of Priapus: anticlericalism, homosocial desire, and Richard Payne Knight," in *Sexual Underworlds of the Enlightenment*, ed. G. S. Rousseau and Roy Porter (Manchester: Manchester University Press, 1987), 101–53, the eighteenth century would not register an interest in Priapus as a symbolic figure of fertility until Richard Payne Knight's *Discourse on the Worship of Priapus, and its Connexion with the Mystic Theology of the Ancients* (1786–87). Giancarlo Carabelli's *In the Image of Priapus* (London: Duckworth, 1996) argues that "the vogue for Priapus" gains new momentum at mid-century with the excavations at Herculaneum (26). For the decline of Priapus and his antiheroic figuration before the eighteenth century, see Lorrayne Y. Baird, "Priapus Gallinaceus: The Role of the Cock in Fertility and Eroticism in Classical Antiquity and the Middle Ages," *Studies in Iconography* 7–8 (1981–82): 81–111; Amy Richlin, *The Garden of Priapus: Sexuality and Aggression in Roman Humor* (New Haven, Conn.: Yale University Press, 1983), 59, 127, 141; and Eugene Michael O'Connor, *Symbolum Salacitatis: A Study of the God Priapus as a Literary Character* (Frankfurt: Verlag Peter Lang, 1989), 16–53. Once a sacred god of generation revered for benevolence and fertility within Greek culture, personified as protector and agricultural benefactor in Virgil's three Priapics of the *Catalepton*, trans. H. Rushton Fairclough (New York: Putnam), 1920–25, 486–89 and worshipped under other names by other cultures, the rituals associated with the ithyphallic god suffered forms of obscene or comic debasement, reducing the once-mighty Priapus to the deformed figure with the grotesquely over-sized phallus whose function was now the ludicrous scarecrow in the garden or the more violent figure who threatened intruders with anal rape. The first of these antiheroic images is used by Henry Fielding in *Joseph Andrews* to introduce young Joey (1742, ed. Martin C. Battestin [Middletown, Conn.: Wesleyan University Press, 1967], Bk. 1, ch. 2, 21). The second is present in the *Priapea* (see *Priapea: Poems for a Phallic God*, ed. and trans. W. H. Parker [London: Croom Helm, 1988]), brought to light by Scaliger and others in the Renaissance.

14. *The Essayes of Michel Lord of Montaigne*, trans. John Florio (1603; reprint London: Oxford University Press, 1906), 3: 90.

15. John Marten, *Gonosologium Novum* (London, 1709), 13.

16. Voltaire, *Philosophical Dictionary*, 199.

17. The penis as trophy in war is discussed in Pierre Darmon's *Le mythe de la procréation a l'âge baroque* (Paris: J.-J. Pauvert, 1977), 18, and Daniel Rancour-Laferriere, "Some Semiotic Aspects of the Human Penis," *Versus: Quaderni di studi semiotici* 24 (1979): 54. For the Athenian phallus as spear or war club, see Keuls, 2.

18. John Oldham, *Sardanapalus*, in *The Poems of John Oldham*, ed. Harold Fletcher Brooks (Oxford: Clarendon Press, 1987), 344–51.

19. Alexis Piron, *Ode à Priape*, in *Oeuvres Complètes Illustrées de Alexis Piron*, ed. Pierre Dufay (Paris: Francis Guillot, 1931), 10: 123–29.

20. John Wilkes, *Veni Creator*, in *The Infamous "Essay on Woman"; or, John Wilkes Seated between Vice and Virtue*, ed. Adrian Hamilton (London: Deutsch, 1972), 244–45.

21. Although they do not deal with the representational history of male reproductive systems, two recent studies which trace these larger cultural shifts are Barbara Maria Stafford's *Body Criticism: Imaging the Unseen in Enlightenment Art and Medicine* (Cambridge, Mass.: MIT Press, 1993) and Jonathan Sawday's *The Body Emblazoned: Dissection and the Human Body in Renaissance Culture* (London: Routledge, 1995).

22. For this reading of the classical legacy regarding male semen, I am indebted to Giulia Sissa's "Subtle Bodies," in *Fragments for a History of the Human Body, Part Three*, ed. Michel Feher et al. (New York: Zone Books, 1989), 133–56. The best modern study of the history of spermatozoa remains F. J. Cole's *Early Theories of Sexual Generation* (Oxford: Clarendon Press, 1930), especially chapters 1–2. Before the prevalence of the two-sex model of male/female differentiation in the seventeenth and eighteenth centuries, women too were believed to produce semen; however, the over-charged rhetoric which was part of the conceptualization of male seed did not extend to descriptions of female seed.

23. See Aristotle, *Generation of Animals*, in *The Complete Works of Aristotle: The Revised Oxford Translation*, ed. Jonathan Barnes (Princeton: Princeton University Press, 1984), 736b33–737a3; Diogenes Laertius, *Life of Pythagoras*, trans. R. D. Hicks (London: Loeb, 1979), 28; Hippocrates, *De Genitura*, trans. W. H. S. Jones, Loeb Classical Library (New York: Putnam, 1920–1925), 7. 470; Galen, *On the Usefulness of the Parts of the Body*, trans. Margaret Tallmadge May (Ithaca, N.Y.: Cornell University Press, 1968), 1: 641.

24. Robert James, *A Medicinal Dictionary*, 3 vols. (1745), 3: s.v. "Venus."

25. Pierre-Louis Moreau de Maupertuis, *The Earthly Venus*, trans. Simone Brangier Boas (1753; reprint New York: Johnson Reprint Corporation, 1966), 10.

26. Quoted in Roy Porter, "The Sexual Politics of James Graham," *British Journal for Eighteenth-Century Studies* 5 (1982): 202.

27. "The Lost Opportunity Recovered," in *Wit and Drollery. Jovial Poems* (London, 1682), 12, 13.

28. *The Joys of Hymen, Or, the Conjugal Directory: A Poem, in Three Books* (London, 1768), 36.

29. Jonathan Swift, *A Tale of a Tub* . . . , ed. A. C. Guthkelch and D. Nichol Smith (1704; reprint Oxford: Clarendon Press, 1958), 261–89. For a provocative and careful account of Swift's ironic game, see Hugh Ormsby-Lennon's "Swift's Spirit Reconjured: Das Dong-An-Sich," *Swift Studies* 3 (1988): 9–78.

30. The first four of sixteen lines makes clear the spirit-semen slang association: "In this strange Town a different Course we take, / Refine ourselves to Spirit, for your Sake. / For Want of you, we spend our random Wit on / The first we find with Needham ["Mother Needham," a notorious brothel-keeper], Brooks, or Briton." For the text of the poem and arguments about its authorship, see *TE* 6: 232–33 and Ralph N. Maud, "Some Lines from Pope," *Review of English Studies*, New Series 9 (1958): 146–51.

31. John Cleland, *Memoirs of a Woman of Pleasure*, ed. Peter Sabor (1749; reprint Oxford: Oxford University Press, 1985), 117, 124, 185.

32. Albrecht von Haller, *First Lines of Physiology Translated from the Correct Latin Edition* (1747; trans. William Cullen. Edinburgh, 1779), 428, 429.

33. The fight between Leeuwenhoek and Hartsoeker over who first "discovered" spermatozoa through microscopic observation spilled into early issues of the *Philosophical Transactions*, and was succinctly recorded in Henry Baker's *The Microscope Made Easy* (London, 1742), 152–3. Leeuwenhoek's 1678 letter to the Royal Society containing the first illustrations of the microscopic spermatozoa of several species can be found in *Philosophical Transactions* 142 (1679): 1040–43. Good modern accounts can be found in Cole (2–15), who includes an English translation of Leeuwenhoek's historic letter to the Royal Society describing in detail his microscopic viewing of fresh sperm (9–12), and, in G. A. Lindeboom's "Leeuwenhoek and the Problem of Sexual

Reproduction," in *Antoni Van Leeuwenhoek, 1632–1723: Studies on the Life and Work of the Delft Scientist Commemorating the 350th Anniversary of His Birthday*, ed. L. C. Palm and H. A. M. Snelders (Amsterdam: Rodopi, 1982), 129–52. Also see chapters 6–9 of Edward G. Ruestow's *The Microscope in the Dutch Republic: The Shaping of Discovery* (Cambridge: Cambridge University Press, 1996).

34. Marjorie Nicholson, "The Microscope and English Imagination," in *Science and Imagination* (Ithaca, N.Y.: Great Seal Books, 1956), 155–234; John Harley Warner, "The Impact of Microscopy on the English Poetry of the First Half of the 18th Century," *Synthesis* 3 (1975): 20–34.

35. Briefly: preformationists debated whether the preformed embryo was located in the male sperm (hence, "animalculists") or the female egg/ovary ("ovists"), although there is obviously much more to the issue than space permits me here. For the history of preformationism and epigenesis, see Joseph Needham's *A History of Embryology* (Cambridge: Cambridge University Press, 1934), Elizabeth B. Gasking's *Investigations into Generation 1651–1828* (Baltimore: Johns Hopkins University Press, 1967), Peter J. Bowler's "Preformation and Pre-existence in the Seventeenth Century: A Brief Analysis," *Journal of the History of Biology* 4 (1971): 221–44, and Clara Pinto Correia's *The Ovary of Eve: Egg and Sperm and Preformation* (Chicago: University of Chicago Press, 1997). Eve Keller has recently made the important point that "though the logic of preformation theory should grant the same kind of subject-status to the preformed miniature in both ovist and animalculist versions, it is only the latter that insistently subjectifies the miniature in its rhetoric" ("Embryonic Individuals: The Rhetoric of Seventeenth-Century Embryology and the Construction of Early-Modern Identity," *Eighteenth-Century Studies* 33 [2000]: 338).

36. See, for example, "Some Account of Mr. Leeuwenhoek's curious Microscopes, lately presented to the Royal Society. By Martin Folkes, Esq; Vice-President of the Royal Society," *Philosophical Transactions* 380 (1723): "It is now above 50 Years, since the late *Mr. Leeuwenhoek* first began his Correspondence with the Royal Society; when he was recommended by *Dr. Regnerus de Graaf*. . . . *Mr. Leeuwenhoek*'s Discoveries" have "given a perfectly new Turn to the Theory of Generation, in almost all the Authors that have since wrote upon that Subject" (446, 449).

37. For versions of this concept see Hippocrates, *De Genitura* 1 [7.470]; Plato, *Timaeus* 86c, 91a; 'Plutarch,' *Moralia* 905a; Diogenes Laertius, 8.28; Censorinus, *De die natali* 5.2 ff.; Isidore, *Origines* 11.1.97, 104, 139. In general, the theory held that seminal matter came mostly from the brain and then was refined in the lumbar region of the spine, kidneys, or testes. Antoine Le Camus's *La Médecine de l'esprit* (Paris, 1753, 1769) went so far as to posit a perfect equivalence between spermatic fluid and cerebral fluid, claiming that the father's semen (emanating from his brain) contains "a little brain that is the seed or kernel from which the fetus is born" (106; quoted in Anne C. Vila, *Enlightenment and Pathology: Sensibility in the Literature and Medicine of Eighteenth-Century France* [Baltimore: Johns Hopkins University Press, 1998], 84).

38. Jean Baptiste Verduc, *A Treatise of the Parts of a Human Body*, trans. J. Davis (London, 1704), 10. Compare Tissot's *Onanism*: " 'We can easily comprehend,' says M. [Friedrich] Hoffman, 'how there is so close a connection between the brain and the testicles; because these two organs secern from the blood the most subtle and exquisite lympha' . . . " (51). The similitude is also maintained in early modern brain terminology such as "testes cerebri" which, as Thomas Willis explained in "A Table of all the hard words . . . " appended to *The Anatomy of the Brain* (1664; trans. S. Pordage, 1681), referred to "Certain tu-

bercles in the brain of a man and beasts, so called because like to the stones of a man" (n.p.). (These so-called "testicles of the brain" are in fact the inferior colliculi which subserve auditory reflexes.) "Testes cerebri" was widely used in neuroanatomical description, found for example in commentaries by Thomas Gibson, La Mettrie, John Harris, and Albrecht von Haller. The only dissenting voice that I know of in this period is that of the Dane, Nicolaus Steno, who, in a section of his *Lecture on the Anatomy of the Brain* (1669) entitled "Meaningless and worthless terminology," asked: "What need was there to use the names, *nates (buttocks), testes, anus, vulva, penis*, when these have so little relationship to the parts that they signify in brain anatomy? Indeed, the resemblance is so slight that what one terms *nates* another terms *testes*, etc." (*Nicolaus Steno's Lecture on the Anatomy of the Brain*, reprinted, with intro. by Gustav Scherz [Copenhagen: Nyt Nordisk Forlag, 1965], 137).

39. It is largely to the work of G. S. Rousseau that we owe a proper understanding of the paradigmatic function of Willis's brain theory as the conceptual bedrock of the eighteenth-century obsession with nerves and nervous conditions, as well as of the socio-medical structure of Sensibility in literature. See his "Nerves, Spirits, and Fibres: Towards Defining the Origins of Sensibility," in *Studies in the Eighteenth Century, vol. 3, Papers Presented at the Third David Nichol Smith Memorial Seminar, Canberra*, ed. R. F. Brissenden and J. C. Eade (Toronto: University of Toronto Press, 1976), 137–57 and "Towards a Semiotic of the Nerve: The Social History of Language in a New Key," in *Language, Self, and Society: A Social History of Language*, ed. Peter Burke and Roy Porter (London: Polity Press, 1991), 213–75. As Rousseau has explained, Willis's paradigmatic leap was to argue that the soul is located in the brain, whose work is performed through the nerves and the animal spirits.

40. Willis's full explanation is as follows: "For truly it seems, that the Arteries instil a spiritous liquor into the Testicles after the same manner as in the Brain; . . . because there, as within the Cortex of the Brain, the spiritous liquor being imbued with a volatile Salt implanted in the part, passes into the most noble *Clyssus, viz.* the Genital humor. But here is not a place to discourse more largely of the nature and origine of the Seed: yet because it is commonly objected, That the Seed is made of nervous Juyce and plenty of Spirits fetched from the Brain, and therefore a large expence of it doth induce quickly on the Brain and Nerves a great debility and enervation; I say, this comes to pass, because after great profusions of the Seed, for the restauration of the same humor, (of which Nature is more solicitous than for the benefit of the individual) presently greater Tributes of the spiritous Liquor are required from the blood to be laid up into the Testicles: wherefore the Brain is made languid, being defrauded of its due stock and afflux of the same spiritous liquor; and the Spirits influencing it and the nervous *System*, because they are deficient in the Fountain it self, are very much depauperated and become flagging. Besides we may add, That the animal Spirits also which actuate the *Prostatae* coming from the spinal Marrow, are consumed about the Venereal acts very much; so that the Loyns are also enervated for this reason" (172–73). Some sense of the pervasive influence of Willis's theory is suggested by the fact that portions of this passage were used verbatim in medical and sexological treatises, as well as scientific dictionaries, from the late seventeenth through to the middle of the eighteenth centuries: for example, in Gibson's *The Anatomy of Humane Bodies Epitomized* (110–12), Marten's *A Treatise of all the Degrees and Symptoms of the Venereal Disease* (361–62), John Harris's *Lexicon Technicum* (London, 1704; s.v. "Testes").

41. The phrase comes from Porter's "The Sexual Politics of James Graham" (202), which discusses Graham's notion of the debilitating physical and social effects of wasting the priceless sperm (through masturbation, excessive venery, or leaky spermatics). The metaphorical extension from notions of precious semen to the idea of ejaculation as "spending" is discussed in Paul-Gabriel Boucé's "Aspects of Sexual Tolerance and Intolerance in XVIIIth-Century England," *British Journal for Eighteenth-Century Studies* 3 (1980): 173–91.

42. Quoted in R. F. Brissenden, "La Philosophie dans le boudoir; or, A Young Lady's Entrance into the World," *Studies in Eighteenth-Century Culture* 2 (1972): 124.

43. Laurence Sterne, *The Life and Opinions of Tristram Shandy, Gentleman*, ed. Ian P. Watt (1759–67; reprint Boston: Houghton Mifflin, 1965), 2: 19, 111–12. Subsequent references to this edition will be cited parenthetically.

44. *A Tale of a Tub*, 2nd edition, ed. A. C. Guthkelch and D. Nichol Smith (Oxford: Clarendon Press, 1958), 287–88. Ever ready to exploit the humorous potential of such body-logic, the Scriblerians would conclude "that the Organ of Generation is the true and only *Seat of the Soul*" (Alexander Pope et al., *The Memoirs of the Extraordinary Life, Works, and Discoveries of Martinus Scriblerus*, ed. Charles Kerby-Miller [New York: Oxford University Press, 1988], 158).

45. Jacques Lacan, "The signification of the phallus," in *Ecrits: A Selection*, trans. Alan Sheridan (New York: Norton, 1977), 287, 288.

46. See Jane Gallop's "Phallus/Penis: Same Difference," in her *Thinking Through the Body* (New York: Columbia University Press, 1988), 126–27. One of the best collections of essays critical of Lacan is the special issue on the Phallus in *differences: A Journal of Feminist Cultural Studies* 4, 1 (1992), especially Kaja Silverman, "The Lacanian Phallus," 84–115; Charles Bernheimer, "Penile Reference in Phallic Theory," 116–32; Judith Butler, "The Lesbian Phallus and the Morphological Imaginary," 133–71.

47. David M. Friedman, *A Mind of Its Own: A Cultural History of the Penis* (New York: Free Press, 2001).

48. Jean-Joseph Goux, "The Phallus: Masculine Identity and the 'Exchange of Women,'" *differences: A Journal of Feminist Cultural Studies* 4, 1 (1992): 45.

49. Daniel Boyarin, "Who Wrote the Dominant Fiction? On the History of the Early Phallus," in *Brief: Intellectual Traditions in Movement*, ed. Mieke Bal et al. (Amsterdam: Amsterdam School for Cultural Analysis, Theory, and Interpretation, 1998), 67, 63, 64.

50. Paul Smith, "Vas," *Camera Obscura* 17 (1988): 102.

51. Susan Bordo, *The Male Body: A New Look at Men in Public and in Private* (New York: Farrar, Straus, and Giroux, 1999), 94, 95.

52. Bordo, 94, 95.

53. See De Graaf's terminological linkage of penis and nervous system: "The internal or contained parts of the penis are the two *corpora nervosa*, 'nervous bodies' . . . " (47).

54. See the important collection of essays in Linda E. Merians, ed., *The Secret Malady: Venereal Disease in Eighteenth-Century Britain and France* (Lexington: University Press of Kentucky, 1996).

55. Michael McKeon, "Historicizing Patriarchy: The Emergence of Gender Difference in England, 1660–1760," *Eighteenth-Century Studies* 28 (1995): 303, 309, 310, 315.

56. Tim Hitchcock makes a related argument in "Redefining Sex in Eighteenth-Century England," *History Workshop Journal* 41 (1996), suggesting

that an earlier norm of mutual touching and orgasmic pleasure between males and females gave way to "sex [which] had become increasingly phallo-centric. Putting a penis in a vagina became the dominant sexual activity. . . . What the eighteenth century saw was the development of an obsession with the penis, and of an assumption that there was only one thing to do with it. . . . [S]exual practice changed, and . . . in a heterosexual context people increasingly restricted their behaviour to forms of phallo-centric, penetrative sex which could be countenanced as procreative" (79, 85).

57. Leo Braudy, "Remembering Masculinity: Premature Ejaculation Poetry of the Seventeenth Century," *Michigan Quarterly Review* 33 (1994): 192, 193, 198.

58. For brief speculation about the period's "new concern with male sexual prowess . . . penis size . . . the frequency of male orgasm . . . as an exchange value dependent on male potency," see Jon Stratton, *The Virgin Text: Fiction, Sexuality, and Ideology* (Norman and London: University of Oklahoma Press, 1987), 15–16.

59. Jill Campbell, " 'When Men Women Turn': Gender Reversals in Fielding's Plays," in *The New Eighteenth Century: Theory, Politics, English Literature*, ed. Felicity Nussbaum and Laura Brown (New York: Methuen, 1987), 68. A similar point is made in Thomas McGeary's " 'Warbling Eunuchs': Opera, Gender, and Sexuality on the London Stage, 1705–1742," *Restoration and Eighteenth-Century Theatre Research* 2nd ser. 7 (1992): 1–22.

60. See Giles Slade, "The Two Backed Beast: Eunuchus and Priapus in *The Country Wife*," *Restoration and Eighteenth-Century Theatre Research* 2nd ser. 7 (1992): 23–34. For the argument that there was a "crisis" in masculinity see Michael S. Kimmel, "From Lord and Master to Cuckold and Fop: Masculinity in Seventeenth-Century England," *University of Dayton Review* 18 (1987): 93–109. Paul Hammond has also written of "a crisis of some kind in masculine sexuality" in "The King's Two Bodies: Representations of Charles II," in *Culture, Politics and Society in Britain, 1660–1800*, ed. Jeremy Black and Jeremy Gregory (Manchester: Manchester University Press, 1991), 42.

61. Quoted in James Grantham Turner, "Pepys and the Private Parts of Monarchy," in *Culture and Society in the Stuart Restoration*, ed. Gerald Maclean (Cambridge: Cambridge University Press, 1995), 96. For the subversive ideological bent and anti-establishment satire of early modern pornography, see David Foxon, *Libertine Literature in England 1660–1745* (New York: University Books, 1965), 48; Roger Thompson, *Unfit for Modest Ears: A Study of Pornographic, Obscene and Bawdy Works Written or Published in England in the Second Half of the Seventeenth Century* (Totowa N.J.: Rowman and Littlefield, 1979), 105–6, 120; Lynn Hunt, "Introduction: Obscenity and the Origins of Modernity, 1500–1800," in *The Invention of Pornography: Obscenity and the Origins of Modernity, 1500–1800*, ed. Lynn Hunt (New York: Zone Books, 1993), 9–45.

62. *John Wilmot, Earl of Rochester: The Complete Works*, ed. Frank H. Ellis (London: Penguin, 1994), 30, lines 11–12.

63. For the argument that current critical approaches lack a tradition for talking about representations of the penis see Peter Lehman, "*In the Realm of the Senses*: Desire, Power, and the Representation of the Male Body," *Genders* 2 (1988): 91–110. A recent example of the modern academic reluctance to consider the penis is apparent in *The Body in Parts: Fantasies of Corporeality in Early Modern Europe* (New York: Routledge, 1997), edited by David Hillman and Carla Mazzio. About the specific bodily sites which this good collection of essays takes up, the editors write that "We should perhaps point out that the

most notably absent sexual organ in this volume is the penis. An argument could be made, however, that the male member functions almost literally as a floating signifier, surfacing throughout this volume in perhaps the most unexpected of places" (xx). Surreal images of floating or surfacing penises notwithstanding, this comment is an emblem of current reluctance to open discussion on the bodily category "penis."

64. For the earliest and most complete inventory of euphemisms and phrases for the yard in *Memoirs*, see B. Slepian and L. J. Morrissey, "What Is *Fanny Hill?" Essays in Criticism* 14 (1964): 65–75.

65. In another context, David Weed's "Fitting Fanny: Cleland's *Memoirs* and the Politics of Male Pleasure," *Novel* 31 (1997): 7–20, offers a persuasive argument that the novel "is less interested in a general celebration of the heroic male engine than in a very particular investigation of the sexual and gender codes that give an emergent class of bourgeois Englishmen the grounds on which they may claim superiority over both their domestic counterparts and men of other classes" (17).

66. I have consulted the following: Thomas Stretzer, *The Natural History of the Arbor Vitae: Or, the Tree of Life (1732); The Ladies Delight. Containing, I. An Address to all well provided Hibernians. II. The Arbor Vitae; or, Tree of Life. A Poem* . . . (London, 1732); *Wisdom Revealed; Or, the Tree of Life Discover'd and Describ'd* (London, 1732?); *Teague-Root Display'd: Being Some Useful and Important Discoveries Tending to Illustrate the Doctrines of Electricity, In a letter from Paddy Strong-Cock* (London, 1746); James Perry, *Mimosa: Or, the Sensitive Plant* (London, 1779).

67. Samuel Butler, *Dildoides* (Kingston, R.I.: Biscuit City Press, 1978), 2, 7.

68. Clive Hart and Kay Gilliland Stevenson, "John Armstrong's *The Oeconomy of Love*: A Critical Edition with Commentary," *Eighteenth-Century Life* 19 (1995): 46, l. 198.

69. *Libertine Lyrics by Various Authors Mostly of the XVII and XVIII Centuries* (Mount Vernon, N.Y.: Peter Pauper Press, n.d.), 55–56.

70. *John Wilmot, Earl of Rochester. The Complete Works*, ed. Frank H. Ellis (London: Penguin, 1994), 71, ll. 15–20.

71. Jean-Joseph Goux (*Symbolic Economies: After Marx and Freud*, trans. Jennifer Curtiss Page [Ithaca, N.Y.: Cornell University Press, 1990]), has written about "the equivalence function of the phallus" which, like gold in the world of commodities and the father in the world of others, serves as universal equivalent. As such, the phallic standard "is necessarily excluded from the imagined body . . . in a logical 'operation,' a *castration* that dramatizes the phantasmic element. . . . The monopoly of gold in its role as general equivalent is recognized through its exclusion, its separation from the relative form; similarly, the phallic primacy could not be validated if the castration reflecting it were not accepted" (23).

72. See Linda Williams, *Hard Core: Power, Pleasure, and the "Frenzy of the Visible"* (Berkeley: University of California Press, 1989), 93–119.

73. Ben Jonson, *Every Man in His Humour* (2.3.71), quoted from the 1616 folio version in *Ben Jonson*, ed. C. H. Herford and Percy Simpson (Oxford: Clarendon Press, 1954).

74. Thomas Hobbes, *Leviathan*, ed. Richard Tuck (Cambridge: Cambridge University Press, 1991), 42.

75. *The Letters of John Dryden, With Letters Addressed to Him*, ed. Charles E. Ward (Durham, N.C.: Duke University Press, 1942), Letter 29, Jan. 1693–4, 65.

76. Comic associations of "yard" as unit of measurement and as penis are not uncommon, as for example later in *Tristram Shandy* when the hot chestnut

which rolls into Phutatorius's crotch causes the epic "ZOUNDS!" which inter-
rupts Yorick's speech: "Yet I say, was *Yorick* never once in any one domicile of
Phutatorius's brain—but the true cause of his exclamation lay at least a yard below" (4: 27, 240–41). James Perry's *Mimosa: Or, the Sensitive Plant* (London,
1779) plays on the same distinction between measuring and phallic yards:
"Who does not pity Lady B. / Fated, nor to *feel*, nor see / The *plant*, altho' she's
wed. / What tho' my Lord is two *yards* high; / She cannot, for her life descry, /
One y— when he's abed" (11).
    77. Nicholas Chorier, *A Dialogue Between a Married Lady and a Maid* (Lon-
don, 1740), 33.
    78. John Oldham, *The Poems of John Oldham*, ed. Harold F. Brooks (Oxford:
Clarendon Press, 1987), 347, 345, 346.
    79. Rochester, *Complete Poems and Plays*, ed. Paddy Lyons (London: J. M.
Dent, 1993), 129.
    80. Harold Weber, "Carolinean Sexuality and the Restoration Stage: Recon-
structing the Royal Phallus in *Sodom*," in *Cultural Readings of Restoration and
Eighteenth-Century English Theater*, ed. J. Douglas Canfield and Deborah C.
Payne (Athens: University of Georgia Press, 1995), 74.
    81. Brean Hammond, *Pope and Bolingbroke: A Study of Friendship and Influ-
ence* (Columbia: University of Missouri Press, 1984), 111.
    82. Timothy Mowl, *Horace Walpole: The Great Outsider* (London: John Mur-
ray, 1996), 92.
    83. *Horace Walpole's Correspondence*, ed. W. S. Lewis (New Haven, Conn.:
Yale University Press, 1961) 30: 35–6.
    84. *The Journals of James Boswell: 1762–1795*, ed. John Wain (New Haven,
Conn.: Yale University Press, 1991), 15, November 1762; 27, December 1762;
42, January 1763.
    85. Lecture XII of Venette's popular *Conjugal Love* had discussed "How
many Times a Man may amorously caress his Wife in a Night," noting at the
outset that "vanity is more particularly exerted in the matters of love" (100).
He concluded "that all the efforts we are able to make near a woman in one
night, cannot amount to above four or five times; these great extravagances in
love, we are told on, being so many fables put on us" (107).
    86. This is not to suggest, however, that impotence was a simple cultural
category, as we will see below in the section on impotence trials. For a complex
instance of the symbolism of impotence in French history, see Antoine de
Baecque's discussion of the political implications of the rumored sexual dysfunction of Louis XVI in *The Body Politic: Corporeal Metaphor in Revolutionary
France, 1770–1800*, trans. Charlotte Mandell (Stanford, Calif.: Stanford University Press, 1993), 29–75.
    87. Quoted in Pierre Darmon, *Le Mythe de la procréation à l'âge baroque* (Paris:
J.-J. Pauvert, 1977), 44.
    88. See also *Wisdom Revealed* (?1732): "Madam, you know as well as I, / The
Rule they Measure Horses by,— / Perhaps it has in all its Strength, / About two
hands of proper Length; / In *Kent* sometimes two Inches more, / But in *Hiber-
nia*'s Three or Four" (9).
    89. Daniel Defoe, *Roxana*, ed. David Blewett (Harmondsworth: Penguin,
1982), 43.
    90. S. A. D. Tissot, *An Essay on Diseases Incidental to Literary and Sedentary Per-
sons*, trans. Charles Dilly (London, 1768), 75–76.
    91. The full story is more complex, with castrati sometimes rumored to be
sexually capable but infertile. For different accounts of the urological and

sexual status of castrati, see Campbell, " 'When Men Women Turn' "; McGeary; James P. Carson, "Commodification and the Figure of the Castrato in Smollett's *Humphry Clinker*," *Eighteenth Century: Theory and Interpretation* 33 (1992): 24–46; Xavier Cervantes, " 'Tuneful Monsters': The Castrati and the London Operatic Public 1667–1737," *Restoration and Eighteenth-Century Theatre Research* 2nd ser. 13 (1998): 1–24.

92. "Large sex organs were considered coarse and ugly. . . . diminutives denoting small penises are used as words of endearment—as, for example, *posthion*, which might be rendered as 'little prick.' . . . [A] huge erect penis . . . to the Greeks was a sign not of manhood but of bestiality" (68, 360).

93. "Upon Some Verses of Virgil," in *The Essayes of Michel Lord of Montaigne*, 91, 115.

94. As often the case, Sterne offers a comical reduction of this cluster of ideas and associations. Speaking of the stranger's prodigious nose/penis in Slawkenbergius's Tale, the narrator comments: "Let it suffice to say, that the riot and disorder it [nose/penis] occasioned in the *Strasburgers* fantacies was so general—such an overpowering mastership had it got of all the faculties of the *Strasburgers* minds. . . . [that] they went so far as to affirm, that there was no cause in nature, why a nose might not grow to the size of the man himself" (4: 191, 193).

95. *Poems on Affairs of State: Augustan Satirical Verse, 1660–1714, vol. 2, 1678–1681*, ed. Elias F. Mengel, Jr. (New Haven, Conn.: Yale University Press, 1965), 158, ll. 64–5; *Poems on Affairs of State: Augustan Satirical Verse, 1660–1714, vol. 1, 1660–1678*, ed. George deF. Lord (New Haven, Conn.: Yale University Press, 1963), 426, ll. 7–10.

96. Rachel Weil, "Sometimes a Scepter is Only a Scepter: Pornography and Politics in Restoration England," in *The Invention of Pornography: Obscenity and the Origins of Modernity, 1500–1800*, ed. Lynn Hunt (New York: Zone Books, 1993), 152.

97. *Satan's Harvest Home: Or the Present State of Whorecraft, Adultery, Fornication, Procuring, Pimping, Sodomy, and the Game at Flatts* (1749; reprint New York: Garland, 1985), 30.

98. Bernard Mandeville, *A Modest Defence of Publick Stews* (London, 1724), 22, 23.

99. Daniel Maclauchlan, *An Essay Upon Improving and Adding, to the Strength of Great-Britain and Ireland, By Fornication* (London, 1735), 44. Maclauchlan's mechanical prescription for male health evidences a casual misogyny whose thoughtlessness is striking: "Our Blood is heated; the Pulse beats high; we are all in a Flame, and can never be cool'd, 'till we have dipped into the soft, the sweet, the bubling Fount of Love: And why should the expelling these superfluous Excrements [semen], these agreeably tormenting Humours, by the *Medium* of a pretty Girl, be a greater Sin than evacuating a distended Bladder in the middle of a clean Piss-Pot?" (44–45).

100. *Consummation: Or, The Rape of Adonis* (London, 1741), 15–16.

101. John Cleland, *Memoirs of a Coxcomb* (Dublin, 1751), 206–7.

102. "No true Love between Man and Woman," in *The Penguin Book of Restoration Verse*, ed. Harold Love (Harmondsworth: Penguin, 1971), 164–65, ll. 5–8, 17–24.

103. Richard Payne Knight, *Discourse on the Worship of Priapus, and its Connexion with the Mystic Theology of the Ancients* (London, 1786–87), 13.

104. For the philosophical contexts of such issues see Yolton's *Thinking Matter: Materialism in Eighteenth-Century Britain* (Minneapolis: University of Minnesota Press, 1983).

105. For important discussions of the scientific background see Oswei Temkin's Introduction to the text of Haller's *A Dissertation on the Sensible and Irritable Parts of Animals* printed in *Bulletin of the Institute of the History of Medicine* 4 (1936): 651–99; R. K. French, *Robert Whytt, the Soul, and Medicine* (London: Wellcome Institute of the History of Medicine, 1969), 63–76; James Rodgers, "Sensibility, Sympathy, Benevolence: Physiology and Moral Philosophy in *Tristram Shandy*," in *Languages of Nature: Critical Essays on Science and Literature*, ed. L. J. Jordanova (New Brunswick, N.J.: Rutgers University Press, 1986), 117–58; Sander L. Gilman, *Sexuality: An Illustrated History Representing the Sexual in Medicine and Culture from the Middle Ages to the Age of AIDS* (New York: John Wiley, 1989), 194–203; Anne C. Vila, *Enlightenment and Pathology: Sensibility in the Literature and Medicine of Eighteenth-Century France* (Baltimore: Johns Hopkins University Press, 1998), 13–42.

106. Quoted in Rodgers, 126. Boerhaave's comments are cited in the anonymous *Tabes Dorsalis, or, the Cause of Consumption in Young Men and Women* (1758), 14.

107. Gilman's analysis of the amputated erection in the medical realm is worth noting in detail, although it seems to me that the contexts of possible significance are much broader than he suggests: "As long as the penis is connected to the body, it remains 'in control,' that is, flaccid. Once the penis is separated from the body, it becomes the erect penis, the penis under control of powerful but non-rational forces of human sexuality. . . . The missing body and the head serve as the normal context for the penis; once they are removed, the penis becomes pathological, taking on a life of its own. . . . The opening of the penis, its dissection, becomes then an analogous action to the opening of the female body. It is the search for the origin of the loss of control, the search for the hidden power that takes control of the penis, a power that is often represented as the female genitalia but that is also the image of the erect penis" (195).

108. Barbara Maria Stafford, *Body Criticism: Imaging the Unseen in Enlightenment Art and Medicine*, 140.

109. For the technical background of De Graaf's syringes this paragraph is indebted to F. J. Cole, "The History of Anatomical Injections," in *Studies in the History and Method of Science*, ed. Charles Singer (Oxford: Clarendon Press, 1921), 285–343, and to Julius Friedenwald and Samuel Morrison, "The History of the Enema With Some Notes on Related Procedures (Part I)," *Bulletin of the History of Medicine* 8 (1940): 68–114.

110. For example, see Thomas Gibson's *The Anatomy of Humane Bodies Epitomized*, 126.

111. Cited in *Making Love: The Picador Book of Erotic Verse*, ed. Alan Bold (London: Pan Books, 1980), 138.

112. Jill Campbell, " 'When Men Women Turn,' " 82.

113. The small amount of helpful scholarship includes Pierre Darmon's important book-length study published in French in 1979, trans. by Paul Keegan as *Trial By Impotence: Virility and Marriage in Pre-Revolutionary France*, as well as a handful of essays: Peter Wagner, "The Pornographer in the Courtroom: Trial Reports About Cases of Sexual Crimes and Delinquencies as a Genre of Eighteenth-Century Erotica," in *Sexuality in Eighteenth-Century Britain*, ed. Paul-Gabriel Boucé (Manchester: Manchester University Press, 1982), 120–40; a chapter on the 1742–43 Beaufort divorce case in Lawrence Stone, *Broken Lives: Separation and Divorce in England 1660–1857* (Oxford: Oxford University Press, 1993), 117–38; Jeffrey Merrick, "Impotence in Court and at Court," *Studies in Eighteenth-Century Culture* 25 (1996): 187–202; Judith Mueller, "Fallen

Men: Representations of Male Impotence in Britain," *Studies in Eighteenth-Century Culture* 28 (1999): 85–102.

114. For the historical details in this paragraph I am indebted to Darmon and Stone.

115. Ephraim Chambers, *Cyclopaedia: Or, an Universal Dictionary of Arts and Sciences* (London, 1738), s.v. "Éjaculation," "Congress."

116. See, for example, the argument on behalf of the husband in *The Case of Impotency Debated in the Late Famous Tryal at Paris. . . .* (London, 1714): "How many Women are now with Impatience expecting the Success of this Enterprise? If Madam *de Gesvres* succeeds, proud of such an Example, how many shall we see the next Day, despising the Yoke of Marriage, and committing the same Insults upon their Husbands? How many Evils would this produce, to the Dignity of a Sacrament, to the Honour of Families, to the Condition of the Subject, and to the publick Tranquility" (1: 99).

117. Jean Barrin, *Venus in the Cloister: Or, the Nun in her Smock* (London, 1725), 111.

118. *The Humours of the Court: Or, Modern Gallantry. A New Ballad Opera. . . .* (London, 1732), 59–60.

119. Cited in Stone, 134, who discusses the case in detail. The passage comes from Walpole's *Correspondence*, 18: 185.

120. Susan Bruce notes that "impotence is paradoxically generated by the very phallocentrism which ought to preclude it" (" 'Rolling About from Whore to Whore': Rochester's Satirico-Sexual Self and the Art of Conspicuous Consumption," *Forum for Modern Language Studies* 30 [1994]: 309).

121. See, for example, G. J. Barker-Benfield's *The Culture of Sensibility: Sex and Society in Eighteenth-Century Britain* (Chicago: University of Chicago Press, 1992).

122. For the cultural capital of the gentleman and politeness see Lawrence E. Klein's *Shaftesbury and the Culture of Politeness: Moral Discourse and Cultural Politics in Early Eighteenth-Century England* (Cambridge: Cambridge University Press, 1994) and Steven Shapin's *A Social History of Truth: Civility and Science in Seventeenth-Century England* (Chicago: University of Chicago Press, 1994). For the enduring power of social and reputational codes of masculinity see Philip Carter's *Men and the Emergence of Polite Society, Britain 1660–1800*.

Chapter 3. The Sexual Traffic in Male Creativity

1. See Eric Partridge, *A Dictionary of Slang and Unconventional English . . .* 7th ed. (New York: Macmillan, 1970): "The *membrum virile* : literary : ca 1790–1880. Perhaps because there was no one that Dr. Johnson was not prepared to stand up to" (229).

2. *The Works of Jonathan Swift* (Dublin: George Faulkner, 1746), 8: 287.

3. J. S. Peters, "The Bank, the Press, and the 'Return of Nature': On Currency, Credit, and Literary Property in the 1690s," in *Early Modern Conceptions of Property*, ed. John Brewer and Susan Staves (London: Routledge, 1995), 372. Other useful studies of the commodity-value of literature, the book trade, meanings of "author," and copyright include Martha Woodmansee, "The Genius and the Copyright: Economic and Legal Conditions of the Emergence of the 'Author,' " *Eighteenth-Century Studies* 17 (1983–84): 425–48; Mark Rose, "The Author as Proprietor: *Donaldson v. Becket* and the Genealogy of Modern Authorship," *Representations* 23 (1988): 51–85; Linda Zionkowski, "Aes-

thetics, Copyright, and 'The Goods of the Mind,' " *British Journal for Eighteenth-Century Studies* 15 (1992): 163–74.

4. Linda Zionkowski, *Men's Work: Gender, Class, and the Professionalization of Poetry, 1660–1784* (New York: Palgrave, 2001), 184.

5. See Zionkowski's argument in "Territorial Disputes in the Republic of Letters: Canon Formation and the Literary Profession," *Eighteenth Century: Theory and Interpretation* 31 (1990): 3–22.

6. Despite the prominence of these metaphors from classical times through to eighteenth-century use, no one has yet written a definitive historical or theoretical study. The work so far published on seventeenth- and eighteenth-century deployments is limited. See, for example, M. H. Abrams's *The Mirror and the Lamp: Romantic Theory and the Critical Tradition* (New York: Oxford University Press, 1953), "Romantic Analogues of Art and Mind," 47–69, which gives the false impression that metaphors of gestation, embryonic growth, and childbirth are absent in the Enlightenment, awaiting renewed use by the likes of Byron and Shelley; Terry J. Castle's "Lab'ring Bards: Birth *Topoi* and English Poetics 1660–1820," *Journal of English and Germanic Philology* 78 (1979): 193–208, wrongly concludes that between the Renaissance and the Romantics the figure of the pregnant male poet was never positively portrayed, but rather becomes the dunce-object of Pope's and Dryden's satires; Garry Sherbert's *Mennipean Satire and the Poetics of Wit: Ideologies of Self-Consciousness in Dunton, D'Urfey, and Sterne* (New York: Peter Lang, 1996), 125–31, comments briefly on Sterne's equation of male wit with the female sexual cycle.

7. Henry Fielding, *The History of Tom Jones*, ed. Fredson Bowers (1749; reprint, Middletown, Conn.: Wesleyan University Press, 1975), Bk. 11, ch. 1, 568. Subsequent references to this edition will be cited parenthetically.

8. *The Posthumous Works of William Wycherley Esq; In Prose and Verse. Faithfully publish'd from His Original Manuscripts, by Mr. Theobald. In Two Parts* (London: 1728), 8.

9. Tobias Smollett, *The Adventures of Peregrine Pickle*, ed. James L. Clifford (1751; reprint, Oxford: Oxford University Press, 1964), 323.

10. Bezaleel Morrice (fl. 1732), *The Present State of Poetry, A Satire* (London, 1726), 22.

11. Samuel Wesley, *An Epistle to a Friend Concerning Poetry* (London, 1700), 9, 12.

12. Colley Cibber, *An Apology for the Life of Mr. Colley Cibber* (1740; reprint, London: Dent, 1914), 2.

13. Ed. Karl K. Hulley and Stanley T. Vandersall (Lincoln: University of Nebraska Press, 1970), 249.

14. At mid-century William Collins's "Ode on the Poetical Character" (1747) would replay the same idea, the sexual conjunction of the creative male god and female Fancy giving birth to male creativity itself: "And Thou, Thou rich-hair'd Youth of Morn, / And all thy subject Life was born!" (in *The Poems of Thomas Gray, William Collins, Oliver Goldsmith*, ed. Roger Lonsdale [London: Longman, 1969], 432, ll. 39–40). A half-century later this *mythos* of origins is still part of a shared metapoetic idiom. In the last stanza of his "Ode to Apollo" (1815), Keats will repeat the story of Apollo and the Muses, impregnation, and the birth of poetry and the tradition of famous male poets: "But when *Thou* [Apollo] joinest with the Nine, / And all the powers of song combine, / We listen here on earth: / The dying tones that fill the air, / And charm the ear of evening fair, / From thee, great God of Bards, receive their heavenly birth" (in *John Keats, Selected Poems and Letters*, ed. Douglas Bush [Boston: Houghton Mifflin, 1959], 6, ll. 42–47).

15. As Frank E. Manuel has argued in *The Eighteenth Century Confronts the Gods* (Cambridge, Mass.: Harvard University Press, 1959), "the bulk of eighteenth-century thought on the origins of religion and the significance of myth was divided between the Euhemerist-historical and the psychological schools" (9). Sir William Temple's comments in his influential essay "Of Poetry" are typical: "The more true and natural Source of Poetry may be discovered, by observing to what God this Inspiration was ascribed by the Ancients, which was *Apollo*, or the Sun, esteemed among them the God of Learning in general, but more particularly of Musick and Poetry. The Mystery of this Fable, means, I suppose, that a certain Noble and Vital Heat of Temper, but especially of the Brain, is the true Spring of these Two Parts or Sciences" (*The Works of Sir William Temple*, 2 vols., ed. Jonathan Swift and Lady Martha Gifford [London, 1720], 1: 236).

16. Part of the attention to the head of the writer can also be explained by the new developments in neuroanatomy and neurophysiology, especially Thomas Willis, whose *Cerebri Anatome* (1664; trans. by Samuel Pordage in 1681 as *Anatomy of the Brain and Nerves*, ed. William Feindel [Montreal: McGill University Press, 1965]) helped bring into mainstream consciousness the rhetoric of nerves, fibers, animal spirits, and brain-body mechanics by which mental phenomena, including creativity, would be understood.

17. John Ogilvie, *Poems On Several Subjects. To Which Is Prefix'd, An Essay On The Lyric Poetry of the Ancients* (London, 1762), xxi–ii.

18. William Harvey, *Disputations Touching the Generation of Animals*, trans. Gweneth Whitteridge (Oxford: Blackwell Scientific Publications, 1981), 452.

19. *Disputations Touching the Generation of Animals*, 445–46.

20. Elizabeth Sacks, *Shakespeare's Images of Pregnancy* (New York: Macmillan, 1980), 4.

21. Julien Offray de La Mettrie, *Man a Machine and Man a Plant*, trans. Richard A. Watson and Maya Rybalka (Indianapolis: Hackett Publishing, 1994), 45.

22. See, for example, Carolyn Merchant's fine assessment of the underlying gender bias of Harvey's embryological system in *The Death of Nature: Women, Ecology, and the Scientific Revolution* (San Francisco: Harper and Row, 1982): "The male sperm endowed the female uterus with the 'plastic power' to create an offspring. Thus the uterus was similar to a brain about to create, in the same way that the painter about to produce a work of art pictured to himself the painting. But this uterine brain was not a free agent. It produced only what was impressed on it by the more perfect male" (161).

23. *Poems by the Earl of Roscommon, To which is Added, An Essay on Poetry . . .* (London, 1717).

24. John Hippisley, *An Essay On Wit: To Which is Annexed, A Dissertation on Antient and Modern History* (London, 1748), 20.

25. William Congreve, *Incognita, or, Love and Duty Reconcil'd. A Novel*, in *Shorter Novels of the Seventeenth Century*, ed. Philip Henderson (1692; reprint, London: Dent, 1930), 241–42.

26. Edward Young, in *Eighteenth-Century English Literature*, ed. Geoffrey Tillotson et al. (New York: Harcourt, Brace and World, 1969), 876.

27. Quoted in Whitteridge's Preface to Harvey's *Disputations*, xv–xvi.

28. Barbara Maria Stafford's claim that "Preformationism . . . fundamentally shaped Neoclassical principles of artistic creation" (*Body Criticism: Imaging the Unseen in Enlightenment Art and Medicine* [Cambridge, Mass.: MIT Press,

1993], 234–5) is certainly not wrong, but fails to explain the substantial presence of aesthetic birth-analogies which parallel the developmental thesis of epigenesis. Her analysis has not considered the huge impact of the female Muse/pregnant male tradition.

29. They were used satirically, too, as in Richard Savage's Scriblerian *An Author To be Lett . . .* (London, 1729), a mock defence of the dunces attacked in Pope's 1728 *Dunciad*: "From these I have extracted curious Hints to assist *Welsted* in his new Satire against *Pope*. . . . 'Tis yet an Embrio, and there are divers Opinions about the Birth of it. Some expect it will spring from his wife['s] Noddle, like *Minerva* from the Head of *Jupiter*. . . . Others, that it will resemble *Milton's* Figure of *Sin* coming from the Brain of the Father of Lies. Then, say they, it will damn its Parent's Reputation. But most are of Opinion, that . . . the Brat will be still-born" (5–6).

30. Laurence Sterne, as quoted in Robert A. Erickson's *Mother Midnight: Birth, Sex, and Fate in Eighteenth-Century Fiction* (New York: AMS Press, 1986), "*Tristram Shandy* and 'The Womb of Speculation,' " 284, note 4.

31. John Vanbrugh, *The Relapse*, ed. Bernard Harris (1696; reprint, London: A. C. Black, 1986), 5.

32. Richard Cumberland, *The Fashionable Lover. A Comedy* (London, 1772), n.p.

33. The satirical tradition of misadventure in these figurative birth-scenes—used to lash out at Grubstreet hacks, scurrilous booksellers and printers, the lifeless stuff of the Moderns, and in general anything that smacked of imaginative failure or insipid mediocrity—will be well-known to my readers. Images of aborted birth, still-born children, monstrous issue, miscarriage, and barrenness are common features. For a fine recent discussion of these ideas see Dennis Todd, *Imagining Monsters: Miscreations of the Self in Eighteenth-Century England* (Chicago: University of Chicago Press, 1995), 199–203.

34. See Maynard Mack, *Alexander Pope, A Life*, 121–25.

35. The phrase comes from Brean S. Hammond's subtitle, *Professional Imaginative Writing in England, 1670–1740: "Hackney for Bread"* (Oxford: Clarendon Press, 1997), which is taken from Fielding's *The Author's Farce*.

36. See Shirley A. Roe, *Matter, Life, and Generation: Eighteenth-Century Embryology and the Haller-Wolff Debate* (Cambridge: Cambridge University Press, 1981), 19, 150, and Angus McLaren, *Reproductive Rituals: The Perception of Fertility in England from the Sixteenth to the Nineteenth Century* (London: Methuen, 1984), 25 ff.

37. Edward Young, in *Eighteenth-Century English Literature*, ed. Geoffrey Tillotson et al. (New York: Harcourt, Brace and World, 1969), 873.

38. *Johnson's Lives of the Poets: A Selection*, ed. J. P. Hardy (Oxford: Clarendon Press, 1971), 312.

39. Percy Bysshe Shelley, as quoted in M. H. Abrams, *The Mirror and the Lamp*, 192. This landmark of literary history has both helped and hindered the study of eighteenth-century literature. Mirrors and lamps, mechanical and organic metaphors are not nearly so neatly separated by historical markers as Abrams suggests.

40. *The Poems and Prose of Mary, Lady Chudleigh*, ed. Margaret J. M. Ezell (New York: Oxford University Press, 1993), 21.

41. *The Poems of John Oldham*, ed. Harold F. Brooks (1677–78; reprint, Oxford: Clarendon Press, 1987), 343, ll. 28–33.

42. For the historical contexts of these beliefs see G. S. Rousseau, "Pineapples, Pregnancy, Pica, and *Peregrine Pickle*," in *Tobias Smollett: Bicentennial Essays*

Presented to Lewis M. Knapp, ed. G. S. Rousseau and Paul-Gabriel Boucé (New York: Oxford University Press, 1971), 79–110. Also see Marie-Hélène Huet, *Monstrous Imagination* (Cambridge, Mass.: Harvard University Press, 1993).

43. Sigmund Freud, "On the Sexual Theories of Children," in *The Standard Edition of the Complete Psychological Works of Sigmund Freud*, trans. James Strachey (London: Hogarth Press, 1959), 9: 219–20. See also "Anxiety and Instinctual Life," 22: 100–1.

44. Carolyn Williams, "Westphalia Revisited," *British Journal for Eighteenth-Century Studies* 9 (1986): 19.

45. See, for example, "Sent to the Compiler from the same. From the Bog-House at Pancras-Wells": "Hither I came in haste to sh-t, / But found such Excrements of Wit, / That I to shew my Skill in Verse, / Had scarcely Time to wipe my A—se" (Hurlothrumbo [pseud.], *The Merry-Thought: or, the Glass-Window and Bog-House Miscellany* [London, 1731], 30).

46. See The Dedication of *The Merry-Thought: or, the Glass-Window and Bog-House Miscellany*, vi.

47. Edward Ward, *The Secret History of Clubs* (London, 1709), 238, 243–44.

48. The finger-pen, anus-inkwell, ink-excrement analogy is not often used, but can be discovered elsewhere, as in Miss W.'s "The Gentleman's Study, In Answer to [Swift's] The Lady's Dressing Room" (1732): "In house of office, when they're bare, / And have not paper then to spare, / Their hands they'll take, half clean their bottom, / And daub the wall, O—rot 'em; / And in a minute, with a t—d, / They'll draw them out a beast or bird, / And write there without ink or pen: / When finger's dry, there's a—se again" (in *Eighteenth-Century Women Poets: An Oxford Anthology*, ed. Roger Lonsdale [Oxford: Oxford University Press, 1989], 130, ll. 7–16).

49. The story of female writers' use of the metaphor of pregnant brains and eroticized Muses to allegorize the processes of female creativity runs a different course, as might be expected, although not a great deal has been written on the subject. The best introduction is Isobel Grundy's "The Poet and Her Muse," in *The Timeless and the Temporal: Writings in Honour of John Chalker by Friends and Colleagues*, ed. Elizabeth Maslen (London: Queen Mary and Westfield College, University of London, Department of English, 1993), 173–93.

50. I use four brief examples to characterize this lesser strand: Alexander Ross's *Mystagogus Poeticus or the Muses Interpreter* (London, 1648) explained that "the Muses were held perpetual Virgins" because "men, that delight in learning, scorn fleshly lusts" (299–300); for John Phillips, the Muses of Homer and Virgil were "chaste as *Vestal Virgins*," and "Were I design'd by Kinder Destiny / To Court a Muse, and follow *Poetry*, / My early care should be to raise a Fence / To guard All-Pure my Native *Innocence*" (*A Reflection On Our Modern Poetry. An Essay* [London, 1695], 1, 8); in Letter XIV of his *Letters Concerning the English Nation* (London, 1733), Voltaire confidently explained Newton's superiority over Descartes as being partly about the former's literal chastity: "that Sir *Isaac*, during the long Course of Years, he enjoy'd was never sensible to any Passion, was not subject to the common Frailties of Mankind, nor ever had any Commerce with Women" (116). In her *Gender and Genius: Towards a Feminist Aesthetics* (Bloomington: Indiana University Press, 1989), Christine Battersby points out how some theories of genius such as William Duff's *Essay on Original Genius* (1767) preferred physical chastity in the mentally-gifted man (79). Anne C. Vila, "Sex, Procreation, and the Scholarly Life from Tissot to Balzac," *Eighteenth-Century Studies* 35 (2002), has written briefly on the

"perceived conflict between thinking and procreation" (239) in later eighteenth-century France.

51. Sir Richard Blackmore, "An Essay Upon Wit," in *Essay Upon Several Subjects* (London, 1716), 196, 213.

52. Joseph Warton, *An Essay on the Writings and Genius of Pope* (London, 1756), 1: 105.

53. J. Amherst, "To the Earl of Roscommon," in *Poems by the Earl of Roscommon . . .* (London, 1717).

54. Joseph Trapp, *Lectures on Poetry Read in the Schools of Natural Philosophy at Oxford* (London, 1742), 8.

55. Figurative markers of an eroticized poet-Muse relationship in its debased forms were sometimes extended, including not only conjugal boredom or indifference, but also the shortness of the honeymoon, venereal disease, divorce, or the figurative sexual troubles of the aging male poet as fumbler.

56. The most eloquent exploration of this trope is in Catherine Gallagher, *Nobody's Story: The Vanishing Acts of Women Writers in the Marketplace, 1670–1820* (Berkeley: University of California Press, 1994), especially her discussion of Aphra Behn.

57. Linda Zionkowski, *Men's Work: Gender, Class, and the Professionalization of Poetry, 1660–1784* (New York: Palgrave, 2001), 9, 8.

58. William Congreve, *The Way of the World. A Comedy*, ed. Kathleen M. Lynch (1700; reprint, Lincoln: University of Nebraska Press, 1965), 6.

59. "Prologue by Mr. Dryden," No. LXIV in William Bradford Gardner, *The Prologues and Epilogues of John Dryden: A Critical Edition* (New York: Columbia University Press, 1951), 107.

60. *The Poetical Works of Robert Lloyd, A.M. To which is prefixed an Account of the Life and Writings of the Author* (London, 1774): 1: 115–16.

61. "A Satyr Against Mankind," in *John Wilmot, Earl of Rochester. The Complete Works*, ed. Frank H. Ellis (London: Penguin Books, 1994), 73.

62. Samuel Wesley, *An Epistle to a Friend Concerning Poetry* (London, 1700), 27.

63. Roscommon, *An Essay on Translated Verse* (London, 1684), 37.

64. Edward Ward, *Durgen. Or, a Plain Satyr Upon a Pompous Satyrist* (London, 1729), 24.

65. Eve Kosofsky Sedgwick, *Between Men: English Literature and Male Homosocial Desire* (New York: Columbia University Press, 1985), 57, 25–6.

66. Plato, *Theaetetus*, in *Plato: The Collected Dialogues*, ed. Edith Hamilton and Huntington Cairns (Princeton, N.J.: Princeton University Press, 1969), 855–56, 150c, 151a. Two literary examples will suffice to characterize this well-known trope: young Pope's letter to Wycherley about his bold editorial handling of the older man's poems: "I have done my best to brush you up like your Neighbours. But I can no more pretend to the Merit of the Production, than a Midwife to the Virtues and good Qualities of the Child she helps into the Light" (*Corr.* 1: 16, 1706); Smollett's reference in *The Expedition of Humphry Clinker* (1771; reprint, ed. Lewis M. Knapp, revised by Paul-Gabriel Boucé [Oxford: Oxford University Press, 1984]) to "this midwife of the Muses" in describing a male bookseller (128).

67. Roy Porter, "A Touch of Danger: the Man-Midwife as Sexual Predator," in *Sexual Underworlds of the Enlightenment*, ed. G. S. Rousseau and Roy Porter (Manchester: Manchester University Press, 1987), 215–16.

68. John Dryden, *The Letters of John Dryden*, ed. Charles E. Ward (Durham, N.C.: Duke University Press, 1942), Letter 29, 68.

69. John Dennis et al., *Letters Upon Several Occasions* (London, 1696), 20.

70. Samuel Wesley, *An Epistle to a Friend Concerning Poetry* (London, 1700), 20, l. 748.

71. James Boswell, *Life of Johnson*, ed. R. W. Chapman (Oxford: Oxford University Press, 1980), 297, Friday, 1 July 1763.

72. Gaius Valerius Catullus, *The Poems of Catullus*, trans. Guy Lee (Oxford: Oxford University Press, 1990), number CV, 140–41.

73. Amy Richlin, *The Garden of Priapus: Sexuality and Aggression in Roman Humor* (New Haven, Conn.: Yale University Press, 1983), 162.

74. Ovid, *The Erotic Poems*, trans. Peter Green (Harmondsworth: Penguin, 1982), 166–7, ll. 25–29.

75. For helpful comments on the *Priapea* see Richlin and Giancarlo Carabelli, *In the Image of Priapus* (London: Duckworth, 1996), 25 ff. The fullest account of backgrounds and literary traditions is the editor's lengthy introduction to *Priapea: Poems for a Phallic God*, ed. and trans. W. H. Parker (London: Croom Helm, 1988), 1–57.

76. *Priapea: Poems for a Phallic God*, ed. and trans. W. H. Parker (London: Croom Helm, 1988), number 1, 67.

77. See *Priapea: Poems for a Phallic God*, 54–55.

78. John Wilmot, Earl of Rochester, "Timon. A Satyr," in *The Complete Works*, ed. Frank H. Ellis (London: Penguin, 1994), 56, ll. 21–22.

79. *The Poems of Sir George Etherege*, ed. James Thorpe (Princeton, N.J.: Princeton University Press, 1963), 42.

80. *Oeuvres Complètes Illustrées de Alexis Piron*, ed. Pierre Dufay (Paris: Francis Guillot, 1931), 10: 123, ll. 1–10. For this translation I am indebted to a colleague who wishes to remain anonymous.

81. Although the reproduction here is taken from a 1790 edition in the British Library, the engraving is a very close copy of the original illustration. The first edition of the novel is one of the rarest of the nearly thirty editions that appeared between 1741 and 1915, and librarians are reluctant to allow photographic reproduction of the early editions which are very often too fragile.

82. Leo Braudy, *The Frenzy of Renown: Fame and Its History* (New York: Oxford University Press, 1986), 108.

83. John Wilkes, *The Infamous "Essay on Woman"; or, John Wilkes Seated between Vice and Virtue*, ed. Adrian Hamilton (London: Deutsch, 1972). On the title pages see Adrian Hamilton, *The Infamous Essay on Woman*, 194–5; Donald W. Nichol and Jacob Larkin, "Wilkes and Editorial Liberty: Attacks on Warburton as Pope's Editor," in *Transatlantic Crossings: Eighteenth-Century Explorations*, ed. Donald W. Nichol with Iona Bulgin, Sandra Hannaford, David Wilson (St. John's, Memorial University of Newfoundland: Department of English Language and Literature, 1995), 53–54.

84. Also see Richard A. Spears, *Slang and Euphemism: A Dictionary of Oaths, Curses, Insults, Sexual Slang and Metaphor, Racial Slurs, Drug Talk, Homosexual Lingo, and Related Matters* (Middle Village, N.Y.: Jonathan David, 1981), 108; and F. Gonzalez-Crussi, *Notes of an Anatomist* (San Diego: Harcourt Brace Jovanovich, 1985), especially the section "On Male Genital Anatomy," 116.

85. *The Odes of Sir Charles Hanbury Williams, Knight of the Bath* (London, 1775), 110–11, ll. 1–12.

86. Thomas Bentley, *A Letter to Mr. Pope, Occasioned by Sober Advice from Horace* (London, 1735), 16.

87. Before Kant and Coleridge, attempts to demonstrate the relationship of the imagination to the conscious will are inchoate, informed primarily by

concepts of opposition between unconscious physical or subrational mental energies and conscious rational faculties. See James Engell, *The Creative Imagination: Enlightenment to Romanticism* (Cambridge, Mass.: Harvard University Press, 1981), 125, 134–6, 344–5.

88. Edward Young, in *Eighteenth-Century English Literature*, ed. Geoffrey Tillotson et al. (New York: Harcourt, Brace and World, 1969), 882.

89. S. A. D. Tissot, *Onanism: or, a Treatise upon the Disorders Produced by Masturbation*, trans. A. Hume (London, 1772), 72.

90. D. T. de Bienville, *Nymphomania, or, a Dissertation Concerning the Furor Uterinus. . . .* trans. Edward Sloane Wilmot (London, 1775), 174. For a discussion of the imagination as the new medical site for sexual disorders in the second half of the eighteenth century, see G. S. Rousseau, "Nymphomania, Bienville and the Rise of Erotic Sensibility," in *Sexuality in Eighteenth-Century Britain*, ed. Paul-Gabriel Boucé (Manchester: Manchester University Press, 1982), 95–119.

91. See John Brewer, *The Pleasures of the Imagination: English Culture in the Eighteenth Century* (London: HarperCollins, 1997).

92. For a helpful overview of metaphorical structures associated historically with masturbation, see the Introduction in Paula Bennett and Vernon Rosario II, eds., *Solitary Pleasures: The Historical, Literary, and Artistic Discourses of Autoeroticism* (New York: Routledge, 1995), 1–18. Also see Thomas W. Laqueur's "Credit, Novels, Masturbation," in *Choreographing History*, ed. Susan Leigh Foster (Bloomington and Indianapolis: Indiana University Press, 1995), which explores the "textual links between credit, novels, and the secret vice to suggest that the common villain is fictionality, the realm of the imagined" (121).

93. The exceptions are Kevin L. Cope's "Squirrel's in the Breeches: Onanism, Diarrhea, and the Aesthetics of Antipanaceatic Discourse," *Eighteenth-Century Life* 17 (1993), which examines Tissot's identification of onanism as "The chief disorder of literary persons" (18); Anne C. Vila's *Enlightenment and Pathology: Sensibility in the Literature and Medicine of Eighteenth-Century France* also calls attention to Tissot's belief that "the dangers of scholarship differ little from those that he associates with other forms of overstimulation" (101).

94. Jean-Jacques Rousseau, *The Confessions*, trans. J. M. Cohen (Harmondsworth: Penguin, 1953), 109.

95. Discussed in Hugh Ormsby-Lennon, "Swift's Spirit Reconjured: Das Dong-An-Sich," *Swift Studies* 3 (1988): 9–78, and in Roy Porter and Lesley Hall, *The Facts of Life: The Creation of Sexual Knowledge in Britain, 1650–1950* (New Haven, Conn.: Yale University Press, 1995), 91–105.

96. *The Poet Finish'd in Prose. Being a Dialogue Concerning Mr. Pope and His Writings* (London, 1735), 18.

97. John Armstrong, "*The Oeconomy of Love*: A Critical Edition with Commentary," ed. Clive Hart and Kay Gilliland Stevenson, *Eighteenth-Century Life* 19 (1995): 44, ll. 106–9.

98. Christopher Fox, "The Myth of Narcissus in Swift's *Travels*," *Eighteenth-Century Studies* 20 (1986): 32.

99. Ormsby-Lennon, "Swift's Spirit Reconjured: Das Dong-An-Sich," 62, 68.

100. George Gordon, Lord Byron, *"Between two worlds": Byron's Letters and Journals*, ed. Leslie A. Marchand (Cambridge, Mass.: Harvard University Press, 1977), 7: 217. Also see Coleridge's "orgasms of a sickly imagination" in *Biographica Literaria*, ed. James Engell and W. Jackson Bate (Princeton, N.J.: Princeton University Press, 1983), 211.

101. Sandra M. Gilbert and Susan Gubar, *The Madwoman in the Attic: The*

Woman Writer and the Nineteenth-Century Literary Imagination (New Haven, Conn.: Yale University Press, 1979), 3.

102. Gilbert and Gubar, 6.

103. There are satirical versions of the writer-fornicator as well, as in Pope's sarcastic response to Lord Hervey's and Lady Mary Wortley Montagu's *Verses Address'd to the Imitator of the First Satire of the Second Book of Horace* (London, 1733) as "this *Witty Fornication*" (*A Letter to a Noble Lord*, in *The Prose Works of Alexander Pope. Vol. 2, the Major Works, 1725–1744*, ed. Rosemary Cowler [Hamden, Conn.: Archon Books, 1986], 447). In "The Reasons that Induced Dr S[wift] to write a Poem call'd the Lady's Dressing Room" (1734), Lady Mary puts the writing-copulating conceit bluntly: "Perhaps you have no better Luck in / The Knack of Rhyming than of ———" (Lady Mary Wortley Montagu, *Essays and Poems and Simplicity, a Comedy*, ed. Robert Halsband and Isobel Grundy [Oxford: Clarendon Press, 1993], 276).

104. *The Whore's Rhetoric, Calculated to the Meridian of London; And Conformed to the Rules of Art. In two Dialogues* (1683; reprint Edinburgh, 1836), A3, recto.

105. Charles Churchill, *The Correspondence of John Wilkes and Charles Churchill*, ed. Edward H. Weatherly (New York: Columbia University Press, 1954), Thursday July 29, 1762, Letter 6, 13.

106. Cynthia Wall, in "Editing Desire: Pope's Correspondence with (and without) Lady Mary," *Philological Quarterly* 71 (1992), discusses "Pope's letters to and about women during his late twenties [which] assume the voice of the sexual gallant, overtly conflating pen with penis" (222).

107. See M. Valerius Martial, *Martial: Epigrams*, ed. Walter C. A. Ker (London: William Heinemann, 1925), 1: 35, 51.

108. For example, in the mid-1720s, two essays in John Sheffield, Duke of Buckingham's *Works*, ed. Alexander Pope (London: 1723), which allegedly contained Jacobite sympaties, were censored and expurgated by the government, and then allowed to be sold. Soon after, Curll circulated a pamphlet with the complete essays, titled *The Castrations* (London, ?1724), and in 1727 appeared *Buckingham Restor'd: Being Two Essays which were Castrated from the Works of the late Duke of Buckingham* (the Hague, 1727) (for background details see Mack, *Alexander Pope: A Life*, 396–99).

109. *The Poems of John Cleveland*, ed. Brian Morris and Eleanor Withington (Oxford: Clarendon Press, 1967), 50, ll. 1–2.

110. James Boswell, *Life of Johnson*, Monday, 22 September 1777, 869.

111. "One Epistle to Mr. A. Pope, Occasioned by Two Epistles lately published" (1730), in *The Works, In Verse and Prose, of Leonard Welsted*, ed. John Nichols (London, 1787), 192.

112. *Two Epistles to Mr. Pope, Concerning the Authors of the Age*, in *The Works . . . of Leonard Welsted*, 39. Related to this is the frequent figure of hostile critics who, to quote from Letter XIII of Oliver Goldsmith's *The Citizen of the World* (London, 1762), "somewhat resemble the eunuchs in a seraglio . . . [being] incapable of giving pleasure themselves, and hinder[ing] those that would."

113. Respectively, *The Case of Impotency, as Debated in England. . . .* (London, 1719), 3; *The Remarkable Trial of the Queen of Quavers* (London, 1778), 34.

114. See Suetonius, *The Twelve Caesars*, trans. Robert Graves, revised with an Introduction by Michael Grant (Harmondsworth: Penguin, 1979), 228.

115. Thomas Gray, *The Progress of Poesy*, in *The Poems of Thomas Gray, William Collins, Oliver Goldsmith*, ed. Roger Lonsdale (London: Longman, 1969), 161–62, ll. 1–4, 7–8.

116. In *John Dryden*, ed. Keith Walker (Oxford: Oxford University Press, 1987), 373, ll. 1–4.

117. As for example in the opening lines of John Denham's *Cooper's-Hill: A Poem* (London, 1655), or in Pope's *Windsor-Forest* (1713), ll. 259–66, 271–72.

118. Sir John Denham, in *Eighteenth-Century English Literature*, ed. Geoffrey Tillotson et al. (New York: Harcourt, Brace and World, 1969), 785.

119. See Eric Partridge, *A Dictionary of Slang and Unconventional English* (New York: MacMillan, 1970), 616.

120. *The Poems of John Oldham*, 342, ll. 22–3.

121. This connection was made by Claude Rawson in his *Satire and Sentiment 1660–1830: Stress Points in the English Augustan Tradition* (New Haven, Conn.: Yale University Press, 1994), 6.

122. John Sheffield, Duke of Buckingham, "A Familiar Epistle . . . ," in *Poems on Affairs of State: Augustan Satirical Verse, 1660–1714*, ed. George deF. Lord (New Haven, Conn.: Yale University Press, 1963), 1: 389, ll. 45–8.

123. Rochester uses a slightly different version of the trope in "On Mistriss Willis" (1680): "Whom that I may describe throughout, / Assist me, bawdy powers; / I'll write upon a double clout / And dip my pen in flowers" (in *The Complete Works*, ed. Frank H. Ellis [London: Penguin, 1994], 199, ll. 5–8). Here, the vagina becomes an ink-well into which the phallic pen can be dipped. The image is as surreal as the scatalogical birthings in which quill and writing were imaged as the author's finger dipped into his own ink-feces.

124. In her discussion of the drunken, physically violent, or sexually promiscuous male body of sixteenth-century Germany, Lyndal Roper has made a different but related point, arguing that the disruptive threat to patriarchal authority had much to do with "a particular way of imagining the male body. Man is understood as a creature who is always breaking through the boundaries of his own body, to the point that he threatens social order. He is a volcano of drives and fluids which constantly threaten to erupt, spilling outwards to dirty his environment through ejaculation, bloodshed, vomiting, defecating. Drinking, which, in the view of the preachers, released all social inhibitions, gave free rein to lusts" (*Oedipus and the Devil: Witchcraft, Sexuality and Religion in Early Modern Europe* [London: Routledge, 1994], 112).

125. For the "lack of a coherent theory of sublimation" as "one of the lacunae in psycho-analytic thought" see Jean LaPlanche and J. B. Pontalis, *The Language of Psycho-Analysis*, trans. Donald Nicholson-Smith (New York: Norton, 1973), 433. On the tendency of "almost all psychoanalytical criticism since Freud . . . to disguise an argument for the regressive nature of art," see Leo Bersani, *The Culture of Redemption* (Cambridge, Mass.: Harvard University Press, 1990), 34.

126. For more detailed analysis of the symbolic sexual terrain in pastoral poetry, see Raymond Stephanson, "The Love Song of Young Alexander Pope: Allusion and Sexual Displacement in the *Pastorals*," *English Studies in Canada* 17 (1991): 21–35.

127. Abraham Cowley, in *The Works of Mr. Abraham Cowley*, ed. Abraham Cowley and Thomas Sprat, 7th ed. (London, 1681), 12.

128. Robert A. Erickson, in "William Harvey's *De motu cordis* and 'The Republick of Literature,' " in *Literature and Medicine during the Eighteenth Century*, ed. Marie Mulvey Roberts and Roy Porter (London: Routledge, 1993), sees the cultural logic of this poem as "a paradigm of the seventeenth-century masculine scientist's domination of Nature which has its analogue in the Restoration libertine-rake's domination of women" (65).

129. Ronald Paulson, *Breaking and Remaking: Aesthetic Practice in England, 1700–1820* (New Brunswick, N.J.: Rutgers University Press, 1989), 57.

130. Hesiod, *Theogony*, in *Works and Days, Theogony, The Shield of Herakles*, trans Richard Lattimore (Ann Arbor: University of Michigan Press, 1959), 134–5, ll. 188–211.

131. Joseph Warton, *An Essay on the Genius and Writings of Pope: In Two Volumes* (London, 1782), 2: 257.

132. For example, from John Garfield's *The Wandring Whore* (Exeter, 1660): "A wandring whore . . . drew out a sharpned [sic] knife for that purpose, and holding of his P— close by the root, she cut it cleer and sheer off, leaving him his member and knife together, where he continued dancing and roaring till some company brought forth lights. . . . [he] went into a Chyrurgeons, who thrust a quil into his pissing place to prevent the stoppage of his Urine . . . and within a day or two following he departed this life" (Part 4, 6).

133. Thomas A. King, " 'Converting *Stones into Bread*': Masculinity, Mimesis and 'Il Ragazzo' Farinelli," 19. I am indebted to Professor King for allowing me to read this unpublished conference paper presented at the ninth DeBartolo Conference in 1995 devoted to "The Eighteenth-Century Male."

134. Gary Taylor's *Castration: An Abbreviated History of Western Manhood* (New York: Routledge, 2000) corroborates this important historical point about which psychoanalysis has been amazingly, ahistorically ignorant: "although they might lack 'the power to breed,' eunuchs were not impotent in any other sense. Castrated human males could be exceptionally powerful" (37).

135. *Rochester: Complete Poems and Plays*, ed. Paddy Lyons (London: J. M. Dent, 1993), 319, ll. 50–61.

136. William Collins, "Ode on the Poetical Character," in *The Poems of Thomas Gray, William Collins, Oliver Goldsmith*, 429, ll. 17–22.

Chapter 4. Pope and Male Literary Communities

1. The most complete account of Pope's medical condition is still Marjorie Nicolson and G. S. Rousseau, *"This Long Disease, My Life": Alexander Pope and the Sciences* (Princeton, N.J.: Princeton University Press, 1968), 56–73.

2. J. V. Guerinot, *Pamphlet Attacks on Alexander Pope, 1711–1744* (New York: New York University Press, 1969).

3. For useful speculations about the known facts supporting or raising doubts about Cibber's claim, see Norman Ault, *New Light on Pope: With Some Additions to his Poetry Hitherto Unknown* (London: Methuen, 1949), 298–307; Helene Koon's Introduction to Cibber's *A Letter . . .* , Augustan Reprint Society 158 (Los Angeles: William Andrews Clark Memorial Library, University of California, 1973), i–xi; and Mack's *Alexander Pope: A Life*, 774–81.

4. Joseph Spence, *Observations, Anecdotes, and Characters of Books and Men Collected from Conversation*, ed. James M. Osborn (Oxford: Clarendon Press, 1966), 1: 32, no. 75.

5. James A. Winn discusses aspects of this pose in "Pope Plays the Rake: His Letters to Ladies and the Making of the *Eloisa*," in *The Art of Alexander Pope*, ed. Howard Erskine-Hill and Anne Smith (London: Vision Press, 1979), 89–118.

6. Maynard Mack, " 'The Least Thing like a Man in England': Some Effects of Pope's Physical Disability on His Life and Literary Career," in *Collected in*

Himself: Essays Critical, Biographical, and Bibliographical on Pope and Some of His Contemporaries, ed. Mack (Newark: University of Delaware Press, 1982), 378.

7. John Hughes, *Letters of Abelard and Heloise*, 10th ed. (Dublin, 1769), Abelard to friend Philintus, Letter I, 94; Heloise to Abelard, Letter II, 105–6.

8. David Clay Jenkins, "Scribblings on the Backside of 'Sapho to Phaon'— An Unpublished Pope Epigram?" *The Scriblerian* 8 (1976): 77–78.

9. See Maynard Mack, "Pope's 1717 Preface with a Transcription of the Manuscript Text," in *Augustan Worlds: Essays in Honour of A. R. Humphreys*, ed. Humphreys et al. (Leicester: Leicester University Press, 1978), 85–106.

10. Even a cursory comparison of Pope's authorized 1737 correspondence with Sherburn's complete record indicates how carefully Pope removed these kinds of sexual tropes.

11. "Martinus Scriblerus of the Poem," in *The Dunciad In Four Books*, ed. Valerie Rumbold (London: Longman, 1999), 71, 70–71. Quotations from the prefatory materials and the poem are taken from this edition, with page, book, and line numbers cited parenthetically.

12. Cibber, *An Apology for the Life of Colley Cibber* (1740; reprint London: Dent, 1914), 23–24.

13. For other approaches to ideas of reproduction, birth, and legitimacy in the *Dunciad* see Rebecca Ferguson, " 'Intestine Wars': Body and Text in *An Epistle to Dr. Arbuthnot* and *The Dunciad*," 137–52, and Carolyn D. Williams, "Breaking Decorums: Belinda, Bays and Epic Effeminacy," 59–79—both in *Pope: New Contexts*, ed. David Fairer (London: Harvester Wheatsheaf, 1990). Feminist critics such as Catherine Ingrassia have examined how the "regressive maternity" or monstrous female fertility of Dulness is linked to female authors, the new breed of commercial writers, and a feminized culture of economic obsessions ("Women Writing/Writing Women: Pope, Dulness, and 'Feminization' in the *Dunciad*," *Eighteenth-Century Life* 14 [1990]: 43). Also see Susan Gubar, "The Female Monster in Augustan Satire," *Signs* 3 (1977): 380–94; Marilyn Francus, "The Monstrous Mother: Reproductive Anxiety in Swift and Pope," *ELH* 61 (1994): 829–51.

14. Pope includes the anal birth idea as well in the Annius-Mummius episode in Book 4. The crafty Annius has swallowed the counterfeit coins which are intended for gullible Mummius, but promises that, "cramm'd with capon" (*TE* 5: 377, Bk. 4, l. 350), he will still make available the coins in a defecatory recovery or anal birth: "There all the Learn'd shall at the labour stand, / And Douglas lend his soft, obstetric hand" (*TE* 5: 380, Bk. 4, ll. 393–94). The grotesque perversion of "labor"—both reproductive and excremental—is not literary, but it still functions as an instance of the new capitalism where all that matters is money, whose literal shitting-forth here parallels the lower-order oozings of Cibber's head.

15. The Loeb edition translates lines 58–60 as "But Phoebus at last appeared, drove off the snake just in the act to bite, and hardened and froze to stone, just as they were, the serpent's widespread, yawning jaws" (*Ovid: Metamorphoses*, trans. Frank Justus Miller [New York: Loeb, 1929], 2: 125).

16. *The Dunciad in Four Books*, 22. John V. Regan suggests "that Pope's artistic achievement represents Orpheus' indestructible song" ("Orpheus and the *Dunciad*'s Narrator," *Eighteenth-Century Studies* 9 [1975]: 96); Patricia Vicari suggests that "For Pope, the severed head is poetry itself and the serpent, by a logical but witty extension, bad poets and carping critics" ("*Sparagmos*: Orpheus among the Christians," in *Orpheus: The Metamorphoses of a Myth*, ed.

John M. Warden [Toronto: University of Toronto Press, 1982], 80); more recently Ronald Paulson reads the epigraph as about Pope's "turning himself into Orpheus, murdered but, even in the act of devourment by the yawning jaws of Dulness, surviving as a poetic voice—while his muse has frozen into the immortality of literature the dunces, hacks, and politicians who have overwhelmed him with personal abuse" (*Breaking and Remaking: Aesthetic Practice in England, 1700–1820* [New Brunswick, N.J.: Rutgers University Press, 1989], 60).

17. See Maynard Mack, *Alexander Pope: A Life* (New Haven, Conn.: Yale University Press, 1985), 32, 656–57. See also Ralph Straus, *The Unspeakable Curll* (1927; reprint New York: Augustus M. Kelley, 1970), 183, 189.

18. Catherine Ingrassia, "Dissecting the Authorial Body: Pope, Curll, and the Portrait of a 'Hack Writer,' " in *"More Solid Learning": New Perspectives on Alexander Pope's Dunciad*, ed. Catherine Ingrassia and Claudia N. Thomas (Lewisburg, Pa.: Bucknell University Press, 2000), 161.

19. Donald W. Nichol, *Pope's Literary Legacy: The Book-Trade Correspondence of William Warburton and John Knapton with Other Letters and Documents 1744–1780* (Oxford: Oxford Bibliographical Society, 1992), xlvii.

20. Owen Ruffhead, *The Life of Alexander Pope, Esq. Compiled From Original Manuscripts; With a Critical Essay on his Writings and Genius* (London, 1769), 532.

21. What little commentary there is can be found in John Aden, "That Impudent Satire: Pope's *Sober Advice*," *Studies in Philology* 4 (1967): 88–106; G. Douglas Atkins, "Strategy and Purpose in Pope's *Sober Advice from Horace*," *Papers on Language and Literature* 15 (1979): 159–74; Howard Erskine-Hill, *The Augustan Idea in English Literature* (London: Edward Arnold, 1983), 304–5; Frank Stack, *Pope and Horace: Studies in Imitation* (Cambridge: Cambridge University Press, 1985), 78–98. The best reading of the poem and its Horatian model is Jacob Fuchs's *Reading Pope's "Imitations of Horace"* (Lewisburg, Pa.: Bucknell University Press, 1989), 85–92.

22. Amy Richlin, *The Garden of Priapus: Sexuality and Aggression in Roman Humor* (New Haven, Conn.: Yale University Press, 1983), 67, 116. The classical tradition includes the three Priapics of Virgil's *Catalepton* in which the deified Priapus speaks; Ovid's *Amores* 3:7 and Petronius's *Satyricon* 132: 6–15 in which the disappointed male berates his impotent yard; Horace's *Satires* 1: 2 in which the man is addressed on behalf of the complaining penis; Martial's *Epigrams* 1: 58, 6: 16, 6: 49, 6: 72, 6: 73, 7: 91, 8: 40, 9:37, 14: 69 in which privy members are variously personified; and Catullus's poems 105 and 115 which feature the personified Mr. Prick or O'Toole.

23. John Wilkes, *The Infamous "Essay on Woman"*, ed. Adrian Hamilton (London: Deutsch, 1972), 244–45. Subsequent references to *An Essay on Woman* will be cited parenthetically by page and line numbers.

24. The most famous of the ancient impotence narratives in which the personified member is addressed is Petronius's *The Satyricon*, ed. and trans. John Sullivan (Harmondsworth: Penguin, 1965), 150–51, and Ovid's *The Erotic Poems*, trans. Peter Green (Harmondsworth: Penguin, 1982), *The Amores* 3: 7, 151.

25. John Wilmot, Earl of Rochester, *The Imperfect Enjoyment*, in *The Complete Works*, ed. Frank H. Ellis (London: Penguin, 1994), 29, ll. 46–61.

26. *Horace's Satires and Epistles*, trans. Jacob Fuchs (New York: Norton, 1977), 5–6, ll. 68–76, 116–19.

27. Michel de Montaigne, *Essays*, 42.

28. Alexander Pope, *A Further Account of the Most Deplorable Condition of Mr.*

Edmund Curll, Bookseller. Since his being Poison'd on the 28th of March (London, 1716), 8.

29. Although it survives only in *Miscellanies. The Third Volume* (London, 1732), the pamphlet may have been published first in 1720. See *Selected Prose of Alexander Pope*, ed. Paul Hammond (Cambridge: Cambridge University Press, 1987), 129.

30. See, for example, "The Lord H-r—y's First Speech in the House of Lords" (London, 1734) and "An Apology for Printing 'The Nobleman's Epistle' " (London, 1734), both anonymous satires of Hervey's politics and effeminate appearance. The latter refers to Hervey as "Lord Fanny" (John, Lord Hervey, *Lord Hervey and His Friends, 1726–38: Based on Letters from Holland House, Melbury, and Ickworth*, ed. Earl of Ilchester [London: John Murray, 1950], 298).

31. Pulteney's *A Proper Reply to a Late Scurrilous Libel* (London, 1731) had openly pointed to Hervey's effeminacy and same-sex proclivities. Hervey's response to this insinuation was to challenge Pulteney to a duel; both were slightly injured. See Robert Halsband, *Lord Hervey: Eighteenth-Century Courtier* (New York: Oxford University Press, 1974), 109–15.

32. Especially in Jill Campbell's "Politics and Sexuality in Portraits of John, Lord Hervey," *Word & Image* 6 (1990): 284–85.

33. Even a casual survey of the Pope-bashing literature, lampoons, and engravings reveals an astonishing degree of malice and scurrility. But we ought not to underestimate Pope's own combativeness, or what G. S. Rousseau has described as the poet's "need to rile his readers with calculated expressions of outrage and contempt" ("Pope and the Tradition in Modern Humanistic Education: ' . . . in the pale of Words till death,' " in *The Enduring Legacy: Alexander Pope Tercentenary Essays*, ed. G. S. Rousseau and Pat Rogers [Cambridge: Cambridge University Press, 1988], 199).

34. For brief but perceptive comment on Ward's poem see Steve Clark, " 'Let Blood and Body Bear the Fault': Pope and Misogyny," in *Pope: New Contexts*, ed. David Fairer (London: Harvester Wheatsheaf, 1990), 84, and Howard D. Weinbrot, *Alexander Pope and the Traditions of Formal Verse Satire* (Princeton, N.J.: Princeton University Press, 1982), 145.

35. Edward Ward, *Apollo's Maggot in His Cups: Or, the Whimsical Creation of a Little Satyrical Poet. A Lyrick Ode* (London, 1729), 7.

36. *Ingratitude: To Mr. Pope* (London, 1733), 3.

37. Lady Mary Wortley Montagu and John, Lord Hervey, *Verses Address'd to the Imitator of the First Satire of the Second Book of Horace* (London, 1733), 4.

38. Jean Astruc, *A Treatise of the Venereal Disease. . .* , trans. William Barrowby (London, 1737), 336.

39. Colley Cibber, *Another Occasional Letter from Mr. Cibber to Mr. Pope. Wherein the New Hero's Preferment to his Throne in the "Dunciad" seems not to be Accepted. And the Author of that Poem His more rightful Claim to it, is Asserted* (London, 1744), 52–53.

40. Eric V. Chandler, "Pope's 'Girl of the Game': The Prostitution of the Author and the Business of Culture," in *"More Solid Learning"*, ed. Ingrassia and Thomas, 125.

41. G. S. Rousseau, " *'et in Arcadia homo'*: Opera, Gender, and Sexual Politics in *The Dunciad*," in *"More Solid Learning"*, ed. Ingrassia and Thomas, 37, 57.

42. Colley Cibber, *A Letter from Mr. Cibber to Mr. Pope, Inquiring into the Motives that might induce him in his Satyrical Works, to be so frequently fond of Mr. Cibber's Name*, ed. Helene Koon (1742; reprint Augustan Reprint Society 158, Los

Angeles: William Andrews Clark Memorial Library, University of California, 1973), 47–49.

43. Laura J. Rosenthal, " 'Trials of Manhood': Cibber, *The Dunciad*, and the Masculine Self," in *"More Solid Learning"*, ed. Ingrassia and Thomas, 103.

44. Eric V. Chandler, "Pope's 'Girl of the Game'," 107–8.

45. Norman Ault, *New Light on Pope*, 302–3.

46. *Sawney and Colley, a Poetical Dialogue: Occasioned by a Late Letter from the Laureat of St. James's, to the Homer of Twickenham* . . . (London, 1742), 5–6.

47. Joseph Spence, *Observations*, 1: 110, no. 251.

48. Joseph Spence, *Observations*, 1: 110, no. 252.

49. Samuel Johnson, *Johnson's Lives of the Poets*, ed. J. P. Hardy (Oxford: Clarendon Press, 1971), 268.

50. Mack, *Alexander Pope: A Life*, 780. Norman Ault has identified the pictorial allusions surrounding the Colley-Pope-whore foreground, linking them to *Three Hours After Marriage* and *The Nonjuror* (*New Light on Pope*, 303).

51. According to Roger Bozzetto and Geneviève Goubier-Robert, the oldest edition known is undated, but bears the following publication information on the title page: "Rome, chez Philotamus, éditeur" ("Lecture," in *Le Portier des Chartreux: Histoire de Dom Bougre*, ed. Roger Bozzetto and Geneviève Goubier-Robert [Actes Sud: Babel, 1993], 259). This is the edition in the Bibliothèque nationale from which my reproduction is taken, which means it is almost certainly from the first edition of 1741.

52. Vincent Carretta, *The Snarling Muse: Verbal and Visual Political Satire from Pope to Churchill* (Philadelphia: University of Pennsylvania Press, 1983), xiii; Philip Stewart, "Indecency and Literary Illustration," *South Atlantic Quarterly* 90 (1991): 149.

53. Carol Wax, *The Mezzotint: History and Technique* (New York: Harry N. Abrams, Inc., 1990), 70. For examples of plates altered to depict different heads and faces see 70–1, 234.

54. Robert Darnton, *The Forbidden Best-Sellers of Pre-Revolutionary France* (New York: Norton, 1995), 73, 104.

55. Erica Jong, *Fanny: Being the True History of the Adventures of Fanny Hackabout-Jones: A Novel* (New York: New American Library, 1980).

56. She was a student of James Clifford in the 1960s and wrote her 1965 M.A. thesis at Columbia University on "The Theme of Women in the Poetry of Pope: A Study of Conventional Sexual Language and Imagery in *Eloisa to Abelard*."

57. Brean S. Hammond, *Pope* (Atlantic Highlands, N.J.: Humanities Press, 1986).

Works Cited

Abrams, M. H. *The Mirror and the Lamp: Romantic Theory and the Critical Tradition*. New York: Oxford University Press, 1953.

Aden, John. "That Impudent Satire: Pope's *Sober Advice*." *Studies in Philology* 4 (1967): 88–106.

Amherst, J. "To the Earl of Roscommon." In Wentworth Dillon Earl of Roscommon, *Poems by the Earl of Roscommon, to Which Is Added an Essay on Poetry*. . . . London, 1717.

Ancillon, Charles. *Traité des eunuques*. 1707. Trans. Edmund Curll as *Eunuchism Display'd*. London, 1718.

Aristotle. *The Complete Works of Aristotle: The Revised Oxford Translation*. Ed. Jonathan Barnes. Princeton, N. J.: Princeton University Press, 1984.

Aristotle [pseud.]. *Aristotle's Master-Piece, or, the Secrets of Generation Displayed in All the Parts Thereof*. . . . London, 1694.

Armstrong, John. "*The Oeconomy of Love*: A Critical Edition with Commentary." Ed. Clive Hart and Kay Gilliland Stevenson. *Eighteenth-Century Life* 19 (1995): 38–69.

Astruc, Jean. *A Treatise of the Venereal Disease*. . . . Trans. William Barrowby. London, 1737.

Atkins, G. Douglas. "Strategy and Purpose in Pope's *Sober Advice from Horace*." *Papers on Language and Literature* 15 (1979): 159–74.

Augustine, Saint, Bishop of Hippo. *De Civitate Dei: The City of God Against the Pagans*. Cambridge, Mass.: Harvard University Press, 1969–1988.

Ault, Norman. *New Light on Pope: With Some Additions to His Poetry Hitherto Unknown*. London: Methuen, 1949.

Ausonius, Decimus Magnus. "Cento Nuptialis." In *Ausonius*. Trans. Hugh G. Evelyn White. 2 vols. 1: 370–93. Loeb Classical Library. London: Heinemann, 1919.

Baecque, Antoine de. *The Body Politic: Corporeal Metaphor in Revolutionary France, 1770–1800*. Trans. Charlotte Mandell. Stanford, Calif.: Stanford University Press, 1993.

Baird, Lorrayne Y. "Priapus Gallinaceus: The Role of the Cock in Fertility and Eroticism in Classical Antiquity and the Middle Ages." *Studies in Iconography* 7–8 (1981–82): 81–111.

Baker, Henry. *The Microscope Made Easy*. . . . London, 1742.

Barker-Benfield, G. J. *The Culture of Sensibility: Sex and Society in Eighteenth-Century Britain*. Chicago: University of Chicago Press, 1992.

Barrin, Jean. *Venus in the Cloister: Or, the Nun in her Smock*. London, 1725.

Battersby, Christine. *Gender and Genius: Towards a Feminist Aesthetics*. Bloomington: Indiana University Press, 1989.

Bennett, Paula, and Vernon A. Rosario, eds. *Solitary Pleasures: The Historical, Literary, and Artistic Discourses of Autoeroticism.* New York: Routledge, 1995.

Bentley, Thomas. *A Letter to Mr. Pope, Occasioned by Sober Advice from Horace.* London, 1735.

Bernheimer, Charles. "Penile Reference in Phallic Theory." *differences: A Journal of Feminist Cultural Studies* 4 (1992): 116–32.

Bersani, Leo. *The Culture of Redemption.* Cambridge, Mass.: Harvard University Press, 1990.

Bienville, D. T. de. *Nymphomania, or, a Dissertation Concerning the Furor Uterinus.* . . . Trans. Edward Sloane Wilmot. London, 1775.

Blackmore, Sir Richard. "An Essay Upon Wit." In *Essay Upon Several Subjects,* 189–235. London, 1716.

Bold, Alan Norman, ed. *Making Love: The Picador Book of Erotic Verse.* London: Pan Books, 1980.

Bordo, Susan. *The Male Body: A New Look at Men in Public and in Private.* New York: Farrar Straus and Giroux, 1999.

Boswell, James. *The Journals of James Boswell, 1762–1795.* Ed. John Wain. New Haven, Conn.: Yale University Press, 1991.

———. *Life of Johnson.* Ed. R. W. Chapman. Oxford: Oxford University Press, 1980.

Boucé, Paul-Gabriel. "Aspects of Sexual Tolerance and Intolerance in XVIIIth-Century England." *British Journal for Eighteenth-Century Studies* 3 (1980): 173–91.

———. "The Secret Nexus: Sex and Literature in Eighteenth-Century Britain." In *The Sexual Dimension in Literature,* ed. Alan Bold, 70–89. London: Vision Press, 1982.

———. "Some Sexual Beliefs and Myths in Eighteenth-Century Britain." In *Sexuality in Eighteenth-Century Britain,* ed. Paul-Gabriel Boucé, 28–46. Manchester: Manchester University Press, 1982.

Bowler, Peter J. "Preformation and Pre-Existence in the Seventeenth Century: A Brief Analysis." *Journal of the History of Biology* 4 (1971): 221–44.

Boyarin, Daniel. "Who Wrote the Dominant Fiction? On the History of the Early Phallus." In *Brief: Intellectual Traditions in Movement,* ed. Mieke Bal et al., 41–83. Amsterdam: Amsterdam School for Cultural Analysis, Theory, and Interpretation, 1998.

Bozzetto, Roger, and Geneviève Goubier-Robert. "Lecture." In *Le Portier des Chartreux: Histoire de Dom Bougre,* ed. Roger Bozzetto and Geneviève Goubier-Robert, 253–82. Actes Sud: Babel, 1993.

Braudy, Leo. *The Frenzy of Renown: Fame and Its History.* New York: Oxford University Press, 1986.

———. "Remembering Masculinity: Premature Ejaculation Poetry of the Seventeenth Century." *Michigan Quarterly Review* 33 (1994): 177–201.

Bray, Alan, and Michel Rey. "The Body of the Friend: Continuity and Change in Masculine Friendship in the Seventeenth Century." In *English Masculinities 1660–1800,* ed. Tim Hitchcock and Michèle Cohen, 65–84. London: Longman, 1999.

Breitenberg, Mark. *Anxious Masculinity in Early Modern England.* Cambridge: Cambridge University Press, 1996.

Brewer, John. *The Pleasures of the Imagination: English Culture in the Eighteenth Century.* London: HarperCollins, 1997.

Brissenden, Robert F. "La Philosophie dans le Boudoir, or, a Young Lady's

Entrance into the World." In *Studies in Eighteenth-Century Culture: Proceedings of the American Society for Eighteenth-Century Studies*, ed. Harold E. Pagliaro, 113–41. Cleveland: Press of Case Western Reserve University, 1972.

Bruce, Susan. " 'Rolling About from Whore to Whore': Rochester's Satirico-Sexual Self and the Art of Conspicuous Consumption." *Forum for Modern Language Studies* 30 (1994): 305–15.

Buckingham, John Sheffield, Duke of. *Buckingham Restor'd: Being Two Essays Which Were Castrated from the Works of the Late Duke of Buckingham*. The Hague, 1727.

———. "A Familiar Epistle to Mr. Julian, Secretary to the Muses" (1677). In *Poems on Affairs of State: Augustan Satirical Verse, 1660–1714*, ed. George deForest Lord, 1: 387–91. New Haven, Conn.: Yale University Press, 1963.

Butler, Judith. "The Lesbian Phallus and the Morphological Imaginary." *differences: A Journal of Feminist Cultural Studies* 4 (1992): 133–71.

Butler, Samuel. *Dildoides*. Kingston, R.I.: Biscuit City Press, 1979.

Byron, George Gordon, Lord. *Byron's Letters and Journals*. Ed. Leslie A. Marchand. 12 vols. Cambridge, Mass.: Belknap Press of Harvard University Press, 1973–82.

The Cabinet of Love. London, 1721.

Cam, Joseph. *A Practical Treatise; or, Second Thoughts on the Consequences of the Venereal Disease. . . .* 3rd ed. London, 1729.

Campbell, Jill. *Natural Masques: Gender and Identity in Fielding's Plays and Novels*. Stanford, Calif.: Stanford University Press, 1995.

———. "Politics and Sexuality in Portraits of John, Lord Hervey." *Word and Image* 6 (1990): 281–97.

———. " 'When Men Women Turn': Gender Reversals in Fielding's Plays." In *The New Eighteenth Century: Theory, Politics, English Literature*, ed. Felicity Nussbaum and Laura Brown, 62–83. New York: Methuen, 1987.

Carabelli, Giancarlo. *In the Image of Priapus*. London: Duckworth, 1996.

Carretta, Vincent. *The Snarling Muse: Verbal and Visual Political Satire from Pope to Churchill*. Philadelphia: University of Pennsylvania Press, 1983.

Carson, James P. "Commodification and the Figure of the Castrato in Smollett's *Humphry Clinker*." *Eighteenth Century: Theory and Interpretation* 33 (1992): 24–46.

Carter, Philip. "James Boswell's Manliness." In *English Masculinities, 1660–1880*, ed. Tim Hitchcock and Michèle Cohen, 111–30. London: Longman, 1999.

———. *Men and the Emergence of Polite Society, Britain 1660–1800*. Harlow: Longman, 2001.

The Case of Impotency, as Debated in England, in That Remarkable Tryal, 1613. . . . London, 1719.

The Case of Impotency Debated, in the Late Famous Tryal at Paris; Between the Marquis de Gesvres, (Son to the Duke de Tresmes, Present Governor of Paris) and Mademoiselle de Mascranny his Lady, Who after Three Years Marriage, Commenc'd Suit against Him for Impotency. London, 1714.

Castle, Terry. "Lab'ring Bards: Birth Topoi and English Poetics 1660–1820." *Journal of English and Germanic Philology* 78 (1979): 193–208.

Catchpole, Hubert R. "Regnier De Graaf 1641–1673." *Bulletin of the History of Medicine* 8 (1940): 1261–300.

Catullus, Gaius Valerius. *The Poems of Catullus*. Trans. Guy Lee. Oxford: Oxford University Press, 1990.

Censorinus. *De Die Natali*. Ed. Otto Jahn. Amsterdam: Rodopi, 1964.

Cervantes, Xavier. " 'Tuneful Monsters': The Castrati and the London Operatic Public 1667–1737." *Restoration and Eighteenth-Century Theatre Research* 2nd ser. 13 (1998): 1–24.

Chambers, Ephraim. *Cyclopaedia: Or, an Universal Dictionary of Arts and Sciences*. 2nd ed. London, 1738.

Chandler, Eric V. "Pope's 'Girl of the Game': The Prostitution of the Author and the Business of Culture," in *"More Solid Learning": New Perspectives on Alexander Pope's Dunciad*, ed. Catherine Ingrassia and Claudia N. Thomas, 106–28. Lewisburg, Pa.: Bucknell University Press, 2000.

Chorier, Nicolas. *Satyra sotadica de arcanis amoris et veneris*. Ca. 1665. *A Dialogue Between a Married Lady and a Maid*, an abridged adaptation in English. London, 1740.

Chudleigh, Lady Mary. *The Poems and Prose of Mary, Lady Chudleigh*. Ed. Margaret J. M. Ezell. New York: Oxford University Press, 1993.

Cibber, Colley. *An Apology for the Life of Mr. Colley Cibber*. 1740. Reprint London: Dent, 1914.

———. *Another Occasional Letter from Mr. Cibber to Mr. Pope. . . .* London, 1744.

———. *A Letter from Mr. Cibber to Mr. Pope. . . .* 1742. Ed. Helene Koon. Augustan Reprint Society 158. Los Angeles: William Andrews Clark Memorial Library, University of California, 1973.

Clark, Steve. " 'Let Blood and Body Bear the Fault': Pope and Misogyny." In *Pope: New Contexts*, ed. David Fairer, 81–101. London: Harvester Wheatsheaf, 1990.

Cleland, John. *Memoirs of a Coxcomb*. Dublin, 1751.

———. *Memoirs of a Woman of Pleasure*. 1749. Ed. Peter Sabor. Oxford: New York, 1985.

Cleveland, John. *The Poems of John Cleveland*. Ed. Brian Robert Morris and Eleanor Withington. Oxford: Clarendon Press, 1967.

Cole, F. J. *Early Theories of Sexual Generation*. Oxford: Clarendon Press, 1930.

———. "The History of Anatomical Injections." In *Studies in the History and Method of Science*, ed. Charles Singer, 285–343. Oxford: Clarendon Press, 1921.

Coleridge, S. T. *Biographica Literaria*. 1817. Ed. James Engell and W. Jackson Bate. Princeton, N.J.: Princeton University Press, 1983.

Collins, William. "Ode on the Poetical Character." In *The Poems of Thomas Gray, William Collins, Oliver Goldsmith*, ed. Roger Lonsdale, 427–35. London: Longman, 1969.

Congreve, William. *Incognita, or, Love and Duty Reconcil'd. A Novel*. 1692. Reprint, in *Shorter Novels of the Seventeenth Century*, ed. Philip Henderson, 237–303. London: Dent, 1930.

———. *The Way of the World. A Comedy*. 1700. Ed. Kathleen M. Lynch. Lincoln: University of Nebraska Press, 1965.

Consummation: Or, the Rape of Adonis. London, 1741.

Connell, R. W. *Masculinities*. Oxford: Polity Press, 1995.

Cope, Kevin L. "Squirrell's in the Breeches: Onanism, Diarrhea, and the Aesthetics of Antipanaceatic Discourse." *Eighteenth-Century Life* 17 (1993): 1–31.

Correia, Clara Pinto. *The Ovary of Eve: Egg and Sperm and Preformation*. Chicago: University of Chicago Press, 1997.

The Countess's Speech to Her Son Roderigo. . . . London, 1731.

Cowley, Abraham, and Thomas Sprat. *The Works of Mr. Abraham Cowley*. London, 1681.

Cowper, William. "An Account of two Glands and Their Excretory Ducts lately Discover'd in Human Bodies." *Philosophical Transactions* 258 (1699): 363–69.

Crawford, Patricia. "Sexual Knowledge in England, 1500–1750." In *Sexual Knowledge, Sexual Science: The History of Attitudes to Sexuality*, ed. Roy Porter and Mikulas Teich, 82–106. Cambridge: Cambridge University Press, 1994.

Cumberland, Richard. "Prologue" for *The Fashionable Lover. A Comedy*. London, 1772.

Darmon, Pierre. *Le Mythe de la procréation a l'âge baroque*. Paris: J.-J. Pauvert, 1977.

———. *Trial by Impotence: Virility and Marriage in Pre-Revolutionary France*. Trans. Paul Keegan. London: Chatto and Windus Hogarth Press, 1985.

Darnton, Robert. *The Forbidden Best-Sellers of Pre-Revolutionary France*. New York: Norton, 1995.

Defoe, Daniel. *Roxana: The Fortunate Mistress*. 1724. Ed. David Blewett. Harmondsworth: Penguin, 1982.

———. *A Review of the State of the British Nation*, 2 February 1710.

De Graaf, Regnier. *Regnier De Graaf on the Human Reproductive Organs: An Annotated Translation of "Tractatus De Virorum Organis Generationi Inservientibus" (1668) and "De Mulierum Organis Generationi Inservientibus Tractatus Novus" (1672)*. Trans. H. D. Jocelyn and B. P. Setchell. Oxford: Blackwell Scientific Publications, 1972.

Denham, John. *Coopers-Hill: A Poem*. London, 1655.

Dennis, John, et al. *Letters Upon Several Occasions. . . .* London, 1696.

Deutsch, Helen. *Resemblance & Disgrace: Alexander Pope and the Deformation of Culture*. Cambridge, Mass.: Harvard University Press, 1996.

Drake, James. *Anthropologia Nova, or, a New System of Anatomy. . . .* London, 1707.

Dryden, John. *John Dryden*. Ed. Keith Walker. Oxford: Oxford University Press, 1987.

———. *Essays of John Dryden*. Ed. W. P. Ker. Oxford: Clarendon Press, 1900.

———. *The Letters of John Dryden, with Letters Addressed to Him*. Ed. Charles Eugene Ward. Durham, N.C.: Duke University Press, 1942.

———. *The Prologues and Epilogues of John Dryden; a Critical Edition*. Ed. William Bradford Gardner. New York: Columbia University Press, 1951.

Engell, James. *The Creative Imagination: Enlightenment to Romanticism*. Cambridge, Mass.: Harvard University Press, 1981.

Erickson, Robert A. *The Language of the Heart, 1600–1750*. Philadelphia: University of Pennsylvania Press, 1997.

———. *Mother Midnight: Birth, Sex, and Fate in Eighteenth-Century Fiction (Defoe, Richardson, and Sterne)*. New York: AMS Press, 1986.

———. "William Harvey's *De Motu Cordis* and 'The Republick of Literature.' " In *Literature and Medicine During the Eighteenth Century*, ed. Marie Mulvey Roberts and Roy Porter, 58–83. London: Routledge, 1993.

Erskine-Hill, Howard. *The Augustan Idea in English Literature*. London: Edward Arnold, 1983.

Etherege, George. *The Poems of Sir George Etherege*. Ed. James Thorpe. Princeton, N.J.: Princeton University Press, 1963.

Fabricant, Carole. "Defining Self and Others: Pope and Eighteenth-Century Gender Ideology." *Criticism* 39 (1997): 503–29.

Ferguson, Rebecca. " 'Intestine Wars': Body and Text in *An Epistle to Dr. Arbuthnot* and *The Dunciad*." In *Pope: New Contexts*, ed. David Fairer, 137–52. London: Harvester Wheatsheaf, 1990.

Fielding, Henry. *The Author's Farce*. 1730. Ed. Charles B. Woods. Lincoln: University of Nebraska Press, 1966.

———. *The Female Husband*. . . . London, 1746.

———. *The History of Tom Jones*. 1749. Ed. Fredson Bowers. Middletown, Conn.: Wesleyan University Press, 1975.

———. *Joseph Andrews*. 1742. Ed. Martin C. Battestin. Middletown, Conn.: Wesleyan University Press, 1967.

Fletcher, Anthony. *Gender, Sex, and Subordination in England, 1500–1800*. New Haven, Conn.: Yale University Press, 1995.

Folkes, Martin. "Some Account of Mr. Leeuwenhoek's curious Microscopes, lately presented to the Royal Society. By Martin Folkes, Esq; Vice-President of the Royal Society." *Philosophical Transactions* 380 (1723): 446–53.

Foster, Susan Leigh. *Choreographing History*. Bloomington: Indiana University Press, 1995.

Fox, Christopher. "The Myth of Narcissus in Swift's *Travels*." *Eighteenth-Century Studies* 20 (1986): 17–33.

Foxon, David. *Libertine Literature in England, 1660–1745*. New York: University Books, 1965.

Francus, Marilyn. "The Monstrous Mother: Reproductive Anxiety in Swift and Pope." *ELH* 61 (1994): 829–51.

French, R. K. *Robert Whytt, the Soul, and Medicine*. London: Wellcome Institute of the History of Medicine, 1969.

Freud, Sigmund. *The Standard Edition of the Complete Psychological Works of Sigmund Freud*. 24 vols. Trans. James Strachey. London: Hogarth Press, 1959.

Friedenwald, Julius, and Samuel Morrison. "The History of the Enema with Some Notes on Related Procedures (Part 1)." *Bulletin of the History of Medicine* 8 (1940): 68–114.

Friedman, David M. *A Mind of Its Own: A Cultural History of the Penis*. New York: Free Press, 2001.

Fuchs, Jacob. *Reading Pope's Imitations of Horace*. Lewisburg, Pa.: Bucknell University Press, 1989.

Galen. *Galen on the Usefulness of the Parts of the Body*. Ed. Margaret Tallmadge May. Ithaca, N.Y.: Cornell University Press, 1968.

Gallagher, Catherine. *Nobody's Story: The Vanishing Acts of Women Writers in the Marketplace, 1670–1820*. Berkeley: University of California Press, 1994.

Gallop, Jane. *Thinking Through the Body*. New York: Columbia University Press, 1988.

Garfield, John, et al. *The Wandring Whore*. . . . Exeter, 1660.

Gasking, Elizabeth B. *Investigations into Generation, 1651–1828*. Baltimore: Johns Hopkins University Press, 1967.

Gervaise de La Touche, Jacques Charles. *Histoire de Dom B***, Portier Des Chartreux*. 1741. Translated as *The Life and Adventures of Father Silas*. London, 1742.

Gibson, Thomas. *The Anatomy of Humane Bodies Epitomized*. . . . London, 1682.

Gilbert, Sandra M., and Susan Gubar. *The Madwoman in the Attic: The Woman Writer and the Nineteenth-Century Literary Imagination*. New Haven, Conn.: Yale University Press, 1979.

Gilman, Sander L. *Sexuality: An Illustrated History: Representing the Sexual in Medicine and Culture from the Middle Ages to the Age of Aids*. New York: Wiley, 1989.

Goldsmith, Oliver. *The Citizen of the World*. . . . London, 1762.

Gonzalez-Crussi, F. *Notes of an Anatomist*. San Diego: Harcourt Brace Jovanovich, 1985.

Goux, Jean-Joseph. "The Phallus: Masculine Identity and the 'Exchange of Women.'" *differences: A Journal of Feminist Cultural Studies* 4 (1992): 40–75.

———. *Symbolic Economies: After Marx and Freud*. Trans. Jennifer Curtiss Page. Ithaca, N.Y.: Cornell University Press, 1990.

Graham, James. *A New and Curious Treatise of the Nature and Effects of Simple Earth, Water, and Air, When Applied to the Human Body.* . . . London, 1793.

Gray, Thomas. "The Progress of Poesy." In *The Poems of Thomas Gray, William Collins, Oliver Goldsmith*, ed. Roger Lonsdale, 155–77. London: Longman, 1969.

Griffin, Dustin H. *Literary Patronage in England, 1650–1800*. Cambridge: Cambridge University Press, 1996.

Grundy, Isobel. "The Poet and Her Muse." In *The Timeless and the Temporal: Writings in Honour of John Chalker by Friends and Colleagues*, ed. Elizabeth Maslen, 173–93. London: Queen Mary and Westfield College, University of London, Department of English, 1993.

Gubar, Susan. "The Female Monster in Augustan Satire." *Signs* 3 (1977): 380–94.

Guerinot, Joseph V. *Pamphlet Attacks on Alexander Pope, 1711–1744: A Descriptive Bibliography*. New York: New York University Press, 1969.

Guerrini, Anita. *Obesity and Depression in the Enlightenment: The Life and Times of George Cheyne*. Norman: University of Oklahoma Press, 2000.

Haggerty, George E. *Men in Love: Masculinity and Sexuality in the Eighteenth Century*. New York: Columbia University Press, 1999.

Haller, Albrecht von. *A Dissertation on the Sensible and Irritable Parts of Animals* . . . *Translated from the Latin.* 1753. Trans. S. A. D. Tissot. London, 1755.

———. *First Lines of Physiology Translated from the Correct Latin Edition.* 1747. Trans. William Cullen. Edinburgh, 1779.

Halperin, David M. "Forgetting Foucault: Acts, Identities, and the History of Sexuality." *Representations* 63 (1998): 93–120.

Halsband, Robert. *Lord Hervey: Eighteenth-Century Courtier*. New York: Oxford University Press, 1974.

Hamilton, Adrian, ed. *The Infamous "Essay on Woman"; or, John Wilkes Seated between Vice and Virtue*. London: Deutsch, 1972.

Hammond, Brean S. *Pope*. Atlantic Highlands, N.J.: Humanities Press, 1986.

———. *Pope and Bolingbroke: A Study of Friendship and Influence*. Columbia: University of Missouri Press, 1984.

———. *Professional Imaginative Writing in England, 1670–1740: "Hackney for Bread"*. Oxford: Clarendon Press, 1997.

Hammond, Paul. "The King's Two Bodies: Representations of Charles II." In *Culture, Politics and Society in Britain, 1660–1800*, ed. Jeremy Black and Jeremy Gregory, 13–48. Manchester: Manchester University Press, 1991.

Harris, John. *Lexicon Technicum: Or, an Universal English Dictionary of Arts and Sciences*. London, 1704.

Hart, Clive, and Kay Gilliland, eds. "*The Oeconomy of Love*: A Critical Edition with Commentary." *Eighteenth-Century Life* 19 (1995): 38–69.

Harvey, Karen. "'The Majesty of the Masculine Form': Multiplicity and Male Bodies in Eighteenth-Century Erotica." In *English Masculinities 1660–1800*, ed. Tim Hitchcock and Michèle Cohen, 193–214. London: Longman, 1999.

Harvey, William. *Disputations Touching the Generation of Animals*. Trans. Gweneth Whitteridge. Oxford: Blackwell, 1981.

Herodotus. *The Histories*. Trans. A. D. Godley. Loeb Classical Library. New York: Putnam, 1920–1925.

Hervey, John, Lord. *Lord Hervey and His Friends, 1726–38: Based on Letters from Holland House, Melbury, and Ickworth*. Ed. Earl of Ilchester. London: Murray Butler & Tanner, 1950.

Hesiod. *Works and Days. Theogony. The Shield of Herakles*. Trans. Richmond Lattimore. Ann Arbor: University of Michigan Press, 1959.

Hill, John. *Lucina Sine Concubitu*. . . . London, 1750.

Hillman, David, and Carla Mazzio, eds. *The Body in Parts: Fantasies of Corporeality in Early Modern Europe*. New York: Routledge, 1997.

Hippisley, John. *An Essay on Wit to Which Is Annexed, a Dissertation on Antient and Modern History*. London, 1748.

Hippocrates. *De Genitura*. Trans. W. H. S. Jones. Loeb Classical Library. New York: Putnam, 1920–1925.

"An Historical Poem." In *Poems on Affairs of State: Augustan Satirical Verse, 1660–1714*. Vol. 2, *1678–1681*, ed. Elias F. Mengel, Jr., 154–63. New Haven, Conn.: Yale University Press, 1965.

The History of the Human Heart or, the Adventures of a Young Gentleman. London, 1749.

Hitchcock, Tim. "Redefining Sex in Eighteenth-Century England." *History Workshop Journal* 41 (1996): 73–90.

Hitchcock, Tim, and Michèle Cohen, eds. *English Masculinities, 1660–1880*. London: Longman, 1999.

Hobbes, Thomas. *Leviathan*. Ed. Richard Tuck. Cambridge: Cambridge University Press, 1991.

Horace. *Horace's Satires and Epistles*. Trans. Jacob Fuchs. New York: Norton, 1977.

Huet, Marie Hélène. *Monstrous Imagination*. Cambridge, Mass.: Harvard University Press, 1993.

Hughes, John. *Letters of Abelard and Heloise*. . . . 10th ed. Dublin, 1769.

The Humours of the Court: Or, Modern Gallantry. A New Ballad Opera. . . . London, 1732.

Hundert, E. J. "The European Enlightenment and the History of the Self." In *Rewriting the Self: Histories from the Renaissance to the Present*, ed. Roy Porter, 72–83. London: Routledge, 1997.

Hunt, Lynn. "Introduction: Obscenity and the Origins of Modernity, 1500–1800." In *The Invention of Pornography: Obscenity and the Origins of Modernity, 1500–1800*, ed. Lynn Hunt, 9–45. New York: Zone Books, 1993.

Hunt, Lynn, and Margaret Jacob. "The Affective Revolution in 1790s Britain." *Eighteenth-Century Studies* 34 (2001): 491–521.

Hurlothrumbo [pseud.]. *The Merry-Thought, or, the Glass-Window and Bog-House Miscellany*. . . . London, 1731.

Ingrassia, Catherine. *Authorship, Commerce, and Gender in Early Eighteenth-Century England: A Culture of Paper Credit*. Cambridge: Cambridge University Press, 1998.

———. "Dissecting the Authorial Body: Pope, Curll, and the Portrait of a 'Hack Writer.' " In *"More Solid Learning": New Perspectives on Alexander Pope's Dunciad*, ed. Catherine Ingrassia and Claudia N. Thomas, 147–65. Lewisburg, Pa.: Bucknell University Press, 2000.

———. "Women Writing/Writing Women: Pope, Dulness, and 'Feminization' in the Dunciad." *Eighteenth-Century Life* 14 (1990): 40–58.

Ingratitude: To Mr. Pope. London, 1733.

Isidore. *Origines*. Loeb Classical Library. New York: Putnam, 1920–25.

James, Robert. *A Medicinal Dictionary*. 3 vols. London, 1745.

Jenkins, David Clay. "Scribblings on the Backside of 'Sapho to Phaon'—An Unpublished Pope Epigram?" *The Scriblerian* 8 (1976): 77–78.

Johnson, Samuel. *A Dictionary of the English Language*. . . . London, 1755.

———. *The History of Rasselas, Prince of Abissinia*. 1759. Ed. J. P. Hardy. London: Oxford University Press, 1968.

———. *Johnson's Lives of the Poets: A Selection*. Ed. J. P. Hardy. Oxford: Clarendon Press, 1971.

Jong, Erica. *Fanny: Being the True History of the Adventures of Fanny Hackabout-Jones: A Novel*. New York: New American Library, 1980.

Jonson, Ben. *Every Man in His Humour*. In *Ben Jonson*, ed. C. H. Herford and Percy Simpson. Oxford: Clarendon Press, 1954.

The Joys of Hymen, Or, the Conjugal Directory: A Poem, in Three Books. London, 1768.

Keats, John. "Ode to Apollo." 1815. In *John Keats, Selected Poems and Letters*, ed. Douglas Bush, 5–6. Boston: Houghton Mifflin, 1959.

Keller, Eve. "Embryonic Individuals: The Rhetoric of Seventeenth-Century Embryology and the Construction of Early-Modern Identity." *Eighteenth-Century Studies* 33 (2000): 321–48.

Keuls, Eva C. *The Reign of the Phallus: Sexual Politics in Ancient Athens*. New York: Harper & Row, 1985.

Kimmel, Michael S. "From Lord and Master to Cuckold and Fop: Masculinity in Seventeenth-Century England." *University of Dayton Review* 18 (1987): 93–109.

King, Thomas A. " 'Converting *Stones into Bread*': Masculinity, Mimesis and 'Il Ragazzo' Farinelli." Conference paper presented at the ninth DeBartolo Conference, devoted to "The Eighteenth-Century Male," 1995.

———. *The Gendering of Men*. Madison: University of Wisconsin Press, forthcoming.

———. *Queer Articulations: Enacting Masculinity and Difference*. Madison: University of Wisconsin Press, forthcoming.

Klein, Lawrence. *Shaftesbury and the Culture of Politeness: Moral Discourse and Cultural Politics in Early Eighteenth-Century England*. Cambridge: Cambridge University Press, 1994.

Klein, Mark. "Regnier De Graaf." In *Dictionary of Scientific Biography*, ed. Charles Coulston Gillispie, 484–55. New York: Scribner, 1972.

Knight, Richard Payne. *Discourse on the Worship of Priapus, and its Connexion with the Mystic Theology of the Ancients*. London, 1786–87.

Koon, Helene, ed. "Introduction." In *Cibber's a Letter from Mr. Cibber to Mr. Pope*, i–xi. Augustan Reprint Series 158. Los Angeles: William Andrews Clark Memorial Library, University of California, 1973.

Kuchta, David. *The Three-Piece Suit and Modern Masculinity: England, 1550–1850*. Berkeley: University of California Press, 2002.

La Mettrie, Julien Offray de. *Man a Machine and Man a Plant*. Trans. Richard A. Watson and Maya Rybalka. Indianapolis: Hackett, 1994.

Lacan, Jacques. "The Signification of the Phallus." In *Ecrits: A Selection*. Trans. Alan Sheridan, 281–91. New York: Norton, 1977.

Lacy, John. "Satire." In *Poems on Affairs of State: Augustan Satirical Verse, 1660–1714*, Vol. 1, *1660–1678*, ed. George deForest Lord, 425–28. New Haven, Conn.: Yale University Press, 1963.

The Ladies Delight. Containing, I. An Address to All Well-Provided Hibernians. II. The Arbor Vitae; or, Tree of Life. A Poem. . . . London, 1732.

Laertius, Diogenes. *Life of Pythagoras.* Trans. R. D. Hicks. London: Loeb, 1979.

Laplanche, Jean, and J. B. Pontalis. *The Language of Psycho-Analysis.* Trans. Donald Nicholson-Smith. New York: Norton, 1974.

Laqueur, Thomas. "Credit, Novels, Masturbation." In *Choreographing History*, ed. Susan Leigh Foster, 119–28. Bloomington: Indiana University Press, 1995.

———. *Making Sex: Body and Gender from the Greeks to Freud.* Cambridge, Mass.: Harvard University Press, 1990.

Le Camus, Antoine. *Mèdecine de l'esprit.* . . . Paris, 1753, 1769.

Leeuwenhoek, Antoni van. "Observations Di. Anthonii Leewenhoeck, de prognatis è Semine genitali Animalculis." *Philosophical Transactions* 142 (1679): 1040–43.

Lehman, Peter. "*In the Realm of the Senses*: Desire, Power, and the Representation of the Male Body." *Genders* 2 (1988): 91–110.

Libertine Lyrics by Various Authors, Mostly of the XVII and XVIII Centuries. Mount Vernon, N.Y.: Peter Pauper Press, 1967.

Lindeboom, G. A. "Leeuwenhoek and the Problem of Sexual Reproduction." In *Antoni Van Leeuwenhoek 1632–1723: Studies on the Life and Work of the Delft Scientist Commemorating the 350th Anniversary of His Birthday*, ed. L. C. Palm and H. A. M. Snelders, 129–52. Amsterdam: Rodopi, 1982.

Lloyd, Robert. *The Poetical Works of Robert Lloyd, A.M., to Which Is Prefixed an Account of the Life and Writings of the Author.* 2 vols. London, 1774.

Locke, John. *An Essay Concerning Human Understanding.* 1690. Ed. Peter H. Nidditch. Oxford: Oxford University Press, 1979.

Lonsdale, Roger H., ed. *Eighteenth-Century Women Poets: An Oxford Anthology.* Oxford: Oxford University Press, 1989.

Lord, George deForest, ed. *Poems on Affairs of State: Augustan Satirical Verse, 1660–1714.* Vol. 1, *1660–1678*. New Haven, Conn.: Yale University Press, 1963.

"The Lost Opportunity Recovered." In *Wit and Drollery. Jovial Poems*, 1–16. London, 1682.

Love, Harold. *The Penguin Book of Restoration Verse.* Harmondsworth: Penguin, 1971.

Mack, Maynard. *Alexander Pope: A Life.* New Haven, Conn.: Yale University Press in association with Norton, 1985.

———. " 'The Least Thing like a Man in England': Some Effects of Pope's Physical Disability on His Life and Literary Career." In *Collected in Himself: Essays Critical, Biographical, and Bibliographical on Pope and Some of His Contemporaries*, ed. Maynard Mack, 372–92. Newark: University of Delaware Press, 1982.

———. "Pope's 1717 Preface with a Transcription of the Manuscript Text." In *Augustan Worlds: Essays in Honour of A. R. Humphreys*, ed. A. R. Humphreys, J. C. Hilson, M. Monica B. Jones and J. R. Watson, 85–106. Leicester: Leicester University Press, 1978.

Maclauchlan, Daniel. *An Essay Upon Improving and Adding, to the Strength of Great-Britain and Ireland, by Fornication.* . . . London, 1735.

Mandeville, Bernard. *A Modest Defence of Publick Stews.* . . . London, 1724.

Manuel, Frank Edward. *The Eighteenth Century Confronts the Gods.* Cambridge, Mass.: Harvard University Press, 1959.

Marten, John. *Gonosologium Novum.* . . . London, 1709.

———. *A Treatise of All the Degrees and Symptoms of the Venereal Disease, in Both Sexes.* 6th ed. London, 1708.

Martialis, M. Valerius. *Martial: Epigrams.* Ed. Walter C. A. Ker. London: Heinemann, 1925.

Maud, Ralph N. "Some Lines from Pope." *Review of English Studies* n.s. 9 (1958): 146–51.

Maupertuis, Pierre-Louis Moreau de. *The Earthly Venus.* 1753. Trans. Simone Brangier Boas. New York: Johnson Reprint Corp., 1966.

Maurer, Shawn Lisa. *Proposing Men: Dialectics of Gender and Class in the Eighteenth-Century English Periodical.* Stanford, Calif.: Stanford University Press, 1998.

McGeary, Thomas. " 'Warbling Eunuchs': Opera, Gender, and Sexuality on the London Stage, 1705–1742." *Restoration and Eighteenth-Century Theatre Research* 2nd ser. 7 (1992): 295–322.

McKeon, Michael. "Historicizing Patriarchy: The Emergence of Gender Difference in England, 1660–1760." *Eighteenth-Century Studies* 28 (1995): 295–322.

McLaren, Angus. *Reproductive Rituals: The Perception of Fertility in England from the Sixteenth Century to the Nineteeth Century.* London: Methuen, 1984.

Mengel, Elias F., ed. *Poems on Affairs of State: Augustan Satirical Verse, 1660– 1714.* Vol. 2, *1678–1681.* New Haven, Conn.: Yale University Press, 1965.

Merchant, Carolyn. *The Death of Nature: Women, Ecology, and the Scientific Revolution.* San Francisco: Harper and Row, 1982.

Merians, Linda E., ed. *The Secret Malady: Venereal Disease in Eighteenth-Century Britain and France.* Lexington: University Press of Kentucky, 1996.

Merrick, Jeffrey. "Impotence in Court and at Court." *Studies in Eighteenth-Century Culture* 25 (1996): 187–202.

Monsieur Thing's Origin: Or, Seignior D——'s Adventures in Britain. London, 1722.

Montagu, Lady Mary Wortley. *Essays and Poems and Simplicity, a Comedy.* Ed. Robert Halsband and Isobel Grundy. Oxford: Clarendon Press, 1993.

Montagu, Lady Mary Wortley, and John, Lord Hervey. *Verses Address'd to the Imitator of the First Satire of the Second Book of Horace.* London, 1733.

Montaigne, Michel de. *The Essayes of Michel Lord of Montaigne.* Trans. John Florio. London: Oxford University Press, 1906.

———. *Essays.* Trans. J. M. Cohen. Harmondsworth: Penguin, 1958.

Morrice, Bezaleel. *The Present State of Poetry, a Satire.* London, 1726.

Mowl, Timothy. *Horace Walpole: The Great Outsider.* London: Murray, 1996.

Mueller, Judith. "Fallen Men: Representations of Male Impotence in Britain." *Studies in Eighteenth-Century Culture* 28 (1999): 85–102.

The Natural History of the Arbor Vitae: Or, The Tree of Life. London, 1732.

Needham, Joseph. *A History of Embryology.* Cambridge: Cambridge University Press, 1934.

Nichol, Donald W. *Pope's Literary Legacy: The Book-Trade Correspondence of William Warburton and John Knapton: With Other Letters and Documents, 1744– 1780.* Oxford: Oxford Bibliographical Society, 1992.

Nichol, Donald W., and Jacob Larkin. "Wilkes and Editorial Liberty: Attacks on Warburton as Pope's Editor." In *Transatlantic Crossings: Eighteenth-Century Explorations,* ed. Donald W. Nichol, Iona Bulgin, Sandra Hannaford, and

David Wilson, 49–58. Department of English Language and Literature, St. John's Memorial University of Newfoundland, 1995.

Nicolson, Marjorie Hope. *Science and Imagination.* Ithaca, N.Y.: Great Seal Books, 1956.

Nicolson, Marjorie Hope, and G. S. Rousseau. *"This Long Disease, My Life": Alexander Pope and the Sciences.* Princeton, N.J.: Princeton University Press, 1968.

"No true Love Between Man and Woman." In *The Penguin Book of Restoration Verse*, ed. Harold Love, 164–65. Harmondsworth: Penguin, 1971.

O'Connor, Eugene Michael. *Symbolum Salacitatis: A Study of the God Priapus as a Literary Character.* Frankfurt: Verlag Peter Lang, 1989.

Ogilvie, John. *Poems on Several Subjects: To Which Is Prefix'd an Essay on the Lyric Poetry of the Ancients.* London, 1762.

Oldham, John. *The Poems of John Oldham.* 1677–78. Ed. Harold Fletcher Brooks. Oxford: Clarendon Press, 1987.

———. *Sardanapalus.* In *The Poems of John Oldham.* 1677–78. Ed. Harold Fletcher Brooks, 344–51. Oxford: Clarendon Press, 1987.

Ormsby-Lennon, Hugh. "Swift's Spirit Reconjured: Das Dong-an-Sich." *Swift Studies* 3 (1988): 9–78.

Ovid. *Amores.* Trans. Grant Showerman. Loeb Classical Library. New York: Putnam, 1920–1925.

———. *The Erotic Poems.* Trans. Peter Green. Harmondsworth: Penguin, 1982.

———. *Metamorphoses.* Trans. Frank Justus Miller. Loeb Classical Library. New York: Putnam, 1920–1925.

Partridge, Eric. *A Dictionary of Slang and Unconventional English.* . . . 7th ed. New York: Macmillan, 1970.

Paulson, Ronald. *Breaking and Remaking: Aesthetic Practice in England, 1700–1820.* New Brunswick, N.J.: Rutgers University Press, 1989.

Perry, James. *Mimosa: Or, the Sensitive Plant; a Poem.* London, 1779.

Peters, J. S. "The Bank, the Press, and the 'Return of Nature': On Currency, Credit, and Literary Property in the 1690s." In *Early Modern Conceptions of Property*, ed. John Brewer and Susan Staves, 365–88. London: Routledge, 1996.

Petronius, Arbiter. *The Satyricon, and the Fragments.* Ed. and trans. J. P. Sullivan. Harmondsworth: Penguin, 1965.

Phillips, John. *A Reflection on Our Modern Poetry. An Essay.* London, 1695.

Phillips, John, and M. E. *Wit and Drollery. Jovial Poems.* London, 1682.

Piron, Alexis. *Ode à Priape.* 1710. In *Oeuvres complètes illustrées de Alexis Piron.* 10 vols. Ed. Pierre Dufay. Paris: Francis Guillot, 1931.

Plato. *Theaetetus.* In *Plato: The Collected Dialogues.* Ed. Edith Hamilton and Huntington Cairns, 845–919. Princeton, N.J.: Princeton University Press, 1969.

———. *Timaeus.* In *Plato: The Collected Dialogues.* Ed. Edith Hamilton and Huntington Cairns, 1151–1211. Princeton, N.J.: Princeton University Press, 1969.

Plutarch. *Moralia.* Trans. Frank Cole Babbitt. Loeb Classical Library. New York: Putnam, 1920–1925.

The Poet Finish'd in Prose. Being a Dialogue Concerning Mr. Pope and His Writings. London, 1735.

The Poetical Tom-Titt Perch'd Upon the Mount of Love. Being the Representation of a Merry Description in Mr. Cibber's Letter to Mr. Pope. July 31, 1742.

Pope, Alexander. *The Correspondence of Alexander Pope*. Ed. George Sherburn. 5 vols. Oxford: Clarendon Press, 1956.

———. *The Dunciad: In Four Books*. Ed. Valerie Rumbold. London: Longman, 1999.

———. *The Iliad of Homer Translated by Alexander Pope*. Ed. Steven Shankman. London: Penguin, 1996.

———. *The Prose Works of Alexander Pope*. Vol. 1, *The Earlier Works, 1711–1720*. Ed. Norman Ault. Oxford: Basil Blackwell, 1936.

———. *The Prose Works of Alexander Pope*. Vol. 2, *The Major Works, 1725–1744*. Ed. Rosemary Cowler. Hamden, Conn.: Archon Books, 1986.

———. *Selected Prose of Alexander Pope*. Ed. Paul Hammond. Cambridge: Cambridge University Press, 1987.

———. *The Twickenham Edition of the Poems of Alexander Pope*. Ed. John Butt et al. 11 vols. London: Methuen, 1961–67.

———. *The Works of Alexander Pope Esq. In Nine Volumes Complete. . . .* Ed. William Warburton. London, 1751.

———. *The Works of Mr. Alexander Pope*. London, 1717.

Pope, Alexander, et al. *Memoirs of the Extraordinary Life, Works, and Discoveries of Martinus Scriblerus*. 1742. Ed. Charles Kerby-Miller. New York: Oxford University Press, 1988.

Porter, Roy, "Introduction." In *Rewriting the Self: Histories from the Renaissance to the Present*, ed. Roy Porter, 1–14. London: Routledge, 1997.

———. "The Literature of Sexual Advice Before 1800." In *Sexual Knowledge, Sexual Science: The History of Attitudes to Sexuality*, ed. Roy Porter and Mikulas Teich, 134–57. Cambridge: Cambridge University Press, 1994.

———. "The Sexual Politics of James Graham." *British Journal for Eighteenth-Century Studies* 5 (1982): 199–206.

———. "Spreading Carnal Knowledge or Selling Dirt Cheap? Nicolas Venette's *Tableau de l'Amour Conjugal* in Eighteenth Century England." *Journal of European Studies* 14 (1984): 233–55.

———. "A Touch of Danger: The Man-Midwife as Sexual Predator." In *Sexual Underworlds of the Enlightenment*, ed. G. S. Rousseau and Roy Porter, 206–32. Manchester: Manchester University Press, 1987.

Porter, Roy, and G. S. Rousseau. *Gout: The Patrician Malady*. New Haven, Conn.: Yale University Press, 1998.

Porter, Roy, and Lesley A. Hall. *The Facts of Life: The Creation of Sexual Knowledge in Britain, 1650–1950*. New Haven, Conn.: Yale University Press, 1995.

Priapea: Poems for a Phallic God. Ed. and trans. W. H. Parker. London: Croom Helm, 1988.

Prior, Matthew [supposed author]. *The Members to Their Soveraign*. London, 1726.

Pulteney, William. *A Proper Reply to a Late Scurrilous Libel. . . .* London, 1731.

Quillet, Claude. *The Joys of Hymen, Or, the Conjugal Directory: A Poem, in Three Books*. London, 1768.

Rancour-Laferriere, Daniel. "Some Semiotic Aspects of the Human Penis." *Versus: Quaderni di studi semiotici* 24 (1979): 37–82.

Rawson, Claude. *Satire and Sentiment, 1660–1830: Stress Points in the English Augustan Tradition*. New Haven, Conn.: Yale University Press, 1994.

Regan, John V. "Orpheus and the *Dunciad*'s Narrator." *Eighteenth-Century Studies* 9 (1975): 87–101.

The Remarkable Trial of the Queen of Quavers. London, 1778.

Richlin, Amy. *The Garden of Priapus: Sexuality and Aggression in Roman Humor*. New Haven, Conn.: Yale University Press, 1983.

Rochester, John Wilmot, Earl of. *Complete Poems and Plays*. Ed. Paddy Lyons. London: Dent, 1993.

———. *The Complete Works*. Ed. Frank H. Ellis. London: Penguin, 1994.

Rodgers, James. "Sensibility, Sympathy, Benevolence: Physiology and Moral Philosophy in *Tristram Shandy*." In *Languages of Nature: Critical Essays on Science and Literature*, ed. L. J. Jordanova, 117–58. New Brunswick, N.J.: Rutgers University Press, 1986.

Roe, Shirley A. *Matter, Life, and Generation: Eighteenth-Century Embryology and the Haller-Wolff Debate*. Cambridge: Cambridge University Press, 1981.

Roger, Jacques. "Two Scientific Discoveries: Their Genesis and Destiny." In *On Scientific Discovery*, ed. Mirko D. Grmek et al., 229–37. Dordrecht: Reidel,1981.

Roper, Lyndal. *Oedipus and the Devil: Witchcraft, Sexuality, and Religion in Early Modern Europe*. London: Routledge, 1994.

Roscommon, Wentworth Dillon, Earl of. *An Essay on Translated Verse*. London, 1684.

———. *Poems by the Earl of Roscommon, to Which Is Added an Essay on Poetry. . . .* London, 1717.

Rose, Mark. "The Author as Proprietor: *Donaldson v. Becket* and the Genealogy of Modern Authorship." *Representations* 23 (1988): 51–85.

Rosenthal, Laura J. *Playwrights and Plagiarists in Early Modern England: Gender, Authorship, Literary Property*. Ithaca, N.Y.: Cornell University Press, 1996.

———. " 'Trials of Manhood': Cibber, *The Dunciad*, and the Masculine Self." In *"More Solid Learning": New Perspectives on Alexander Pope's Dunciad*, ed. Catherine Ingrassia and Claudia N. Thomas, 81–105. Lewisburg, Pa.: Bucknell University Press, 2000.

Ross, Alexander. *Mystagogus Poeticus, or the Muses Interpreter. . . .* London, 1648.

Rousseau, G. S. " *'et in Arcadia homo'*: Opera, Gender, and Sexual Politics in *The Dunciad*." In *"More Solid Learning": New Perspectives on Alexander Pope's Dunciad*, ed. Catherine Ingrassia and Claudia N. Thomas, 33–61. Lewisburg, Pa.: Bucknell University Press, 2000.

———. " 'In the House of Madame Van Der Tasse': Homosocial Desire and a University Club During the Enlightenment." In *The Pursuit of Sodomy: Male Homosexuality in Renaissance and Enlightenment Europe*, ed. Kent Gerard and Gert Hekma, 311–48. New York: Harrington Park Press, 1989.

———. "Love and Antiquities: Walpole and Gray on the Grand Tour." In *Perilous Enlightenment: Pre- and Post-Modern Discourses Sexual, Historical*, 172–99. Manchester: Manchester University Press, 1991.

———. "Nerves, Spirits, and Fibres: Towards Defining the Origins of Sensibility." In *Studies in the Eighteenth Century*, vol. 3, *Papers Presented at the Third David Nichol Smith Memorial Seminar, Canberra*, ed. Robert F. Brissenden and J. C. Eade, 137–57. Toronto: University of Toronto Press, 1976.

———. "Nymphomania, Bienville and the Rise of Erotic Sensibility." In *Sexuality in Eighteenth-Century Britain*, ed. Paul-Gabriel Boucé, 95–119. Manchester: Manchester University Press, 1982.

———. "Pineapples, Pregnancy, Pica, and *Peregrine Pickle*." In *Tobias Smollett: Bicentennial Essays Presented to Lewis M. Knapp*, ed. G. S. Rousseau and Paul-Gabriel Boucé, 79–110. New York: Oxford University Press, 1971.

———. "Pope and the Tradition in Modern Humanistic Education: '. . .in the pale of Words till death.' " In *The Enduring Legacy: Alexander Pope Tercentenary Essays*, ed. G. S. Rousseau and Pat Rogers, 199–239. Cambridge: Cambridge University Press, 1988.

———. "The Pursuit of Homosexuality in the Eighteenth Century: 'Utterly Confused Category' and/or Rich Repository?" *Eighteenth-Century Life* 11 (1986): 132–69.

———. "Scriblerians." In *The Gay and Lesbian Literary Heritage*, ed. Claude J. Summers, 645–48. New York: H. Holt, 1995.

———. "The Sorrows of Priapus: Anticlericalism, Homosocial Desire, and Richard Payne Knight." In *Sexual Underworlds of the Enlightenment*. Ed. G. S. Rousseau and Roy Porter, 101–53. Manchester: Manchester University Press, 1987.

———. "Towards a Semiotic of the Nerve: The Social History of Language in a New Key." In *Language, Self, and Society: A Social History of Language*, ed. Peter Burke and Roy Porter, 213–75. London: Polity Press, 1991.

Rousseau, Jean-Jacques. *The Confessions*. Trans. J. M. Cohen. Harmondsworth: Penguin, 1953.

Ruestow, Edward G. *The Microscope in the Dutch Republic: The Shaping of Discovery*. Cambridge: Cambridge University Press, 1996.

Ruffhead, Owen. *The Life of Alexander Pope, Esq. . . .* London, 1769.

Rumbold, Valerie. *Alexander Pope: The Dunciad In Four Books*. London: Longman, 1999.

Sacks, Elizabeth. *Shakespeare's Images of Pregnancy*. London: Macmillan, 1980.

Sade, Marquis de. *Juliette*. Trans. Austryn Wainhouse. New York: Grove Press, 1968.

Sandys, George. *Ovid's Metamorphosis Englished, Mythologized, and Represented in Figures*. Ed. Karl K. Hulley and Stanley T. Vandersall. Lincoln: University of Nebraska Press, 1970.

Satan's Harvest Home: Or the Present State of Whorecraft, Adultery, Fornication, Procuring, Pimping, Sodomy, and the Game at Flatts. 1749. Reprint, New York: Garland, 1985.

Savage, Richard. *An Author to Be Lett. . . .* London, 1729.

Sawday, Jonathan. *The Body Emblazoned: Dissection and the Human Body in Renaissance Culture*. London: Routledge, 1995.

Sawney and Colley, a Poetical Dialogue: Occasioned by a Late Letter from the Laureat of St. James's, to the Homer of Twickenham. . . . London, 1742.

Sedgwick, Eve Kosofsky. *Between Men: English Literature and Male Homosocial Desire*. New York: Columbia University Press, 1985.

Setchell, Brian P. "The Contributions of Regnier De Graaf to Reproductive Biology." *European Journal of Gynecology and Reproductive Biology* 4 (1974): 1–13.

Shapin, Steven. *A Social History of Truth: Civility and Science in Seventeenth-Century England*. Chicago: University of Chicago Press, 1994.

Sharp, Jane. *The Midwives Book, or, the Whole Art of Midwifry Discovered*. Ed. Elaine Hobby. New York: Oxford University Press, 1999.

Shelley, Percy Bysshe. "Defence of Poetry." 1821. In *Prose of the Romantic Period*, ed. Carl R. Woodring, 488–513. Boston: Houghton Mifflin, 1961.

Sherbert, Garry. *Mennipean Satire and the Poetics of Wit: Ideologies of Self-Consciousness in Dunton, D'urfey, and Sterne*. New York: Peter Lang, 1996.

Sheridan, Richard Brinsley [supposed author]. "The Geranium." In *Libertine Lyrics by Various Authors, Mostly of the XVII and XVIII Centuries*. Mount Vernon, N.Y.: Peter Pauper Press, 1967.

Shoemaker, Robert Brink. *Gender in English Society, 1650–1850: The Emergence of Separate Spheres?* London: Longman, 1998.

Silverman, Kaja. "The Lacanian Phallus." *differences: A Journal of Feminist Cultural Studies* 4 (1992): 84–115.

Singer, Charles. "The History of Anatomical Injections." In *Studies in the History and Method of Science*, 2nd ser., ed. Charles Singer, 285–342. Oxford: Clarendon Press, 1921.

Sissa, Giulia. "Subtle Bodies." In *Fragments for a History of the Human Body, Part Three*. Ed. Michel Feher et al., 133–56. New York: Zone Books, 1989.

Slade, Giles. "The Two Backed Beast: Eunuchus and Priapus in *The Country Wife*." *Restoration and Eighteenth-Century Theatre Research* 2nd ser. 7 (1992): 23–34.

Slepian, B. and L. J. Morrissey. "What Is *Fanny Hill*?" *Essays in Criticism* 14 (1964): 65–75.

Smith, Paul. "Vas." *Camera Obscura* 17 (1988): 89–111.

Smollett, Tobias. *The Adventures of Peregrine Pickle*. 1751. Ed. James L. Clifford. Oxford: Oxford University Press, 1964.

———. *The Expedition of Humphry Clinker*. 1771. Ed. Lewis M. Knapp and revised by Paul-Gabriel Boucé. Oxford: Oxford University Press, 1984.

Spears, Richard A. *Slang and Euphemism: A Dictionary of Oaths, Curses, Insults, Sexual Slang and Metaphor, Racial Slurs, Drug Talk, Homosexual Lingo, and Related Matters*. Middle Village, N.Y.: Jonathan David, 1981.

Spence, Joseph. *Observations, Anecdotes, and Characters of Books and Men, Collected from Conversation*. 2 vols. Ed. James Marshall Osborn. Oxford: Clarendon Press, 1966.

Stack, Frank. *Pope and Horace: Studies in Imitation*. Cambridge: Cambridge University Press, 1985.

Stafford, Barbara Maria. *Body Criticism: Imaging the Unseen in Enlightenment Art and Medicine*. Cambridge, Mass.: MIT Press, 1993.

Steno, Nicolaus. *Lecture on the Anatomy of the Brain*. 1669. Introduction Gustav Scherz. Copenhagen: Nyt nordisk forlag, 1965.

Stephanson, Raymond. " 'Epicoene Friendship': Understanding Male Friendship in the Early Eighteenth Century, with Some Speculations About Pope." *Eighteenth Century: Theory and Interpretation* 38 (1997): 151–70.

———. "The Love Song of Young Alexander Pope: Allusion and Sexual Displacement in the *Pastorals*." *English Studies in Canada* 17 (1991): 21–35.

———. "The Symbolic Structure of Eighteenth-Century Male Creativity: Pregnant Men, Brain-Wombs, and Female Muses (with some comments on Pope's *Dunciad*)." *Studies in Eighteenth-Century Culture* 27 (1998): 103–30.

Sterne, Laurence. *The Life and Opinions of Tristram Shandy, Gentleman*. 1759–67. Ed. Ian P. Watt. Boston: Houghton Mifflin, 1965.

Stevenson, David. *The Beggar's Benison: Sex Clubs of Enlightenment Scotland and Their Rituals*. East Lothian: Tuckwell Press, 2001.

Stewart, Philip. "Indecency and Literary Illustration." *South Atlantic Quarterly* 90 (1991): 111–52.

Stone, Lawrence. *Broken Lives: Separation and Divorce in England, 1660–1857*. Oxford: Oxford University Press, 1993.

Stratton, Jon. *The Virgin Text: Fiction, Sexuality, and Ideology*. Norman: University of Oklahoma Press, 1987.

Straub, Kristina. *Sexual Suspects: Eighteenth-Century Players and Sexual Ideology*. Princeton, N.J.: Princeton University Press, 1992.

Straus, Ralph. *The Unspeakable Curll; Being Some Account of Edmund Curll, Book-*

seller, to Which Is Added a Full List of His Books. 1927. Reprint, New York: A.M. Kelley, 1970.

Stretzer, Thomas. *The Natural History of the Arbor Vitae: Or, The Tree of Life.* London, 1732.

Suetonius. *The Twelve Caesars.* Trans. Robert Graves. Revised with an introduction by Michael Grant. Harmondsworth: Penguin, 1979.

Swartz, Richard G. "Patrimony and the Figuration of Authorship in the Eighteenth-Century Literary Property Debates." *Works and Days* 7 (1989): 29–54.

Swift, Jonathan. *A Tale of a Tub, to Which Is Added the Battle of the Books, and the Mechanical Operation of the Spirit. . . .* 1704. Ed. A. C. Guthkelch and D. Nichol Smith. Oxford: Clarendon Press, 1958.

———. *The Works of Jonathan Swift.* Ed. George Faulkner. Dublin, 1746.

Taylor, Gary. *Castration: An Abbreviated History of Western Manhood.* New York: Routledge, 2000.

Teague-Root Display'd: Being Some Useful and Important Discoveries Tending to Illustrate the Doctrines of Electricity, in a Letter from Paddy Strong-Cock. London, 1746.

Temkin, Oswei. "Introduction to the Text of Haller's *A Dissertation on the Sensible and Irritable Parts of Animals.*" *Bulletin of the Institute of the History of Medicine* 4 (1936): 651–99.

Temple, Sir William. *The Works of Sir William Temple.* Ed. Jonathan Swift and Lady Martha Giffard. London, 1720.

Thompson, Roger. *Unfit for Modest Ears: A Study of Pornographic, Obscene, and Bawdy Works Written or Published in England in the Second Half of the Seventeenth Century.* Totowa, N.J.: Rowman and Littlefield, 1979.

Tillotson, Geoffrey, Paul Fussell, and Marshall Waingrow, eds. *Eighteenth-Century English Literature.* New York: Harcourt Brace and World, 1969.

Tissot, S. A. D. *An Essay on Diseases Incidental to Literary and Sedentary Persons.* Trans. Charles Dilly. London, 1768.

———. *Onanism, or, a Treatise Upon the Disorders Produced by Masturbation, or, the Dangerous Effects of Secret and Excessive Venery.* Trans. A. Hume. London, 1772.

Todd, Dennis. *Imagining Monsters: Miscreations of the Self in Eighteenth-Century England.* Chicago: University of Chicago Press, 1995.

Tosh, John. "The Old Adam and the New Man: Emerging Themes in the History of English Masculinities, 1750–1850." In *English Masculinities 1660–1800,* ed. Tim Hitchcock and Michèle Cohen, 217–38. London: Longman, 1999.

Trapp, Joseph. *Lectures on Poetry Read in the Schools of Natural Philosophy at Oxford.* Trans. William Clarke, ed. William Bowyer. London, 1742.

Trumbach, Randolph. *Sex and the Gender Revolution.* Vol. 1, *Heterosexuality and the Third Gender in Enlightenment London.* Chicago: University of Chicago Press, 1998.

———. "London's Sapphists: From Three Sexes to Four Genders in the Making of Modern Culture." In *Body Guards: The Cultural Politics of Gender Ambiguity,* ed. Julia Epstein and Kristina Straub, 112–41. New York: Routledge, 1991.

———. "The Birth of the Queen: Sodomy and the Emergence of Gender Equality in Modern Culture, 1660–1750." In *Hidden from History: Reclaiming the Gay and Lesbian Past,* ed. Martin Bauml Duberman, Martha Vicinus and George Chauncey Jr., 29–40. New York: New American Library, 1989.

———. "Gender and the Homosexual Role in Modern Western Culture: The 18th and 19th Centuries Compared." In *Homosexuality, Which Homosexuality?*, ed. Dennis Altman, Carole Vance, et al., 149–69. London: GMP Publishers, 1989.

———. "Sodomitical Assaults, Gender Role, and Sexual Development in Eighteenth-Century London." *Journal of Homosexuality* 16 (1989): 407–29.

Turner, James Grantham. "Pepys and the Private Parts of Monarchy." In *Culture and Society in the Stuart Restoration*, ed. Gerald Maclean, 95–110. Cambridge: Cambridge University Press, 1995.

———. "Pope's Libertine Self-Fashioning." *Eighteenth Century: Theory and Interpretation* 29 (1988): 123–44.

Vanbrugh, John. "Prologue," *The Relapse*. 1696. Reprint, ed. Bernard Harris. London: A & C Black, 1986.

Venette, Nicolas. *Conjugal Love or, the Pleasures of the Marriage Bed*. London, 1750.

Verduc, Jean Baptiste. *A Treatise of the Parts of a Human Body*. Trans. J. Davis. London, 1704.

Vicari, Patricia. "*Sparagmos*: Orpheus Among the Christians." In *Orpheus: The Metamorphoses of a Myth*, ed. John Warden, 63–83. Toronto: University of Toronto Press, 1982.

Vila, Anne C. *Enlightenment and Pathology: Sensibility in the Literature and Medicine of Eighteenth-Century France*. Baltimore: Johns Hopkins University Press, 1998.

———. "Sex, Procreation, and the Scholarly Life from Tissot to Balzac." *Eighteenth-Century Studies* 35 (2002): 239–46.

Virgil. *Catalepton*. Trans. H. Rushton Fairclough. Loeb Classical Library. New York: Putnam, 1920–25.

Voltaire. *Letters Concerning the English Nation*. Trans. John Lockman. London, 1733.

———. *Philosophical Dictionary*. Trans. Theodore Besterman. Harmondsworth: Penguin, 1971.

A Voyage to Lethe; By Capt. Samuel Cock; Sometime Commander of the Good Ship the Charming Sally. Dedicated to the Right Worshipful Adam Cock, Esq; Of Black-Mary's-Hole, Coney-Skin Merchant. London, 1741.

Miss W—. "The Gentleman's Study, In Answer to [Swift's] The Lady's Dressing Room." 1732. In *Eighteenth-Century Women Poets: An Oxford Anthology*, ed. Roger Lonsdale, 130–34. Oxford: Oxford University Press, 1989.

Wagner, Peter. "The Pornographer in the Courtroom: Trial Reports About Cases of Sexual Crimes and Delinquencies as a Genre of Eighteenth-Century Erotica." In *Sexuality in Eighteenth-Century Britain*, ed. Paul-Gabriel Boucé, 120–40. Manchester: Manchester University Press, 1982.

Wall, Cynthia. "Editing Desire: Pope's Correspondence with (and without) Lady Mary." *Philological Quarterly* 71 (1992): 221–37.

Walpole, Horace, et al. *Horace Walpole's Correspondence*. . . . Ed. W. S. Lewis. 39 vols. New Haven, Conn.: Yale University Press, 1961.

Ward, Edward. *Apollo's Maggot in His Cups: Or, the Whimsical Creation of a Little Satyrical Poet. A Lyrick Ode*. London, 1729.

———. *Durgen. Or, a Plain Satyr Upon a Pompous Satyrist*. London, 1729.

———. *The Secret History of Clubs*. . . . London, 1709.

Warner, John Harley. "The Impact of Microscopy on the English Poetry of the First Half of the 18th Century." *Synthesis* 3 (1975): 20–34.

Warton, Joseph. *An Essay on the Genius and Writings of Pope: In Two Volumes*. London, 1782.

————. *An Essay on the Writings and Genius of Pope*. London, 1756.

Wax, Carol. *The Mezzotint: History and Technique*. New York: H.N. Abrams, 1990.

Weber, Harold. "Carolinean Sexuality and the Restoration Stage: Reconstructing the Royal Phallus in *Sodom*." In *Cultural Readings of Restoration and Eighteenth-Century English Theater*, ed. J. Douglas Canfield and Deborah Payne, 67–88. Athens: University of Georgia Press, 1995.

Weed, David. "Sexual Positions: Men of Pleasure, Economy, and Dignity in Boswell's *London Journal*." *Eighteenth-Century Studies* 31 (1997–98): 215–34.

————. "Fitting Fanny: Cleland's *Memoirs* and the Politics of Male Pleasure." *Novel* 31 (1997): 7–20.

Weil, Rachel. "Sometimes a Scepter Is Only a Scepter: Pornography and Politics in Restoration England." In *The Invention of Pornography: Obscenity and the Origins of Modernity, 1500–1800*, ed. Lynn Hunt, 125–53. New York: Zone Books, 1993.

Weinbrot, Howard D. *Alexander Pope and the Traditions of Formal Verse Satire*. Princeton, N.J.: Princeton University Press, 1982.

Welsted, Leonard. *The Works, in Verse and Prose, of Leonard Welsted, Esq. . . .* Ed. John Nichols. London, 1787.

Wesley, Samuel. *An Epistle to a Friend Concerning Poetry*. London, 1700.

The Whore's Rhetoric, Calculated to the Meridian of London; and Conformed to the Rules of Art. In Two Dialogues. 1683. Reprint, Edinburgh, 1836.

Whytt, Robert. *An Essay on the Vital and Other Involuntary Motions of Animals*. Edinburgh, 1751.

Wilkes, John. *The Infamous "Essay on Woman"; or, John Wilkes Seated between Vice and Virtue*. Ed. Adrian Hamilton. London: Deutsch, 1972.

————. *Veni Creator; Or, The Maid's Prayer*. In *The Infamous "Essay on Woman"; or, John Wilkes Seated between Vice and Virtue*. Ed. Adrian Hamilton, 244–45. London: Deutsch, 1972.

Wilkes, John, and Charles Churchill. *The Correspondence of John Wilkes and Charles Churchill*. Ed. Edward H. Weatherly. New York: Columbia University Press, 1954.

Williams, Carolyn. "Breaking Decorums: Belinda, Bays and Epic Effeminacy." In *Pope: New Contexts*, ed. David Fairer, 59–79. London: Harvester Wheatsheaf, 1990.

————. "Westphalia Revisited." *British Journal for Eighteenth-Century Studies* 9 (1986): 19–32.

Williams, Sir Charles Hanbury. *The Odes of Sir Charles Hanbury Williams, Knight of the Bath*. Ed. Joseph Ritson. London, 1775.

Williams, Linda. *Hard Core: Power, Pleasure, and the "Frenzy of the Visible"*. Berkeley: University of California Press, 1989.

Willis, Thomas. *The Anatomy of the Brain and Nerves*. Trans. Samuel Pordage. 1681. Ed. William Feindel. Montreal: McGill University Press, 1965.

Winn, James A. "Pope Plays the Rake: His Letters to Ladies and the Making of the *Eloisa*." In *The Art of Alexander Pope*, ed. Howard Erskine-Hill and Anne Smith, 89–118. London: Vision Press, 1979.

Wisdom Revealed; or, the Tree of Life Discover'd and Describ'd. London, 1732(?).

Woodmansee, Martha. "The Genius and the Copyright: Economic and Legal Conditions of the Emergence of the 'Author.' " *Eighteenth-Century Studies* 17 (1984): 425–48.

Wycherley, William. *The Country-Wife, A Comedy*. 1675. Ed. James Ogden. London: A & C Black, 1991.

———. *The Posthumous Works of William Wycherley, Esq.* . . . Ed. Mr. Theobald. London, 1728.

Yolton, John W. *Thinking Matter: Materialism in Eighteenth-Century Britain.* Minneapolis: University of Minnesota Press, 1983.

Young, Edward. *Conjectures on Original Composition.* . . . 1759. Reprint in *Eighteenth-Century English Literature*, ed. Geoffrey Tillotson et al., 871–89. New York: Harcourt, Brace and World, 1969.

———. *Two Epistles to Mr. Pope Concerning the Authors of the Age.* London, 1730.

Zionkowski, Linda. "Aesthetics, Copyright, and 'the Goods of the Mind.' " *British Journal for Eighteenth-Century Studies* 15 (1992): 163–74.

———. *Men's Work: Gender, Class, and the Professionalization of Poetry, 1660–1784.* New York: Palgrave, 2001.

———. "Territorial Disputes in the Republic of Letters: Canon Formation and the Literary Profession." *Eighteenth Century: Theory and Interpretation* 31 (1990): 3–22.

Index

Acknowledgments

I owe many thanks to the two readers for the University of Pennsylvania Press, whose expert comments and criticism improved my focus and organization. Over the years various sections of this project have also benefitted from the shrewd readerly advice and kindly suggestions of Lesley Biggs, Ron Cooley, Bob Erickson, Isobel Grundy, Jim King, Peter Loptson, the late Peter Millard, the late Roy Porter, George Rousseau, Bill Slights, and Larry Stewart. I have had help with translations, queries, references, or resources from David Blewett, Peter Burnell, Moishe Black, Peter Hynes, Tom King, Richard Morton, Carl Spadoni, Randolph Trumbach, and staff at the University of Saskatchewan Interlibrary Loans department. The electronic challenges of computer files, software disasters, document management, and digital sanity have on many occasions been solved or rescued by Allison Muri. Research librarians at the British Library, the Bibliothèque Nationale de France, the Huntington Library, and the Wellcome Library have helped with rare book materials, but in particular I want to acknowledge the friendly treatment I received from staff at my two favorite research libraries: the William Andrews Clark Memorial Library in Los Angeles, and the William Ready Division of Archives and Research Collections, McMaster University Library in Hamilton. To the following I owe various kinds of moral support: to my Department Chair Paul Bidwell and colleagues in the University of Saskatchewan Department of English (especially my friends Bob Calder, Len Findlay, Dave Carpenter, David Parkinson), to colleagues in the Canadian Society for Eighteenth-Century Studies (especially Benoît Melançon and Peter Sabor), and to colleagues here (especially Lisa Vargo) who have helped to make Eighteenth-Century Studies at the University of Saskatchewan (Research Unit) so great a pleasure.

Portions of Chapters 1, 3, and 4 first appeared in *Studies in Eighteenth-Century Culture* (27 [1998]: 103–30), and portions of Chapters 1 and 4 in *Eighteenth Century: Theory and Interpretation* (38 [1997]: 151–70). I am grateful to the editors for permission to reprint this material, as well as to the following institutions for permission to reproduce illustrations:

Wellcome Library; William Ready Division of Archives and Research Collections; History & Special Collections Division, Louise M. Darling Biomedical Library, UCLA; British Library; the Bibliothèque Nationale de France, and the Huntington Library.

At various times my work and research travel have been happily improved by grants and fellowships from SSHRC, McMaster University, William Andrews Clark Memorial Library, and the Dean of Arts and Science at the University of Saskatchewan.

My greatest debt is to Lesley Biggs, who has patiently helped me and my project from beginning to end.